What's Left of the Left

What's Left of the Left

*Democrats and Social Democrats
in Challenging Times*

Edited by
James Cronin, George Ross, and James Shoch

Duke University Press
Durham and London
2011

© 2011 Duke University Press
All rights reserved.
Printed in the United States of America
on acid-free paper ∞
Typeset in Charis by Tseng Information Systems, Inc.
Library of Congress Cataloging-in-Publication Data
appear on the last printed page of this book.

Contents

Acknowledgments

The editors of this book have a long and interconnected history, and the book itself has been long in the making. Having participated in the upheavals of the 1960s and spent the next two decades on the socialist left in different parts of the country, the three of us met in the late 1980s on the Boston collective of the journal *Socialist Review*. Although our faith in the socialist project subsequently ebbed, we remained both committed to progressive politics and fast friends.

As our political views evolved, our friendship endured and was nurtured over the next fifteen years through regular outings to action movies of uneven quality that our vastly more discriminating wives refused to see. When one of us departed for California in 2003, we looked over the next several years for ways to keep in touch beyond the occasional e-mail and visit. It was then that the fourth member of our movie group, Lou Ferleger, suggested to Jim Cronin that with our collective expertise on European and American politics, the three of us should collaborate on a book. With the center-left parties that we all studied and agonized over in difficult straits, Jim proposed an edited volume on the parties on both continents. The other two of us jumped at the chance to work together on a project close to all our hearts.

We pulled together a stellar cast of contributors who wrote draft chapters that were presented and discussed at a stimulating conference at the Center for European Studies at Harvard in May 2008. A conference in spring 2009 to celebrate George Ross's retirement at the Brandeis Center for German and European Studies was also used to present work based on some of the chapters in this book. After several rounds of revision by our authors and two lively, scotch-fueled editorial meetings near Lake Tahoe and on Cape Cod, we produced the book before you.

In pulling this volume together, we have of course accumulated many debts. First and foremost, we wish to thank our authors, who we think have contributed chapters of exceptional quality. We also appreciate the help of Valerie Milholland and Miriam Angress at Duke University Press in shepherding this book through the editorial process.

Lou Ferleger deserves another mention, both for suggesting this volume and for being our great friend through all these years. Thanks too to Peter Hall and Patricia Craig at the Center for European Studies and to Sabine von Mering, Karen Hansen, and Judy Hanley at the Brandeis Center for German and European Studies and Department of Sociology for supporting and hosting our two meetings. Thanks as well to Joanne Barkan, Andrea Campbell, Joel Krieger, Michel Löwy, Richard Valelly, Eleni Varikas, and Kathrin Zippel for joining us and commenting on the chapters presented at the Harvard conference. We also want to thank James Clifton for his excellent work on the references.

Last but by no means least, we want to thank our wives—Laura Frader, Jane Jenson, and Barbara Baran—exemplary scholars and professionals all, for contributions to this book and to our lives, too numerous to mention. We love you all and appreciate your tolerance.

Introduction

The New World of the Center-Left

James Cronin, George Ross, and James Shoch

Left History and Its Crossroads

The idea of the "left" has varied greatly since its first appearances on the benches of France's revolutionary assemblies. Born of rebellion against perceived injustices in capitalist development, the left has had to adapt constantly, often painfully, to the dynamics of capitalism and the changing dimensions of capitalist societies. The subject of this book is how parties and movements of the center-left have responded to the vast shifts that have occurred in worlds around them since the 1970s. But before turning to this, it is worth reviewing some of the left's experiences with crossroads in the past.[1]

Faced with early industrialization, different lefts had tense discussions about whether the socialist movement should work through the state or work from the ground up through social movements like trade unions. Would social democracy come from high-level political action, or action at the very base of society? These discussions led to divisions between anarchists and socialists, memorialized in Marx's vivid anti-anarchist polemics. In some places, like the United States, divisions between advocates of politics and advocates of trade unionism reproduced these earlier arguments in different forms. These early disputes have continued to help shape the trajectories of many, if not most, labor and socialist lefts since then.

In the early twentieth century, after it had become clear that industrial capitalism had more staying power than earlier lefts had anticipated, there came new and bitter splits between revolutionaries and social democrats—Kautsky versus Bernstein being but one example. For social democrats, if capitalism was not about to implode, leftists had to settle in for the long haul by building and deepening a democracy which would eventually empower the people to demand changes to humanize harsh market societies. Revolutionaries concluded, quite differently, that if capitalism had unexpected staying power, quasi-military vanguards of professional revolutionaries should transcend it by putchist force. The vanguardists, inspired by the success of the October revolution in Russia, advocated disciplined party centralization to seize power and the building of socialism from above by technocrats of revolution acting in the name of the "masses." The legacies of this division permeated and often poisoned the left's twentieth century.

Earlier left theorists had also assumed that the left would naturally be internationalist. "Workers of the world unite, you have nothing to lose but your chains" was one famous statement of this thesis. But in 1914, when real, existing socialists marched eagerly into the trenches in national uniforms to massacre one another, there came a shocking correction. The lesson was that from then on lefts would be national.[2]

Postwar Crossroads and Golden Ages

The lefts that we are about to analyze emerged from another crossroads that began after the Great Depression and the Second World War. In Western Europe countries rushed to emulate the mass production consumer capitalism pioneered in the United States, while the United States deepened its own version. Lefts in these nations were deeply touched by the general issues raised by this new society and economy, which often came simultaneously with new democratization, particularly in the societies where fascism and authoritarianism had won in the interwar period. The puzzle of this period, now seen by many nostalgically as a golden age, was whether left parties and movements would seek to transform capitalism into a new form of socialism or rather "settle" for the new compromises between capital and labor that postwar welfare states, Keynesianism, and new economic growth seemed to allow.

Answers varied, and the world of postwar lefts became an exotic mosaic. Where lefts were divided between social democrats and communists, as in Latin Europe, they had difficulty winning power, and even extensive welfare states and protective employment relations systems were often promoted by others. British Labour occasionally won power, but had problems conciliating Labourism with economic dynamism. The Swedes, the great success story, were never particularly Keynesian, but they built an egalitarian middle-class system which created stakeholders for social democracy and also had mechanisms to compete in the international economy. The Germans succeeded, again without much Keynesianism, when strong unions and innovative private sector exporters cooperated on wage restraint and flexibility, carefully supervised by a very demanding central bank. Americans, with fewer socialists and weaker socialist dreams, continued their waning New Deal trajectory, falling well behind their European counterparts.

The left's key claims in this golden age are familiar. Capitalism was deeply flawed, unable to manage the risks that it created, prone to waste and periodic crises, and an incubator of inequality. Capitalist markets left to themselves paid little attention to human needs, often corrupted political life, and were imperfect in the terms of economics textbooks. Left politics had strong remedies to propose, mainly through action by the national state. Keynesianism might help states shape their macroeconomic policies by managing demand to limit the chaos, even out ups and downs, achieve full employment, and target particular groups through welfare state programs and industrial policies. The world of the golden age was industrial, and in it workers counted most because they created value and had the most significant needs. They were, or would be, well organized into trade unions, they would support left visions of change, and they voted for progressive political parties.

Lefts after the Golden Age?

Four decades later this left world and its slogans have disappeared. Indeed one rarely hears the term "left" these days: instead, electable left parties of the world are almost always labeled "center-left." Center-lefts now include a variety of political forces, among them social liberals, social democrats, democratic socialists, progressives, greens, and human rights campaigners. They accept markets and a mixed economy, but favor limited state intervention, are "moderate" in most ways, and are somewhat "libertarian." Perhaps the most important thing, however, is that this new center-left accepts the multiple constraints of economic internationalization. With the limited exception of the brief period at the onset of the current crisis, it has abandoned Keynesianism in favor of "sound" budgetary practices involving low deficits, low debts, and restrained spending. The dream of full employment has been replaced by an emphasis on achieving price stability and promoting national competitiveness in the broader world. Commitments to redistribution have been attenuated, and center-lefts have learned to live with greater income inequality. Postwar ideas about social policies and employment relations systems to provide lifetime security have been leavened by notions about choice and "flexibility." The center-left remains reformist, but with a changed repertory that now includes environmentalism, civil and human rights, and individual cultural liberties on top of older concerns like economic security and cross-class redistribution. The idea of transcending capitalism and creating "socialism" has completely disappeared.

Center-lefts now live in a changed environment and work with changed political technologies. There are fewer workers, and unions are weaker. Mass-based political parties are in decline. Politics, even on the left, has been professionalized, and sophisticated specialists now track potential voters and issues into every nook and cranny of ever more complicated, individualized societies. Money also talks louder, along with wealthy lobbies, in a world where extensive and expensive media attention counts hugely. Last but not least, the transition from left to center-left has made for political orphans who often do not recognize their concerns in what center-lefts are proposing. Some of these would earlier have been in what were once called "mass organizations." Others, in "new social movements," issue-focused NGOs, or lobbies, would earlier have looked to left parties for inclusion of their issues in party programs and outlooks. They are now much more likely to take their appeals directly to engaged audiences and to policymakers, often through the Internet. From the point of view of center-left parties, these orphans can be politically volatile and unpredictable. Some, like anti-globalization activists, see themselves as the "left of the left" whose protests will keep the center-left "honest." Others will stick to their own issues even if it hurts the center-left's electoral chances. Still others venture into a fluid world of populism to oppose freer trade and immigration, or even join mobilizations over "values" or "threatened identities."

It would be wrong to conclude that the coming of center-lefts marks the dead end of the left's long march, however. Labour and social-democratic parties and, in the United States the Democratic Party, have remodeled their outlooks, organizations, and relationships with constituents in response to very large, often global, changes. The political space within which they operate has changed greatly. But neoliberalism, which vaunts markets as the appropriate place for all social decision making, has not succeeded in banishing all effective opposition. Left-right competition is still the most prominent feature of our politics (Noel and Therien 2008); center-lefts still advocate serious reformist programs, and they still win support and elections.

This book seeks to explore the center-left's new political space and the content that fills it in different places. What is the demand out there for center-left reformism? What are the hopes of the center-left and the projects that it proposes in response? The chapters that follow will explore these issues historically and comparatively through a range of case studies covering various nations, including the United States. They will consider why and how the old world of the left has given way, what the new world of the center-left looks like, and how promising its future may be. What we will see is a patchwork of different center-lefts, some with serious problems, others just barely coping, and still others doing very well. We insist that new political spaces for the center-left have emerged everywhere, however, and our interest is in illuminating how different parties have acted to fill them and to take advantage of the opportunities they offer.

From Left to Center-Left: Three "Crises"

Sometime in the 1970s the long postwar boom came to an end for western democracies, beginning a long crisis that challenged the certainties of the world in which the left had lived for a quarter-century after 1945. Inflation, built into postwar settlements in many western democracies, had already been slowly rising in the 1960s. Successful Fordist reindustrialization in Western Europe and Japan had slowly diminished America's competitive advantages. The American decision in 1971 to abandon the commitment to gold enshrined in the Bretton Woods agreement began a lengthy process of readjustment. This process was then massively complicated by the oil shocks of 1973 and 1979, which fused rising unemployment and uncontrollable inflation in a "stagflation" that in theory could not happen.

The slump that followed ended the Keynesian era and its consensual assumptions about running the economy, including the compatibility of a large state sector, high public expenditure, and prosperity. For left and social democratic parties throughout the industrial world, including the Democratic Party in the United States, Keynesianism had for a time made it possible to maintain that market-constraining social and economic policies—large welfare states, protective labor laws, high redistributive taxation, and an activist, regulatory state—were good for the economy and society and in the national interest.[3]

With Keynesianism challenged, this understanding of the public good was no longer compelling. This was particularly true when ascendant neoliberalism argued for reversing Keynesian priorities, asserting that large government, centralized planning, high taxes, and social spending were antithetical to growth and should be considered obstacles to prosperity. The most visible reversal came in the realm of macroeconomic policy. The notion that smart demand management could fine-tune otherwise unruly markets and produce consistent growth was largely abandoned. What replaced it was a turn to what some have labeled a "market fundamentalism," which largely conquered public servants, politicians, economists, and the news media. Monetarism and fiscal retrenchment quickly became the norm, and emphasis shifted to "supply-side" policies and efforts to produce competitiveness through higher productivity, greater flexibility, and constant innovation.

Neoliberalism promoted a vastly different view of the state and its roles. Where American liberals and social democrats elsewhere had seen the state as an essential and largely benign instrument, the new advocates of the market saw it as detrimental and sought to restrict its scope and impact. This meant, in the first instance, ceasing to see the state as the solution to social and economic problems and abandoning commitments to full employment—probably the most important legacy of the 1930s. The more extreme formulations of neoliberalism insisted on the need to permanently reduce taxes, privatize nationalized industries, and pursue deregulation, thus depriving the state of the means to steer the economy. Beyond that, the state itself should be restructured so as to use market mechanisms to deliver services and market criteria to assess its performance. Wherever possible, the state should not provide services directly but rather contract or partner with private companies to do so.

This shift posed a huge challenge to the center-left: would it also make the turn toward the market or would it resist? The answer was a long time in coming, for it required the experiences of policy failure and electoral defeat to produce a major rethinking. It was the sorry fate of many of the social-democratic, labor, and democratic parties to be in power during the 1970s and early 1980s and to suffer the frustrating consequences of changing environments around them. In Britain the Labour governments led by Harold Wilson and then James Callaghan responded to the oil shocks by adopting income policies that the party's core supporters came to reject in a defiant wave of strikes, leading to the election of Margaret Thatcher and nearly two decades of neoliberal Conservative rule. In the United States Jimmy Carter, facing stagflation and foreign policy crises, was equally ineffective and also prepared a turn to the right in 1980. In France, the Mitterrand government, elected in 1981 and committed to strong Keynesian and statist reforms, had to retreat rapidly on almost every front. Center-left parties in general, including those that built the "Nordic model," had difficulty adapting economic and social policies to the problems of the new era, problems with which voters were overwhelmingly concerned.

A second crisis, more political than economic, was soon to follow, involving the collapse of socialism in Eastern Europe in 1989 and the disappearance in 1991 of the Soviet Union.[4] These huge events further narrowed the discursive and programmatic political space within which the center-left could operate, putting paid to what remained of any nineteenth-century vision of replacing capitalism with a wholly different system. There was great irony in this, because parties of the democratic left had long been at pains to distance themselves from communism and "actually existing socialism." But in fact, while western democratic socialists had vehemently deplored the illiberal, antidemocratic practices of communism, they had nonetheless held many abstract beliefs and predispositions in common with their communist rivals. Although the intensity of the most utopian of these passions had slowly attenuated in most of the left since 1945, what happened between 1989 and 1991 nonetheless forced a reckoning with the socialist past and its thinking about the world. The dream of transcending capitalism disappeared, making a political life bounded by capitalism and markets look permanent. This shift dictated a more restricted definition of what was politically possible and desirable. It is important to add that the end of the cold war and the Soviet experiment occurred when campaigns for hard-line neoliberalism—the political consequence of the economic crisis that opened in the 1970s—were reaching their apogee. The western victory over "already existing socialism" was thus a huge gift to market fundamentalists.

Globalization is our third critical event, or process, and its effects on the center-left have already been very powerful. Beginning in the 1990s fast-moving trends that expanded world trade, opened product and financial markets, and heightened international capital mobility combined to place new limits on how national states could manage their economics, protect workers and their environments, and pursue fiscal policies, including those that provided social services. The crisis of the 1970s and computer technologies had opened the door to financial globalization, which came on strong in the 1990s with the growth of multinational companies, tentacular investment banks, mutual and hedge funds, futures, swaps, derivatives, and rapidly flowing hot money. Over the same period successive GATT rounds had lowered tariffs and opened trade, culminating in 1995 in the new World Trade Organization. The Bretton Woods institutions—the World Bank and the IMF—had also done their part by energetically imposing the "Washington consensus" on countries that resisted the new orthodoxies. In Europe the move toward more open markets had also been pushed forward gradually by European integration, but it took the single market program and Economic and Monetary Union (EMU) after 1985 to institutionalize fully open markets and the new paradigms of price stability and budget balancing. Less encompassing regionalizing efforts in North America had similar results. Economic and policy borders became more permeable, affecting sovereignty and narrowing what national governments could do.

The limits created by globalization were also in part discursive and ideological. Motivated by either sincere belief or perceived political imperatives, politicians and intellectuals of the left and the right now ruled out all sorts of policy options because of the supposed dictates of the global economy. The reality beneath the rhetoric was nevertheless sobering enough. The global economy and new technologies clearly made it easier to move capital and jobs to places with fewer rules and lower labor costs. They also allowed employers and, more broadly, investors to threaten such moves and thus enhance their political leverage to insist that states adopt their preferred fiscal, monetary, and regulatory policies. The impact of globalization was made still more real as it became itself more truly global. While the United States and Europe might have begun the processes that created a more open world market and to that extent laid the ground rules for its operation, other nations joined in and thus acquired an interest in keeping it open and functioning. Specifically, China, India, Russia, Brazil, and other "emerging" economies entered global manufacturing with a vengeance, marching forward on the back of huge comparative advantages in labor costs and growing economically at rates not seen since the nineteenth century. Energy producers like Russia, the leading Arab oil exporters, Venezuela, Nigeria, and South Africa were no less invested in the world market, whatever the ideological complexion or rhetoric of their regimes. The effect was to reinforce the trend toward international economic interdependence and to underline the dictates of globalization.

Taken together, these three shocks remade the world in which center-left parties and movements operate. It is only a slight exaggeration to say that the contemporary center-left is itself a product of this new world and the constraints and opportunities that it presents. In this transformed world, the alternative to actually existing capitalism is not socialism, but a better and more just capitalism. Scholars and activists now study not transitions to socialism but the "varieties of capitalism" or the virtues and vices of distinctive "worlds of welfare" and state provision (Hall and Soskice 2001; Esping-Andersen 1990; Schröder 2008).[5] This is not a time bereft of possibilities, but it is a moment when possibilities need to be located within the global economy rather than outside or in opposition to it. This is, most important, a moment when to be effective the center-left must be creative and find opportunities in new policies and strategies.

From Left to Center-Left: Large Social Changes

The effects of the passing of the Keynesian era, the collapse of socialism in Eastern Europe and then the Soviet Union, and the coming of a more intense era of global economic competition were felt at the levels of both ideology and policy. It was hard to know what to believe, what to hope for, and what actually to do. But the center-left confronted yet another set of problems about electability. To be successful in the new era it had also to come to grips with a fourth major challenge: the shifting social bases of its political appeal. The left's utopias, legends, programs, and practices had historically been grounded in the social movement of the industrial working class, especially its most organized sectors and occupations. This fact, true even if electoral success also typically required support from the middle and professional classes, had been built upon long and storied historical struggles. The rich lore that surrounded the Paris Commune, the Haymarket, the struggle for the eight-hour workday, the October Revolution, the British General Strike, the French strikes of 1936, the struggle against fascism, the French May and Italian Hot autumn of the 1960s, to list but a few headline moments, nourished the politics of generations.

In recent decades, however, these stories, traditions, and utopias have become far less meaningful. The social bases of "progressive politics" have dramatically shifted, mainly because of the transition to what has been variously termed a "post-industrial," "service," or "knowledge-based" economy. Starting in the 1920s, if not earlier, services began to grow faster than industry in developed economies (Clark 1940). The trend accelerated with the information and communications revolution that began in the 1970s. The introduction of labor-saving technologies, including computer-based technologies, together with rising consumer affluence and demand for new goods and services substantially transformed the nature of the workforce.

The first consequence is that the industrial working class has literally shrunk. In 1950 agriculture had accounted for 28.3%, industry for 34%, and services for 37.7% of employment in developed countries. By 1971, with Fordist mass production at its peak, the figures were 12.7%, 37.9%, and 49.4%. By 1998 they were 4.8%, 27.0%, and 67.4%. While the added value of manufacturing to GDP hovered at around 35% of the total throughout this period, deindustrialization proceeded apace and the number of industrial workers, relative to other wage earners, steadily declined (Feinstein 1999). Much of the manufacturing not already relocated to developing countries is now capital- and skills-intensive, and the workers who remain are better educated and trained, live better and differently, partake in mass consumption and culture, and are no longer encapsulated in the working-class subcultures that informed the mythologies of the left's pasts. Many are also women, now somewhat better off when compared to men even if not yet equal, and in most countries male breadwinner status and pay scales are in retreat. Rising living standards have also blurred the line between workers and the lower middle class, while service work is often hard to categorize as either blue- or white-collar, manual or non-manual. The demographic underpinnings for what Eric Hobsbawm (1978) once labeled the "forward march of labour" have thus dissipated.

Similar things can be said of the organizational structures that sustained older left projects. In some countries—mainly smaller ones—union membership remains practically obligatory (because of what is called the Ghent system) and therefore at high levels. Since the 1980s, however, union membership in the EU-15, the heartland of traditional social democratic politics, has declined by roughly 20%. And where trade unionism has not been quasi-obligatory, unions have had a particularly rough ride. In France union membership has halved since 1970 and is now at 8% of the workforce (around 3% in the private sector); in Germany it is 22% and falling; in the United Kingdom it is down one-third, to roughly 30%; and in the United States it is down to 12.5%. In most of Europe declines may be mitigated somewhat by legal extensions of collective agreements to non-unionized workers. Even there, however, over time the membership drop is likely to undermine these extensions and the overall meaningfulness of collective bargaining. And in more liberal industrial environments, where contract extensions don't exist, the situation is much worse (Visser 2006). In the United States 13.8% of workers are covered by contracts, as are 30% in the United Kingdom. Moreover, most union organizations, however powerful, have themselves changed. Earlier efforts to fuel broader working-class cultures have given way to the provision of highly professionalized and bureaucratized representational services for members.

Lefts and center-lefts have needed middle-class help to "march forward," and this in turn has always necessitated complicated strategic calculations and compromise (Przeworski 1985; Przeworski and Sprague 1986). With the relative decline of the organizations, culture, and size of the working class, this need is now overwhelming. Average employment in services in the EU-15 area in 2006 was 70% of the labor force, compared to 78% in the United States (OECD 2008a). "Services" are not an undifferentiated group, however, and involve occupations ranging from low-paid precarious work, through social service workers in caring and teaching work, to relatively secure public sector functionaries, professors, and investment bankers. The challenge of formulating appeals to capture the needs and aspirations of such a diverse population is daunting. At one end of the spectrum, low-paid personal and distributional service workers are the core of a growing "working poor" whose needs for dignity and "social inclusion" are widely recognized but not easily addressed by the existing repertoire of center-left policy prescriptions. That these populations often consist of immigrants or ethnic minorities compounds the danger of an emerging social dualism between market insiders and outsiders, a split that can and occasionally has become political and is almost always detrimental to the center-left.

Attending to the concerns of more middle-class and professional constituencies is more complicated still. Political science literature has made much of the emergence of "post-material values" among educationally credentialed new middle strata (Inglehart 1990). The strategic problem is that center-lefts have problems conciliating traditional "material" issue outlooks with the more "libertarian," individualist, and universalist passions of new middle-class groups (Kitschelt 1994). Concerns for the environment or for human rights or the rights of women and minorities might well be compatible with the traditional goals and visions of the left, but they sometimes seem not to be. In any event, engineering the ideological, programmatic, and organizational changes needed to reconcile the conflicting demands of constituents who have "material" needs and demands with others who have "left libertarian" or "quality of life" concerns is now a baseline for center-left success. Achieving it remains a struggle, however.

As if the changing social bases of center-left parties were not enough of a challenge, the ways of doing politics have changed as well. In the United States after the Second World War—earlier than in Europe—new worlds of political campaigning opened up, connected to the decline of traditional party organizations and their constituent groups, especially labor unions, and the simultaneous rise of modern mass communications, particularly television and later the Internet. As costly "air wars," including positive and negative TV ads, replaced the grassroots, labor-intensive "ground wars" of old, political consultants of various kinds—strategists, pollsters, media experts, and fundraisers—assumed control of political campaigns from traditional party leaders. More recently, American parties have adopted sophisticated, computer-assisted "micro-targeting" techniques, through which vast amounts of consumer data are analyzed to identify likely sympathizers. Messages are then delivered to these voters by direct mail, phone calls, and increasingly, with the rediscovery of the value of face-to-face contact, in person by grassroots volunteers.

In the new style of electoral campaigning, issues have remained important for attentive voters. Advanced polling techniques are used to ascertain voters' preferences on salient issues, while "issue ads" and other media tactics are used to "frame" issues in language favorable to particular candidates, to "prime" voters to judge candidates on the basis of issues that a particular party "owns," and in some cases to persuade voters to change their preferences. In complex post-industrial societies, however, the rise in salience of new social, cultural, environmental, and other non-economic issues alongside traditional economic ones means that candidates have to position themselves on multiple issue dimensions to win the support of some groups without alienating others that have conflicting preferences. To avoid such dilemmas, politicians often take vague or ambiguous issue positions. Beyond this, because most voters are relatively inattentive to politics and have little awareness of candidates' issue positions, one contemporary trend, greatly reinforced by the growing role of the mass media, is for electoral campaigns to downplay issues and instead foreground themes that demand less from viewers and listeners. These include incumbents' performances and candidates' personal characteristics—their integrity, honesty, experience, leadership ability, religiosity, patriotism, affability, race or gender, physical attractiveness, etc.

These new media-centered and computer-aided campaign techniques are very costly and would thus seem likely to disproportionately benefit conservative parties tied to powerful business interests and other wealthy donors. Parties on the center-left may also have more qualms and hesitations about making use of these tactics than their opponents. But the very newest of these campaign techniques, enabled by the emergence of the Internet, may actually be of greatest value to parties of the center-left. For example, in the United States Barack Obama—through his own campaign website, social networking sites like Facebook, MySpace, and Twitter, YouTube videos, e-mail, and text messaging—was able to raise vast sums of money from small donors and mobilize tens of thousands of grassroots volunteers, both processes contributing immensely to his innovative and successful presidential campaign. In the French presidential campaign in 2007 Ségolène Royal used analogous techniques to short-circuit her Socialist rivals and win her party's nomination, even though, unlike Obama, she did not win the general election.

All this is not to suggest that the new forms of campaigning are of decisive importance in determining election outcomes. The so-called fundamentals—the balance of partisan identification in the electorate, the state of the economy and international relations, and the popularity and effectiveness of the executive—retain a dominant role. But especially in close elections, campaigns can definitely matter; and the changed character of political campaigning adds yet another challenge to the parties of the center-left.

Policy Dilemmas

Shifting bases of political allegiance, combined with the new economic constraints and new campaigning techniques, vastly complicate the task of putting together stable and long-term center-left coalitions. They also make it harder to develop policies to bring and hold together fragmented and hetero-geneous constituencies and then to govern effectively. In the policy realm, for example, center-left parties—especially in Europe—must adapt to new monetary policies that emphasize price stability and deemphasize counter-cyclical spending, constraints limiting their ability to reward old and new constituencies. They also confront difficult issues of welfare state reform prompted in part by aging populations that have produced skewed pension dependency ratios and rapidly rising healthcare costs. They must devise pro-grams in response to new social needs—childcare for new single-parent and two-breadwinner families and support programs for the working poor, for example. Most controversially, they are expected to promote flexible labor markets without undermining employment security, to reform institutions governing industrial relations, and to promote new patterns of cooperation between labor and capital. An equally difficult challenge involves reforming educational systems to promote lifelong learning, training, and retraining. Finally, they need to find new revenue sources without damaging national economies engaged in global competition. These strategic dilemmas have cre-ated new political minefields.

There is another side to this, however. The new conditions also open up new political space for center-left parties and political entrepreneurs. With older certainties gone, there is much greater room for more persuasive and creative center-left politicking than earlier. Navigating the contemporary maelstrom of changing economies, social bases, and political technologies is obviously difficult. But recent setbacks notwithstanding, there is ample evi-dence that parties of the center-left remain capable of winning elections. The American presidential election of 2008 provides some evidence, but other data are easy to find in contemporary European history. The changes that we have listed have not eliminated the political space for strategies and policies beyond, and often against, the neoliberal paradigm. In a number of countries humanized "supply-side" alternatives to Keynesian demand management have produced successes. Productivity-enhancing public investment—in education and training, infrastructure, and new technologies—has been ex-panded without abandoning fiscal restraint. It also seems possible, given the right raw materials, to make labor markets more flexible and liberalize them without turning them into the sites of wars among the insecure. This, plus innovative attention to equal opportunities and public services, and absent severe macroeconomic shocks, can generate levels of growth, employment, and other benefits sufficient to produce electoral victories. Policies aimed at and premised on delivering economic growth thus remain prominent. They have not dominated center-left policymaking quite as much as they did in the past, however, as new issues, backed by new constituencies, have become more prominent. In part this is because the same economic processes that have led to fewer manual workers have also produced more white-collar professionals who can be mobilized by the center-left on social and cultural rather than economic issues. The increase in women's employment likewise contains possibilities as well as challenges. The declining significance of class more broadly creates room for a politics that broaches questions of racial and sexual equality, human rights, war and peace, the environment, and lifestyles—questions that cut across electorates differently from earlier class cleavages. Center-left parties, which have long debated the electoral significance of these shifts, by now have come to understand them reasonably well and have begun to successfully incorporate new issues into their electoral appeals and programs. On old and new issues, with old and new constituencies, there are real possibilities for the center left even in a different world.

There Are Center-Lefts and Center-Lefts . . .

All center-lefts have had to confront these crises and changes, but it would be misleading to argue that there is *one* center-left everywhere challenged in the same way. Histories and policy legacies vary tremendously from country to country in ways that may either facilitate or hinder adaptive responses to new conditions. In addition, differences among national constitutional, institutional, and political systems can result in a wide range of policy responses to similar economic and other circumstances. Specific location in the uneven development of the unfolding global economy is also important. The chapters in this book will illustrate these different variables at work through case studies.

Different narratives about recent political changes tend to have different heroes. Many center-leftists grant pride of place to the Nordic countries. These countries, perhaps uniquely, have been able simultaneously to adapt public financial practices to new international standards, promote public investment and flexible internal labor markets to facilitate rapid innovation, and sustain generous welfare states. Denmark and Sweden have been particularly good at active labor market "flexicurity" policies that liberalize labor regulations while providing support to wage earners looking to make employment transitions and reskill. There are specific reasons for this. The Nordic countries, each different, are all very small—the population of Denmark is about the same as that of greater Boston, for example. Their size has long obliged them to be open to international trade, and over time they have internalized the lesson that success on international markets demands high levels of national cross-class cooperation. Active labor market policies and monetary policy prudence have long been central parts of the package. The Swedes were never extravagantly Keynesian, for example, and the Danes tied their currency to the D-Mark early in the 1980s, binding themselves to the tough monetarism of the German Bundesbank. As conditions changed around them, therefore, Denmark and Sweden began with helpful policy legacies, although even being so endowed none of the Nordic countries has avoided severe moments of crisis and change.[6] Moreover, their much-admired labor market flexibility, monetary soundness, and admirable welfare states have not always helped the center-left. In Denmark social democrats have been relatively weak and the country is now run by a center-right coalition. Finnish politics has almost always involved centrist governing coalitions. In Sweden once-hegemonic social democrats are now out of power and, if they return, will only do so as part of a complex coalition. The Norwegians are exceptional in this discussion because they have had oil to grease their economic wheels.

The United Kingdom has provided a very different northern European success story, although it now seems over. Here good recent results for the center-left are in large part the product of radical discontinuities caused by Thatcherite neoliberalism. The Thatcher years undid much of Old Labour's postwar heritage of a vast, inefficient, public sector, decentralized collective bargaining that fed chronic inflation, and persistent budgetary difficulties. They left a lean, mean liberal environment, and until its defeat in 2010, New Labour achieved success through its intelligent acceptance of this as a basis upon which to build. The point of departure for its Third Way was thus an extreme market fundamentalism that cried out for a move to the center and an effort to restore public services. New Labour was also blessed until recently by a decade of steady economic growth, which it helped sustain through prudent public financial management. New Labour thus had resources for a series of modest innovations, particularly in social policy. To be sure, it took policy creativity to zero in on what to do, and the good if also flawed leadership of Tony Blair to carry it out. The present financial crisis profoundly challenges the New Labour formula, however.

The EU's continental political economies, in contrast to the Nordic countries and the United Kingdom, have been more troubled, with center-lefts deeply implicated. Excepting brief interludes, France has had low growth and high employment since the early 1990s. The French left, obliged to work radical changes in financial and monetary policies in the 1980s, has been slow at adapting to the need for a more liberal and flexible labor market. These two processes may have been linked. French governments of the center-left and sometimes of the center-right, afraid of electoral reactions to labor market reform, reduced the size of the workforce at taxpayers' expense in ways that may have made economic matters worse. One consequence has been high, and not terribly productive, levels of public spending. Moreover, despite incremental but serious welfare state reforms, there has been growing division between insiders and outsiders. The center-left has had huge problems developing attractive, coherent programs and has lost almost all major elections since 1993.

Germany started out better placed than France for the new world. It did not need to abandon Keynesianism, because the long-standing monetarist practices of its Bundesbank had ruled it out in the first place. Also, Germany pursued an export-oriented development strategy built around very competitive manufacturing operations, whose success had trickled down to finance a generous welfare state. Thus while virtually everyone else faced trauma in the 1980s, Germany sailed as *Modell Deutschland*. But the end of the cold war and globalization proved more troublesome. German unification, a huge political success, was promoted in economically unsound ways and led to huge and chronic internal west-east transfers (upward of 5% of GDP annually), a huge jump in unemployment, and chronic budgetary problems. Germany remains the world's leading exporter, but at the cost of increased capital investment and labor shedding. Germany's exporting companies now employ fewer well-paid, highly skilled, and flexible workers. But German society has been more and more troubled. Recent social policy reforms have helped, but the German welfare state remains expensive, and trickle-down effects from successful exporting no longer reliably float broader living standards. The result has been insider-outsider dualism. The German center-left, held responsible by parts of its working class base for painful welfare state reforms, has lost electoral support to a new left competitor, die Linke, whose stock in trade is defensive resistance to social policy change.

In southern Europe the distinctive character of political regimes has affected prospects of the center-left. In Italy the left long meant the Italian Communist Party (PCI), which had deep working-class roots, solid experience in local government, and a leadership less craven in its relations with Moscow than its counterparts in the rest of Europe, France especially. It would for all these reasons become Eurocommunism's best hope in the 1970s. But the PCI was also ghettoized, and its dominance of the working-class vote produced for most of the postwar era a rallying of right-wing and centrist political forces around the Christian Democratic Party (DC), which had an effective lock on central government. That firm grip allowed Italian politics to remain clientelist and corrupt, and the corruption enveloped nearly everyone, including the socialists under Bettino Craxi. The end of the cold war and of Christian Democratic domination had the effect of undermining both left and right: the PCI became a shadow of its former self; the DC suffered massive defections and was replaced by smaller, more erratic, and often right-wing groupings; and the socialists never recovered from the scandals known collectively as Tangentopoli. One consequence was a center-left that was fragmented and lacked a history, vision, and program; a second was the rise of the clownish, populist, but electorally successful Silvio Berlusconi; the third was a policy stasis, as no party or coalition could muster the will or the means to reform the welfare state and economy. Italy as a society has thus also moved toward the dualism—the insider-outsider pattern visible elsewhere—but with more corruption and, it must be admitted, much better style.

Spain, Portugal, and Greece, in contrast, all lived under authoritarian dictatorships that did not end until the mid-1970s. In both Spain and Greece they ended in ways that helped lefts to become center-lefts and then gave them an unusual record of electoral success. In part this was because in both countries rights had been tainted by complicity with the dictatorships. The center-lefts thus had access to power which, in the context of joining the EU and modernizing their societies and economies, gave them a widely shared national mission and, with success, strong new credibility. The Portuguese left did less well, losing its post-dictatorship advantage through excess revolutionary posturing and internal divisions.

The new lefts of Eastern European countries provide different illustrations of the importance of historical legacies. Revulsion with the communist past ruled out the emergence of strong forms of traditional social democracy. As they democratized and built market societies, these countries started out on a more liberal path than their Western European neighbors. Ironically, this tendency has not prevented center-lefts, often formed from the remnants of communist parties, from winning elections. The policies that they then carried to power have been very different from those in the West. Two decades of transition are not long enough to discern permanent trends, however, and the situation remains unsettled.

Including the American Democratic Party in a comparative analysis of center-left parties is unorthodox, since unlike Europe, America has not produced a socialist movement tied to a strong union movement.[7] Yet the Democrats may have become center-left before anyone else, obliged by their different historical trajectory to build complex alliances with social groups other than the working class and to deal with unusually powerful capitalists. At the same time, from the New Deal through the 1960s the Democrats followed many of the policy trajectories of their European brethren. But constrained by an anti-statist political culture, a fragmented federal state, and a weak labor movement, the American welfare state was a "residual" one, combining tax-subsidized, employer-provided retirement and healthcare benefits for workers in the core, mostly unionized sectors of the economy, government-sponsored pension and healthcare programs for the elderly, and means-tested programs for the poor. Momentum in the growth of an already limited welfare state was largely stopped in the early 1980s by a deeply rooted and long-lived conservative political reaction that lasted until Barack Obama's victory in 2008.

Ironically, owing to the size and global strength of its economy, the United States has been able to circumvent some of the crises that have bedeviled European countries. The United States spearheaded the international shift away from Keynesianism, but the administration of Ronald Reagan, while hawkish about the practices of other governments, was able to engineer a quick and politically beneficial recovery from transitional recession by running budget deficits that could, thanks to American international monetary and financial centrality, be financed in global capital markets by foreign investors and central bankers. It was only during the Democratic, center-left presidency of Bill Clinton that the United States turned toward obeying standard rules of fiscal responsibility; these were swiftly abandoned by President George W. Bush, who returned to the use of internationally financed budget deficits to fund sweeping, politically driven tax cuts for corporations and the upper class. Rule violations and role reversals have seemed eminently feasible for a country that has been the biggest elephant in the international economic zoo, at least until very recently.

The negative consequences of these practices and of the harsh conservatism that pushed them forward are in part why even as Europe continued to liberalize, the Democratic Party in the United States began to move toward a more active government economic role. With the bursting of the technology and housing bubbles, economic growth and job creation in the United States slowed, while globalization, technological change, the weakening of labor unions, a declining minimum wage, and regressive Republican tax policy contributed to stagnant wages, eroded retirement and healthcare benefits, and increased inequality. In response to all these developments, as well as to the resulting shift of American public opinion to the left since the mid-1990s, and with the continued availability of capital in global markets, Democratic policy intellectuals and politicians themselves moved a bit to the left. Reconsidering the economic and political primacy of reduced budget deficits, Democratic elites, in some cases drawing on the example of the European experience, began to call for universal healthcare, increased public investment, wage insurance for workers displaced by globalization, and progressive tax reform.

This Democratic shift to the left accelerated briefly in the wake of Obama's victory and the global economic crisis, which at least temporarily relaxed traditional constraints on an expanded government role. In addition to rescuing failing financial institutions and auto companies, Obama and congressional Democrats, in the face of vociferous Republican opposition, passed a massive economic stimulus program and a budget resolution—including aid to the states and big increases in public investment in infrastructure and "green jobs"—to spark an economic recovery and strengthen the foundations for long-term growth. After an epic battle, Obama and his allies then successfully restructured the nation's healthcare system and later enacted an important if modest financial reform bill. However, a persistently weak economy and mounting public concern over bailouts, rising spending and deficits, and "Big Government" led to significant Republican gains in the congressional midterm elections in 2010, jeopardizing the durability of the recent shift to the left in United States politics.

There is therefore considerable variety in the economies and societies where center-left parties operate and hope to make gains. There are also very different histories, whose legacies may not quite determine the future but nevertheless matter greatly. Still, the center-left parties work within strikingly similar electoral maps across Europe and North America, confront surprisingly similar social and economic problems, and must find their way within a common world economy. We believe that it is therefore worth examining their situations and prospects together.

The Book and Its Goals

The book explores the post-Keynesian, globalized political world in which the center-left finds itself after the cold war and assesses its consequences and implications. It is premised on a belief that it is unhelpful to lament the recent narrowing of political debate and to regard the acceptance of new constraints as betrayal. Instead, it will probe the new political structures faced by the center-left with an eye toward realizing, seizing, and expanding the political possibilities that they offer. We shall investigate the center-left's more successful initiatives and analyze when and where they occurred, which conditions facilitated the most useful political responses, which barriers blocked their emergence in other places, and how they were subject to limitations even where they were politically feasible. Our work as presented here will often be historical, but we shall try consistently to look forward. It will be broad in its reach but necessarily selective; and it will be transatlantic, but also aware of the very real differences that separate the European experience from that of the United States.[8]

The first chapter focuses on the unique history of social democracy in Europe and its roles in securing democracy, prosperity, and a measure of social justice and social protection in the postwar years. It also makes clear the pitfalls, detours, and false starts that accompanied what the author, Sheri Berman, considers the victory of social democracy, and the continuing difficulties that social democrats have had in understanding their own achievements, sustaining them in hard times, and building upon them in the most recent era. Gerassimos Moschonas follows with a comparative essay on the shifting electoral fortunes and social bases of center-left parties over the past quarter-century. The story he tells is mixed and complicated, like Berman's, in which achievements and setbacks are carefully balanced through time and space. Less mixed, but unsurprisingly so, is the record of center-left parties in eastern and central Europe surveyed by Jean-Michel De Waele and Sorina Soare. In that unfortunate region the legacy of "actually existing socialism" and Soviet domination cast doubt on the legitimacy of anything calling itself socialist or social democratic, even as the economic and social wreckage left behind called out for a political vision offering more than neoliberalism and "shock therapy."

Three case studies follow: on Britain, France, and Sweden. Britain and Sweden illustrate two potentially viable paths for center-lefts. France, in contrast, embodies many of the obstacles to taking any path. James Cronin reviews the unhappy history out of which New Labour emerged and argues that this history, and the desire to transcend it, explain a great deal of what New Labour has been about. Viewed in that historical context, New Labour has achieved more than it is usually credited with having achieved. It may or may not be a model for the center-left, but despite its defeat in the elections of May 2010, it is at the least a model worth studying. Art Goldhammer and George Ross undertake a similar analysis of the lengthy process by which the French center-left reached its present impasse. They see a record of incoherence and factionalism that has prevented French socialists from capitalizing on the many failures of their opponents and from undertaking the sorts of policies that might give them a more lasting purchase on voters' preferences. Jonas Pontusson tells a different story about Sweden, where, he explains, a period of political uncertainty and economic distress in the 1980s afforded social democrats the opportunity to sort out what was central in their vision and program. That involved a reaffirmation of the party's commitment to work rather than to a particular job, to the skills and training and social supports required for obtaining and keeping work, and to a world market in which workers and firms would find their just rewards. If properly understood and locally tailored, this slimmed-down and updated Swedish model can, Pontusson insists, inspire the center-left in countries far different from Sweden and its Scandinavian cousins.

What form of center-left politics is likely or even possible in a place as different as the United States? That is part of what the three chapters focused on the American experience seek to determine. In his chapter on electoral dynamics, Ruy Teixeira makes the argument that for all of America's real and imagined "exceptionalism," and notwithstanding its setback in the congressional midterm elections in 2010, the party of the center-left is in the process of becoming politically dominant. Democrats have emerged as the party of professionals in the "knowledge" industries and the service sector as well as of women, the young, and ethnic and racial minorities. The party has lost support among its traditional bases in the white working class, but offsetting this to a considerable extent is that those workers who do vote Democratic, mainly those in trade unions, turn out in large numbers to do so. Teixeira differs sharply from those who argued before the last two election cycles that the unusual strength of the religious right, the effects of Republican-controlled redistricting, and the enduring attraction of tough rhetoric on national security, immigration, and divisive social issues had given Republicans a permanent edge. Teixeira concludes his highly useful corrective by predicting that despite the current decline in Obama's popularity and the Democrats' substantial midterm losses in 2010, due in both cases mainly to the weak economy, the subsequent economic turnaround and the continued growth of the Democrats' demographic coalition will likely produce a reelection victory for Obama in 2012 and a broader Democratic revival. Time will tell if Teixeira's relatively optimistic forecast is borne out.

Chris Howard breaks with the conventional wisdom about the supposed retrenchment of American social policy, describing a record of consistent and not insignificant increases in what would normally be considered government social expenditure. Spending in the United States does not match that in other developed nations, but America is not quite the laggard it is often thought to be. Howard stresses three additional and critical features of the American welfare state: a reliance on the tax system to transfer funds to those in need; the tendency of government programs to miss those most in need and to focus instead on those with real but less pressing needs; and, because the United States economy generates very unequal incomes and distributes wealth disproportionately to the very top, the failure of increases in social spending to do much to redress inequality. Howard further shows that the

Democratic Party bears considerable responsibility for the recent growth in social spending, although the enactment of social programs and the shift in the distribution of social benefits has often required cooperation from Republicans. Assessing the future of the American welfare state in the wake of the current economic crisis, Howard notes the many positive provisions of the recently enacted economic stimulus and healthcare reform bills. He concludes somewhat pessimistically, however, that for a number of economic and political reasons, Obama and congressional Democrats are unlikely to make more than a dent in poverty and inequality.

James Shoch's chapter on globalization begins by noting that European social democrats have long recognized the benefits of free trade while both compensating "losers" with various social policies and expanding public investment to boost national competitiveness and save and create jobs. The Democratic Party, however, once committed to free trade, has in the past few decades charted a different course. Democratic presidents representing broad national constituencies have continued to promote trade liberalization. But congressional Democrats, under strong pressure from trade-battered labor constituents while also unable or unwilling to press for significant compensatory or public investment programs in the face of Republican attacks on them as "tax-and-spend" liberals, have instead opposed and in some cases blocked recent free trade initiatives. Barack Obama's victory and the expansion of the Democrats' congressional majorities in 2008 initially appeared to signal a new era of increased social and public investment spending and thus also a possible eventual decline of labor and Democratic opposition to freer trade. But Democratic midterm losses in 2010 and likely further Senate setbacks in 2012, Shoch concludes, have seriously diminished these prospects.

Taken together, the three chapters devoted to the United States show that the center-left in America faces much the same set of problems as elsewhere and, especially in light of the election results from 2008, that the Democratic Party's potential to win elections, despite its current slide in approval, may be at least equal to that of any center-left party in Europe. The American chapters also show, however, that historically center-left policies are perhaps harder to develop, implement, and maintain in America than in Europe. Still, policy and politics go together everywhere, and some of the most pressing policy concerns will pose difficulties for center-left parties on both sides of the Atlantic. The last three chapters in the book demonstrate this very clearly. Jane Jenson looks closely at what have been termed "new social risks" and the policy responses they have provoked. New risks come in part from the changing demography of the workforce, as more women work and family structures shift, and from the changed nature of work itself, which is now less secure, more variable over time, and more highly concentrated in sectors and regions. Specifically, there are now more single mothers as well as more women working, and more of the so-called working poor. The main response to this set of changes has been to try to get more people into the workforce—labor market activation is the term for this—or to make work pay better, either by subsidizing low-paid work or by supplementing wages with social supports. Jenson demonstrates that these problems and responses are shared across different countries with historically rather different welfare systems and types of political economy. The implication is that systems and regimes and parties can and will learn from each other, because whatever the policy legacy, the problems are converging in a more and more global economy.

Sofía Pérez makes a very similar argument about an issue that is equally important for the center-left: immigration. All over Europe there are more immigrants than before, and some of them, especially those from Africa, Asia, and the Middle East, are by definition more different from Europeans than earlier immigrants and in that respect less easily integrated in the societies to which they have come. The effects of immigration have varied between countries, Pérez shows, but everywhere it matters in unprecedented ways and, one might add, in ways that have affected American politics for a very long time. The center-left has problems with immigration, since part of its natural base (organized labor) may find immigrants an economic threat, but the center-right faces similar problems (with employers). Both factions try to avoid these problems through symbolic political positions which tend to cancel the partisan effects.

The penultimate piece in our collection is George Ross's analysis of the impact of the European Union on the center-left. When the EU began as a Common Market, many on the left regarded it as either a capitalist plot or an irrelevancy for national politics. Then from the mid-1980s, when the EU came to exercise new and extensive power over its member states, lefts had to pay more attention. For a while some hoped for a "social Europe," but recently the EU has looked more like a force for globalization and market liberalization. Ross provides a tour of these moves and what each has meant for parties of the center-left across the continent. His is a particularly intimate and, at base, disenchanted view, but he sees possibilities as well as constraints in EU institutions which are obliged to speak in, if not seek, broad consensus. Ross's account of the EU is in many ways an account of the present state of the world economy and of the institutions and assumptions that govern it, and so also of their impact on the prospects of the center-left in Europe and elsewhere. It is a reminder again of the novel mix of constraints and opportunities, limits and possibilities, within which center-left politics now operates, and which must be mastered if it—or rather they, for the constituents of the center-left are many and varied—are to prosper and fulfill the hopes of supporters.

The book ends not with a summary but a set of reflections on what the center-left and its components—be they socialists or social-democrats or democratic socialists or members of the Labour Party or just plain Democrats in the United States—have meant in the past and how the world they inhabit today requires that they evolve new identities, meanings, and means of being effective. The portrait which emerges is varied and nuanced. Some center-lefts are better placed than others to conciliate the demands of economic management, humane policy innovation, and popular support. Some live in institutional environments that favor success; for others this is less true. Some have been able to sustain support among a large number of voters, while others live in fragmented political landscapes that vastly complicate the tasks they need to undertake. All face a new historical crossroads, created by the collapse of the global financial sector that spread from the United States outward beginning in 2008.

It is too soon to know what this crisis will bring for center-lefts, but significant change is likely. Initial responses pointed to a blunting of the excessive faith in markets that had colored politics everywhere where center-lefts had operated for the past quarter-century, a return to government and politics in the making of key economic and social decisions, enhanced regulation of markets, and perhaps even more extensive global governance. All these initial efforts were first aid, designed to save North America, Europe, and the rest of the world from the catastrophic collapse of the global financial sector. They did not necessarily indicate a fundamental shift, and in any case history tells us that major economic crises have not immediately helped lefts. The "Great Recession" lingers, its effects still spreading, but if recent electoral cycles are an indication, it has benefited center-right parties for the most part. This is predictable, as is the way in which conservatives have sought to turn what was initially a crisis of capitalism, for which capital itself was largely blamed, into a crisis of the welfare state and social provision. The big question not yet answered is whether, as has often happened in the past, center-lefts will eventually be able to regroup, gain strength, and bring new and needed reforms. Crises can present great political opportunities, but one can never be sure just who will be able to seize these opportunities. Center-lefts should be in a position to profit if they are able to recognize that this crisis is an invitation not to resurrect the past but rather to innovate in ways that could enhance and restore economic security and produce sustainable new development and greater distributional justice and opportunity for their supporters.

Notes

1. The editors are more than aware of their debt to the enormous and thoughtful literatures on which they build. Some of that is reflected in the references, but surely not all.

For a sampling of the best literature and extensive references see Sassoon 2010 and Bartolini 2007.

2. The only really effective left internationalism of the twentieth century turned out to be imposed and enforced on communists by the Soviet Union.

3. Whether the experience of the 1970s truly disproved Keynesian notions and policy prescriptions remains controversial. So too are the questions of how and when Keynesian ideas were adopted and implemented in various countries. Even in Britain, where Keynes himself was intimately involved in policymaking from the 1920s until his death in 1945, it can be argued that Keynesianism triumphed as a means to fight inflation during the Second World War rather than as a means to counter depression and stimulate the economy. See Hall ed. 1989.

4. The narrowing is especially evident among those who seek to resist it. See, for example, the review by Therborn (2007) of the ideas and projects of those who place themselves to the left of the center-left.

5. A number of authors, most notably Iversen and Stephens (2008), have sought to combine the "varieties of capitalism" and "welfare state regimes" frameworks in a notion of "welfare production regimes." See also Schröder 2008.

6. Denmark's crisis, like that in the Netherlands, came earlier in the 1980s. The Swedes had several years of inflation, high unemployment, and financial instability in 1990 which led them to join the EU. Finland had a massive crisis with higher unemployment than anyone in the EU 15 after the end of the cold war in the 1990s. The Norwegians had oil. See Dølvik 2008 and, on the Netherlands, Visser and Hemerijk 1997.

7. The question of whether to study the United States alongside other advanced industrial societies is often debated but seldom resolved. Does "American exceptionalism" render comparison meaningless, or is the United States similar enough to justify comparison? See among many others Lipset and Marks 2000, Kopstein and Steinmo eds. 2008, and Baldwin 2009.

8. As noted above, this volume builds upon the efforts of many other scholars. There are a number of admirably broad studies on the center-left, most of which unfortunately end chronologically at roughly the point where our volume will begin. These works also focus almost exclusively on Europe. One classic example is Scharpf 1987, which treats only the end of the Keynesian postwar boom years. Other large-scale and important studies—including Bartolini 2007, Sassoon 2010, Eley 2002, and Pierson 2001a—bring their stories to a close at roughly similar points. Kitschelt 1994 is an impressive analysis whose focus is primarily on parties and voting rather than policy, and its database may now be somewhat out of date. Moschonas 2002 comes close chronologically to what we propose, even if it remains European in its focus, but Moschonas's presence among our contributors indicates that he has a great deal

more to say. Another impressive and more current study, focused on the experience of parties in power in six countries, is Merkel, Petring, Henkes, and Egle 2008. On recent developments in social democracy, including the turn toward "third way" reforms, see Bailey 2009a and Huo 2009. In more of a political theory vein see Meyer with Hinchman 2007. More prescriptively see Giddens 1998.

In addition to these general works there are a number of very good studies of the prospects of social democracy for sustaining electoral coalitions or achieving success in key policy areas: generating growth, managing industrial relations, and maintaining welfare states in the face of the new constraints. For good examples on parties and politics see Berman 2006 and two important earlier studies: Piven ed. 1992 and Anderson and Camiller 1994. There is also an extensive pertinent literature on policy areas. On economic policy per se see Boix 1998, Glyn 2001, and Blyth 2002. On social policy and the welfare state there is a huge literature. See for example the classic work by Esping-Andersen (1990), as well as Garrett 1998, Hicks 2000, Pierson 2001b, Stephens and Stephens 2001, Swank 2002, Esping-Andersen, Gallie, Hemerijk, and Myles 2002, Rieger and Leibfried 2003, Bonoli and Powell eds. 2004, Ferrera, Hemerijk, and Rhodes eds. 2006, Giddens, Diamond, and Liddle eds. 2006, Pierson 2007, Svallfors and Taylor-Gooby 2007, Rueda 2008, and Häusermann 2010.

Part I

Ideas, Projects, and Electoral Realities

Social Democracy's Past and Potential Future

Sheri Berman

The aim of this book is to figure out "what's left of the left," that is, what the left or center-left stands for and should aspire to accomplish in our current globalized world. Globalization is seen as particularly problematic for the left because it has thrown into question many of the left's traditional policies and principles. Many insist, for example, that the increasing mobility and internationalization of capital have permanently shifted the balance of power in society in capital's favor. As the exit options of capital grow, so does the bargaining power of employers vis-à-vis labor, thereby complicating efforts to regulate and control business decisions and development. Similarly, increasing international competition is said to make things like generous welfare states and high tax rates an impediment to efficiency and therefore luxuries that states can no longer afford. But perhaps more important than globalization's impact on policies traditionally associated with the left is its direct challenge to many of the postwar left's key ideological principles. Among the most striking features of contemporary globalization debates is the widespread belief in the primacy of economics. In the world envisioned by neoliberals, markets would be allowed as great a degree of freedom and as wide a scope as possible and states would be knocked from the "commanding heights" that they occupied during the postwar era (Yergin and Stanislaw 1998). Given the historic connection between social democracy and the use of the state to provide services, facilitate growth, and generally tame the market and temper its effects, the logic of this position is that at the beginning of the twenty-first century there is not much "left of the left" at all. In fact, a number of commentators have announced that "socialism is dead" and, as Ralf Dahrendorf pointedly insisted, "none of its variants can be revived." It is now time, according to Anthony Giddens, to begin the process of "burying socialism."[1]

This chapter argues that such pessimism and the reading of history that underlies it are not merely premature but wrong. Indeed, the very conditions that have led so many observers to proclaim the left's demise provide an excellent context for its reexamination and perhaps even rejuvenation. This is because for all its purported novelty, the issue at the heart of contemporary globalization debates—whether states can and should dominate market forces or must bow before them—is in fact very old. Social democracy, the most successful version of leftist thinking and politics during the twentieth century, emerged from similar debates within the international socialist movement a century ago. It is only because these debates have been forgotten or misunderstood—at least until the onset of the global financial and economic crisis of 2008—that contemporary discussions of left and contemporary political alternatives are so superficial and intellectually impoverished, and why it is so important to refresh the democratic left's collective memory about its past. This chapter will endeavor to do just that, providing a brief summary of the emergence and rationale of social democracy. It will then use this history to provide a foundation upon which to begin thinking about possible paths forward for the democratic left today.

The Origins of Social Democracy

Social democracy's intellectual origins lie in a debate that began within the international socialist movement at the end of the nineteenth century. Like now, this was a period of rapid globalization. Spurred on by new technologies in communications and transportation, capitalism had developed renewed vigor and was rapidly spreading its tentacles across the globe. These changes made many question the "orthodox" version of Marxism that had established itself as the official ideology of much of the international socialist movement by this time.[2] The most distinctive features of this doctrine (which was largely codified by Marx's collaborator and leading apostle, Friedrich Engels, and popularized by the "pope of socialism," Karl Kautsky) were historical materialism and class struggle, according to which history was propelled forward not by changes in human consciousness or behavior but rather by economic development and the resulting shifts in social relationships. As Engels put it, "The materialist conception of history starts from the proposition that . . . the final causes of all social changes and political revolutions are to be sought, not in men's brains, not in man's better insight into eternal truth and justice, but in changes in the modes of production and exchange. They are to be sought, not in the *philosophy* but in the *economics* of each particular epoch" (Engels 1962, 365–66). As one observer noted, what historical materialism offered was an "obstetric" view of history: since capitalism had within it the seeds of the future socialist society, socialists had only to wait for economic development to push the system's internal contradictions to the point where the emergence of the new order would require little more than some midwifery (Cohen 1999). And in this drama the role of midwife was played by class struggle and in particular by the proletariat. In Kautsky's words, "economic evolution inevitably brings on conditions that will compel the exploited classes to rise against this system of private ownership" (Kautsky 1910, 90–91). With each passing day, ever larger would grow the group of "propertyless workers for whom the existing system [would become] unbearable; who have nothing to lose by its downfall but everything to gain" (Kautsky 1910, 119).

By the end of the nineteenth century, however, it was becoming increasingly clear that many orthodox Marxist predictions were not coming true. The proletariat was not experiencing a steady "immiserization," small farming and businesses were not disappearing, economic growth was continuing, and general economic collapse seemed increasingly far off. Just as Marxism's failings as a guide to history and economic development were becoming clear, moreover, criticism arose within the international socialist movement regarding its inadequacy as a guide to constructive political action. Parties acting in Marx's name had become important political players in a number of European countries by the end of the nineteenth century, but orthodox Marxism could not furnish them with a strategy for using their power to achieve any practical goals. Orthodox Marxist thought had little to say about the role of political organizations in general, since it considered economic forces rather than political activism to be the prime mover of history.

Around the beginning of the twentieth century, therefore, many on the left faced a troubling dilemma: capitalism was flourishing, but the economic injustices and social fragmentation that had motivated the Marxist project in the first place remained. Orthodox Marxism offered only a counsel of passivity—of waiting for the contradictions within capitalism to bring the system down, which seemed both highly unlikely and increasingly unpalatable.

Orthodox Marxism's passive economism also did little to meet the psycho-political needs of mass populations under economic and social stress. As noted above, the last years of the nineteenth century, like those at the end of the twentieth and the beginning of the twenty-first, were marked by a wave of globalization and rapid, disorienting change. This caused immense unease in European societies, and critics, not just on the left but increasingly now on the nationalist right, railed against the glorification of self-interest and rampant individualism, the erosion of traditional values and communities, and the rise of social dislocation, atomization, and fragmentation that capitalism brought in its wake (Hughes 1977). Orthodox Marxism had little to offer those interested in actively responding to capitalism's downsides (rather than merely waiting for its collapse) and little sympathy or understanding for growing nationalist sentiment. It was against this backdrop and in response to these frustrations that revisionism emerged.

As the nineteenth century drew to its close, several socialists realized that if their desired political outcome was not going to come about because it was inevitable (as Marx, Engels, and many of their influential followers believed), then it would have to be achieved as a result of human action. Some, such as Lenin, felt that it could be *imposed*, and set out to spur history along through the politico-military efforts of a revolutionary vanguard. Others, not willing to accept the violence or élitism of such a course, chose to revamp the socialist program so as to attract the support of a majority of society. They felt that if the triumph of socialism was not going to be inevitable, it could be made *desirable* and emerge through the active, collective efforts of human beings motivated by a belief in a better, higher good.

These democratic revisionists rejected the pseudo-scientific and materialist justifications of socialism proffered by orthodox Marxists and called for a rediscovery of socialism's moral roots, for an emphasis on the ideals and spirit underpinning the original Marxist project. (As some contemporary observers noted, they wanted to exchange Hegel for Kant.) Although their thoughts and actions often emerged independently and differed according to local context, democratic revisionists shared an emphasis on the desirability rather than the necessity of socialism, on morality and ethics as opposed to science and materialism, and on human will and cross-class cooperation rather than irresistible economic forces and inevitable class conflict. The most influential member of this group was Eduard Bernstein, an important figure in both the international socialist movement and its most powerful party, the Sozialdemokratische Partei Deutschlands (SPD).

Bernstein attacked the two main pillars of orthodox Marxism—historical materialism and class struggle—and argued for an alternative based on the primacy of politics and cross-class cooperation. His observations about capitalism led him to believe that it was not heading toward its collapse but rather was becoming increasingly complex and adaptable. Thus instead of waiting until capitalism's demise for socialism to emerge, he favored trying to actively reform the existing system. In his view the prospects for socialism depended "not on the decrease but on the increase of . . . wealth," and on the ability of socialists to come up with "positive suggestions for reform" capable of spurring fundamental change (Bernstein 1898).

Bernstein's loss of belief in the inevitability of socialism led him to appreciate the potential for political action. In his view, orthodox Marxists' faith in historical materialism had bred a dangerous political passivity that would cost them the enthusiasm of the masses. He felt that the doctrine of inevitable class struggle shared the same fatal flaws, being both historically inaccurate and politically debilitating. There was actually a natural community of interest between workers and the vast majority of society that suffered from the injustices of the capitalist system, he argued, and socialists should regard dissatisfied elements of the middle classes and peasantry as potential allies ready to be converted to the cause.

Bernstein's arguments were echoed by a small but growing number of revisionist socialists across Europe, who shared an emphasis on a political path to socialism rather than its necessity, and on cross-class cooperation rather than class conflict. During the last years of the nineteenth century and the first years of the twentieth, revisionism progressed in fits and starts, within and across several countries, and although Bernstein and his fellow revisionists insisted that they were merely "revising" or "updating" Marxism, their fiercest critics—the defenders of orthodoxy—saw clearly what the revisionists themselves were loath to admit: that they were arguing for a replacement of Marxism with something entirely different. By abandoning historical materialism and class struggle, they were in fact rejecting Marxism as thoroughly as Marx had rejected liberalism a half-century earlier. But the revisionists were not yet ready to fully accept the implications of their views and make a clean break with orthodoxy. The result was growing tension and confusion, which left the international socialist movement, like many of its constituent parties, a house divided against itself. The First World War and its aftermath brought the house down.

The vast changes unleashed by the Great War led many on the left to explicitly reject class struggle and historical materialism and to openly embrace their antitheses—cross-class cooperation and the primacy of politics. The doctrine of class struggle suffered a critical blow with the outbreak of the war. Socialist parties across the continent abandoned their suspicion of bourgeois parties and institutions and threw their support behind the states they had hitherto pledged to destroy. The doctrine came under even more pressure in the postwar era, as the democratic wave that spread across much of Europe confronted socialists with unprecedented opportunities for participation in bourgeois governments. Given a chance to help form or even lead democratic administrations, many were forced to recognize the uncomfortable truth that workers alone could never deliver an electoral majority and that cooperation with non-proletarians was the price of political power. The war also revealed the immense mobilizing power of nationalism and bred a generation that valued community, solidarity, and struggle. Populist right-wing movements across the continent were riding these trends, and many socialists worried that clinging to orthodox Marxism's emphasis on class conflict and proletarian exclusivity would prevent them from responding to the needs of ordinary citizens and thus cause them to lose ground to competitors.

The second pillar of orthodox Marxism, historical materialism, was also dealt a critical blow by the war and its aftermath. The pivotal position occupied by socialist parties in many newly democratized countries after the Great War made it increasingly difficult to avoid the question of how political power could contribute to socialist transformation, and the subsequent onset of the Great Depression made submission to economic forces tantamount to political suicide. Protests against liberalism and capitalism had been growing since the end of the nineteenth century, but war and depression gave these protests a mass base and renewed momentum, with the legions of the disaffected ready to be claimed by any political movement promising to tame markets. Orthodoxy's emphasis on letting economic forces be the drivers of history meant that here too it ceded ground to activist groups on the right.

As socialist parties stumbled and fell in country after country, a growing number of socialists became convinced that a whole new vision was necessary for their movement—one that would supplant rather than tinker with orthodoxy. So they turned to the themes set out by revisionism's pioneers a generation earlier: the value of cross-class cooperation and the primacy of politics. In the context of the interwar years and the Great Depression this meant first and foremost using political forces to control economic ones. Where orthodox Marxists and classical liberals preached passivity in the face of economic catastrophe, the new, truly "social democratic" leftists fought for programs that would use the power of the state to tame the capitalist system. Neither hoping for capitalism's demise nor worshipping the market uncritically, they argued that the market's anarchic and destructive powers could and should be fettered at the same time that its ability to produce unprecedented material bounty was exploited. They thus came to champion a real "third way" between laissez-faire liberalism and Soviet communism. These themes found their advocates within all socialist parties. In Belgium, Holland, and France, for example, Hendrik De Man and his *Plan du travail* found energetic champions. De Man argued for an activist strategy to combat economic depression, an evolutionary transformation of capitalism, and a focus on the control rather than the ownership of capital. Activists in other parts of Europe echoed these themes: in Germany and Austria reformers advocated government intervention in the economy and pseudo-Keynesian stimulus programs; and in Sweden the Swedish social democratic party, the SAP, initiated the single most ambitious attempt to reshape capitalism from within (Berman 2006).

Regardless of the specific policies they advocated, one thing that joined all budding interwar social democrats was a rejection of the passivity and economic determinism of orthodox Marxism and a belief in the need to use state power to tame capitalism. In order to do this, however—and finally relegate historical materialism to the dustbin of history—they had to win majority support for their programs and fight back the advances of the growing nationalist right. Hence during the interwar years many returned to the themes of cross-class cooperation that Bernstein and other revisionists had preached a generation earlier. In an era of dislocation and disorientation, these social democrats realized that appeals to the "people," the "community," and the common good were much more attractive than the class struggle perspective of orthodox Marxism or the individualism of classic liberals. Therefore they often embraced communitarian, corporatist, and even nationalist appeals and urged their parties to make the transition from workers' to "people's" parties.

It was only in Scandinavia and in Sweden in particular that a unified party embraced this new approach wholeheartedly. This is why one must turn to the Swedish case to observe the full dimensions, and potential, of the social democratic experiment at this time. During the interwar years the SAP began to develop a comprehensive economic program designed to harness the powers of the market and reshape the Swedish polity. In selling this program to the electorate, especially during the depression, the SAP stressed its activism and commitment to the common good. For example, during the election campaign of 1932 a leading party paper proclaimed: "Humanity carries its destiny in its own hands. . . . Where the bourgeoisie preach laxity and submission to . . . fate, we appeal to people's desire for creativity . . . conscious that we both can and will succeed in shaping a social system in which the fruits of labor will go to the benefit of those who are willing to . . . participate in the common task" (Social-Demokraten, 15 September 1932).

The SAP's leader Per Albin Hansson, meanwhile, was popularizing his theme of Sweden as the "folkhemm" or "people's home." He declared, "The basis of the home is community and togetherness" and stressed that social democracy strove to "break down the barriers that . . . separate citizens" (Hansson 1982 [1928]). The result was that while in countries such as Germany and Italy the populist right assumed the mantle of communal solidarity and put together devastatingly effective cross-class coalitions, in Sweden it was the social democrats who became seen as the champions of the "little people," the party that was "one with the nation" and was taking critical steps toward becoming a true "people's party." These positions helped the SAP to form a majority government through an alliance with the peasantry, and reap political rewards from the economic recovery that eventually occurred.

By the mid-1930s the democratic strand of revisionism had therefore blossomed into a powerful and creative political movement all its own. Orthodox Marxism's historical materialism and class struggle were jettisoned for a belief in the primacy of politics and cross-class cooperation, and these principles were translated into a distinctive and viable policy agenda based on a "people's party" approach together with a commitment to using the state to control markets. Together this added up to social democracy. It was only in Sweden, however, that social democrats were able to take charge of a political party, and so it was only there that the social democratic agenda was fully implemented during the interwar period.

The Postwar Era

If during the interwar years social democrats generally lost the battle for the soul of the left, except in Scandinavia and particularly in Sweden, the story changed after the Second World War as many of the social democrats' ideas and policies ultimately triumphed, on the left and across much of the political spectrum. The political chaos and social dislocation of the 1930s were held to have been caused by the Great Depression, which in turn was held to have been caused by unregulated markets—and so actors from across the European political spectrum agreed on the inadvisability of taking that path again. And so as Europe struggled to rebuild economically while trying to head off the political and social instability that had led to ruin in the past, there was widespread agreement that unchecked capitalism could threaten goals in all three spheres. After 1945, therefore, Western European nations started to construct a new order, one that could ensure economic growth while at the same time protecting societies from capitalism's destructive consequences (Marglin and Schor 1991; Armstrong, Glyn, and Harrison 1991). As John Ruggie has put it, postwar policymakers "seized upon the state in the attempt to reimpose broader and more direct social control over market forces," redefining the "legitimate social purposes in pursuit of which state power was expected to be employed in the domestic economy" (Ruggie 1982, 386). No longer would states be limited to ensuring that markets could grow and flourish; no longer were economic interests to be given the widest possible leeway. Instead, after 1945 the state became generally understood as the guardian of society rather than the economy, and economic imperatives were often forced to take a back seat to social ones. Throughout Western Europe states explicitly committed themselves to managing markets and protecting society from its most destructive effects.

Across Europe, in short, the postwar order represented something quite unusual. Crosland pointed out that it was "different in kind from classical capitalism . . . in almost every respect that one can think of" (Crosland 1967, 34), while Andrew Shonfield questioned whether "the economic order under which we now live and the social structure that goes with it are so different from what preceded them that it [has become] misleading . . . to use the word 'capitalism' to describe them" (Shonfield 1969, 3). But of course capitalism did remain—even though it was a very different capitialism than before. After 1945 the market system was tempered and limited by political power, and the state was explicitly committed to protecting society from the market's worst consequences. Scholars have long recognized that this new order represented both a decisive break with the past and a repudiation of the radical left's hopes for an end to capitalism (Maier 1981; Offe 1983). What they have often failed to appreciate is just how much it was a repudiation of traditional liberalism as well. The core principle of the new system—that political forces should control economic ones—was a reversal of both classical liberalism's theory and its long-standing practice. The most common term used to describe the postwar system—Ruggie's "embedded liberalism" (Ruggie 1982)—is thus a misnomer. If liberalism can be stretched to encompass an order that saw unchecked markets as dangerous, that had public interests trump private prerogatives, and that granted states the right to intervene in the economy and society to protect a "common" or "public" interest, then the term is so elastic as to be nearly useless. In fact, rather than a modified, updated form of liberalism, what spread like wildfire after the war was really something quite different: social democracy.

Although the postwar order represented a clear triumph for social democratic principles, and marked the first time that Western Europe was able to combine economic growth, well-functioning democracy, and social stability, social democracy's victory was not complete. Many on the right accepted the new system out of necessity alone: once their fear of economic and social chaos (and the radical left) faded, their commitment to the new order also faded. But more interestingly, many on the left failed to understand or wholeheartedly accept the social democratic compromise. Although after 1945 almost all democratic socialist parties eventually turned themselves into champions of policies that helped temper and redirect market forces, this practical reorientation was not always matched by an equivalent ideological one. Many democratic leftists may have embraced social democratic words but still didn't hear the music, and they continued to proclaim their dedication to classic, pre-war ideological goals such as transcending capitalism entirely and avoiding too-close relationships with non-proletarian groups.

The classic unfolding of this drama occurred in Germany. Despite a radically changed environment, after the war the German social democratic party, SPD, offered Germans a rehashed version of its pre-war program and appeal.[3] The theoretical and historical sections of the party's program spoke in traditional Marxist tones not dramatically different from those invoked at Erfurt more than half a century earlier. Kurt Schumacher, who dominated the leadership until his death in 1952, proclaimed: "The crucial point [of the SPD's contemporary agenda] is the abolition of capitalist exploitation and the transfer of the means of production from the control of the big proprietors to social ownership, the management of the economy as a whole in accordance not with the interests of private profit but with the principles of economically necessary planning. The muddle of the capitalist private-economy . . . cannot be tolerated. Planning and control are not socialism; they are only prerequisites for it. The crucial step is to be seen in drastic socialisation" (Schumacher 1986 [1945], 274).

In addition to offering a bleak, intransigent view of capitalism's possibilities and calling for widespread nationalization, the SPD more or less returned to its traditional emphasis on workers and suspicion of other parties. Under Schumacher "the party slid all too easily into the oppositional stance of the Weimar days, supremely confident that it could spurn co-operation with bourgeois parties and win power effortlessly through the logic of history" (Carr 1987, 194). But if Schumacher and his cronies were comfortable with such a position, others in the party, and especially its younger echelons, were not. As the SPD's membership declined in the 1950s, it became painfully clear that without a change it was heading for permanent minority status. Meanwhile, the contrast between an increasingly dictatorial regime in the East and the Federal Republic's prospering economy helped many to realize that a fully socialized economy was inimical to both democracy and growth (Carr 1987, 196). As a result, in 1955 Schumacher's successor Erich Ollenhauer set up a commission to reevaluate the party's direction and appeal.

The outcome was a full reconsideration of the SPD's course in German politics, the famed Bad Godesberg program. Essentially this committed the SPD to the twin aims of a modern social-democratic program: a people's party strategy and a commitment to reform capitalism rather than destroy it. In particular, Bad Godesberg proclaimed that the party "no longer considered nationalization the major principle of a socialist economy but only one of several (and then only the last) means of controlling economic concentration and power" (Braunthal 1994, 18). In the program's well-known phrase, it committed the SPD to promoting "as much competition as possible, as much planning as necessary." Bad Godesberg also attempted to reach beyond the working class by making clear the party's desire for better relations with the churches and its commitment to defending the country and supporting its military. Finally, the Bad Godesberg program marked the triumph of social democracy through its clear, if implicit, severing of socialism from Marxism:

> Democratic socialism, which in Europe is rooted in Christian ethics, humanism and classical philosophy, does not proclaim ultimate truths — not because of any lack of understanding for or indifference to philosophical or religious truths, but out of respect for the individual's choice in these matters of conscience in which neither the state nor any political party should be allowed to interfere.
>
> The Social Democratic party is the party of freedom of thought. It is a community of men holding different beliefs and ideas. Their agreement is based on the moral principles and political aims they have in common. The Social Democratic party strives for a way of life in accordance with these principles. Socialism is a constant task — to fight for freedom and justice, to preserve them and to live up to them. (Miller and Potthoff, 1986, 275)

Bad Godesberg marked a clear shift in the SPD's stated identity and goals. Yet if somewhere Bernstein was smiling about his ultimate triumph over Kautsky, he might also have been a bit troubled, because the shift was at least as much pragmatic as it was principled, motivated by a desire to break out of a political ghetto rather than a decision to chart a bold course for the future. In a country where national socialism was a recent memory and "real, existing" socialism was being built next door, the wish to avoid ideology and grand projects is perhaps easy to understand. And it was made possible by the leadership transition to Ollenhauer, "a solid, loyal party functionary, a man dedicated to oiling the wheels of a smoothly running bureaucratic machine [who] was as far removed from the consuming political passions that fired Kurt Schumacher as anyone in the SPD could be" (Parness 1991, 60). But if the SPD's de-ideologizing made it more palatable and less scary to voters — and it did indeed eventually lead to an expansion of the party's support and its participation in government — it also had its drawbacks. In particular, it "rendered [the SPD] unserviceable as a nexus for creating and reproducing utopian aspirations" (Gorski and Markovits 1993, 44), alienating from the party those dissatisfied with the status quo and looking to transform it into something better.

By the 1960s the SPD's reorientation had thus opened a political space to the party's left, a trend furthered by its increasing intolerance of intraparty disputes and its own activists, and the fall-out from its "Grand Coalition" with the CDU. When the pragmatic and centrist Helmut Schmidt became chancellor after Willy Brandt resigned in 1974, the SPD's postwar transformation was complete. Competent and determined but lacking transformative goals and an ideological temperament, Schmidt focused on proving that his government, and the SPD more generally, were the most capable caretakers of Germany's domestic economy and international standing. Schmidt committed himself to maintaining and improving the living standards of Germany's citizens and committed the country to accepting NATO missiles on European soil. Although successful on their own terms, these stances further alienated the left, and by tying the party's fortunes ever closer to the country's economy they made the SPD vulnerable to the economic downturn that began in the 1970s.

In short, by the 1970s the SPD had become so fully integrated into the system, and so inflexible and ideologically exhausted, that the partial discrediting of its leadership by economic turmoil dealt it a blow from which it has yet to recover. Over the next generation the party hemorrhaged members and increasingly became a home for the elderly and beneficiaries of the status quo. It lost the support of the young and the radical (many of whom turned left to the Greens), as well as many of the poor, unemployed, and alienated (some of whom have lately turned to right and left-wing populism and some to the left, die Linke). Lacking anything distinctive to offer, the hollowed-out SPD now finds itself electorally vulnerable, subject to internal dissension, and increasingly unable to generate either enthusiasm or commitment from anybody.

In Italy and France the left's trajectories were not entirely dissimilar, although it took even longer for socialists in both countries to make their peace with reality. In Italy the socialists "jettisoned what remained of [their] Marxist heritage" only in the 1970s (De Grand 1989, 161–62). When the Partito Socialista Italiano (PSI) reestablished itself after the war it quickly returned, like the SPD, to many of the same patterns and practices that had doomed it to irrelevance in the 1920s. Its initial postwar leader, Pietro Nenni, sought to ally, and even merge, with the Communists (the PCI), and believed that the party's foremost goal should be the immediate formation of a "socialist Republic." His stances alienated the party's more moderate and social democratic elements, leaving the PSI weakened by infighting.

By 1947 Nenni's opponents had split off, leaving him free to dally with the Communists and reorganize the party along Leninist lines, thereby turning it into probably the "most radical and, in a Marxist sense, fundamentalist, of all

European socialist movements" (Laqueur 1970, 155). Despite or probably because of this, the PCI soon overwhelmed the hapless PSI, becoming the main party of the left and wresting away control of many of the affiliated organizations of the labor movement (Di Scala 1998, 280). This left the Italian center up for grabs, a situation of which the Christian Democrats took full advantage to become Italy's dominant party.

After many years of political irrelevance the PSI was finally turned around by Bettino Craxi, who transformed it into a moderate reformist center-left party by the 1970s. At least initially this strategy paid off, and Craxi became the first socialist prime minister of Italy in 1983. Yet the party proved unable to build on this success and construct a distinctive and dynamic movement with broad appeal. It was "too late to wrench the PCI's strong grip from the masses" (Colarizi 1996, 151), and in any case the PSI now lacked the type of clear ideological profile that might attract committed followers and engender real enthusiasm. Making matters worse, Craxi suffered from the same weaknesses as other Italian politicians, and in the 1990s he was convicted of accepting bribes and kickbacks. With a discredited leader and no particular raison d'être, Italian socialism found its renewal short-lived.

French socialism offers yet another dreary version of the same theme. After the war the Section Française de l'Internationale Ouvrière (SFIO) abandoned many of its traditional policy stances, and most importantly ended its long-standing internal battles over whether to accept a position as a junior partner in a governing coalition. Nevertheless, despite such changes the party was unable to make a full break with its past or drop its Marxist rhetoric. Its most prominent member, Léon Blum, vociferously urged a change of course and pushed for a socialism based on evolutionary rather than revolutionary change, one committed to appealing to "people in every walk of life" rather than one steeped in class warfare and worker exclusivity (Graham 1994, 271–76; Halperin 1946). Yet his pleas were rejected, and at its first postwar congress in August 1945 the SFIO proclaimed: "The Socialist party is by its nature a revolutionary party. It aims at replacing capitalist private property by a society in which natural resources and the means of production are socially owned and classes have been abolished. Such a revolutionary transformation, though in the interest of all mankind, is to be achieved only by the working class. . . . The Socialist party is a party of class struggle founded on the organized working class" (Braunthal 1967, 24).

During the following years the orthodox faction of the party continued to gain in strength. At the party's congress in 1946, for example, this wing, under the leadership of Guy Mollet (who soon became the party's general secretary), attacked Blum's "watering down" of the party's principles and "all attempts at revisionism, notably those which are inspired by a false humanism whose true significance is to mask fundamental realities—that is, the class struggle" (Colton 1966), 459.

Unsurprisingly, as a result the party's membership declined from 354,000 in 1946 to 60,000 in 1960, while its share of the vote dropped from 23% in 1945 to 12.6% in 1962. Its bastions of support ended up being not the working classes, the young, or the more dynamic sectors of the economy but rather middle-aged civil servants and professionals along with those who stood to lose from rapid social and economic change (such as textile workers and small farmers). As in Germany and Italy, meanwhile, one consequence of the SFIO's rhetorical radicalism was that it provided an opening for the center-right—here in the form of Gaullism—to capture those groups alienated by the left and form a true cross-class coalition on the other side of the aisle, thereby becoming the dominant force in French political life.

The SFIO remained stuck in a rut through the 1960s; yet continual electoral defeats, culminating in routs in 1968 and 1969, finally led to change. Mollet retired in 1969 and a new, more pragmatic organization, the Parti Socialiste (PS), arose in 1971. It insisted on maintaining a clear left-wing profile, at least in part so that it could form an alliance with the Communists. The two forces eventually agreed on a unity program, the Programme Commun, which committed the Communists to democracy and pluralism and the socialists to economic radicalism, including large-scale nationalizations. This combined front came to power in 1981 during an economic downturn by convincing voters that it had the most promising and innovative solutions to France's problems.

Unfortunately the socialists' economic program did not work out as hoped, and the long-awaited socialist government soon found itself overseeing an economy in turmoil. Forced to act but with little else to fall back on, the socialists ended up making a dramatic volte-face: by 1982 the PS had moved from advocating one of the most radical economic programs of any socialist party in Europe to implementing deflationary measures and dramatically cutting public spending. By the end of the twentieth century the French socialists, like their German and Italian counterparts, had shown themselves able to win elections but could no longer explain to themselves or others why anyone should care.

Not all socialist parties suffered the same fate. As might be expected, the Swedes did well—largely because they, unlike most socialist parties elsewhere, understood and believed in what they were doing. The SAP was able to prosper at the polls and maintain its distinctiveness by recognizing that the two tasks were in fact complementary: the party's ability to integrate individual policy initiatives into a larger social democratic whole ensured that it remained more vibrant and successful than most of its counterparts in the rest of Europe.

To be sure, the Swedish social democrats started off the postwar era in a better position than parties on the left elsewhere. They could build on their own governing record rather than struggle to reestablish their very existence as a party, and their country emerged in better shape from the war than did most others. But even more than luck and a head start, their success was due to their having fully internalized the core elements of social democratic ideology and devoted themselves to developing creative policies for putting them into practice.

Politically the SAP worked during the postwar years to strengthen its hold over a broad cross-section of the Swedish electorate. Continuing the strategy that it had embraced during the interwar years, the party directed its appeals not to workers alone but to the Swedish "people" (*folk*) in general. In doing so it exploited its wartime leadership role, loudly proclaiming its commitment to social solidarity and the national interest. There was no conflict between these positions and social democracy, the party insisted, because social democracy properly understood was all about advancing collective interests rather than those of a particular group or class. SAP appeals were saturated with references to "solidarity," "cooperation," and "togetherness." This was especially true in discussions of plans for an expanded welfare state, which was presented as part of the SAP's strategy for creating "the strong society" (*starka samhället*) and protecting the public from the uncertainties and insecurities inherent in modern capitalism. Meanwhile the SAP also continued along its pre-war path of using state intervention to manage the economy and sever the link between individuals' market position and their broader life chances (Stephens 1986; Svensson 2002; Pontusson this volume). What made these efforts so distinctive was not only the sizable amount of intervention and decommodification they involved, but also the way they were presented as part of a larger, transformative project. The Rehn-Meidner model, for example, was sold not merely as a practical package of wage regulations but as a case study in the party's strategy of increasing "social control" over the economy without resorting to full-scale nationalization (Meidner 1993, 211). The Swedish welfare state was understood in a similar way. Its comprehensiveness and universalism helped "manufacture broad class (even cross-class) solidarity and social democratic consensus," while at the same time marginalizing "the market as the principal agent of distribution and the chief determinant of peoples' life chances" (Esping-Andersen 1985, 245). The party consciously used social policy to expand its hold over the electorate and develop a sense of common interests across classes.

Recognizing the growing importance of white-collar workers, for example, the SAP explicitly designed social policies that would appeal to them and tie their interests to those of other workers. This was particularly clear in the fight over supplemental pensions at the end of the 1950s, when the SAP "stressed the common interests of manual and white-collar workers [in these pensions] and the struggle for the[m] as of vital interest for all wage-earners" (Svensson 1994, 272). As with increased economic management, moreover, welfare state enhancements were presented as valuable not only on their own terms but as steps toward a better future. The party insisted that the welfare state itself represented a form of socialism, since under it "the total income of the people was regarded as a common resource and a portion of it was transferred to those with inadequate incomes" (Sainsbury 1990, 66).

All these strategies proved quite successful, and in the years after the war the SAP was able to remain firmly anchored in the working class while strengthening its support well beyond it. Still by far the largest party in the Swedish political system, it used its dominance to shift the country's center of political gravity to the left, and built the greatest record of political hegemony of any party in a democratic country during the twentieth century.

Even so, the party did not escape unscathed from some of the problems that set back its counterparts elsewhere. Like them, in the 1970s it was forced to reevaluate some of its traditional tactics and even strategies (Blyth 2002). It went through a period in the late 1980s when it appeared to be drifting intellectually and politically (Blyth 2002). But because it had strong reserves of political, ideological, and intellectual capital to draw on, and had reshaped the political and social structure of Swedish society so extensively, in the end the party was able to weather the storm better than others. It bounced back politically, recaptured power in the 1980s, and although currently out of office, remains the dominant party in the Swedish political system (although it is not as hegemonic as before). It has maintained its ability to appeal to voters across much of the political spectrum and managed to coopt many new "postmaterialist" issues such as environmentalism and women's rights. And economically it recovered from the fiasco surrounding wage earners' funds by essentially promising the electorate that it would maintain traditional social democratic policies while updating them as appropriate to deal with contemporary challenges—something at which it has been relatively successful, overseeing impressive economic growth in recent years during its time in office, while still maintaining high levels of social spending and a commitment to egalitarianism and social solidarity.

Perhaps the SAP's greatest success has been to preserve a sense of social democratic distinctiveness in Sweden (Castles 1978). Despite all the changes that have occurred in both the domestic and international economy over recent decades and the current existence of a bourgeois government, the vast majority of Swedes acknowledge and accept the SAP's basic ideas about the virtues of social solidarity, egalitarianism, and political control over the economy. Rather than question whether these social democratic concepts are worthwhile, political debate in Sweden has tended to be about whether the socialists or the bourgeois parties are best able to implement them together with steady growth.

UNDERSTANDING SOCIAL DEMOCRACY'S original rationale and gaining a renewed appreciation for its role in twentieth-century political development is reason enough to reconsider the movement's history. It turns out that there are other pressing reasons to do so as well, since many of the hard-earned insights of earlier ideological battles have been forgotten in recent years, as a shallow version of neoliberalism has come to exert an almost Gramscian hegemony over mainstream public debate.

Globalization, it is often said, marks a new era. The spread of markets across the globe, and the deepening and quickening of economic interconnections accompanying it, is creating a fundamentally new environment for leaders and publics, imposing burdens while constraining choices. You can either opt out of the system and languish, or put on what Thomas Friedman has called neoliberalism's "Golden Straitjacket"—at which point "two things tend to happen: your economy grows and your politics shrinks" (Friedman 1999, 87).

Globalization's onward march has produced a backlash too, of course, and anti-globalization protests have become a regular feature of contemporary life. Yet if contemporary neoliberals of the right and center dismiss concerns about globalization's individual and social costs, large sectors of the left exhibit the opposite tendency and dismiss the huge gains that the global spread of capitalism has brought, particularly to the poor in the developing world. These debates resemble nothing so much as those that took place a century ago, out of which the social democratic worldview first emerged (Berman 2006).

Democratic revisionists such as Bernstein saw that capitalism was not collapsing and seemed likely to be around for at least the medium term. They decided accordingly to try to reform and reshape it rather than destroy it. Democratic revisionists also recognized the need to counter the immense mobilizing power of nationalism and offer something to the vast majority of people suffering from the injustices and dislocations of capitalism. Their successors a generation later built upon this foundation, arguing that the time had come to put aside calls for capitalism's collapse and instead focus on managing and directing markets. By the 1930s social democrats recognized that markets and capitalism were not only here to stay but were an invaluable tool for producing growth and wealth. At the same time, they never wavered in their insistence that while markets made great servants, they also made terrible masters. Capitalism might be necessary to ensure an ever-increasing economic pie, but it had to be carefully regulated by states so that its negative social and political consequences could be kept in check. During the 1930s social democrats came to see as never before how widespread and powerful was the longing for some sort of communal identity and social solidarity, and that if they did not come up with some convincing response to this longing, other more nefarious movements would do so in their place.

Whether or not the participants recognize it, in other words, today's battles over globalization are best viewed as simply the latest chapter in an ongoing debate over how to reconcile capitalism with democracy and social stability. Now as before, liberals who venerate markets uncritically and old-style leftists who are unwilling to recognize any good in them have little to offer the vast majority of people who recognize and want to share in capitalism's material benefits but who fear its social and political consequences. Then as now, many liberals only see capitalism's benefits while many on the left only see its radical flaws, leaving it to social democrats to grapple with a full appreciation of both.

Participants at both extremes of today's globalization debates need to be reminded that it was only through the postwar settlement that capitalism and democracy found a way to live together amicably in much of the West. Without the amazing economic results generated by the operations of relatively free markets, the dramatic improvements of mass living standards throughout the West would not have been possible. Without the social protections and limits on markets imposed by states, in turn, capitalism's benefits would never have been distributed so widely and political and social stability would have been infinitely more difficult to achieve. One of the great ironies of the twentieth century is that the very success of this social democratic compromise led it to become a background condition of modern life, letting us forget how new and controversial it was at one time.

Thus the appropriate response to contemporary conditions is neither to worship capitalism nor scorn it, but to recognize its advantages *and* disadvantages and figure out ways to deploy the former against the latter. The challenge is to dust off the principles underlying the postwar settlement and generate from them new initiatives that address today's new problems and opportunities. Many of the policies that worked during the postwar era have run out of steam, and the left should not be afraid to jettison them. The important thing is not the policies but the goals—encouraging growth while at the same time protecting citizens from capitalism's negative consequences. In the era opened up by capitalism's most recent crisis, the opportunity for such political creativity is great, but it will not last forever.

Building on the best traditions, the center-left must reiterate its commitment to managing change rather than fighting it, embracing the future rather than running from it. This might seem straightforward, but in fact it is not generally accepted. Many European and American liberals and social democrats are devoted to familiar policies and approaches regardless of their practical relevance or lack of success. And many peddle fear of the future, fear of change, and fear of the other. Increasing globalization and the dramatic rise of giants in the developing world such as China and India are seen as threats rather than opportunities.

At its root, these fears stem from the failure of many on the center-left to appreciate that capitalism can be a positive-sum game, not a zero-sum one— that over the long run the operations of relatively free markets can produce net wealth rather than simply shift it from one pocket to another. Because social democrats understand that basic point, they want to do what they can to encourage trade and growth and cultivate as large a net surplus as possible— all the better to tap it to pay for measures that can equalize life chances and cushion publics from the terrors and blows that markets can inflict.

Helping people adjust to capitalism, rather than engaging in a hopeless and ultimately counterproductive effort to hold it back, has been the historic accomplishment of the social democratic left, and it remains its primary goal today in those countries where the social democratic way of thinking is most deeply ensconced. Many analysts have remarked, for example, on the impressive success that countries like Denmark and Sweden have had in managing globalization—promoting economic growth has increased competitiveness even as the state has ensured high employment and social security. The Scandinavian cases show conclusively that social welfare and economic dynamism are not enemies but natural allies. Not surprisingly, according to surveys it is precisely in these countries that optimism about the future and opinions of globalization are highest. In other parts of Europe, on the other hand, fear of the future is pervasive and opinions of globalization astoundingly low. Since the election of 2008 opinion in the United States has been decidedly more mixed. The goal of the American center-left should therefore be to advocate policies and programs that promote both growth and social solidarity, rather than forcing a choice between them. Concretely this means agitating for policies—like reliable, affordable, and portable healthcare, tax credits and other government support for retraining, investment in education, and unemployment programs that are both more generous and characterized by properly aligned incentives—that will help workers adjust to change rather than make them fear it.

Just as important is for the center-left to regain its former optimism and vision. Many self-described parties of the left and center-left win elections, but few inspire much hope or offer more than a kinder, gentler version of a generic centrist platform. Given the left's past, this is simply astonishing. The left has traditionally been driven by the conviction that a better world is possible to achieve and that it is the left's job to bring it into being. But somehow this conviction was lost during the last few decades. As Michael Jacobs has noted, "Up through the 1980s politics on the left was enchanted—not by spirits, but by radical idealism; the belief that the words could be fundamentally different. But cold, hard political realism has now done for radical idealism what rationality did for pre-Enlightenment spirituality. Politics has been disenchanted" (Jacobs 2002). Many have welcomed this shift, believing that transformative projects are passé or even dangerous. But this loss of faith in transformation "has been profoundly damaging, not just for the causes of progressive politics but for a wider sense of public engagement with the political process."

As social democratic pioneers of the late nineteenth century and the early twentieth recognized, the most important thing that politics can provide is a sense of the possible. Against Marxism's and liberalism's laissez-faire and ultimately passive views of history, they pleaded for the development of a political ideology based on the idea that people working together could and should make the world a better place. The result was the most successful political movement of the twentieth century, one that shaped the basic politico-economic framework under which we still live. The problems of the twenty-first century may be different in form, but they are not different in kind. There is no reason that the accomplishment cannot be developed and extended.

Notes

1. See Sassoon 1996, 647, for quotes from Alain Touraine, Dahrendorf, and Giddens.
2. There is a great debate in the literature about whether "orthodox Marxism" is a logical continuation or betrayal of Marx's thought. Since I am not concerned here with the true nature of Marxism but rather with how a generation of socialists interpreted or perceived Marxism, this debate is not directly relevant to the argument presented here. Nonetheless, it is clear that Marx's relative lack of concern with politics, combined with his emphasis on the primacy of economic forces in history, created a fateful

dynamic for the generation of socialists that followed him. See, for example, Miliband 1977; Tucker 1970; Gouldner 1980; Schwartz 1995; and Cohen 1999.

3. This is perhaps easier to understand if one recognizes that many of the party's initial postwar leaders came from its pre-war ranks. Carr 1987; Miller and Potthoff 1986.

Historical Decline or Change of Scale?

The Electoral Dynamics of European
Social Democratic Parties, 1950–2009

Gerassimos Moschonas

I wish it was the sixties.
–Radiohead, "The Bends" (quoted in Glyn 2006)

Is Something Important Happening to Electoral Social Democracy?

In this period of significant political and ideological change, electoral developments have attracted lively research on an international scale. Paradoxically, however, the electoral dynamics of party families have not been sufficiently studied from a comparative and historical point of view. As regards social democracy, a very limited number of works are devoted to the diachronic development of its electoral strength although arguments about electoral trends are everywhere (Merkel 1992a; Merkel 2001; Delwit 2005; Bergounioux and Grunberg 1996; and, for the European elections, Grunberg and Moschonas 2005). What hasn't been written and said, by scholars and pundits and politicians themselves, about the sudden weakness or strong resurgence, the stagnation or golden age, the crisis, the decline, the stability, or indeed the end of social democracy?

The question of the electoral development of social democracy will be the principal subject of this chapter, which charts the electoral condition of European socialism decade by decade from the 1950s to 4 October 2009; 1950 is chosen as the starting point for observation because an analysis of electoral trends can only usefully begin then. The immediate postwar period was certainly a critical moment, but the lack of electoral crystallization and consolidation renders it highly anomalous and hence inappropriate as a point of departure.

The performance of socialist and social democratic parties will be observed in sixteen West European states (including, since the 1970s, Greece, Portugal and Spain). Italy will be excluded from the statistics, even though it is a country where the left has been (and remains) influential, and not only electorally. The bankruptcy of the Italian Socialist Party (PSI) in the 1990s (a unique case of the actual disappearance of a socialist party) and its "replacement" by a communist party putatively transformed into a "fully fledged social-democratic party" (Favretto 2006, 163)—today's Democratic Party—make diachronic comparison inappropriate. This is all the more true because the electoral bases of these two parties, which were rivals for many years, were historically very different in terms of electoral sociology. Including Italy would complete the general picture but would also lead to distortions of the "dynamic" picture that is our main focus.[1]

This effort will provide a comprehensive empirical grounding to help answer the questions that swirl around the state and fate of the center-left, and of social democracy in particular. Is it possible to craft a reliable periodization of the electoral development of European socialism? Was there an electoral golden age? Is the hypothesis of decline corroborated by the electoral facts? Is the thesis of overall stability (or "slight decline"), which is dominant in the specialist literature, confirmed? Which national parties have been the big winners and the big losers over these last sixty years? What happened in the late 1990s, during a "brief spell of social-democratic hegemony" (Bonoli 2004, 197), when social democrats dominated governments in Europe? To these questions I shall try to provide a "quantitative" response, while being fully conscious that the quantitative necessarily prompts interpretive or explanatory reflections, which will be taken up in the final part of this chapter.

The central question is of course whether something important is happening to social democracy as an electoral force. The answer is an unequivocal yes. Social democracy is in electoral crisis, albeit not in all countries, and where it is, not to the same degree and not in the same way. Despite local variations, the qualifications suggested by the specialist literature have now been overtaken by the steady march of electoral indicators. The trend is neither cyclical nor random. This crisis is not "historic," and there is probably nothing inexorable about it, but it is serious. The solidity of the "old house" (to borrow a phrase from Léon Blum) is shaken, and the decline is profound and serious. Social democracy is experiencing a new electoral era, even if the dynamics of electoral change proceed in zigzags. The medium-term prospects for social democrats look bleak, and the recovery will not be easy.

Is there then "nothing but doom and gloom in the house of social democracy"? (Berger 2004, 393). The answer is paradoxical: in terms of electoral arithmetic the crisis is serious; in terms of its political significance for governance it seems less so. This is a new electoral era, and the center-left is not the only political force to be affected, so the concept of "electoral crisis" does not have the same content as it did in the past. There appears to be a "broken equilibrium" in politics, rather than a paradigm shift (Jouke de Vries, quoted in Becker and Cuperus 2007). Social democracy is thus not "a threatened species" (Hinnfors 2006, 32), at least not yet. Furthermore, it is not the first time in history that social democracy is perceived (to borrow Stathis Kaly-vas's expression regarding Catholicism) as "a declining and spent force, re-treating in front of modernization" (Kalyvas 2003, 303). This does not alter the fact that social democratic parties are in the process of changing stature and dimension. They have become smaller and less imposing and also less stable and robust. There has been a change in scale.

The Three Phases of Electoral Social Democracy

Over the long term (1950–2009) socialists, considered as a political family, have become weaker electorally. In the thirteen countries where diachronic comparison is possible (table 1), electoral contraction was marked and reached a peak in the years after 2000. Social democracy declined from an unweighted average of 33.2% in the 1950s and 1960s to 26.6% in the period 2000–2009, a fall of 6.6 percentage points, or 19.8%; eleven of thirteen parties registered scores inferior to those of the 1950s. Only two parties, in France and Germany, improved their performance, and these parties had been decidedly weak in the 1950s—a decade which for them, against the general trend, was the worst of the postwar period. From another perspective, if one compares the period 2000–2009 with the best decade of each party, the universality of the decline is still more impressive (see table 5). All parties, without exception, were electorally less successful in the 1990s and 2000s than they had been in the past.

Social democratic parties obtained their best results in the 1950s and 1960s (an unweighted average of 33.2%), fell back moderately in the 1970s (to 31.7%), stabilized at a somewhat lower level in the 1980s (31.1%), and then returned to the path of decline in the 1990s (29.2%) and 2000–2009 (26.6%). The decline had been steady, with each decade being less good elec-torally than the previous one (−1.5% in the 1970s; −0.6% in the 1980s; −1.9% in the 1990s; and −2.6% in the 2000s). Thus the decline tended to become more marked in the 1990s and 2000s, although social democracy was already weaker in these years. The data in table 1 indicate that the performance of so-cial democracy can be meaningfully broken up into three phases of approxi-mately twenty years each:

    1. The first involved an electoral bright spell (the 1950s and 1960s). While

Table 1. Electoral Performance in Legislative Elections as Measured by Percentage of Votes for Socialist Parties by Decade, 1950–2009

	1950–59	1960–69	1970–79	1980–89	1990–99	2000–2009
Austria	43.3	43.3	50.0	45.4	37.3	33.7
Belgium	35.9	31.0	26.6	28.0	23.3	24.6
Denmark	40.2	39.1	33.6	30.9	36.0	26.8
Finland	25.3	23.4	24.5	25.4	24.4	23.0
France	15.2	15.9	21.0	34.5	20.6	24.4
Germany	30.3	39.4	44.2	39.4	36.9	31.9
Ireland	10.9	14.7	12.7	8.9	14.9	10.5
Luxembourg	34.1	33.5	24.8	29.0	23.9	22.5
Netherlands	30.7	25.8	28.6	31.0	26.5	21.2
Norway	47.5	45.5	38.8	37.4	36.0	30.8
Sweden	45.6	48.4	43.7	44.5	39.8	37.5
Switzerland	26.5	25.1	24.1	20.6	20.9	21.4
United Kingdom	46.3	46.1	39.1	29.2	38.8	38.0
Unweighted average of 13 countries	33.2	33.2	31.7	31.1	29.2	26.6
Greece			19.5	43.4	42.3	41.6
Portugal			33.4	26.4	39.0	39.9
Spain			29.9	43.9	38.2	40.2
Unweighted average of 16 countries	33.2	33.2	30.9	32.4	31.2	29.2

Source: The data presented here and in the following tables are mostly based on voting statistics published by the relevant government agencies. For the most recent period much of the information is available online at various websites. The data have been gathered, checked, and assembled into their current form by the author.

not quite a "golden age" (other than in a small number of countries, social democracy's performance was not extraordinary), it was unquestionably the European center-left's best.[2] Equally important was the remarkable electoral stability of the social democratic parties (Spyropoulou 2008, 51–52). The 1950s and 1960s represent an electoral summit in two respects—high electoral scores and low volatility—that has not been attained since.

2. This positive period was followed by a generally moderate process of erosion during the 1970s and 1980s. This was also a phase marked by electoral disorder and significant national fluctuations. This was apparently a transitional phase distinguished by sharp and contradictory movements. Thus social democracy became significantly weaker in more than half of the thirteen countries included in table 1 (Denmark, Britain, Norway, Luxembourg, Sweden, Belgium, and Switzerland). Second, in a number of these countries (Denmark, Britain, and Norway) spectacular defeats were suffered. In the

1980s some of the parties in retreat (the Social Democratic Labour Party of Sweden, or SAP; the Belgian Socialist Party, or PS; and the Luxembourg Socialist Workers' Party, or LSAP)—recovered some of their lost ground, while others continued on their downward slope (the Danish Social Democrats, or SD; and the Social Democratic Party of Switzerland, or SP) or dramatically accelerated it (the British Labour Party). By contrast, four social democratic parties registered considerable success: the Social Democratic Party of Germany (SPD), the Dutch Labour Party (PvdA), the Social Democratic Party of Finland (SDP), and most notably the Social Democratic Party of Austria (SPÖ).[3]

Spectacular defeats coexisted with dazzling successes, contraction with progress, violent decline with rapid recovery of influence, volatility with stability. Thus throughout these twenty years the electoral facts seem to lack any consistent pattern. Nevertheless, if the overall picture is mixed, three new trends are evident:

— A moderate electoral decline which, though not general, affected a majority of center-left parties. Since the electoral losses were modest in the aggregate, and since national developments were decidedly mixed, this was probably not the most important trend.
— A small number of "catastrophic" electoral results (Denmark and Norway in 1973, the United Kingdom in 1983). These indicate that something unprecedented was occurring at the core of social democracy's electoral support—something beyond conjunctural oscillations. But this "something" applied to only a very limited number of elections and parties.
— The increased volatility of social democratic performance is the third and arguably the most important development. Table 2 measures the number of elections per decade in which socialists won or lost five or more percentage points compared with their score in the previous election. The pattern is crystal-clear. Instability strongly increases after the 1960s. The behavior of social democratic voters becomes more volatile and anarchic during the 1970s, and this pattern persists.

In sum, the contrast with the past was neither consistent nor systematic in the years 1970–89. But it did exist. Mixed signals predominated and increased weakness involved only a small number of countries. Further, the impressive performance of the Greek, Spanish, and French socialists in the 1980s, together with quite good results in Belgium, the Netherlands, Finland, and Luxembourg, constituted reasons for optimism (see also Delwit 2005, 63). Whether from the standpoint of electoral arithmetic or that of the psychology of actors and voters, this was not tantamount to electoral crisis. No

Table 2. Changes of More Than 5% in Socialist Vote between Two Legislative Elections

	Number of Cases					
	1950s	1960s	1970s	1980s	1990s	2000s
Increase of More Than 5%	2	4	2	7		3
Decrease of More Than 5%	1	4	7	8		8

Note: Includes Austria, Belgium, Denmark, Finland, France, Germany, Ireland, Luxembourg, Netherlands, Norway, Sweden, Switzerland, and United Kingdom.

retrospective reading of the period can alter this fundamental reality. On the other hand, if there was no electoral crisis, there were clear indications of partial or selective retreat—and of great instability. In the 1970s and 1980s European socialism entered a new era.

3. The third period—the 1990s and 2000s—was marked by a new process of electoral retreat. Throughout these nineteen years social democracy's earlier losses were confirmed. Worse, it lost further ground and lost it more rapidly. Relative to the high point of the 1950s and 1960s, more than two-thirds of the losses (to be precise, −4.5 points, or 68.2% of the total decline) occurred in this period. Individual parties, with the notable exception of British Labour, all turned in average performances in the 2000s that were decidedly inferior to those of the 1970s and 1980s. Certainly the simultaneous victories of the social democrats in the second half of the 1990s—an event rare in the annals of electoral history—created the impression of a strong resurgence and a change in trends. In fact the recovery of influence in the late 1990s was modest and certainly very brief (see discussion below). In addition, since 2000 the process of decline has again intensified and deepened. During this third phase (1990s and 2000s) signs of weakening abounded, instability was strongly on the increase, and electoral earthquakes multiplied, demonstrating the extent to which socialist parties had become vulnerable.[4] The electoral base of social democracy became less broad and far less solid.

The Complexity of the Decline:
North and South, Big and Small, and the European Union

The preceding analysis has not taken into account results in Spain, Portugal, and Greece, for the Iberian countries were long dominated by authoritarian regimes and there was no social democratic party in Greece. When we include the Spanish Socialist Workers' Party (PSOE), the Panhellenic Socialist Movement of Greece (PASOK), and the Socialist Party of Portugal (PS) in our calculations, the image of electoral decline is considerably attenuated.

If one compares the thirteen countries counted for the early years with the sixteen relevant to the later years, the unweighted average declines from 33.2% for the 1950s and 1960s to 29.2% for the years 2000–2009. Viewed this way, socialists lost four points of the total vote, or 12% of their own vote (as opposed to a drop of 19.8% for the thirteen parties for which we possess an uninterrupted series of electoral statistics). A calculation of this sort is methodologically debatable (because it compares thirteen parties for the 1950s with sixteen for the 2000s), but it does offer a more rounded sense of the "state we are in." It is also important to note, from this overall perspective, the very good performances of the socialist parties during the 1980s, often viewed as a period of social democratic setback and "held up as the decade of the wave of triumphant neo-liberalism" (Delwit 2005, 63).

The most interesting aspect of the positive news from the south is not quantitative but qualitative: when, against the "general" trend, a group of parties shows signs of lasting success, it is the significance of the general trend that warrants reexamination. Thus an integrated reading yields a "dual" image of the electoral dynamic of contemporary social democracy. These two electoral faces of the socialist and social democratic family, both of which are "true," bring out the unique and somewhat contradictory character of the current situation. The southern performance illustrates the complexity of social democratic decline.

A further illustration of the political complexity that lies behind the general decline can be seen in the different dynamics of parties from large countries and those from small countries. Figure 1 graphs the data. It is apparent that socialist parties from large countries (Germany, Britain, France, and Spain), which are the main contributors to the socialist group in the European Parliament and exercise greater influence within the European Union (EU) system, do *markedly better* than those from small countries (in the 2000s, 33.6% as opposed to 27.8% for small and medium-sized countries), the reverse of what prevailed in the 1950s. In addition, they do markedly better than the socialist family as a whole.[5] While the 1950s were the worst decade for socialists from large countries (because of the extreme weakness of the French socialists and the mediocre performance of the German SPD), the period of the last thirty years was an era of moderate success, with strong British and Spanish results making a particular contribution. Nevertheless, in spite of this trend the most recent electoral developments in Germany (2009) did not help to improve the social democratic influence inside the EU.

Yet another useful approach to the data is to focus on the performance of the center-left in the European Economic Community (EEC) and European Union (EU). Successive enlargements seem to have led to political consolida-

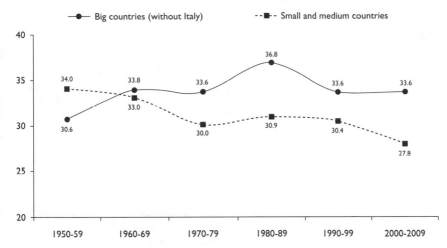

Figure 1. Average percentage of votes cast for socialist parties by decade in large and in small or medium-sized countries, 1950–2009.

tion for the socialist family inside the EEC/EU institutional system. Figure 2 displays the trajectory of social democratic electoral strength in legislative elections in the countries of the European Communities (from the "inner six" of 1957 to the larger group that existed after the "Big Bang" expansion of 2004). The center-left achieved better results in the period 1986–2004 than in the first three decades of the EEC. From a level of 29.3% in the period 1957–72 for five countries (France; the Federal Republic of Germany, or FRG; Luxembourg; Belgium; and the Netherlands, with Italy again excluded), the average rises to 31.3% for fourteen countries for 1996–2004. Among the new entrants the parties of southern Europe (PASOK since 1981, PSOE and the Portuguese PS since 1986) have made the greatest contribution to this upward trend. The enlargement of 1995 (Sweden, Finland, and Austria) also improved center-left influence, albeit only slightly. As a result, the losses of some of the founding members, notably in the Benelux countries, have been more than made up for by the new entrants. The consequence has been an enhanced socialist presence in European institutions, notably the European Council.[6] Only the recent (but, it must be noted, the largest) enlargement of 2004 served to weaken the center-left.

These different calculations qualify the extent of social democratic decline over time and also change the political significance of the decline. The development and maturation of the European Union, which in the 1990s became a much more influential political entity than the European Economic Community of previous years, increased the interdependence between national

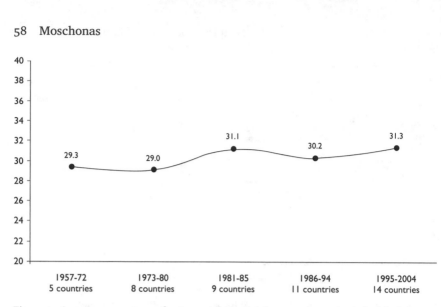

Figure 2. Average percentage of votes cast for social democratic parties in legislative elections within EEC and EU, 1957–2004 (Italy excluded).

states and altered the centers of decision making. Especially since the 1980s social democracy has become weaker as an electoral phenomenon than it was in the past. However, its forces are now better distributed geographically and are also rather more concentrated in decision-making sites. In consequence, it is not unreasonable to think that we are witnessing a decline of social democratic political influence that is much less important than the strictly arithmetical tendencies might imply. Paradoxically, and fortunately for social democracy, electoral and political dynamics do not fully converge.

Classical Social Democracy: The Locomotive Breaks Down

This complex and varied pattern of social democratic performance can be further clarified by two exercises that group parties in more politically and historically meaningful categories. The first centers primarily on the governmental capacity of parties and their rootedness in the working class; the second effort involves a categorization based on the type of policy regime, specifically the different "worlds of welfare" that social democratic parties helped to create and have then inhabited.

In tables 3 and 4 center-left parties are divided into three groups using a typology developed by Merkel and further refined for this chapter (Merkel 1992a). By far the most important criterion is electoral status and resulting governmental capacity. The second is the relationship between parties and

Table 3. Electoral Performance in Legislative Elections as Measured by Percentage of
Votes for Social Democratic Parties Classified by Type, 1950–2009

	Social Democratic and Labourist Parties: High Electoral Status						
	1950–59	1960–69	1970–79	1980–89	1990–99	2000–2009	Relative Change, 1950–2009
Austria	43.3	43.3	50.0	45.4	37.3	33.7	−22.2
Denmark	40.2	39.1	33.6	30.9	36.0	26.8	−33.3
Germany	30.3	39.4	44.2	39.4	36.9	31.9	5.3
Norway	47.5	45.5	38.8	37.4	36.0	30.8	−35.2
Sweden	45.6	48.4	43.7	44.5	39.8	37.5	−17.9
United Kngdom	46.3	46.1	39.1	29.2	38.8	38.0	−17.9
Unweighted average	42.2	43.6	41.6	37.8	37.5	33.1	−21.5

	Pragmatic Coalition-Oriented Parties: Medium Electoral Status						
	1950–59	1960–69	1970–79	1980–89	1990–99	2000–2009	Relative Change, 1950–2009
Belgium	35.9	31.0	26.6	28.0	23.3	24.6	−31.6
Finland	25.3	23.4	24.5	25.4	24.4	23.0	−9.3
Netherlands	30.7	25.8	28.6	31.0	26.5	21.2	−30.9
Luxembourg	34.1	33.5	24.8	29.0	23.9	22.5	−34.0
Switzerland	26.5	25.1	24.1	20.6	20.9	21.4	−19.2
Unweighted average	30.5	27.8	25.7	26.8	23.8	22.5	−26.1

trade unions (no matter which side historically has preceded or dominated the other) and the extent of parties' integration in working-class milieus. The third and least important criterion is a judgment based largely upon the party's history which allows me—only when it comes to borderline cases—to include in the same group parties with similar historical trajectories.[7]

The question of electoral status is fundamental, for it determines whether social democratic parties can govern alone or as dominant coalition partners and whether as a consequence they have the necessary resources to decisively influence key policy decisions and policy outcomes and hence the capacity to "narrow or widen the 'corridor of action' for the subsequent choices" (Merkel 2001, 34). In this sense electoral influence is an indirect identity factor, a constitutive element of party identity dynamics. Using these criteria makes it possible to place parties in one of three quite distinct categories.

1. Social democratic and Labourist parties: high electoral status. The

Table 4. Electoral Performance in Legislative Elections as Measured by Percentage of Votes for Socialist Parties in New Democracies by Decade, 1950–2009

	1950–59	1960–69	1970–79	1980–89	1990–99	2000–2009
Spain			29.9	43.9	38.2	40.2
Portugal			33.4	26.4	39.0	39.9
Greece			19.5	43.4	42.3	41.6
Unweighted average			27.6	37.9	39.8	40.6

parties in this group—Sweden, Austria, Denmark, Norway, Great Britain, and Germany—represent governmental social democracy par excellence. Four of them (the Swedish, Austrian, Danish, and Norwegian parties) possess the distinctive characteristics of the "classical" social democratic model and pursue policies characteristic of the "welfare statist model" (Merkel 1992a, 144–45). The British Labour Party, representing a different, so-called Labourist model, is also included in this group. Its high electoral status, its ability to govern in single-party governments (largely the result of the electoral system in the United Kingdom), and its historically great penetration in the working class justify this choice. These five parties were by far the most strongly working-class parties in the 1950s and 1960s.[8] The SPD, a party with heavy history, completes the picture of this first group. Its consistently solid electoral performance (fluctuating around or above 35% of the electorate) and its status as the dominant partner in governmental coalitions (the practice of forming "great coalitions" being less frequent in Germany than in the consensus-based democracies of the second group) explain its inclusion in this category.[9] Typically forced to govern in coalition governments and characterized by a more cross-class base of support, the German party represents something of a borderline case, but on balance it fits better in this group than in any other. Included in this first group are the world's strongest social democratic parties. Their strength and durability have led some of them to be labeled huge "tankers," to use Peter Glotz's term, that turn around very slowly (quoted in Kitschelt 1992, 198).

2. Pragmatic coalition-oriented parties: medium electoral status. This grouping contains the social democratic parties of Belgium, the Netherlands, Luxembourg, Finland, and Switzerland, which are distinguished by their intermediate competitive status and less dominant role in government. Since 1945 they have been relatively frequent participants in coalition governments, most often with moderate center, center-right, or Christian democratic parties. In general they have developed a mainstream and moderate

social democratic profile with a connection to trade unions. Most important, they have been more or less systematically involved in the "consensus-based" politics typical of polities that discourage the exercise of classical majoritarian politics.[10] (This group coincides with the "pragmatic coalescent type" of Merkel's typology, with Germany excepted and Luxembourg added.)

3. Late-developing socialists. The center-left parties of Greece, Spain, and Portugal constitute a third category. Despite their recent electoral successes these parties differ from classical or labourist social democracy on account of their overall constitution and historical context. They exhibit medium or weak cooperation with fragmented unions; working-class tradition is weaker in these countries, and there is thus lower electoral penetration in the working class; they face or have faced strong competition from the left; and the political system in which they operate has historically less developed democratic institutions and a less extensive welfare state.[11]

Using this admittedly partial and necessarily somewhat arbitrary classification, it can nevertheless be seen fairly clearly that the parties of the first group were the electoral locomotive of European socialism after the Second World War. In the 1950s the average for these parties was 42.2% (if we exclude the German SPD, 44.6%). This impressive performance makes it possible to say that a golden age of social democracy definitely existed. However, it only involved five socialist parties—the Swedish SAP, the Norwegian Labour Party (DNA), the Danish SD, the British Labour Party, and the Austrian SPÖ[12]—and did not last much beyond the 1960s.

Adverse trends became evident in the 1970s with a decline in the group's average performance, but the news was not all bad, particularly in Germany and Austria. Two subsequent and abrupt regressions—the first in the 1980s and the second in the 2000s—nevertheless signaled the effective end of the propellant power of this group of five parties.

In the 2000s the average of their performance stood at 33.1%, which meant that for the full 1950–2009 period the average losses amounted to 9.1%. The large social democratic parties had lost 21.5% of their previous influence. Losses of this magnitude clearly mattered, and they were rendered more significant because they often came in the form of electoral earthquakes—as in Denmark and Norway in the 1970s, Britain in the 1980s, and Denmark and Norway again in the 2000s. Thus the old electoral locomotive of European socialism went into a dangerous spiral. The electoral retreat appears as a slow, steady slide, almost without interruption, that is still in progress. The electoral golden age now seems far removed. The years since 2000 have also inflicted a lot of damage. In the period 2000–2009 none of the parties in the first group received more than an average of 38% of the vote, whereas during the 1960s none of them averaged less than 39.1%. Thus *the best average results for the 2000s are inferior to the worst results for the 1960s*. This is a clear indication of electoral "banalization" of this distinguished company of parties.

The fate of parties with intermediate electoral status was if anything worse. This group registered even greater losses than the group of most classically social democratic parties. Their performance dropped 8 percentage points, hence a loss of 26.1% of their electoral strength during the 1950s. The LSAP lost 34% of its strength since the 1950s, the Belgian PS 31.6%, and the PvdA 30.9%, while the Dutch compete with the Norwegians for the gold medal for electoral instability (cf. Spyropoulou 2008, 53). Losses for parties in this category differ from those of the first group in one important respect: they are more randomly distributed in time and less structured.[13] It is therefore less easy to locate a precise turning point or cause. On the other hand the decline is cumulatively stronger, and the warning signs appeared earlier for the social democratic parties more systematically involved in consensus-oriented decision making. These "pragmatic coalition-oriented parties" are suffering more than other parties of the center-left.

The picture of declining strength of social democratic parties changes considerably when one looks to the south (table 4). The southern European parties, which turned in excellent electoral performances during the 1980s (with the exception of the Portuguese socialists), consolidated their strong positions and improved their average in the 1990s and 2000s. The improvement was above all due to the strong resurgence of the Portuguese PS, which obtained its best historical result (45.1%) in the 2005 elections—the best score of any socialist party anywhere in Europe for 2000–2009. The PSOE achieved its best results in the 1980s but also consolidated its position in the 2000s after a significant drop in the 1990s. By contrast, PASOK, although performing very solidly overall, appears to have entered a phase of soft electoral decline (see Voulgaris 2008) despite its triumphal return to power in 2009.[14] The southern pole is by far the strongest in European socialism today—a major novelty in the electoral history of socialism.

These results can be refined still further by looking at social democratic parties in countries with different kinds of welfare states. In table 5 we classify parties based on whether they operate in states with social democratic, Christian democratic, or liberal welfare regimes and compare their performance for the period 2000–2009 with their best average performance in any decade since the 1950s (no matter which decade was the best).[15] The results are stark and surprising: parties in classic "social democratic" welfare states (relative average change −26.7%) and those in Christian democratic welfare regimes (−28.2%) have been more adversely affected than those in

Table 5. Welfare Regimes and Change in the Social Democratic Vote, Best Decade versus 2000–2009 (percentage of votes)

Social Democratic		Liberal		Christian Democratic	
Austria	−32.5	Australia	−15.7	Belgium	−31.6
Finland	−9.6	New Zealand	−15.8	France	−29.3
Denmark	−33.3	United Kingdom	−17.9	Germany	−27.8
Norway	−35.2			Ireland	−29.6
Sweden	−22.6			Netherlands	−31.6
				Switzerland	−19.2
Unweighted average	−26.7	Unweighted average	−16.5	Unweighted average	−28.2

Note: Classification of welfare regime types according to Stephens, Huber, and Ray 1999.

liberal regimes (−16.5%). Interestingly enough, in the list of big losers we find some of the most prominent and most recognizable brands of European social democracy: the Norwegian DNA (−35.2%), the Danish SD (−33.3%), the Austrian SPÖ (−32.5%), the Belgian PS (−31.6%), the Dutch PvdA (−31.6%).

Much the same picture emerges if we use the classification offered by Esping-Andersen in his *The Three Worlds of Welfare Capitalism* (1990). Thus figure 3 displays the electoral influence of the socialist parties in two extreme groups of countries: the so-called high decommodification group, which includes the classic social democratic models of Sweden, Norway, and Denmark as well as the "traditionalist-conservative" welfare states such as the

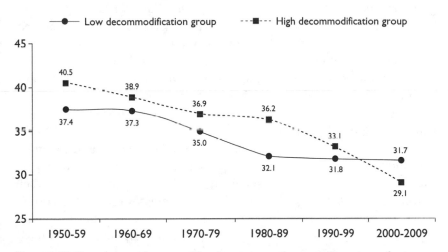

Figure 3. Welfare regimes, decommodification status, and average percentage of votes cast for social democratic parties in legislative elections, 1950–2009.

Netherlands, Belgium, and Austria; and the "low decommodification" group of liberal regimes, including the United Kingdom, Ireland, New Zealand, and Australia (Esping-Andersen 1990, 52, 47–54).[16] For parties belonging to the high decommodification group, the decline is extraordinary (a proportional change of −28.15% compared to the 1950s), while for parties belonging to the low decommodification group the losses are much less serious (−15.24% in relative terms). Again the contrast is too strong not to matter.

Parties operating in liberal environments or Labourist parties that are more market-friendly appear to be resisting decline better than those in social democratic environments.[17]

Taken together, these data show fairly convincingly that the parties which have fared worse electorally are those at the very center of the social democratic project. The implications would seem to be serious indeed.

The Myth of the Landslide of the Late 1990s: A New Golden Age?

The principal unit of analysis employed here—electoral average by decade—does not capture short-term fluctuations, which are what in fact determine a party's transition to opposition or its arrival in government. In addition, it artificially fractures electoral time, because political dynamics do not obey the logic of rounded-up figures. Thus according to our data the 1990s represented yet another stage in the sequence of the electoral erosion of social democracy (see table 1). However, toward the end of the 1990s twelve out of fifteen governments in the European Union were either single-party social democratic governments or coalition governments with social democratic participation. The "magical return of social democracy," as it has been called, does not feature prominently in our data (Cuperus and Kandel 1998, 11). It was quite real, but it was also fleeting and modest in its scope and consequences.

The data in table 6 describe the electoral cycle of the 1990s. They show, first of all, that the peak of social democratic influence was not at the end of the 1990s but toward the middle of the decade. In this period social democrats, scoring 32.3%, advanced by 2 points compared with the previous election, an undoubtedly solid achievement. Ironically, however, at the moment (the late 1990s) when the governmental power of social democratic parties was "at an historic peak" (Merkel 2001, 35), they had already begun their transition to electoral regression (31.1% is the average for the last election in the 1990s, as against 32.3% for the penultimate one). To a certain extent this explains the short-lived character of their governmental domination. Already on a downward electoral slope at the end of the decade, they saw things get worse: socialists only obtained 29.6% in the first election in the 2000s (−1.5%

Table 6. Electoral Performance of the Socialist Parties in Electoral Cycle of the 1990s
(Percentage of Votes)

	Ante-penultimate election of 1990s	Penultimate election of 1990s	Last election of 1990s	First election of 2000s
Unweighted average (without Spain, Portugal, Greece)	29.0	29.7	28.9	27.5
Total unweighted average (all 16 countries)	30.3	32.3	31.1	29.6

* For countries with only two elections in the 1990s, average of antepenultimate election is calculated by taking into account the last election of the 1980s.

compared with the late 1990s and −2.7% compared with the mid-1990s). The decline being rapid and marked, the new century very soon put an end to the socialist majority in the European Council.

Not only was the revival brief, it was also modest. If one excludes the southern parties from the calculations, the image of electoral progress is considerably attenuated. The peak achieved toward the middle of the decade (29.7% for the thirteen countries) was in fact *below* the average social democratic score—not the peak—for the 1980s (31.1%), well below the score for the 1970s (31.7%), not to mention the scores for the 1950s and 1960s (33.2%; see table 1). Thus there was nothing extraordinary about the electoral rise of the period, which did not exceed the habitual electoral ceiling of performances in this era.

Third, the governmental swing in Europe was the result of mixed tendencies at a national level. Significantly, nine of the sixteen parties considered here were in electoral decline by the last election of the 1990s, while only seven were in ascent. The electoral trend was not general, which explains how socialists dominated governments in Europe on the basis of an electoral advance that was limited in aggregate terms but remarkable at the level of certain national political systems. The modest impetus that imparted power (when one thinks in European terms) often concealed landslides at a national level.

On balance, the widespread view of commentators at the time that Europe was experiencing a kind of social democratic "resurrection" is not confirmed by the data. What made this image plausible was the roughly simultaneous coming to power of center-left parties in France, Britain, and Germany. The image of an electoral "renaissance" of social democracy was fashioned after these victories. Given the demographic, geopolitical, and in part intellectual

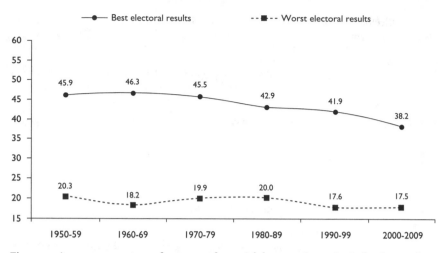

Figure 4. Average percentage of votes cast for social democratic parties in five best and five worst elections for parties in each decade, 1950–2009 (Greece, Portugal, and Spain excluded).

influence of the three countries concerned, it was politically legitimate. But it was electorally exaggerated. Social democracy (with Greece, Spain, and Portugal excepted) dominated governments in Europe on the basis of crisis figures. In retrospect we know that these figures (concerning the thirteen parties of our analysis) were by far the best for the whole period extending from 1990 to 2009. But they were inferior to previous ones. Such performances do not call into question the cycle of erosion.

A rather more accurate understanding of the modest gains of the 1990s can perhaps be gained by looking at the best and worst performances by social democratic parties over the longer period, 1950–2009. Figure 4 shows the average of the five best and five worst results for center-left parties for each decade. The decline is very clear. What is equally clear is that the best showings of the 1990s, which led to social democrats coming to office, did not come close to matching the achievements of earlier periods. Nor did they reverse the long-term trend.

Put another way, the truly extraordinary electoral achievements of the 1950s and 1960s now seem to be out of social democratic reach. Since the 1980s social democracy has achieved successively smaller victories than in the previous decades. From this perspective the results of the late 1990s were electorally rather ordinary. Social democracy as a political phenomenon has become smaller, its "carrying electoral capacity" correspondingly weaker. It was this smaller social democracy, semi-strong and semi-exhausted, that found itself temporarily in power at the end of the 1990s. In a sense the return to power was genuinely "magical."

What Kind of Crisis?

The electoral retreat of social democracy transcends spatial boundaries and national borders within Europe; it even transcends "oceanic frontiers" (cf. Horn 2007, 190). It is a complex, multilayered process, and several causes act together to produce it. On this very fluid terrain, where a whole host of parameters is in play and where the share of hypothesis and deduction is large, we won't venture to propose a "general theory" of social democratic electoral dynamics. Accordingly, this discussion will attempt an answer to three questions: How are we to explain the divergent electoral dynamics in northern and southern Europe? Is the social democratic electoral decline inexorable or irreversible? And how serious is the electoral crisis of social democracy, and how temporary or enduring could it be? The discussion aims to outline a general framework of influences; it will offer nothing more than some reference points, "some indices of weighting."

Understanding the Winners

The excellent performances of the Spanish, Portuguese, and Greek parties represent the major exception to the long-term process of social democratic decline. Their successes, moreover, have lasted nearly as long as the downward slope of the other socialist parties. During the period of initial success (in the 1980s) it was reasonable to argue that there was a *two-speed* or *two-track* electoral pattern in operation—the old "mature" Nordic parties versus the "new," expanding, but not yet consolidated parties in the south—which might be merely temporary. Today this makes less sense, for the southern "latecomers" have experienced not only the initial upturn of the 1980s but also serious setbacks and proud recoveries. There is clearly more at work here than a matter of "catching up" or "maturation."

PASOK and PSOE are by far the most successful group of parties in the European socialist and social democratic family.[18] The puzzle of their success is all the more intriguing for three reasons. In the first place, these two parties have followed rather different political and economic itineraries. Second, they have failed to honor numerous electoral promises. Finally, their economic records have generally not been brilliant (examples: the Spanish socialists' disappointing jobs record or the shipwreck of Greek Keynesianism during the 1980s). An extensive discussion of their accomplishments is not possible here, but one obvious historical comparison stands out: these two parties managed to create, in much the same fashion as the Swedish SAP in the 1930s and the Austrian SPÖ in the early 1970s, a new mainstream that was ultimately accepted and broadly legitimated by all political forces. They exercised prolonged ideological and political domination, though shorter than in Scandinavia.

A further and related factor contributed to the initial success (at the end of the 1970s and during the 1980s) of both PASOK and PSOE: the lack of credibility of the principal right-wing parties, a deficit linked to the black pages of history of both countries (party system factor). Nonetheless, a favorable ideological framework does not lead to a long-lasting electoral dominance.

In effect, above and beyond the initial ideological weakness of the right, three policy factors explain the electoral dominance of PASOK (1981–2004) and PSOE (1982–96 and from 2004 to the present): first, the implementation of more advanced social policies than those of right-wing or centrist parties (socialist policies on health, pensions, social benefits, education, and reducing regional inequalities largely explain the two parties' initial momentum and the persistence, especially in the case of PSOE, of their electoral success); second, the institutional modernization undertaken by the socialist governments (a key dimension of which was the deepening of democratization); third, measures of cultural modernization (the implementation of "progressive" reforms affecting private life and relations in civil society).

Overall the socialists proved capable of clearly dominating their center-right opponents in these three areas (social policy and the welfare state, political liberalism, and cultural liberalism), and it was these reforms that were supported by a majority of public opinion throughout the socialist reign (Moschonas and Papanagnou, 2007, 75–81). By contrast, their advantages in economic modernization and European policy (joining the EEC) were either less strong (PSOE) or, in an initial phase, nonexistent (PASOK from 1981 to 1985). In this regard the adoption of a European perspective and the neoliberalization of their economic policy are in themselves insufficient to explain the two parties' electoral domination even though within the European social democratic family PSOE found itself in the vanguard of economic liberalism and Europeanization. Now, socialist ascendancy in the areas of social policy, institutional modernization, and cultural modernization was combined with an *advantage of physiognomy* in the sense that this triple domination was profoundly in tune with significant distinguishing features of PASOK's and PSOE's initial ideological and programmatic profiles. In terms of identity, these thematic areas constituted—after the abandoning of the "radical scenario"—the main reference points of southern specificity in the social democratic family. Over the long term the two parties—in spite of severe contradictions, broken promises, ideological treasons, and corruption—took a lead over their opponents on all these fronts. This created a composite political cycle in which the economy was an important but not necessarily or always a determinant aspect (Moschonas and Papanagnou 2007).

All this underlines the reality that electoral ascendancy and decline are not produced simply by sociological trends nor by deft political management of electoral clienteles but are more a matter of having a credible political project, symbolic framework, and set of political opportunities. The southern case therefore demonstrates that ideas and policies as well as strong leadership count; that political and ideological factors are critical in establishing class alignments and obtaining good electoral results. Sweden in the 1930s, 1950s, and 1960s (because of the remarkable Swedish model) and Austria in the 1970s (because of the Austro-Keynesian stance) undoubtedly reinforce this thesis. So too does the more controversial British case in the 1990s and early 2000s.

Britain is especially instructive. The "Third Way" project, an aggressive strategy that aimed to liberate Labourism once and for all from the image of a "tax-and-spend" party, acquired a central place in British politics. The adoption of an inventive version of economic liberalism—with an emphasis on "supply-side" interventions in education and training, a "huge investment" in public services, many measures taken to raise the income of the poorest—along with constitutional reforms and more generally a proven capacity to dominate the political agenda, were essential in producing repeated favorable electoral results (Seldon 2007, 646; Stewart 2007, 432; Shaw 2007, 201–3; Cronin in this volume). Labour's neoliberal macroeconomic management, complemented by an innovative and bold set of social policies (not always social democratic in the traditional sense of the term), appears to have generated a new policy mainstream in the British political system. It is highly significant that even David Cameron, the leader of the Conservative Party, has come to embrace much of the Labour's public service reform agenda (Seldon 2007, 650).

Undoubtedly New Labour "killed" the old collectivist Labourist spirit and outlook (Cronin 2006, 53, 63). It also may have encouraged "the nation's values to move in a more conservative direction" and at least indirectly undermined its capacity "to achieve electoral success over the long term" (Curtice 2007, 52). Under Blair overall income inequality remained "fairly static" (Stewart 2007, 432–35). However, the most striking electoral fact of the period 1997–2005 is the Labour Party's very good performance among the non–manual labor categories of the population. This improvement, much stronger than that of other social democratic parties, is largely explained by Tony Blair's modernization strategy (Moschonas 2008b). New Labour's aggressive adoption of new policies and ideas (in other countries the set of new policies and ideas was more defensive) enabled British social democrats to penetrate part of the Conservatives' natural social base. Despite its obvious lack of a central "ethical motivational core," its neoliberal macroeconomic options, and its extremely catch-all discourse, New Labour chalked up an important number of thematic victories that elicited public approval and served to shape voting. This ideologically "eclectic" party (Shaw 2007, 186) thus became the driving force of a significant political change. The British case demonstrates that political factors are important in establishing new electoral (and class) alignments even though after twelve years in power Labour was ultimately defeated in the elections of 2010. Obviously the wearing effect of being in power for a long period seems today to exact a high electoral price—in all probability higher than in the past. It also seems to involve a kind of programmatic exhaustion. In a case like this, the theme of "change"—a central one in the strategy of the British conservatives ("it's time for change")—emerges as a "super issue" and probably a decisive one.

The current situation in Scandinavian countries tends to confirm the thesis that ideas and policies count: "if the Swedish party dropped the 'big idea' early, it has had over the years a number of 'big issues' around which to mobilize a wider base of support. . . . Today, however, the Scandinavian, and in particular the Swedish Social Democrats' policy agendas, appear bereft of big issues" (Arter 2003, 97). Put slightly differently, if ideas and big issues count, their lack counts too. The weakening performance of the SAP—a party that is nevertheless in a much better electoral position than its counterparts in Denmark and Norway—is powerfully consistent with the analysis developed here: in 2006 the Swedes suffered "their worst score in a parliamentary election since 1920—that is, since the advent of fully democratic politics" (Aylott and Bolin 2007, 621). The recent difficulties of the Swedish SAP, whose party story still ranks as one of the best of all times, seem to be intimately connected to a crisis of "policy horizons."

Certainly Sweden is still a social democratic nation, and the social democratic legacy is not really affected by the electoral retreat of the SAP, which although weakened remains a powerful electoral (and programmatic) machine. Scandinavian social democrats, compared to the Spanish, Greek, and Portuguese socialists or the British Labourists, are not less effective in achieving the traditional leftist goals of full employment and social justice; quite the contrary. Scandinavian social democrats remain by far the best "social brand" in the world. Scandinavia's social experiment still represents a unique mix of universal ideals and efficient policies (see Pontusson 2005; Pontusson in this volume). But after racking up ideological and policy successes for more than five decades, Scandinavian social democracy has entered a new phase. It now has great trouble repeating its previous achievements (and electoral results). It has lost the way, its own unique way, to connect with its constituencies' soul. In effect Scandinavian social democrats, confronted with a modernized and "social" right in their own countries, failed to sufficiently renew their policy agenda and rearticulate—in a hegemonic manner—their own historical legacy. Thus they became less effective in dominating their right-wing opponents.

To sum up, the core of our argument is not that southern socialism has the mastery of ideas and policy renewal within European social democracy. The Scandinavians, British, French, and partly the Germans continue to be the programmatic avant-gardes within the European social democratic family. For example, PASOK's triumphal return to power in October 2009 was based on, among other things, the promise that Greece will become the "Denmark of southern Europe." This promise says a great deal about the influence of the Scandinavian model. Northern and central Europe's social democracy remains ideologically pivotal and its programmatic and policy centrality, despite its decreasing electoral influence, is as pronounced as ever within the center-left family.

Hence our argument—and hypothesis—is that programmatic and policy novelty currently find a more favorable political and social terrain in non–social democratic societies (southern Europe) or liberal societies (Great Britain, etc.) rather than in classically social democratic ones (Scandinavia). In the latter countries social democracy's "ability to differ" is smaller, partly because of its previous successes. By contrast, in countries with less developed welfare states, less modern institutional structures, or both, we are witnessing a structure of opportunities more favorable to a left-wing agenda. In consequence, our argument is not "ideational." If ideas count, ideas and imagination are not constraint-free or circumstance-free.

From this point of view, while the ideological and policy center of social democracy remains largely in central and northern Europe, Southern socialist parties seem to be in a better position to prevail ideologically over right-wing parties. Among the factors contributing to their good electoral results, modernization (frequently under the form of Europeanization) ranks high (Moschonas 2002). The goal of modernization entails solving a series of puzzles that are specific to these countries and enhance the innovative and problem-solving part of social democratic action. Obviously this is less the case in northern and central Europe, although investment of the terms "modernity" and "modernization" by social democrats is not a new phenomenon (examples: the SPD's promise in 1969 to create a "modern Germany" and the project of Harold Wilson's Labour Party of modernizing the British economy). In short, liberal and non–social democratic environments create and recreate a living space for social democratic and left-wing forces. They make the occurrence of programmatic and policy ascendancy a little easier for the left. The latest Spanish (2007) and Greek (2009) elections brought this reality into sharp focus.

In more general terms, the problem with the current ideological and programmatic profile of classical social democracy is that it does not project a genuine "reformist imaginary." Contemporary social democracy is bereft of *big political—and policy—ideas* in its electoral arsenal, ideas capable of capturing intense public attention and structuring the vote. The whole history of social democracy, from the Erfurt Programme to the Stockholm School and Austro-Keynesianism, demonstrates that social democratic parties have succeeded in establishing themselves as majority forces when they have taken an ideological lead over their right-wing opponents by embracing programmatic ideas and implementing policies which the latter were not yet ready to accept or implement—like universal suffrage and political rights for the working class, inventive policies against unemployment, the welfare state and Keynesianism, or an institutionalized role for trade unions. Parties are sites of policy-oriented ideas. Only if parties differ can they endure and dominate their opponents. It is thus hard to see how social democratic parties can remain highly competitive if for more than thirty years they remain unable to generate an image of genuine ideological originality. And their deep commitment to "a new round of catch-all policies" (Allen 2009, 641) has not made things easier.

In conclusion, though it is impossible to quantify and therefore difficult to prove definitively, the thematic victories won by southern socialists (and by New Labour) and the current "thematic" or "agenda" crisis of "old" social democratic parties would seem to go a long way toward explaining the contrasting electoral dynamics in both the South and the North.

Inexorable Decline? The Class Factor and the Ideological Retreat

The question of thematic victories and defeats leads us to the question of the nature of the electoral crisis that social democracy experiences. Is the decline "inexorable" or "historical," reflected as it seems to be in a shrinking of its core working-class clientele and a decreasing propensity of workers to vote for the left, phenomena described by Hobsbawm (1981) and Adam Przeworski and John Sprague (1986) more than two decades ago? Undoubtedly the retreat is in part a "class affair" and a result of the shifting contours of class. But is it not also a product of a political and ideological transformation?

The point of departure for the penetrating—and elegantly formulated—argument of Przeworski and Sprague is the minority status of the working class *stricto sensu*. Given this inescapable social reality, it is argued, socialist parties are condemned to minority electoral status when they pursue "pure" class strategies, but they also lose votes among the working class when they follow cross-class strategies. Confronted with this dilemma (i.e., a persistent trade-off between working-class and middle-class votes), social democrats have been "unable to win either way," and the situation only worsens with time (Przeworski and Sprague 1986; Przeworski 1985, 102–36).

This view has been widely—and in part rightly—criticized on methodological and empirical grounds (Sainsbury 1990; King and Wickham-Jones 1990; Merkel 1992b). Certainly much has changed since these arguments were first made. Nevertheless the curve of recent electoral developments, notably what we could identify as the second wave of electoral results (1990s and 2000s), shows that the paths of social democratic retreat closely resemble Przeworkski's and Sprague's scenario of "irreversible" decline.

First, the development of social democracy's electoral performances in the long run possesses all the characteristics of a decline that is difficult to arrest. Second, sociological data for the full period of 1967–2007 show that social democracy's positions within the working class have been gradually but considerably weakened since the 1970s. At the same time, social democratic parties that have in recent years pursued the most strongly cross-class strategies have resisted decline much better and even made progress among the middle classes (Moschonas 2002 and 2008b). Third, the class structure of social democracy has changed in such a way that two social poles of almost equal arithmetical importance now coexist within social democratic electorates: the working class and the middle strata (Moschonas 2002; cf. Merkel 1992b, 27). On balance, and despite the many criticisms of the thesis presented by Przeworski and Sprague in *Paper Stones* (1986), it would appear that the dilemmas and trade-offs discussed nearly a quarter-century ago are real enough. And despite the changing terms of the trade-off (because of the gradual consolidation of new dividing lines, such as the cultural one, or the new polarization between winners and losers of European integration and globalization), the hard core of the argument (not some follies of the statistical calculations) seems to me solid.

Without offering a full account of the issue, let us however notice some stubborn facts which seem to contradict, or at least qualify, this line of argument. First, the electoral trade-off between working-class and middle-class votes did not take place (as far as classical social democratic parties are concerned) in the 1950s and 1960s, when social democracy was at its ideological best, but later. It was really only with the breakdown of the Keynesian paradigm that social democracy's positions were weakened, both electorally and in the working-class milieu. Furthermore, the available evidence indicates that disaffection with social democratic parties tends to accelerate after a governmental failure of the left, especially in social policy. Bad results in government precipitate and structure working-class defection (Cautrès and Heath 1996, 566–68; also Kitschelt 1999, 324, 344).

Second, the "new" economic policies adopted by social democratic governments since the mid-1980s have for the most part not lacked coherence, technocratic effectiveness, inventiveness, or social compassion. However, all poll research indicates that they did not produce positive electoral and identity effects equivalent to those of the Keynesian era. Thus the politico-economic originality of the social democratic alternative — or, to put it better, the understanding by voters of its originality and virtues — has been impaired. It would seem that the decline in the politics of growth makes it impossible to interpret social democracy "as quite dramatic evidence of the politics of solidarity" (Hibbs 1993, 66). This evolution, together with the collapse of communism, constituted a major turning point. It created what Laclau (2005, 138) has labeled a "drastic rearticulation of the political imaginary," which has been accompanied by the tendency to class dealignment since the 1970s and 1980s.

These factors would support either an analysis that favors political (and policy) explanations of the electoral decline over more narrowly sociological explanations or one that insists on the impossibility of effective political management of complex sociological dynamics (Przeworski's and Sprague's view). If so, the trade-off between working-class and middle-class votes should be seen primarily as part of the wider process of political and ideological retreat brought about by the end of the so-called social democratic consensus. In fact the economic setting for left-wing political ideas changed dramatically after the 1970s and 1980s. The new economic policies of social democratic parties, together with, to paraphrase George Ross (1987, 32), the sudden absence of plausible ideological ways of being a social democrat, generated a break in social democratic identity. In this broader context the working-class defection was less the inevitable effect of an inescapable electoral dilemma than an effect of the end of the postwar economic and ideological cycle. It was precisely the inability of social democrats, with or without their enduring "electoral dilemma," to reestablish the conditions for more egalitarian policies that generated (and later amplified) the defection of the working-class electorate (Lavelle 2008). It was also this failure that favored, albeit indirectly, the consolidation of a cultural vote and to some extent amplified the electoral trade-off between working-class and middle-class votes. In consequence, the electoral trade-off became important within the new horizon of the political and ideological evolution of left politics. In the absence of a credible social democratic project for the future, ideological dynamics and class dynamics converged and created the electoral crisis.

Let us return for a moment to the "winners"—the winners of the 1990s and 2000s, but also those of previous decades. The Swedish party in the 1930s, the social democrats as a family in the first postwar period, the Austrian party in the 1970s, the French PS in the 1970s and 1980s, the southern parties since the 1980s—all demonstrated that political action and policy-oriented ideas count. These were instances of successful "hegemonic" political strategies, and in pursuing these strategies electoral trade-offs were not crucial for determining electoral outcomes. However much Przeworski's and Sprague's arguments are tempting, however well they highlight the real trade-off between worker and nonworker votes, "they deny," as Merkel perceptively notes, "the possibility to pursue the interests of different classes in a single synthetic political strategy" (Merkel 1992b, 17; see also Sainsbury 1990, 48). In reality the "dilemma of electoral socialism" denies the best moments of social democratic history. But it describes much better the current situation.

The current problem of the socialist leaderships is thus not so much one of tactics concerning electoral target groups (middle classes or lower classes) nor one of political strategy, be it classical (positioning oneself more to the left or more to the right) or less classical (positioning oneself along the left-libertarian versus right-authoritarian political dimension). It is rather, and most importantly, a basic ideological and programmatic problem: How is the ideological and programmatic ascendancy of social democracy to be restored? To define the problem this way is not to deny the importance of the question of strategic options—market-liberalizing centrist, left-libertarian, or a mixture of both—or social and cultural divides (Kitschelt 1994; Kitschelt 1999). It is to suggest, however, that national strategic options and therefore electoral performances are subordinate to a broader balance of ideological forces. From this point of view the end of the "old" ideological and programmatic ascendancy explains why approaches emphasizing strategic dilemmas and agency, no matter how valid they are, cannot sufficiently account for the major fact that in the last decades, in all kinds of possible trade-offs and strategic scenarios, social democracy experienced an unprecedented electoral downturn.[19] In essence the data and analysis presented here both point to a *tendance lourde* that transcends national strategic subtleties: whatever the strategic posture adopted, whatever the social democratic response to its "strategic dilemmas" (Kitschelt, 1999, 321–44), social democracy has proved incapable of making up the electoral ground it lost in the 1970s and 1980s. National strategic options and different configurations of competition are especially salient for any detailed understanding of national or short-term electoral tendencies (see Kitschelt and Rehm 2005; Kitschelt 1999), but they do not account for the general downward electoral trend.

To summarize, if past social democratic electoral dominance was the result of powerful historical forces that brought about the rise and consolidation of social democratic ideas, another powerful movement has led to the rise of neoliberal ideas and so has reversed the earlier pattern. The new social democratic ideological and programmatic stance—formulated in the second half of the 1990s around the ideas of the "Third Way"—lacks the "stature and the coherence" of previous social democratic projects (cf. Bonoli 2004, 197). Social democrats are no longer one step ahead of the right-wing parties on issues such as social policy, welfare, economic efficiency, or modernization, and they are losing votes. They are, it can be argued, one step ahead in the domain of cultural liberalism or cultural libertarian orientation, and they are accordingly gaining votes among the educated middle strata. As Arthur Schlesinger put it (1986, 276), "politics in the end is the art of solving substantive problems."

All this does not attenuate the depth of the current social democratic electoral decline; rather the contrary. But in ideological and programmatic matters, there is nothing "inexorable." A hegemonic relation can always, sooner or later, be overturned or reversed. If so, nothing can prove that possibilities for a new cycle of social democratic ideological domination have been permanently lost. The thesis that the current electoral decline is "historical" (or "inexorable") is rather difficult to sustain. Electoral prospects remain an open-ended battlefield, even if the terrain and the advantage have shifted.

Relativizing Recovery Prospects, Relativizing Crisis

So how serious is the electoral crisis of social democracy? And how temporary or enduring might it be? The answer is that there is no easy recovery, no easy and rapid exit. The medium-term prospects for social democrats look bleak. They look bleak first of all because of the "rationale of numbers," which are clear. The tendency is neither circular nor one of trendless fluctuation. The electoral erosion is present in all but the three southern countries in Europe; it is similar everywhere and without any reversions to the status quo ante. The scope, the phases, the highs and lows may differ, but the trend is universal and well structured. There has occurred a non-conjunctural attenuation of the bond between socialist parties and the electorate.

Prospects are also bleak because the electoral erosion does have sociological underpinnings in the process of class dealignment. The tendency toward a gradual distancing between working-class voters and social democratic parties has lasted for nearly forty years. It is a sociological tidal wave (less pronounced in some countries such as Sweden, unmistakable and aggressive in some others such as Denmark) that reduces social democracy's natural level of support and renders a recovery more difficult. In addition, social democracy's restructured base has become the locus of a profound tension between two economically and culturally distinct groups, the working class and the salaried middle strata. The "fragmented" social composition of social democratic electorates may add numbers on occasion, but it is also a constraining factor reducing the freedom to maneuver of socialist leaderships. It is an internal constraint in a period when the "external" constraints are all but rare.

Third, and much more importantly, the electoral weakening of social democratic parties coincides with a parallel crisis of political projects and imaginaries (see discussion above). A host of economic and institutional factors, national and international—rather than some lack of imagination on the part of social democratic headquarters—explains social democracy's incapacity to provide "new clues" for perceiving economic and social reality. In particular, the combined forces of globalization and Europeanization (in great part put in place by social democrats themselves) have not only changed the balance between politics and markets but created a redoubtable problem of collective action and coordination for all those aspiring to a left-wing reform strategy (Moschonas 2009). The extraordinary strengthening of the EU from 1985 until the end of the 1990s has functioned as a "conservative" institutional trap for the future, by locking in a neoliberal policy logic both at the EU level and in part at the national level (McGowan 2001; Moschonas 2009; Bailey 2009b; Ross in this volume). Moreover, the "nationalism paradox" of European unification (Cuperus 2007) reinforces cultural voting and becomes an additional factor of electoral weakness for parties of the social democratic type as well as a factor favoring the consolidation of new populist parties.

Could this situation change easily? The answer is an unqualified no, because these "internal" and "external" factors represent sizable and not short-term obstacles to any policy reorientation. In a sense, today the "old" difficulty of effective political management of complex class dynamics is largely aggravated by the "new" difficulty of effective political management of even more complex *economic* and *institutional* dynamics. Thus the lack of a winning ideological and programmatic formula, of a "single synthetic political strategy," already at the source of the recent electoral crisis, risks being a relatively lasting phenomenon. With respect to the social democratic electoral prospects, globalization and the EU are obstacles to a sustained electoral recovery of social democracy.

A Less Serious Crisis of Social Democratic Governance?

Is there nothing but gloom and doom ahead for European socialists? Here we must take note of an irony, a contradiction between electoral trends and the prospects for getting and holding office and for governing that offers a less depressing picture. Nearly all the available evidence suggests that the social democratic decline is part of a deeper and vaster electoral change which affects other political forces—Christian democracy in particular—as much as it does the center-left. It is a period of fluid electoral landscapes and greater fragmentation that is inauspicious for parties of majority aspiration or parties in office, whether they are social democrats or their opponents. Thanks to the consolidation of new party actors—the average number of relevant political parties is clearly on the rise in western democracies (Henjak 2003)—and new or renewed party families (extreme right, greens, or radical left), the phenomenon of electoral erosion must be relativized.

The real political force of social democracy is obviously reduced by its declining electoral performances, but it is indirectly enhanced by the splintering of the competition and the slumping fortunes of its main opponents. If the present is judged in the light of past electoral achievements, from the viewpoint of electoral history the crisis is indeed serious. But if the present is judged relative to itself, from the viewpoint of the actual balance of forces, it is less serious and different in kind. The unique moment of the 1990s, when modest aggregate gains for the center-left generated great governmental change, showed clearly that electoral power is a relative quantity in the contemporary world. Electoral power is not merely a matter of percentages.

Social democratic parties have in this sense not fundamentally changed their competitive status—as certain Christian democratic parties have done. They have not become politically bankrupt, and they remain everywhere key forces in the political system, situated in an electoral zone close to the governmental threshold (Bergounioux and Grunberg 1996, 279). This is a strategic position that slows the process of erosion in difficult times, and accelerates the process of recovery in better times. Even in countries where the downward trend in social democratic voting was marked by brutal "ruptures," there was always a reverse, if not quite equal, subsequent swing of the pendulum, which has typically brought back the defeated socialist party close to the governmental threshold. This tendency to recover indicates a margin of safety and offers a timely reminder of the capacity of social democracy to remain a "credible contender for power" (Kalyvas 2003, 294) in a political context characterized by "chronic political instability" (Wolfreys 2006). We would argue therefore that the electoral crisis of social democracy might be—in its political and, notably its governmental consequences—less marked and less serious than the data suggest.

Conclusions: A Change of Scale

Social democracy is between a rock and a hard place. In a way it put itself there. But in several other ways numerous "outside" factors—sociological, cultural, institutional—exerted important influence on its electoral dynamics. Social democratic parties in Europe are caught in a net of multicausal constraints, including shifting demographics, ideological waves, European integration, globalization, governmental performances, and programmatic choices. Some of these factors are part of the explanatory background; others (governmental performances, programmatic choices, strategic leadership) are "direct causes."

In any case, a full explanation of the social democratic electoral retreat was outside the scope of this chapter. As for its structure, my main and central ambition was to document and specify the extent, contradictions, and true scale of social democratic electoral influence. My purpose was also to discuss two questions: First, how is one to explain the divergent electoral dynamics in northern and southern Europe? Second, is the electoral decline inexorable; is it "historical," as described by Adam Przeworski and John Sprague more than two decades ago?

Let us now try to recapitulate, clarify, and in part reformulate some of the theses of this chapter.

The process of social democratic decline is highly systematic: it is relatively strong; it encompasses nearly all countries (with the exception of southern Europe); it is confirmed from one decade to the next; it becomes deeper as it progresses; it already has a past and a history; even when the electoral pendulum swings back it systematically yields "smaller" victories than in the past; and it provokes occasionally "catastrophic" results and temporary "minor" collapses. The electoral dynamic of European social democracy is clearly declining and, at the same time, the volatility of its performances is on the increase.

The dynamic of decline is nevertheless complex, with the crisis proceeding in zigzag fashion. It is evidenced in narrow defeats and victories, and landslide defeats and victories. It does not progress in a linear fashion but largely takes the form of volatile performances (supported by volatile voters). A gradual, slow decline at the aggregate level is however frequently violent at a national level. While it is conjuncturally discontinuous, it is persistent over the long term.

Our initial—chronological—option to regroup electoral performances by decade, and not into political and economic cycles, actually yields a better description of the electoral development of social democracy. However our data are interpreted, the available electoral evidence fully justifies a division of the electoral time span of social democracy into three phases (each lasting approximately twenty years: the 1950s and 1960s, the 1970s and 1980s, and the 1990s and 2000s). This kind of division underscores better the specificity of the intermediate phase (the 1970s and 1980s: a period full of contradictory trends), as well as the scale of the electoral crisis of the 1990s and 2000s, and refines approaches, such as Merkel's, that distinguish between the period prior to 1973 and subsequent years. Developments in Australia and New Zealand also confirm, even more emphatically, that the period of weakening par excellence is the last twenty years. Broad economic and ideological cycles hold an important independent power in influencing electoral performances, but have no direct, self-evident, and immediate influence on electoral results. In any case, within the small sphere of numbers and symbols one can consider 1973, the year of the two dramatic defeats in Denmark and Norway, as the defining moment of electoral change.

A particularly troubling finding is that those parties closest to the "classical" social democratic model (whatever its definition) have been affected more strongly than others and are to this extent more than others in the eye of the storm. It is the epicenter of historical social democratic forces, the hard core of the socialist family, which is under the most intense pressure (with the partial exception of Sweden). On the other hand, and perhaps for some equally troubling, Labourist parties of the Anglo-Saxon type have been more resilient. In addition, and again somewhat surprisingly, parties of high electoral status and parties in more majoritarian political systems have resisted better than those in "consensus-based" democracies. It is of course impossible to draw firm lines between these different experiences, but it is surely noteworthy that parties belonging to liberal environments (the United Kingdom, Ireland, but also New Zealand and Australia) or non–social democratic environments (Spain, Portugal, Greece: the fourth world of welfare capitalism, see Leibfried 2000, 193) have been doing better than those in more social democratic environments. The tendency opens new research agendas and suggests new and stimulating topics of inquiry.

Given these realities, it would seem that those arguing for only a "slight decline" in center-left fortunes have underestimated the magnitude and nature of the electoral erosion (Merkel 2001; Delwit 2005).[20] In addition, the very widespread belief in an electoral renaissance of social democracy in the late 1990s is largely misleading. Even the triumphant social democracy of the late 1990s clearly had less mastery over its electorate and its environment than its predecessors prior to 1980. The current influence of social democracy in fact oscillates at around 80% of its level in the 1950s and 1960s (Spain, Greece, and Portugal not included). The drop is strong, although it is not cataclysmic. Thus we are not witnessing the "end" or the "death" of electoral social democracy. Nevertheless, the paths of retreat show that the electoral ebbing and greater instability of social democratic parties is a genuinely firm trend, a tendance lourde.

It is clear as well that the "political power of economic ideas," to borrow the apt expression of Peter Hall (Hall ed. 1989), which was an asset in the past, has become a liability for today's social democratic parties. The domination of liberal economic ideas has destabilized social democracy. To some extent social democracy was able to integrate the neoliberal register into its own political rhetoric and governmental output. But this "grafting"—the left's absorption of the right's economic agenda (Duncan 2006, 483)—while electorally successful when first tried in the 1990s, might well serve to undermine its capacity "to achieve electoral success over the long term" (Curtice 2007, 52; also Bailey 2009a, 32). In addition, the competitive security of social democracy seems affected by a certain revival of the radical left (communists, post-communists, left socialists).

If the center-left's ability to contest the neoliberal paradigm may have been limited in the period since 1980, it is also quite possible that the new hegemony can be undermined from within, from the difficulty of achieving a self-regulation of market forces. As the subprime mortgage crisis and the broader economic recession have recently demonstrated, the blind mechanics of markets and the "irrational exuberance" of financial forces (Krugman 2005, 30) may well reactivate core social democratic ideas about the regulatory role of politics and states. Moreover, and fortunately for social democracy, there is abundant evidence that in the OECD countries "popular support for egalitarianism is very much alive" (Glyn 2006, 177). Even so, recent social democratic moves to the left, evident at the level of discourse, risk being without important policy consequences because of European constraints (in part put in place by social democrats themselves).

Recent developments in Europe offer fresh evidence. Despite the exceptional emergency circumstances, social democratic leaders, always trapped by European institutional constraints and poor cooperation, had great difficulty in inventing new policies attuned to both the scale of the crisis and the requirements of the European stage. In reality they were seeking Keynesian solutions to the crisis while at the same time striving to maintain a neoliberal status quo and to preserve the Stability and Growth Pact. In this sense social democracy's moves to the left are institutionally "rootless." For now social democracy is still lacking a winning ideological and programmatic formula in the domain of economic and social policy.

It is too soon to determine the influence of the economic crisis on the electoral cycle. Nonetheless, early post-crisis election results do not show promise of much better times. In sum, two parties, the Norwegian DNA (+2.7%) and the Greek PASOK (+5.8%), registered important electoral progress (compared with their previous electoral performance), while four are in decline (Austria, Luxembourg, Portugal, and Germany). Among the latter, for the Austrian SPÖ (−6%), the Portuguese PS (−8.5%), and of course the German SPD (−11.2%) the losses are highly significant. To these three cases of electoral setback we should doubtless add the "catastrophic" result—a defeat without precedent—in the European Union elections of June 2009. Yet the number of elections is too limited to provide sufficient data to (re)establish a trend. In any case, in a time of distrustful electorates and of ideological and policy uncertainty, a long-term trend will not change without a good political reason.

Overall, our findings largely confirm the thesis that social democratic parties have come down a notch in the political market; they have become "smaller." And they will probably remain so for a long time to come. Being "smaller," whether in the South or the North, will not prevent socialists from governing or winning elections, but it could prevent them from being consistently successful over a long period. Social democracy has changed in stature and dimension, but its level of influence is still close to the governmental threshold. It remains in the game of governmental alternation and is still a "credible contender for power." Any further losses beyond the current point of electoral erosion, however, could at least in some countries make less credible the strategy of acting like the natural party of government, or one of several. Is social democracy at the point of crossing this "critical threshold"? Probably not, for political traditions take "a long time to establish and a long time to break down" (Wolfreys 2006). Historical parties, like spirits, live on and persist. Nevertheless, the major defeat in the European elections of 2009 is a powerful warning signal. Concerning the long-term future, the evidence is far from clear.

Social democratic parties have changed in scale. In a sense—in just the sense that I have tried to develop in this chapter—this change of scale is "historical." It describes a new condition. But this "new" condition does not imply that the downward trend (at the aggregate level) will expand and deepen. It does imply, however, that there is no easy return to the electoral status quo ante. There is nothing contradictory in the supposition that social democracy at the aggregate level is likely neither to easily recover nor suffer further dramatic weakening. Both tendencies may be part of what makes the new situation "new."

I shall permit myself a final thought that mixes optimism and pessimism. In my view, the more time passes—and this is something that does not emerge from the figures presented here—the more northern socialists and southern socialists will come to have the "same shadow," the same electoral future. This tendency will likely persist until the moment when a new reversal occurs, as it surely will. This too does not emerge from the figures. But it represents the great lesson of the last 130 years of the history of European capitalism, a history intimately bound up with that of social democracy.

Notes

Part of this research was carried out in 2005, during my three-month residence as a visiting scholar at Yale University (Political Science Department and the Yale Center of International and Area Studies) under a grant from the Fulbright Foundation in Greece. I am indebted to Stathis Kalyvas, who made my stay at Yale easier and more productive. I am grateful to James Cronin, George Ross, and James Shoch, whose patient and meticulous editing and critical advice have significantly improved the quality of this contribution. I would like to thank Vassia Stagia for her valuable help in updating my data base and constructing some of the tables. I would also like to thank Vivian Spyropoulou for generously allowing me access to her data, thereby facilitating my work in checking figures.

1. The decision by Merkel (2001) and Delwit (2005) to include the Italian center-left in their calculations is no doubt intellectually legitimate, since the space of the center-left, with or without the PSI, has always been occupied by an organized political force. In my view my choice has the merit of greater consistency. In any event, with or without Italy the aggregate trend does not change significantly.

2. The designation (Golden Age) produces "a false impression of social democratic potency in the years of the 'long boom'" (Callaghan 2000, 436).

3. For the Austrians and the Germans the 1970s were the best decade of the entire postwar period (with an average score that was impressive for the SPÖ—50%—and excellent for the SPD—44.2%). For the Dutch (31%) and the Finnish (25.4%) the 1980s were their best years.

4. Some examples illustrate the new situation with perfect clarity: −17.1% for the

French socialists in 1993 (1988: 34.7%; 1993: 17.6%); −10.8% for the Norwegians in 2001; −7.9% for the Dutch in 1994 and another −13.9% in 2002; −8.9% for the Swedes in 1998; −7.9% for the Austrians in 1994; −6.8% for the Danish in 2001; −6.7% for the Belgians in 2007. Notwithstanding its small size, even the Irish Labour Party experienced great instability. It more than doubled its electoral strength in 1992 and then lost 8.9% in the subsequent election (1989: 9.5%; 1992; 19.3%; 1997: 10.4%).

5. Overall we witness the same trend in European elections (Grunberg and Moschonas 2005).

6. In the European Parliament as well, successive enlargements of the EEC/EU have played an important role in the electoral consolidation of the socialist family (Grunberg and Moschonas 2005).

7. Contra Merkel (1992a, 142), I do not group the French SFIO/PS and the Greek PASOK with parties of the "roman" variety (despite important similarities), and conversely, in an analysis focused on electoral trends, I find it difficult to consider the German SPD and the Austrian SPÖ as belonging to different typological groups (despite important dissimilarities).

8. These parties, from the standpoint of electoral sociology, were characterized during the 1960s by an electoral penetration that approximated or exceeded two-thirds of the working-class vote in Sweden and Norway, 60% in Great Britain, Denmark, and Austria, and just over 50% in Germany (Moschonas 2002, 50).

9. Merkel includes the SPD in the "pragmatic coalescent" group. He also constructs a "Labourist" group containing the British and Irish Labour parties (Merkel 1992a, 144–45). Historical and profile affinities partly justify this choice. Nevertheless, the political role assumed by the above-mentioned parties in their respective political systems is very dissimilar because of their differing electoral size.

10. The border case here is the Finish SDP. A powerful party in the 1930s, it suffered from the consolidation of an influential communist pole and the division of the labor movement. The era of consensualism in Finish politics, which began in the mid-1960s and ended only recently, allowed for SDP's frequent participation in government. The intermediate competitive status of the party explains its inclusion in the second group (see Sundberg 1999, 57, 59).

11. The French SFIO/PS party is not included in this group. The marked specificity of French socialism makes it a "unique" case (medium electoral status but in a majoritarian political system; often governing in single-party governments; no connection with the trade-union movement; well-developed democratic institutions and welfare state; and last but not least, an uninterrupted series of electoral data). The French party, traditionally capable of the best and the worst, is characterized by a congenital instability. Badly weakened in the 1950s and 1960s and thus a mere shadow of its former self in the run-up to 1968 (Horn 2007, 163, 136; Ross and Goldhammer in this volume), it made significant breakthroughs in the 1980s. Overall it tends to stabilize at a higher level compared to the 1950s.

12. Although this party experienced its real national golden age a little later, in the 1970s.

13. In the light of this picture of abrupt declines and destabilization, the Finnish distinguish themselves by their remarkable stability. The exception came in the 1990s, when they made a modest breakthrough in 1995 (28.3%), only to return immediately afterward to more traditional results (22.9% in 1999).

14. In the elections of 2007 PASOK posted its worst electoral performance (38.1%) since the late 1970s. However, we should note the excellent performance of the Greek socialists in 2009 (43.92%).

15. Here we use the definitions offered by Stephens, Huber, and Ray (1999).

16. Two more countries, Canada and the United States, included by Esping-Andersen in the low decommodification group (1990, 52) are not part of our calculations for evident reasons.

17. The partial exception would be Sweden, though the SAP is rather friendly toward a market economy. See Hinnfors (2006) and Pontusson (this volume).

18. The Portuguese PS has been moderately successful, but not on the scale of the Spanish and Greek parties (see Magone 2007; Delwit 2007).

19. Thus according to Kitschelt, "given that social democratic politicians are rational . . . the current search for new 'winning electoral formulas' on the political left may yield considerable electoral and programmatic instability of social democratic parties across Europe rather than uniform and progressive decline" (1999, 344–45). Since Kitschelt wrote, we have seen both electoral and programmatic instability *and* an (almost) uniform and progressive decline.

20. Our individual country data confirm Merkel's findings with only rare and slight differences. By employing Merkel's periodization and approach (inclusion of Italy, exclusion of Luxembourg), I recalculated the average electoral results for the periods 1950–73 and 1990–99 (see Merkel 2001, 34). According to this calculation, the inclusion of Italy in the Merkel's data attenuates the social democratic retreat by 1.3 points, and the inclusion of Spain, Greece, and Portugal in the diachronic comparison adds 2.1 more points to the downward trend for the period in question.

In his detailed study, however, Pascal Delwit clearly highlights the main tendency: the downward trend "for the great majority" of social democratic parties as well as the "structural erosion" of the Scandinavian ones (Delwit 2005, 66–67).

Part II

Varieties of Social Democracy and Liberalism

Once Again a Model

Nordic Social Democracy in a Globalized World

Jonas Pontusson

What are the prospects for social democracy in the current era of global economic crisis? The answer to this question surely depends on what we mean by "social democracy." And to specify this we need empirical referents. By my reading of public debates as well as academic literature on both sides of the Atlantic, it has become increasingly common over the last couple of decades to conflate "social democracy" with "Social Europe." This is unfortunate on two counts. First, the economic performance of continental Europe has been sluggish by comparison to that of liberal market economies such as the United States and the United Kingdom. Second, the notion of "Social Europe" usually connotes institutional arrangements—patient capital, codetermination, vocational training—that cannot readily be transposed to other settings. To the extent that this is what social democracy is all about, its relevance to contemporary politics in the United States or other liberal market economies would appear to be very limited.

The basic aim of this chapter is in a sense to rescue social democracy from the economic travails of continental Europe by reinstating the Nordic countries as the main exemplars of the social democratic approach to managing capitalism. The reasons why the Nordic countries have figured so prominently in discussions of social democracy hardly need to be rehearsed. In a nutshell, unions and social democratic parties have historically been stronger and more influential in the Nordic countries than in any other liberal democracies. Social democratic parties governed Sweden, Denmark, and Norway more or less continuously from the 1930s into the 1970s and remain major contenders for government power in all the Nordic countries, including Finland.[1] As commonly noted in the existing literature, moreover, even center-right parties in the Nordic countries have to a large extent embraced social democratic policy priorities. All of this is well established. The "news" that my discussion builds on is that the Nordic countries again became economic success stories over the period stretching from the mid-1990s until the onset of the global economic crisis in 2008. Not only did the Nordic countries experience more rapid growth than just about any other OECD economies in this period (except Ireland), they also appear to have adjusted successfully to changes in the global economy by shifting into more knowledge-intensive services and manufacturing. The question becomes whether there is something social democratic about the recent success of the Nordic economies. If the answer to that question is yes, then it becomes plausible to argue that social democracy represents a realistic alternative to market liberalism, worthy of examination and perhaps emulation by progressive political forces outside the Nordic area.

The chapter consists of three parts. In the first part, I delineate what is distinctively social democratic about the four Nordic countries by identifying policies (and policy outcomes) on which these countries differ from Germany and other "social market economies" in continental Europe. Building on several existing typologies, I use the term "social market economies" (SMEs) to encompass France as well as Germany and its smaller next-door neighbors: Austria, Switzerland, Belgium, and the Netherlands.[2] In essence I consider policies that the Nordic countries have in common to be core social democratic policies provided that they also distinguish the Nordic countries from continental SMEs and that they can be traced to social democratic initiatives. This exercise yields the following broad features of what I will refer to as the "social democratic policy regime": universalism in the design of social insurance schemes, direct public provision of social services, solidaristic wage bargaining, active labor market policies, policies to promote female employment and gender equality in the labor market, and finally, high levels of investment in public education and policies to equalize educational opportunity. Throughout the following discussion I emphasize complementarities among these policies. I also emphasize that these policies were designed to promote labor mobility and productivity as well as to redistribute income and equalize opportunity.

In the second part of the chapter I address the institutional conditions for the success of social democratic policies by engaging with the varieties-of-capitalism literature. Contrary to what this literature seems to imply, I do not believe that the economic benefits of social democratic policies are contingent on the persistence of "patient capital" and manufacturing systems that rely on the kinds of skills acquired by workers through vocational training along German lines. I argue that social democratic policies have benefits for a wide range of business activities and that more footloose or short-term investors should be able to recognize these benefits. At the same time, I argue that the effective implementation of core components of the social democratic policy regime depends on the participation of organized business and above all on the existence of encompassing and cohesive unions.

In the third part I contrast the economic performance of the Nordic countries since 1995 with that of continental SMEs. Here my core arguments are that the welfare states of the Nordic countries facilitated the adoption of deregulatory reforms that contributed to economic growth and restructuring and that the egalitarianism of these countries, particularly in the realm of education, has also contributed directly to their economic success. In addition to developing these arguments, I present data showing that the growing gap between labor-market "insiders" and "outsiders" is first and foremost a continental phenomenon. This and other dualist trends have been much less pronounced in the Nordic countries.

By way of conclusion, I will briefly address the implications of the current economic crisis for the social democratic project as I understand it, as well as the lessons that progressive forces in the United States might draw from the Nordic experience.

Nordic Egalitarianism versus Continental Social Protection

In emphasizing differences between Nordic and continental political economies, my discussion builds on the insights of Esping-Andersen (1990) and subsequent comparative welfare-state literature (notably Huber and Stephens 2001 and Swank 2002). This literature teaches us that the "conservative" welfare states of continental Europe—above all Germany and France—provide insurance against income losses associated with unemployment, poor health, and old age that is roughly comparable to the insurance provided by Nordic welfare states, but they do so in ways that to a much greater extent preserve existing income and status differentials. Generalizing, we might say that the two core pillars of social protection in continental Europe are legislation and regulatory practices that restrict the ability of employers to fire workers, and mandatory social insurance based on earnings-differentiated benefits.

Relative to the continental model, the welfare states built up by Scandinavian social democrats in the 1940s and 1950s were based on the idea of "social citizenship," which concretely manifested itself in the emphasis on flat-rate benefits and government-provided services financed out of general taxes (rather than earmarked payroll contributions). Starting with the introduction of supplementary pension schemes in the 1960s, earnings-related benefits assumed a prominent role, but the emphasis on the public sector has remained a distinctive feature of Nordic welfare states. Equally important, these welfare states incorporated the principle of earnings-differentiated benefits into comprehensive social insurance systems that covered everyone, as distinct from the occupationally (and sometimes sectorally) segregated insurance schemes characteristic of continental welfare states.

Setting aside the public provision of services, the Nordic countries do not spend significantly more of their GDP on income transfers, yet they achieve a much larger reduction of household income inequality through income transfers than most of their continental neighbors do.[3] Redistribution through taxes and transfers is clearly one crucial reason why the Nordic countries have a much more equal distribution of disposable income and also lower poverty rates than the social market economies of continental Europe, let alone the liberal market economies of the Anglophone world (see table 1).[4]

It is important to note that redistribution was not the only motivation behind the distinctive approach to welfare-state design adopted by Scandinavian social democrats. Another important motivation was the idea that public provision of benefits, organized on a universalistic basis, would facilitate labor mobility across firms and across sectors of the economy and thereby provide for a more efficient allocation of labor. The attitude toward employment security adopted by the Swedish social democrats in the 1950s and 1960s is also very relevant in this context. Cognizant of Sweden's export dependence and the need for economic restructuring in response to changes in world markets, Swedish union leaders and social democratic politicians very explicitly eschewed the idea that the government should provide workers with security in their current jobs. Their stated goal was to provide for "security in the labor market," as distinct from "job security." Pursuing this goal entailed generous unemployment compensation to protect workers against the income losses associated with unemployment, but also active labor market policies to help workers find new, higher-paying, and otherwise better jobs.

In the context of severe industrial adjustment problems, the Swedish labor movement in the 1970s pushed for new laws restricting the ability of employers to fire workers. By recent OECD measures, employment protection in Sweden is slightly stricter than in Germany and less strict than in France (Pontusson 2005a, 120). Yet Denmark stands out as one of the West European countries with the least restrictive laws governing the ability of employers to fire workers. In this respect Denmark might be said to have remained more true to traditional social democratic principles than Sweden, but it should also be noted that standard OECD measures ignore the fact that Swedish employment protection legislation gives firms and unions the right to negotiate alternative arrangements, and the typical tendency is for collective bargain-

Table 1. Measures of Inequality, circa 2000

	(1) Household Income Inequality	(2) Poverty Rate	(3) 90–10 Full-Time Wage Ratio	(4) Female/ Male Full-Time Wage Ratio	(5) Female/ Male Employ- ment Rate Ratio	(6) 95–5 Ratio on Literacy Tests	(7) Information- Age Literacy
LME average	.332	14.4	3.58	.767	.812	2.53	52
United States	.370	17.7	4.35	.755	.857	2.79	53
Continental average	.267	7.3	3.00	.797	.781	2.00	58
Germany	.275	8.4	2.93	.760	.797	1.73	59
Nordic average	.244	5.9	2.23	.817	.919	1.76	68
Denmark	.225	5.4	2.16		.893	1.65	65
Finland	.247	5.4	2.41	.788	.929	1.86	63
Norway	.251	6.4	2.00		.906	1.75	69
Sweden	.252	6.5	2.35	.845	.949	1.79	74

Limited market economy (LME) average = unweighted average for Australia, Canada, Ireland, the United Kingdom, and the United States

Continental average = unweighted average for Austria, Belgium, France, Germany, the Netherlands, and Switzerland in columns 1–5, Belgium, Germany, the Netherlands, and Switzerland in columns 6–7

Nordic average – unweighted average for the four Nordic countries (except for column 4)

(1) Gini coefficient for disposable household income (adjusted for household size). The figures refer to 2000 except for Australia (2001), the United Kingdom (1999), and the Netherlands (1999). Source: http://www.lisproject.org/keyfigures.htm.

(2) Percentage of population living in households with less than 50% of the median disposable household income. Same years and source as column (1).

(3) The ratio of earnings in the 90th percentile to earnings in the 10th percentile, gross earnings for full-time employees. The figures refer to 1999–2000 except for Denmark (1990). Source: Organisation for Economic Cooperation and Development (OECD) Relative Earnings Database (unpublished).

(4) The ratio of the median female wage to the median male wage, full-time employees only. Same years and source as column (3).

(5) The ratio of the female employment rate to the male employment rate in 2000 (employment rate = employed individuals as a percentage of the population between the ages of 15 and 64). Source: OECD 2004, 295–96.

(6) The ratio of 95th-percentile test scores to 5th-percentile scores on literacy tests for population aged 15–65 in 1994–98. Source: OECD 2000, 135–36.

(7) Percentage of the population scoring at level 3 or better on literacy tests. Same years and source as column (6).

ing agreements to be more flexible than what the law prescribes. Particularly if we extend our perspective to encompass additional issues such as health and safety, the Nordic countries are still distinguished not only from France but also from Germany by their (de facto) reliance on collective bargaining rather than government legislation to regulate employment conditions.

Alongside welfare-state universalism, the so-called Rehn-Meidner model deserves a prominent place in most discussions of Nordic social democracy as a distinctive policy regime. Conceived by economists working for the Swedish confederation of blue-collar unions in the 1950s, this intellectual construct became the justification for an aggressive union push for wage leveling and for the expansion of active labor market policies in the 1960s and 1970s. To varying degrees and with some modifications, unions and social democratic parties in the other Nordic countries emulated the policies associated with the Rehn-Meidner model.

The Rehn-Meidner model articulated the egalitarian goals of the labor movement as part of a strategy to promote productivity growth and contain wage inflation. On the one hand, a concerted union effort to provide low-wage workers with higher wage increases than market forces dictated would squeeze the profits of less efficient firms (or sectors) and force them either to rationalize production or go out of business. On the other hand, wage restraint by well-paid workers would promote the expansion of more efficient firms (or sectors). For the unions to pursue this strategy the government needed to develop active labor market measures that would ease the transition of workers from less efficient to more efficient firms and sectors and also to curtail wage drift caused by bottlenecks in the supply of labor.[5]

The insight at the core of the Rehn-Meidner strategy is that low wages represent a subsidy to inefficient capital. At the same time, Rehn and Meidner recognized that wage differentials were necessary as an incentive for workers to acquire skills and take on more responsibility in the production process. The goal of union wage policy should be to eliminate differentials based on corporate profitability while maintaining differentials based on skills and effort. In other words, the goal of union wage policy should be "equal pay for equal work," as distinct from "equal pay for everyone."

In practice it proved difficult for Swedish unions to maintain the distinction between "good" and "bad" wage differentials in the context of full employment and economy-wide wage bargaining. Solidaristic wage policy may have become too egalitarian in the course of the 1960s and 1970s, producing a generalized profits squeeze and ultimately a campaign by employers to decentralize wage bargaining in the 1980s (Pontusson and Swenson 1996). While Norway has retained peak-level wage negotiations, the locus of Danish wage bargaining has also shifted to the industry level (Wallerstein and Golden 2000). With respect to formal institutional arrangements, we can no longer speak of a Nordic model of wage bargaining that is clearly distinct from the continental model. In marked contrast to the social market economies of continental Europe, however, union membership held up quite well in the Nordic countries in the 1980s and 1990s (see table 2), and partly as a result of this, Nordic unions appear to have retained a greater capacity to coordinate their wage demands based on solidaristic principles. As table 1 shows, wage compression remains a distinctive characteristic of the Nordic countries as a group.

The Nordic social democrats began to articulate gender equality as a core component of their reformist project in the 1960s and policies to promote women's participation in the labor force—chiefly parental leave insurance and public childcare—emerged as a widely admired feature of the Nordic model in the 1970s. The literature on gender and the welfare state (e.g., Sainsbury 1999) commonly draws a sharp contrast between the progressive, gender-egalitarian approach to family policy characteristic of the Nordic countries and the conservative, "male-breadwinner" approach of Germany and other continental countries in which Christian democratic ideology has been influential. Relatedly, I want to emphasize the affinity between gender-egalitarian policies adopted in the 1970s and existing social democratic commitments to the public sector and to solidaristic wage policy. While the expansion of welfare-related public services became the principal source of new employment for women from the 1960s through the 1980s, the closing of the pay gap between men and women was from the beginning a major objective of solidaristic wage policy.

Column 4 in table 1 reports on gendered pay differentials, measured as the ratio of the median female wage to the median male wage, but these data pertain to full-time employees alone, and we only have data for two of the Nordic countries, Sweden and Finland. Combining these two, quite disparate observations yields an average that is two percentage points higher than the average for continental SMEs, but there is also a lot of variation among continental SMEs in this regard. The contrast between the Nordic countries and the continental SMEs is much clearer in column 5, which reports on employment-rate differentials between men and women. Women have a much higher labor force participation rate in Nordic countries than in either continental SMEs or Anglophone LMEs.

The final contrast that I wish to draw between Nordic and continental political economies concerns education and skill formation. This is a topic that has recently caught the attention of students of comparative political economy. In the Varieties-of-Capitalism (VofC) tradition, skill formation has come to be seen as the crucial link between social provisions and production strategies (cf. Estevez-Abe, Iversen, and Soskice 2001; Iversen 2005; and Iversen and Stephens 2008). In a nutshell, the standard VofC argument is that high levels of employment protection and social insurance in the Nordic countries as well as continental Europe are associated, as both cause and effect, with the fact that these economies rely more heavily than liberal market economies do on firm- and industry-specific skills. Investment in specific skills is riskier than investment in general skills, and if this sort of investment is to be undertaken, there must be some assurance of good long-term employment prospects in the firm or industry to which the skills apply, as well as some assurance of income support during possible spells of unemployment. In turn, firms that rely on specific skills can be expected to join with skilled workers in a cross-class alliance in support of social protection as well as vocational training.

In my view this argument captures something quite essential about the social market economies of continental Europe, but it misses several important things about the Nordic experience. To begin with, the tension between vocational training that follows the German model and social democratic ambitions to remove barriers to class mobility through educational achievement deserves to be noted. In Sweden education reforms in the 1950s and 1960s incorporated vocational training for fifteen- to eighteen-year-olds into the new (comprehensive) secondary schools, effectively eliminating apprenticeship-based training (Pontusson 1997). Though some apprenticeship-based training survived in Denmark, the thrust of postwar educational changes in the other Nordic countries appears to have been similar to what we observe in Sweden. While the UNESCO sources cited by Iversen and Stephens (2008, 616) indicate that the proportion of school-age cohorts engaged in "vocational training" is about the same in the Nordic countries as in Germany (and much higher than in Austria or Switzerland), the question becomes whether the figures are really comparable. Based on the results of adult literacy tests, there is good reason to believe that the general-skills component of vocational training is more pronounced in the Nordic countries.

A second and related point is that Denmark, Norway, and Sweden stand out as the three OECD countries that spend the largest share of their GDP on public education, with Finland ranked fifth (following New Zealand) on this measure (Iversen and Stephens 2008, 616; see also Pontusson 2005a, 134). Partly in response to deteriorating employment conditions, the Nordic countries increased spending on higher education quite dramatically in the 1980s and 1990s, but their most remarkable achievement in this realm has to do with basic skills. In the international adult literacy study carried out by the OECD and Statistics Canada in the second half of the 1990s, the four Nordic countries stood out not only as the countries with the highest mean scores but also as the countries with the most compressed distributions of test scores (see table 1, column 6). The proportion of the population that passed the study's threshold for "information age literacy" was also higher in the Nordic countries than in any of the countries included in the study (table 1, column 7).

The Nordic experience suggests that educational equality and economic equality are closely linked. As Blau and Kahn (2005) point out, compression of educational achievement can be invoked to explain cross-national variation in wage inequality. At the same time, we might reasonably suppose that children from low-income households are better able to take advantage of educational opportunities when the distribution of household income and living conditions is more equal (cf. Iversen and Stephens 2008, 621–22). The very low rates of child poverty in the Nordic countries deserve to be mentioned in this context (see Pontusson 2005a, 160).

Relatively high skill levels at the bottom of the skill hierarchy may have enabled employers in the Nordic countries to contend with the challenges posed by solidaristic wage policy, allowing them to deploy new technologies and thereby improve productivity with low-skilled workers. Also, the expansion of higher education has undoubtedly curtailed the growth of returns to education in these countries. In both these ways public investment in education has made it easier for unions to practice wage solidarity. In the realm of traditional manufacturing, the argument about skills facilitating the deployment of new technologies surely pertains to technical as well as general skills. What is most distinctive about the skill profile of the Nordic countries, however, is the quality of general skills at the bottom of the distribution. Public investment in education is particularly relevant to explaining why the Nordic economies have outperformed the continental economies in knowledge-intensive manufacturing and private services over the last fifteen years (a topic to which I shall return).

To sum up, the preceding discussion calls into question the attempt by Esping-Andersen (1990) to capture what Nordic social democracy has been about with the concept of "decommodification." Socializing social benefits or, in other words, reducing the role of firms (and families) as providers of social benefits has indeed been an objective of Nordic social democracy, but none of the policies enumerated above have entailed decommodification in the broader sense of an emancipation of workers from their dependence on the labor market. Quite the contrary, the thrust of the social democratic project is to bring people into the labor market and then to *empower them as sellers of labor power*. In a sense the concept of decommodification is more applicable to policies associated with Christian democracy and other strands of traditional conservatism on the European continent (including the Mediterranean countries): employment protection, early exit from work, and policies designed to keep women in the role of homemakers.

From a social democratic perspective the empowerment of workers as sellers of labor depends not only on the existence of a finely meshed social safety net but also on full employment, access to education (skills), and union representation. These should be considered core components of the social democratic project. My discussion also suggests that egalitarianism represents a more prominent feature of Nordic social democracy than Esping-Andersen's seminal interpretation recognized.

As indicated above, rejection of the idea of a trade-off between equality and efficiency is a defining feature of Nordic social democracy. In this regard I want to emphasize that the main intellectual tradition of Nordic social democracy conceives "economic efficiency" in terms that are quite consistent with mainstream economics. At least as I understand them, Nordic social democrats do not deny that egalitarianism might conflict with efficiency. Their core claim is rather that it is possible to redistribute income in ways that also promote productivity growth and a more efficient allocation of resources.

Social Democracy and Varieties of Capitalism

The question of why social democratic ideas have been particularly influential in the Nordic countries lies well beyond the scope of this chapter, but I want to briefly address the related question of the extent to which social democratic policies presuppose a particular type of capitalism. Specifically, I wish to question—or at least qualify—what I take to be an implication of the VofC literature, namely that the institutional framework characteristic of "coordinated market economies" (CMEs) constitutes a precondition for successful social democracy.[6]

According to the VofC literature, encompassing and organizationally coherent (more or less centralized) unions and employer organizations are an important part of what distinguishes coordinated market economies from liberal market economies, but the distinction between these two types of capitalism ultimately hinges on corporate finance and ownership (cf. Soskice 1999; Hall and Soskice 2001). Coordinated market economies are first distinguished by limited firm exposure to capital markets, with banks providing long-term finance to the corporate sector and ownership being concentrated in the hands of a few long-term stakeholders. Cross-share holdings among firms are also common in coordinated market economies, protecting firms against volatile capital markets and the threat of hostile takeovers while also providing the basis for coordination among firms.

We can distinguish several arguments that construe the dynamics of co-ordinated market economies as supportive of social democracy—and conversely, construe "stock-market capitalism" as a force working against social democratic policies. To begin with, patient capital arguably allows firms to provide long-term employment for their employees, and long-term employment in turn provides the basis for trust and employees' commitment to the success of the firm. Partly as a result of cooperative labor relations within firms, the comparative advantage of CMEs lies in the production of industrial goods of high quality. Their production strategies in turn allow for the high wages and taxes upon which the social democratic project depends. They may also allow for the compression of wage differentials. More specifically, as we have already seen, recent contributions to the VofC literature argue that reliance on specific skills makes employers in coordinated market economies interested in employment protection and generous social insurance schemes.

These arguments pertain to the congruence of social democratic policies with the production strategies of dominant business segments. In a different vein, one might also argue that the effective implementation of social democratic policies depends on the cooperation of organized business as well as organized labor or, in other words, that the effective implementation of these policies presupposes "corporatist" institutional arrangements. From this perspective firms in liberal market economies might stand to gain from social democratic policies, but they do not have the capacity to help governments implement these policies (e.g., Martin 2004).

For the VofC literature, then, social democracy does not represent a viable policy regime for liberal market economies, while its prospects in coordinated market economies are quite favorable. At the same time the VofC literature argues strenuously against the proposition that capital mobility and in tensified international competition favor LMEs over CMEs. The standard VofC argument on this score is that the institutional differences between CMEs and LMEs are the source of different comparative advantages: CME firms and LME firms pursue different innovation and production strategies, but these strategies are equally viable. Rather than generate pressures for convergence on the liberal model, globalization actually serves to crystallize differences between the two types of capitalist economies (Soskice 1999).

In my view the implications of capital mobility and the globalization of finance over the last two decades are more far-reaching than VofC scholars typically recognize. On average, European firms may still be less exposed to capital markets than American firms are, but ownership structures and corporate governance practices have clearly shifted in a "liberal" direction across the coordinated market economies. In addition, the VofC argument about comparative advantage is strikingly manufacturing-centered and ignores the macroeconomic implications of differential growth rates across industrial sectors.[7] CME firms specializing in "incremental innovation" may well be able to thrive in the new world economy, but if sectors in which competition hinges on "radical innovation" grow at a much faster rate, this surely poses a problem for countries that have a comparative advantage in incremental innovation.

On the other hand, I want to suggest that the VofC literature exaggerates the extent to which the fate of social democracy is tied to the persistence of "patient capital" and manufacturing systems that rely on the kinds of skills that workers acquire through vocational training of the sort given in Germany. As noted above, what distinguishes the Nordic countries in the realm of education and skill formation is not vocational training but rather public investment in human capital in a much broader sense. Such investment facilitates productivity growth across a wide range of business activities, and more footloose or short-term investors should be quite readily able to recognize its benefits. The same basic argument holds, it seems to me, for other components of the social democratic policy regime, notably the promotion of women's participation in the labor force, the emphasis on getting the unemployed back to work, and the mobility-enhancing implications of universalistic social insurance schemes. As for wage solidarity, let me simply reiterate that it is a policy designed to benefit any and all firms with above-average profits. In short, I fail to see any compelling reason why the economic and social benefits of social democratic policies should be more pronounced in coordinated market economies than in liberal market economies.

The proposition that the effective implementation of social democratic policies presupposes institutional arrangements of the CME type cannot be as readily dismissed. Solidaristic wage bargaining and active labor market policies surely require participation and coordination by employers as well as unions. While this is less obviously so for other components of the social democratic policy regime, such as parental leave insurance and public spending on primary and secondary education, the notion of a "policy regime" implies interdependence among different policies. However, the argument about institutional capacity has more to do with encompassing unions and employer associations than with corporate finance and governance institu-

Table 2. Unionization Rates, 1980 and 2000

	1980	2000	Change
LME average	43	27	−16
United States	22	13	−9
Continental average	35	23	−12
Belgium	54	56	2
Germany	35	25	−10
Nordic average	72	71	−1
Denmark	79	74	−5
Finland	69	76	7
Norway	58	54	−4
Sweden	80	79	−1

Note: Continental average excludes Belgium; otherwise
countries included in group averages are the same as in
table 1 (columns 1–5).
Source: OECD 2008b, 24–25, 34–35.

tions. Historically the concentration of ownership and capitalists with interests in a number of different firms may have been a precondition for the
emergence of relatively centralized employer and trade associations in northern Europe, but it does not follow that recent changes in the structure of
ownership and control undermine existing corporatist arrangements.

Even more so than strong business organizations, strong unions must be
considered an institutional prerequisite for successful social democracy. By
"union strength" I have in mind both high levels of unionization and an organizational structure that makes coordination among unions possible. The
latter feature is not adequately captured by centralization of authority in
the hands of national union officials. Union strength involves limits on the
autonomy of locals and shop stewards but also, perhaps more importantly,
clear jurisdictional boundaries and the absence of inter-union competition
over members. As emphasized by Kjellberg (1983), Nordic unions are distinguished by strong locals as well as strong peak associations.

Strong and coordinated industrial unions are clearly critical to the implementation of solidaristic wage policy. Here I want to emphasize the less commonly recognized point that strong local unions have made it possible for
Nordic social democrats to eschew detailed government regulation of employment and working conditions, instead relying on local unions to protect
workers in this realm. I have yet to puzzle through the micro-foundations of
this argument, but I am strongly inclined to believe that collective bargaining provides a more flexible path to employment security than government

legislation and that reliance on this method attenuates the trade-off between employment security and employment growth.

Does union strength ultimately depend on the broader (or deeper) institutional conditions emphasized by the VofC literature? Leaving aside Belgium, average union density in continental SMEs was actually lower than in Anglophone LMEs in 1980 and fell by nearly as much over the last two decades of the twentieth century (see table 2). It is possible that some of the institutional features of continental SMEs actually contributed to union decline. The practice of extending bargained wage contracts to firms (or workers) that were not party to the contract poses the obvious question of why workers would choose to join unions in these countries. Similarly, employment protection legislation and works councils would seem to deprive unions of an important role at the local level. Here is another complementarity (or "virtuous circle") that deserves to be noted: the social democratic policy regime depends on strong unions, but it also sustains strong unions.[8]

Economic Growth and Social Solidarity, 1995–2007

As Martin and Thelen (2007) have recently asserted, using Denmark and Germany as illustrative cases, the trajectories of the Nordic countries and continental Europe have diverged since the early 1990s. Economic growth and cooperation between unions and employers have been restored and social solidarity has been maintained in the Nordic countries. By contrast, Martin and Thelen observe an erosion of social-market institutions and rising labor-market dualism in Germany and other continental countries. In what follows I will elaborate on this divergence and relate it to my earlier discussion.

To begin with, table 3 brings out the contrast between the Nordic countries and continental Europe with respect to overall economic performance. To summarize, the Danish, Norwegian, and Swedish economies have grown by an average annual rate of about 3% per capita while the Finnish economy has grown by an annual rate of nearly 4% since the end of the economic crisis of the early 1990s. For Finland and Sweden in particular, but also for Denmark, this represents a strong improvement on the 1980s and early 1990s, when Nordic growth—except for Norway, which benefited from oil exports—lagged behind not only the United States but also continental Europe by a significant margin. Over the thirteen years from 1995 through 2007 even Denmark, which grew more slowly than the other Nordic countries, grew at the same rate as the average for Anglophone LMEs (slightly higher than the United States growth rate) and outperformed the average for continental SMEs by one percentage point per year.[9]

Table 3. Average Annual Growth Rate of Real GDP per Capita

	1984–94	1995–2007
LME average	2.8	2.9
Ireland	4.0	7.5
United States	3.0	2.8
Continental average	2.3	1.9
Germany	2.8	1.5
Nordic average	1.9	3.2
Denmark	2.0	2.9
Finland	1.2	3.8
Norway	2.8	3.1
Sweden	1.4	3.1

Note: Countries included in group averages are the same as in table 1 (columns 1–5), except that LME average excludes Ireland.
Source: OECD 2008a, 249.

Like the rest of Western Europe, the Nordic countries have relied heavily on productivity growth to achieve economic growth, and employment growth has been sluggish. In Sweden and Finland unemployment remains much higher than it was before the economic crisis of the early 1990s. Without minimizing this problem, which was the main reason why the Swedish social democrats lost the election of 2006, it is noteworthy that Sweden and Finland managed to avoid the pattern of Germany and other continental SMEs from the mid-1970s through the mid-1990s, when each successive recession was associated with a ratcheting up of the "equilibrium rate" of unemployment. In Sweden open unemployment jumped from 1.2% in 1991 to 9.9% but subsequently fell back, fluctuating in the range of 5 to 7% between 2001 and 2007. In Finland the rate of unemployment peaked at 15.1% in 1995 and fluctuated between 7% and 9% in 2001–7. It also deserves to be noted that Norway and Denmark have successfully maintained very low rates of unemployment over the last ten years, significantly below the United States rate, let alone the EU rate.[10] Perhaps most importantly, economic growth has been accompanied by a very significant reduction in the duration of average unemployment spells in the Nordic countries since the mid-1990s (see table 8).

Nordic economic success over the last ten to fifteen years has occurred in the context of a continued shift to services as the principal source of employment. As table 4 illustrates, the continental SMEs experienced the biggest shift toward a postindustrial employment structure in the 1990s and early 2000s, but the Nordic economies had gone farther down this path by the late 1980s and the Nordic economies remained more postindustrial than the con-

Table 4. Services as Percentage of Total Civilian
Employment, 1991–2007

	1991	2007	Change
LME average	68.1	74.7	6.6
United States	71.8	78.8	7.0
Continental average	60.5	71.2	10.7
Germany	55.0	67.7	12.7
Nordic average	67.0	73.9	6.9
Denmark	66.6	73.6	7.0
Finland	62.3	69.7	7.4
Norway	70.5	76.0	5.5
Sweden	68.4	76.1	7.7

Note: Countries included in group averages are the
same as in table 1 (columns 1–5).
Source: OECD 2008b, 24–25, 34–35.

tinental SMEs by the end of the recent boom. The continued shift to service
employment is particularly noteworthy because the public sector's share of
total employment has either contracted or remained constant in the Nordic
countries since the early 1990s.

By all accounts the embrace of information-processing and communication technologies was a very important component of economic recovery in
Sweden and Finland in the 1990s. Alongside the rise of Ericsson and Nokia as
global ICT firms, these countries have become home to clusters of smaller ICT
companies (Richards 2004). Relatedly, the spread of ICT use across manufacturing and public as well as private services appears to have been an important factor behind rapid productivity growth not only in Sweden and Finland
but also in Denmark and Norway.

For 1995–2006 table 5 reports on annual growth of value added in four
broad sectors: (1) low-technology manufacturing, (2) high and medium-to-
high (HMH) technology manufacturing, (3) finance and business services,
and (4) other private services.[11] As the table indicates, the United States outperformed Germany and the average for continental SMEs in every one of
these sectors, but the performance gap was particularly pronounced for HMH
manufacturing and other private services. Interestingly, HMH manufacturing and other private services are also the two sectors in which Sweden and
Finland clearly outperformed the continental SMEs in this period. The very
strong performance of these countries in HMH manufacturing, with growth
rates one and a half times the United States rate, is particularly striking. It

Table 5. Average Annual Growth of Value Added by Sector, 1996–2006

	Low-Technology Manufacturing[a]	High and Medium-to-High-Technology Manufacturing[b]	Financial and Business Services[c]	Other Private Services[d]
United States	1.1	6.0	3.7	4.5
Continental average[e]	0.7	3.4	2.8	2.4
Germany	0.4	1.0	3.5	2.1
Denmark	−1.0	1.7	2.9	3.1
Finland	2.5	9.1	2.5	4.7
Norway	1.0	1.5	4.3	4.2
Sweden	0.9	9.1	3.2	4.0

[a] Food products, beverages, tobacco, wood and wood products, pulp and paper products, printing and publishing, other manufacturing and recycling.

[b] Chemicals and chemical products, machinery and equipment, transport equipment.

[c] Finance, insurance, real estate, and business services (computer and related activities, research and development, renting of machinery and equipment, etc.).

[d] Wholesale and retail trade, restaurants and hotels, transportation, storage, and communications.

[e] Same countries as in table 1 (columns 1–5).

Source: OECD, STAN Structural Analysis Database, version 2008 (http://stats.oecd.org/).

is also noteworthy that all four Nordic countries enjoyed stronger output growth than the continental SMEs in a wide range of private services.

The emergence of the Nordic countries as models of how high-wage countries can meet the challenges of globalization by shifting to more knowledge-intensive manufacturing and service production is reflected in recent reports by the World Economic Forum (WEF). According to the forum's most recent report on information-age preparedness (released in April 2008), Denmark is the most "networked economy" in the world, followed by Sweden in second place, Finland in sixth place, and Norway in tenth place. On the forum's broader index of global competitiveness, Denmark, Sweden, and Finland ranked third, fourth, and fifth in 2008. By contrast, continental SMEs other than Switzerland are notably absent from the top-ten list on both WEF indexes.[12]

The WEF rankings take into account the regulatory environment as well as the quality of human capital, infrastructure, and government support for research and development. It is commonplace in OECD publications to attribute the recent successes of the Nordic economies to deregulatory, liberalizing reforms undertaken in the 1980s and 1990s (e.g., OECD 2007a). Let me briefly illustrate the kinds of reforms involved here with reference to Sweden. To begin with, the Swedish social democrats engaged in deregulation of capital markets and financial services on a scale quite similar to Mrs. Thatcher's "Big Bang" in the second half of the 1980s. By all accounts this reform contributed to the ensuing assets bubble and the banking crisis of 1991–92, but it also seems to have improved access to capital for Swedish firms—and certainly had important consequences for the ownership and governance of Swedish business. Foreign capital entered on a massive scale through the foreign acquisition of Swedish firms as well as portfolio investment in the 1990s (Henrekson and Jakobsson 2005).

In eliminating a variety of tax expenditures while lowering the nominal rate of profits taxation, the Swedish tax reform of 1990 was also inspired by market-liberal thinking. Less commonly noted, the social democrats presided over a comprehensive dismantling of price supports and other regulations of agriculture in 1990. Furthermore, successive Swedish governments in the 1980s and 1990s enacted measures that effectively broke up public utilities and telecommunications monopolies and partially privatized the ownership of relevant state enterprises. Across the entire range of markets for manufactured goods and private services, government reforms have sought to encourage competition and entrepreneurship.

With Norway as something of a laggard, the other Nordic countries have engaged in similar deregulatory reforms. A systematic comparative analysis lies far beyond the scope of this chapter, but I doubt that anyone would contest the proposition that Sweden, Denmark, and Finland have embraced and implemented the deregulation of capital markets, product markets, and private services to a considerably greater extent than continental SMEs like Germany and France.[13]

The Nordic countries reduced the income replacement provided by various social insurance programs and also cut spending on public services in the early 1990s, but reforms of the welfare state were far more circumscribed than the deregulatory reforms enumerated above. Budgetary pressures rather than market-liberal ideas clearly constituted the primary motivation behind these reforms, and spending cuts were restored as economic growth picked up in the second half of the 1990s. Under the umbrella of "flexicurity," Denmark reformed its system of unemployment support in the 1990s, restricting the duration of passive income support while expanding the rights of the long-term unemployed to individually tailored retraining (Madsen 2002), but this reform can hardly be described as "market-liberal." To the contrary, it represents an embrace of the principles of Swedish active labor market policy. Other social policy reforms can also be said to have shored up existing welfare states. Perhaps most importantly, it is striking that after two decades of reform, public monopolies in the provision of education, healthcare, child-care, and elderly care remain effectively intact in the Nordic countries.

The trajectory of Nordic political economies might thus be characterized as one of far-reaching but targeted or "asymmetric" liberalization, as distinct from the across-the-board liberalization of Thatcher's Britain. As I have emphasized throughout this chapter, the asymmetric embrace of markets in some realms and rejection of market solutions in other realms has long been a hallmark of Nordic social democracy. With the benefit of hindsight, the de-regulatory reforms enumerated above may have been an essential part of the political process that enabled the social democrats to regain their capacity to define the terms of economic and social policy debate. At the same time, it seems plausible to argue that the Nordic countries have been able to engage in far-reaching deregulation precisely because their citizens enjoy generous, publicly provided welfare provisions that render them less sensitive to the fate of the companies in which they work. In other words, the Nordic experience of the last couple of decades suggests that the compensatory logic of social welfare articulated by Katzenstein (1985) applies to domestic liberalization as well as trade liberalization.

Released shortly before the election of 2006, a report on the Swedish economy by a team of American and Swedish economists (Freeman, Swedenborg, and Topel eds. 2006) concluded that "excessive egalitarianism" remained a drag on economic growth and that the economic boom provided a favorable environment for allowing income differentials to rise. By contrast, I suggest that the egalitarianism of the Nordic countries has contributed positively to their economic success since the early 1990s. As I see it, three mechanisms are at work. First, coordinated wage bargaining with strong unions has limited wage differentials resulting from corporate profitability and kept pressure on firms to improve productivity. Even within the private service sector, the logic of the Rehn-Meidner model still seems to work.[14] Indeed, it is tempting to argue that the shift from peak-level to industry-level wage bargaining has reduced the need for unions in the Nordic countries to pursue inter-occupational leveling and hence enabled them to pursue wage policies based more exclusively on Rehn-Meidner principles.

Second, there can be little doubt that high levels of public investment in families and education since the 1970s (or earlier) contributed to the strong performance of the Nordic economies in the 1990s and 2000s, and especially to the growth of more knowledge-intensive sectors. The broad base of general skills—or in other words, the relatively high level of general skills at the bottom of the skill distribution—clearly represents the distinctive ad-

vantage of the Nordic countries, not only in allowing for the use of information technology in the production of goods and services but also in making
for more sophisticated consumers of ICT products. As noted earlier (table 1),
"information-age literacy" is more widespread in the Nordic countries than
in any other OECD countries.

Finally, the Nordic economies have benefited in more or less tangible ways
from high levels of female labor force participation and gender equality.
Though I have no quantitative evidence on this score, the large-scale entry of
women into managerial positions in the corporate sector represents an important new development in the Nordic countries over the last two decades.
There is every reason to suppose that the quality of management improves as
the pool of potential managers increases.

The final contrast that I want to draw between Nordic and continental trajectories since the early 1990s concerns labor-market dualism. The growth
of precarious forms of employment and conflicts of interest between labor
insiders and outsiders has recently emerged as a prominent theme in the
comparative political economy of advanced industrial states. While King and
Rueda (2008) treat dualist tendencies as a common feature of all OECD countries, others (e.g., Iversen and Stephens 2008, 605) conceive growing dualism
as a distinctively continental European phenomenon. In the latter vein Palier
and Thelen (2010) argue that growing labor-market dualism in France and
Germany is a result of the distinctive political dynamics of labor-market and
social policy reforms in these countries.

Tables 6–9 present some preliminary evidence in support of the proposition that dualist tendencies have been less pronounced in the Nordic countries than in continental Europe over the last ten to fifteen years. To begin
with, table 6 reports on the percentage of the labor force employed under
fixed-term contracts. In the mid-1990s fixed-term contracts were more common in the Nordic countries than in Germany and the continental SMEs as
a group. However, the incidence of fixed-term employment declined in the
Nordic countries (except for Sweden) while it increased on the European continent in the late 1990s and early 2000s. In this respect the Nordic experience
seems to resemble the experience of the United States more than that of continental Europe.

Part-time employment is commonly viewed as another form of precarious employment (e.g., King and Rueda 2008). As shown in table 7, part-time
workers as a proportion of all workers increased very markedly in Germany
from 1994 to 2007. The incidence of part-time employment also increased in
the other continental SMEs over this period, but it declined in Sweden and
Norway, as in the United States, and remained constant in Denmark. Start-

Table 6. Fixed-Term Employment as Percentage of
Total Labor Force, 1994–2002

	1994	2002	Change
LME average	8.1	7.1	−1.0
United States	5.1	4.0	−1.1
Continental average	9.3	11.3	2.0
Germany	10.3	12.0	1.7
Nordic average	14.5	12.4	−2.1
Denmark	12.0	8.9	−3.1
Finland	18.3	16.1	−2.2
Norway	12.9	9.9	−3.0
Sweden	14.6	14.8	0.2

Note: LME average excludes Australia; otherwise countries included in group averages are the same as in table 1
(columns 1–5). Figures in column 1 are from 1997 for Finland and Sweden, 1996 for Norway.

Source: OECD Labour Market Statistics Database (down-
loaded and compiled by David Rueda).

Table 7. Part-Time Employment as Percentage of
Employed Population, 1994–2007

	1994	2007	Change
LME average	17.3	18.6	1.3
United States	14.2	12.6	−1.6
Continental average	18.8	28.8	10.0
Germany	13.5	22.2	8.7
Nordic average	15.9	16.1	0.2
Denmark	17.3	17.7	0.4
Finland	8.9	11.7	2.8
Norway	21.5	20.4	−1.1
Sweden	15.8	14.4	−1.4

Note: Part-time employment defined as less than 30 hours
per week in one's main job. For lack of data for 1994, LME
average excludes Australia and continental average excludes Austria; otherwise countries included in group averages are the same as in table 1 (columns 1–5).

Source: OECD 2008c, 352.

Table 8. Long-Term Unemployment (More
Than 6 Months) as Percentage of Total
Unemployment, 1994–2007

	1994	2007	Change
LME average	49.9	30.2	−19.7
United States	20.3	17.6	−2.7
Continental average	60.0	60.1	0.1
Germany	63.8	71.3	7.5
Nordic average	48.1	27.3	−20.8
Denmark	54.0	29.5	−24.5
Finland		37.9	
Norway	43.7	25.1	−18.6
Sweden	46.7	27.3	−19.4

Note: To capture change over time, Nordic average excludes Finland; otherwise the countries included in group
averages are the same as table 1 (columns 1–5).
    Source: OECD 2008c, 355.

Table 9. Incidence of Low Pay, 1994–2004

	1994	1996	1997	1999	2002	2003	2004
United States	25.1					23.3	
United Kingdom	19.5				21.4		
Germany	11.6				15.8		
Netherlands	11.9			14.8			
Denmark		7.3				9.3	
Finland					7.3		
Sweden			5.7				6.4

Note: Figures represent percentage of full-time employees earning less than two-thirds of the
median wage for full-time employees.
    Source: OECD Relative Earnings Database.

ing at a much lower level, Finland is the only Nordic country that conforms
to the continental European pattern with respect to the growth of part-time
employment.

    Trends in the incidence of long-term unemployment constitute another
point of contrast between the Nordic countries and continental Europe that
is relevant to the theme of labor-market dualism. Table 8 reports on the percentage of the unemployed who have been unemployed for more than six
months. During the economic crisis of the early 1990s this figure shot up in
the Nordic countries, but it never quite reached continental levels, and it has

subsequently been more or less halved in Denmark, Norway, and Sweden (with data for the mid-1990s missing for Finland). Again, the contrast with continental Europe is striking. In Germany the incidence of long-term unemployment rose dramatically while the overall unemployment rate held more or less steady from 1994 to 2007. Averaging across six continental SMEs, the incidence of long-term unemployment remained constant while the overall unemployment rate dropped.

Finally, table 9 presents some fragmentary data on the incidence of low-pay employment, defined here as the percentage of full-time workers earning less than two-thirds of the median wage. The evidence suggests that the low-pay labor force has grown in the Nordic countries as well as continental Europe, but the increases in Denmark and Sweden are notably smaller than those observed in Germany and the Netherlands. As the incidence of low-pay employment in continental Europe has begun to approach levels characteristic of liberal market economies, represented by the United Kingdom and the United States in table 9, the Nordic countries stand out even more by this measure.

It deserves to be noted that overall wage inequality among full-time employees and inequality of gross earnings among working-age households have actually increased more in Sweden than in Germany since the 1990s (Pontusson 2005a, 45). In Sweden low-skilled and low-paid workers have fared relatively well while highly educated workers have gained relative to the middle. This pattern of inequality growth, which resembles that of liberal market economies, may be more conducive than the continental pattern to the persistence of a redistributive coalition of low-income and middle-income voters (cf. Lupu and Pontusson 2010). For our purposes, suffice it to say that the recovery and successful restructuring of the Nordic economies over the last fifteen years have not brought about any dramatic increase in the gap between labor-market insiders and outsiders.[15] Relative to continental SMEs, the Nordic economies may be less in need of labor-market dualism because they rely more extensively on general skills and because their labor markets are more flexible.

THE POLICY REGIME associated with Nordic social democracy cannot be captured by a simple formula along the lines of "politics against markets" (Esping-Andersen 1985). Rather, this policy regime represents an essentially pragmatic approach to managing contemporary capitalism, characterized by a combination of collective bargaining and government intervention to regulate labor markets, direct government provision of public goods, and redistributive taxes and incomes transfers to correct for inequalities generated by markets. Nordic social democrats have not only been willing to concede a lot of terrain to markets, they have celebrated the efficiency of markets as mechanisms to allocate productive resources. The "market-friendliness" of social democracy became more pronounced in the 1980s and 1990s, but it was also quite pronounced in the 1950s and 1960s, and the generous boundaries that social democratic ideology sets for market solutions to societal problems remain. To my mind, it is the radical trade-union initiatives of the 1970s (Pontusson 1992) rather than the deregulatory reforms and budget-balancing measures of the 1990s that represent a radical break with the social democratic tradition. In particular, it is noteworthy that postwar Nordic governments pursued quite restrictive fiscal policies (premised on full employment, the Rehn-Meidner model incorporated this policy stance).

What are the consequences of the global economic crisis that began to unfold in the fall of 2008 for the social democratic policy regime as I have conceived it in this chapter? A few brief comments must suffice. The origins of the crisis clearly call into question the laissez-faire approach to financial markets adopted by Nordic social democrats, along with just about all other major political parties, in the 1980s and 1990s. It also seems clear, already, that recovery from the crisis will require fiscal stimulus on a scale that exceeds anything the Nordic countries have experienced since the 1930s. The Nordic countries are neither immune to the crisis nor particularly vulnerable. Most importantly for present purposes, the main policy challenges would seem to lie outside the realm of the social democratic policy regime. The social democratic policy regime itself does not prescribe a particular fiscal policy stance, restrictive or expansionary, and macro-economic conditions do not alter the (desirable) effects of its core components. The same argument holds, I think, with respect to the question of how financial markets should be regulated. These observations imply an important clarification of the preceding discussion: the social democratic policy regime as I conceive it is not a comprehensive regime that encompasses all aspects of economic and social policy.

I have argued that the social democratic policy regime remains viable under conditions of globalization and liberalization. To clarify further, this part of my argument pertains specifically to the political and economic viability of the social democratic policy regime. Throughout this chapter I have quite deliberately shied away from the question of which conditions will enable parties pursuing social democratic policies to be electorally successful. As Moschonas (this volume) shows, a secular decline of electoral support for mainstream social democratic parties has occurred across northern Europe over the last two or three decades. The reasons for this are complex, but one thing seems clear: societal demand for social democratic policies has not diminished. With rising inequality and employment insecurity, the opposite is surely true. One might plausibly argue that the decline of unions and other social and political trends have diminished the voice of those who benefit most from social democratic policies. The Nordic experience suggests another possibility, namely that other political parties—other left parties as well as centrist and center-right parties—have embraced social democratic policies and thereby weakened the electoral appeal of social democratic parties. In my mind the extent to which the social democratic policy regime depends on electoral mobilization by social democratic parties is an open question.

In closing, let me very briefly address the question of the relevance of the social democratic policy regime for progressive politics in the United States and other liberal market economies. In contrast to adherents of the Varieties-of-Capitalism school, I have emphasized in this chapter that core policies associated with Nordic social democracy are broadly conducive to productivity growth and benefit more efficient and knowledge-intensive firms across manufacturing and services. In addition, I have tried to suggest that "stock-market capitalism" does not necessarily render these policies inoperative. The pragmatic nature of the social democratic approach also deserves to be noted in this context. With regard to wage solidarity, for example, the social democratic approach does not prescribe some particular leveling of wage differentials that must be obtained: any standardization of wages across firms with variable profitability is considered desirable.

In short, I believe that there is quite a lot of room for social democracy in liberal market economies. At the same time, I have emphasized that the implementation of solidaristic wage policy and other components of the social democratic policy regime presuppose relatively strong unions. To some extent government may be a "functional substitute" for strong unions. Most obviously, we might think of minimum wage legislation as a substitute for solidaristic wage bargaining, curtailing the extent to which low wages subsidize inefficient firms. Similarly, government legislation can obviously provide workers with protection against unfair dismissals and serve to enforce occupational health and safety standards. I do not wish to imply that government should desist from these activities, but the comparison of the Nordic countries and continental Europe introduces a cautionary note, for it suggests that extensive government regulation of labor markets and employment conditions may preempt unionization. Building stronger unions must surely be an indispensable part of any effort to move economic and social policies in the United States in a social democratic direction.

Notes

I thank Jim Cronin, George Ross, and Jim Shoch for their comments and, above all, their patience. For help with table 5, I am grateful to my research assistant, Michael Becher. Above all, I am very much indebted to Mary O'Sullivan, whose criticisms forced me to make major revisions at a stage when I thought that I was almost finished with this paper.

1. Perhaps it is needless to say that I use the term "Nordic" rather than "Scandinavian" because I think that Finland deserves to be included among the countries with a social democratic policy regime. From a comparative Nordic perspective, the Finnish experience is exceptional on at least two counts: the country industrialized much later than in Scandinavia, and political and ideological struggles on the left divided the labor movement. As a result, the Finnish social democratic party never assumed the same position as its Scandinavian sister parties held in the 1950s and 1960s, yet Finnish politics clearly shifted in a social democratic direction in the 1970s and 1980s. Arguably, policy diffusion among the Nordic countries contributed to this development.

2. "Liberal market economies" (LMEs) constitute another comparison group to which the following discussion will refer. Exemplified by the United States, this group also includes Australia, Canada, Ireland, and the UK. Pontusson 2005a juxtaposes LMEs and SMEs and then distinguishes between Nordic and continental SMEs. To emphasize differences between Nordic and continental political economies, I here reserve the term "social market economies" (coined by German Christian Democrats in the 1950s) for continental countries with comprehensive systems of social protection. This terminological change is part of an effort to correct what I now consider a fundamental ambiguity in *Inequality and Prosperity* (2005). See Pontusson 2006 for an earlier "correction" along similar lines.

3. Among continental welfare states Belgium stands out as comparable to the Nordic welfare states in terms of its redistributive impact. See Pontusson 2005a, 153–62.

4. Like most of the tables that follow, table 1 sorts countries into three groups and reports group averages as well as individual figures for the United States, Germany, and the four Nordic countries. Of course group averages sometimes hide significant variation within groups: the main instances of divergence within the continental and Nordic groups will be noted in the text.

5. See Pontusson 1992 for a more detailed discussion of solidaristic wage policy as a form of industrial policy.

6. To clarify, the Nordic countries and the continental European countries that I call "social market economies" are all (with the possible exception of France) "coordinated market economies" by the criteria of the VofC literature. Japan is commonly thought to exemplify yet another CME variant.

7. See Pontusson 2005b for a more comprehensive critique of the VofC approach.

8. Rothstein (1992) makes a similar argument about unemployment insurance. It is hardly a coincidence that public subsidies to union-administered unemployment

funds play a very prominent role in the unemployment insurance systems of Sweden, Denmark, and Finland and that these countries also have very high and apparently resilient rates of unionization. Among continental SMEs Belgium alone has a Ghent system of unemployment insurance. For the Nordic countries this feature represents a very notable departure from welfare-state universalism.

9. Note that in making these comparisons I do not include Ireland in the LME average, for the simple reason that Ireland grew at twice the rate of any other country included in table 3 during the 1990s.

10. At 2.6%, the Norwegian unemployment rate was the lowest of any OECD country in 2007. Three other countries performed better than Denmark (3.8%) by this measure: Korea, the Netherlands, and Switzerland. The unemployment rates reported here are standardized rates from the OECD (2008b, 335).

11. I follow OECD convention in classifying manufacturing sectors as either "low-technology" or "HMH."

12. In 2008 the Netherlands ranked seventh on networked readiness while Germany ranked tenth on global competitiveness. For further details see http://www.weforum.org.

13. See OECD 2007, 44, for comparative data on product market regulations.

14. By contrast, Iversen and Wren (1998) seem to posit (for reasons that I do not fully understand) that the logic of the Rehn-Meidner model only applies to manufacturing.

15. The pioneering discussion by Rueda (2007) of the politics of insider-outsider conflict misses this contrast between Nordic and continental political economies (which all score high on his measure of "corporatism").

Embracing Markets, Bonding with America, Trying to Do Good

The Ironies of New Labour

James Cronin

Not long after Labour won office in 1997, Tony Blair and Gerhard Schröder put their names to a book entitled *The Third Way* (Blair and Schröder 1999). It was not destined to be a best-seller, but it did capture the feeling in the late 1990s that perhaps New Labour had solved the problem of how to be a social democratic party in an era largely inhospitable to parties and movements of the left. The party came to power armed with a supposedly new outlook and program and it had ridden its new message to an overwhelming electoral victory. Was New Labour the future?

A decade later very few progressives, whether European social democrats or American liberals, would assign to New Labour such a historic role. The war in Iraq largely discredited Blair's government at home and abroad, and the fallout from Iraq served to confirm for many, especially on the left, the suspicion that Labour under Blair's leadership had sold its soul for political power (Shaw 2007). Gordon Brown's tenure was worse, for although he sought to separate himself from what were seen as the negatives of Tony Blair, he did not succeed in regaining popular support. Brown had some bad luck, though no more than is normal for a leader, and he suffered as the economy collapsed as well, but these factors alone cannot account for the dramatic decline in his, and the party's, support. At least three other factors would appear to have been at work: Brown's unattractive persona; a perhaps normal but in this case unusually rapid shift away from the party that had held power for over a decade; and the quite important fact that the Tories had not only a new and younger and more attractive leader but also a new set of policies that at least in theory were much closer to those of Labour than its earlier policies had been.

The effect of all this has been a kind of amnesia and absence of context in the assessment of what Labour achieved in its decade in power. Critics focus reasonably, but far too narrowly, on the recent defeat or on the party's difficulties over Iraq, and their eagerness to pronounce the "end of New Labour" suggests an antipathy masking itself as history. The newly elected leader, Ed Miliband, largely based his campaign on the need to go beyond New Labour and in this way abetted those who never liked it. The unfortunate effect is to largely pass over the actual record of Labour in government. There is also a tendency to forget that the appropriate context for assessing New Labour is the record of failure and frustration that preceded it: specifically, the eighteen years that Labour spent in the wilderness after 1979, as Thatcher and her successors effectively destroyed what Labour had built over generations and in the process transformed the political landscape in Britain. This particular piece of forgetting has also allowed people to believe that because Labour won large parliamentary majorities in 1997 and again in 2001, the party was free to do more or less whatever it chose to do while in office. Forgetting the context affects the assessment of foreign policy as well and, because the war in Iraq turned out so badly, critics have not been compelled to confront the very complicated question of what a "progressive" foreign policy would look like in an age of globalization, "rogue states," jihadist terror, and international uncertainty. It has been enough to denounce what was done and those who did it. Fair enough for debate, not good enough as history or as political analysis, and quite unhelpful in answering the perennial but now especially urgent question: "What is to be done?"

Forged in Adversity: The Making of New Labour

New Labour's claims to be new were, and indeed still are, sometimes disputed. Inevitably the party in its current form bears the marks of its origins and its long history, not least in its name. Nevertheless it is also the product of a protracted and systematic effort to "modernize" the party, to reimagine its vision, to remake its program, and to develop new sources of support.[1] The effort was a response to the challenges confronting all social democratic and liberal parties, but it is important to understand just how, and how seriously, these challenges presented themselves in Britain. Everywhere the center-left was forced to deal with the perceived ineffectiveness of Keynesian formulas in solving the economic problems of the 1970s and 1980s. This is not to say that Keynesian solutions were by themselves wrong or their theoretical underpinnings less firm than those supporting rival policy frameworks. The point is that the conventional wisdom associated with Keynesianism—

the priority in policymaking given to full employment, the assumed compatibility between large state expenditures and sustained growth, the notion that moderate shifts in fiscal and monetary policy could effectively manage economic problems—ceased to be compelling and so came to be less widely accepted.

Nowhere did this process go further or have more devastating effects than in Britain. The "stagflation" of the 1970s was superimposed upon a pattern of long-term economic decline in the United Kingdom, and policymakers were asked to address both the short-term crisis and the secular trend. They failed on both counts, calling into question all their policy nostrums and discrediting mainstream, consensually oriented Conservatism as well as the Labour Party. Labour was particularly vulnerable because it was in office during the period 1974–79, the worst of the crisis, and so bore much of the blame, and because even while it was in office its policies were incoherent. The party was deeply split between the left, centered increasingly on the figure of Tony Benn, and those on a looser right, though it is perhaps more accurate to call them centrists or simply moderates. The left wanted more state ownership and planning, more spending and taxes, and a "fundamental and irreversible" shift in power away from corporations and elites—what together became the "alternative economic strategy." The strategy was premised on withdrawal from the European Community and the need to construct an autarchic "siege" economy during the transition. Centrists within the party were more corporatist in approach, keen to build on the party's historic ties to the trade unions to craft a social contract that would hold down wages and prices while redistributing wealth toward the poorest by increasing "the social wage."[2] This was basically a strategy to manage the economic crisis of the 1970s and do some good for the least well-off workers in the process. Actual policy was decided and implemented by party moderates, though the left won many rhetorical battles and the unions exercised a veto over initiatives from wherever they came. By 1979 policy had failed dramatically, and the Labour government led by James Callaghan found itself presiding over a "winter of discontent" brought on by a rebellion from within the ranks of trade unionists, especially in the public sector. Pictures of garbage piling up in the streets, reports of graves undug and of ambulance drivers refusing to drive the sick to hospitals, paved the way for the election of Margaret Thatcher and a dramatic break with all the orthodoxies of the Labour Party, those of its right as much as its left. The shift away from Keynes would be truly seismic in Britain, and it would be ongoing.

The turn away from Keynes and the state and toward the market was the defining and enduring feature of Thatcherism. Its "neoliberal" program had enormous effects on the economy and society: it shifted the burden of taxes away from the wealthy; it abolished exchange controls and deregulated industry and finance; it renounced the government's traditional commitment to full employment and replaced it with commitments to fiscal orthodoxy and the control of inflation; it abandoned previous "corporatist" policies, according to which key decisions were discussed with representatives of industry and the trade unions—instead the government chose to confront the trade unions and restrict the scope and effectiveness of industrial action. Thatcherism divested the state of ownership and hence control of key industries and to that degree gave away critical levers over the economy, and it sold off the bulk of the public housing that half a century of progressive urban policy had built.

What was decisive and brilliant about these moves was that they were largely irreversible. Once the state has given up control and ownership over essential industries and resources, it is hard or at least prohibitively expensive to get them back; once taxes on the well-to-do are reduced, raising them again is nearly impossible short of a national emergency; once working people get a taste of homeownership, they do not want to lose what they now own; once the unions have been reduced in membership and political influence, they stay relatively powerless. Thatcher's governments left a huge legacy that was very hard to displace, and it was this institutional inheritance that Labour was forced to deal with. New Labour has often been criticized for accepting too much of this legacy.[3] The party's record in office, it followed, would amount to little more than a "humane Thatcherism" or, as one analyst labeled it, a kind of "compensatory neoliberalism."[4] Such criticism, however, is fundamentally and historically naïve, for it vastly underestimates the weight and durability of what Thatcher brought about.

Labour in Britain also confronted, more sharply than the center-left elsewhere, a rapidly changing electorate. The transition from an industrial to a postindustrial economy, from the production of goods to the provision of services, was more drastic and abrupt in Britain than elsewhere in Europe or even in America. As of the 1960s Britain still had hundreds of thousands of workers employed in industries like mining, textiles, and shipbuilding. These were among the leading industries of the first industrial revolution and, appropriately, were often Victorian in their use of technology, their management structures, and their approach to marketing. They were old and destined to disappear. The United Kingdom also had its share of firms operating in the industries characteristic of the second industrial revolution—steel, chemicals, later motor cars and other consumer durables—but even here productivity lagged and techniques compared poorly with those prevalent among

Britain's continental competitors and in the United States. But neither Labour nor the Tories had much of a plan for managing the rundown of old industries and the shift into newer lines of work. The historic strength of finance and services did provide employment for an ever-expanding share of the workforce, prompting endless discussions during the 1950s and especially the 1960s about the "black-coated worker" (Britain's term for the white-collar worker) and "affluent worker" and their impact on politics. But into the 1970s very large numbers continued to work in manual jobs in older industries. The effect on Labour as a party was twofold: first, it only gradually and inconsistently redirected its appeal toward white-collar workers and did little to adapt its message and appeal; and second, its policies were overwhelmingly oriented to protecting a workforce whose physiognomy was already changing and about to change even more. The clearest manifestation of this social fact was the enormous clout of coal miners within the counsels, thinking, and lore of the party: mining strikes in the early 1970s virtually brought down the Conservative government led by Edward Heath, for example, and served as the template for what "direct action" could achieve; and it would be the miners whose desperate but doomed strike in 1984–85 sealed the fate of the enduring tradition of Labour as the party committed overwhelmingly to the defense of manual workers.

For the Labour Party, therefore, the transformation from a party of the workers to a catch-all cross-class party came very late and all of a sudden. During the Thatcher period, in fact, entire industries and working-class communities simply disappeared, and when the economy slowly began to grow again in the 1980s it did not in any sense revive; rather, it expanded by means of new industries in new locations and in the process created the outlines of a new social structure. The Labour Party was therefore forced in the 1980s not only to develop new policies but to do so while confronting a new electorate. It was this novelty that *Marxism Today*, the most thoughtful and engaged advocate of a reoriented Labour Party, tried to capture with the phrase "New Times." Deploying the classically Marxian trope of "base and superstructure," the New Times were said to be rooted in the transformation from a "Fordist" to a "post-Fordist" economy and required that ideas and policies be updated accordingly. The party had to alter its traditional rhetoric, policy assumptions, and even emotional attachments if it was to compete effectively in a post-Fordist, Thatcherite, neoliberal world. As with the shift away from Keynes, the Labour Party was pushed to reconstruct its social base, the constituencies and interests that it spoke for, dramatically and abruptly.

The need to reshape the Labour Party was made still more urgent by the electoral landscape of the 1980s. The split within Labour actually worsened after 1979. The left effectively took over the party and prompted secession by the right, which in 1981 launched the Social Democratic Party (SDP) with the specific aim of capturing the center ground of British politics. Labour's first response was to hold firm, and it chose to fight the general election of 1983 on the most left-wing program it had ever espoused—what one MP called "the longest suicide note in history." The party's worst defeat since 1931 led to the election of Neil Kinnock as party leader. Kinnock was seen as a man of the left and elected as such, but he was ultimately to lead the party back toward the center. However, he was forced to spend his first two years dealing with the miners' strike and the influence on the so-called Militant Tendency (a small but surprisingly effective Trotskyist sect) within the local parties in Liverpool and parts of London. By 1985 Kinnock turned to an effort to re-shape the party's message and, in effect, to compete for the centrist voters lost to the SDP and the Tories. To do so he gathered around himself a coterie of "modernizers" including Charles Clarke, Patricia Hewitt, and Peter Mandelson. The immediate focus was presentation, but after the defeat of 1987 it would include policy as well. The Policy Review of 1987–89 moved the party's program decidedly to the center. By certain standards it could be argued that Labour only became a genuinely social democratic party in 1989, when it finally reconciled itself to working within the "mixed economy" and gave up its aspiration, never realistic but nevertheless never relinquished, for socialist transformation.

Despite this major policy reorientation, Labour failed again to dislodge the Tories in the election of 1992. It had seen off the threat from the SDP, but it was still far from being able to beat the Conservatives. This fourth successive defeat was in some respects even more traumatic than earlier ones. After all, the party had reformed itself, purged itself, fashioned a new and more attractive message, and still lost. The effects were mixed in the short term, profound and utterly decisive in the long term. Kinnock resigned straightaway and was replaced by John Smith, a moderate Scot whose selection signaled a period of consolidation and whose supporters believed that with "one more shove" Labour could win. The modernizers, who by this time were led by Tony Blair and Gordon Brown, were appalled, for they believed that the lesson of 1992 was the need for further reform. When Smith died in 1994 he was replaced by Blair, who chose to push even harder on the modernizing agenda. His first big achievement was to convince the party that it should replace clause IV, the commitment to public ownership, in its constitution. The move was largely symbolic, but it had the right effect, for it sent a message to voters, the press, and potential rivals that Labour had become a quite new and different party.

These final moves toward modernizing and centering the party were at least partly stimulated by the two other forces that have recently constrained center-left parties across Europe: the collapse of communism and the progress of globalization. The Communist Party (CPGB) was never a major force within British politics, in part because it effectively chose to cast its fate with the Labour Party from the 1930s. Marxist ideas of various sorts had nevertheless a fairly wide influence on the left. The collapse of communism had an effect that was only modest practically, but large symbolically and emotionally. It was a signal that notions of socialist transformation, and hopes of transcending capitalism, really were the stuff of nostalgia and served no useful purpose even in the rhetoric of the Labour Party. To some, like Jack Straw, this meant that it was time to alter the party's image and discourse by finally abandoning claims about socialism and in particular by ridding the constitution of clause IV (Straw 1993). Blair, as party leader, would agree.

Britain's place in the world economy, and its unique dependence on international trade and finance, has long been an important factor in British politics. As the first and most consistent of free trade nations, Britain has been much more exposed to the opportunities and vulnerabilities that stem from that stance than its rivals and competitors have been (Trentmann 2008). This exposure was increased massively and deliberately after the election of Margaret Thatcher: the Tories quickly announced the abolition of exchange controls, for example, and sought to make London once again the world's leading financial center, albeit through the activities of American banks and investment houses. The "big bang" of 1986 was the key milestone in this process. The Conservatives also welcomed foreign investment in industry and, perhaps most important, were willing to see British firms perish if they could not effectively compete internationally. Britain was also keen on creating a European "single market" in the 1980s. All of this made globalization more real for Britain than for other major economies and made it easy and logical for the modernizers in the Labour Party to insist that their policies were to a considerable extent dictated by the need to compete in international markets. Some within the party might be tempted to object, of course, for there had been strong support within the party for policies that would constrain or counteract the world market and protect industry and jobs from its devastating effects. These were in fact the assumptions and intentions of the "alternative economic strategy" proposed in the late 1970s. But the implementation of that strategy was effectively preempted by the decision to secure an IMF loan in 1976. The need for the loan, though disputed then and since, offered a choice between participating fully in the world economy and not doing so. Once made, the choice was difficult to reverse; and the modernizers within the party insisted that opting out was inconceivable (Burk and Cairncross 1982; Fay and Young 1978; Callaghan 2000).

So party competition, shifts in the sociology of the electorate, and the repeated failures of the Labour Party while in office and the consequent discrediting of its policy assumptions, as well as the more diffuse but no less important effects of the end of communism and the advance of globalization—all put enormous pressure on the Labour Party to become something very different. As the modernizers, Blair especially, came to understand this imperative, they sought to transform three of the defining features of the party. First, they worked hard to refashion the party's image and rhetoric. This meant embracing modern campaign techniques and the instruments required to make them effective—polls, focus groups, and the employment of public relations staff rather than researchers or organizers. It also led to the selection of leaders and spokesmen who looked, talked, and acted the part. The second task was to redefine the message: Labour's program during the 1970s and into the late 1980s was on the whole quite radical, but it had by the 1990s been rejected again and again. The major work in revising the program was done in the late 1980s under Kinnock, but the process would continue under Smith and Blair. With the accession of Blair to the leadership, moreover, revision became more intense and aggressive. So long as Kinnock and Smith were leaders, the move to the center was seen and understood as a tactical necessity, not something done out of conviction. Blair set out to convince voters that he really meant it, that he and Brown and their allies genuinely believed that the market was a good thing and not merely something to be accommodated, that New Labour could make a market economy work better and produce more humane outcomes, and that they embraced the future and the role of the market and of business within it rather than merely acquiescing in its inevitability. Not everyone within the party agreed, and many grumbled privately and a few openly, but the grumbling was much diminished when the party won office in 1997.

The third and less often noted set of changes had to do with organization (Russell 2005). The structure of the Labour Party differed qualitatively from that of other parties in Britain and, it would seem, from social democratic parties elsewhere. Labour in origin was a projection of the trade union interest into politics, formed largely to protect that interest industrially, and the trade unions were built directly into its organization. Thus most members of the party were members by virtue of their membership in trade unions; the great bulk of party finances came from the unions rather than from individual subscriptions or donations; at the annual party conference, which defined the party's principles and set out its program, trade unions controlled fully 90%

of the votes until the early 1990s; and trade unions long had substantial built-in representation on the National Executive Committee. Inevitably the connection largely defined the underlying outlook and culture of the party also, even if there was a gloss of ethical socialism and Marxism laid on top. And it served the party well over many years, providing financial support and the backbone of electoral mobilization.

Over time, however, the union link had two further and ultimately unhappy consequences. During the 1960s and especially the 1970s the party in government had tried to do three things simultaneously: to generate as much growth and employment as possible; to move the economy, or society, in a more collectivist and egalitarian direction; and to do these things while keeping prices under control. The problem was that the first two objectives largely contradicted the third. Labour governments in Britain, like governments elsewhere, had very few mechanisms at hand for maintaining price stability. The best they could do was ask the trade unions to help. Trade union leaders were willing, but their members were not. The effect was a series of botched efforts to get the trade unions' cooperation in controlling inflation. In 1968–69, for example, the government produced a white paper, "In Place of Strife," which proposed that union leaders be given the power to rein in unofficial strikes. In return unions and their members would be accorded an impressive array of rights and privileges. The effort got nowhere, and the government was forced into a retreat that showed its impotence in the fact of union resistance. A decade later a still weaker Labour government tried to manage the economic crisis it faced by asking unions to agree to another year of wage restraint. Such a policy had worked from 1974 through 1977, as the government had offered increases in the "social wage"—i.e., in pensions and social services—and in the wages of the poorest workers as part of a broad "social contract." It finally failed, in the "winter of discontent."

The effect was not merely the election of Mrs. Thatcher. The inability to make the trade union connection work for Labour in power discredited the connection itself as well as the trade unions. The fiasco over "In Place of Strife" demonstrated that trade union leaders wielded a de facto veto over Labour policy; the winter of discontent demonstrated that the disaffected rank and file could veto what their leaders had decided on high. The party was rendered doubly ineffective. Leaders like Wilson and Callaghan and later Kinnock found the situation embarrassing; Blair regarded it as intolerable, and his allies were determined to overcome it. They were aided in this by Margaret Thatcher, who beat the miners into submission, rewrote labor law, and presided over a decade of industrial transformation that left the unions severely weakened. For their part the Labour modernizers were careful in opposition not to promise to reverse Tory industrial relations policy; they also made it clear that the unions were not to enjoy special access to a future Labour government. More important, they initiated a series of alterations in the internal organization of the party that reduced the influence of the trade unions. The aim was not merely to distance themselves from the unions but to prevent the unions from ever exercising the decisive influence they had wielded during previous Labour regimes.

New Labour in Power

These decisions, the problems they were meant to solve, and the constraints they were intended to overcome all had a very big impact on what New Labour did in power after 1997. So too did the party's promise not to exceed Tory spending limits for the first two years and the decision, made shortly after the election, to let the Bank of England set interest rates outside the control of the government. The effect of a moderate program, a rhetoric aimed at consensus, and policies designed not to upset but reassure financial markets made for a first term with only modest achievements. Gradually, however, New Labour gained the confidence and experience to begin seriously to implement its program. It also profited from the brute fact of economic success, which meant that the proceeds of growth could be used to direct money to Labour's preferred objectives. In the election of 2001, moreover, the government hinted at least at the prospect of an increase in national insurance contributions—in theory not a tax increase, but everyone understood it as such—and another decisive victory led to its adoption. Labour now had the money and the experience to put its stamp upon policy and upon society.

What did it do, and how well? The answer depends in part on where one looks, on what area of policy one chooses to emphasize. Any list is arbitrary, but any moderately comprehensive one would presumably include: economic performance and employment; the funding and administration of public services such as health, education, and transport, and how these translate into outcomes; the constitution and distribution of power and authority; and issues of personal and national security, from crime to foreign policy. What is perhaps most interesting about the experience of New Labour is that in most of these areas the government claimed to be doing something new and distinctive, different not only from the Tories but also from what past Labour governments had done or at least tried to do. In assessing its performance, it is therefore useful to ask both how New Labour did and also whether success or failure had anything to do with the distinctive innovations, if any, made by New Labour in government. A thorough analysis would take volumes, but a brief inventory is possible (Shaw 2007; Seldon 2007; Toynbee and Walker 2010).

The Economy and Employment

Labour had the good fortune to inherit an economy in recovery. The party promised, of course, to manage growth better than the Tories, but it offered few specific proposals. Labour would essentially continue to provide a stable macroeconomic framework with only minor alterations. The most visible move was the decision to let the Bank of England set interest rates free from detailed government involvement. Did this matter economically? It is difficult to say definitively, but the decision did send a message to financial markets that Labour was committed to market mechanisms and to the fight against inflation. The message was a welcome one to business and certainly did much to reassure investors that they had little to fear from New Labour. Whether that belief conduced to greater economic growth is, again, very hard to determine. What can be said is that this initial decision, coupled with a decade of generally prudent fiscal policy under Gordon Brown's supervision, did nothing to derail an economy that was already growing substantially. In fact, the record of sustained economic growth compiled during the first decade of New Labour rule exceeded that of any previous administration. It is of course possible that New Labour was merely profiting from policies begun earlier by its opponents and was unfairly given credit that others deserved, but that is how politics works.

What was new about Labour's economic and employment policies, then, was not any departures from what the Tories had put in place, but rather how they differed from the party's history. New Labour broke decisively from what was seen as the pattern of previous Labour governments, which promised to do a great deal, to spend and (inevitably) to tax, and to make use of the state to spur economic growth and create jobs. New Labour no longer believed this was possible, and so did not promise it. What it did offer was a range of policies to increase employment by making people more employable and giving them greater incentives to work. The theoretical underpinnings of the approach were found in "endogenous growth theory," which focused on skills and knowledge. Practically speaking, getting more people into work—insertion, as some would call it, or labor market activation in another parlance—would simultaneously reduce the number on welfare and promote "social inclusion." A prominent initiative, partly modeled on the welfare reform efforts of President Bill Clinton, was the so-called New Deal, which offered financial support as well as childcare to those willing to enter approved training schemes, vocational education, or subsidized work (King and Wickham-Jones 1990). The first program aimed at the young; subsequent ones focused on single parents, the disabled, and the long-term unemployed. A related set of policies sought to reduce the disincentives to work: free or subsidized childcare, for example, would eliminate or at least lower that barrier to employment; a minimum wage would make work pay better for the poorest; and the "Working Families Tax Credit" together with the Child Tax Credit would allow a kind of "top-up" beyond what they ordinarily earned. The aim was to escape the so-called poverty trap that rendered work less profitable than relief. Alongside these "active labor market policies" was a broader interest in encouraging human capital development through increased investment in education and policies aimed at nurturing "knowledge-based" industries through more research and development. Labour chose to call this mix of policies "supply-side socialism," and they did work on the supply side, though to call this socialism is rather a stretch (Romano 2006).

Whatever the label, the consensus is that the New Deal, tax credits, training, and improved daycare arrangements have been moderately effective: more people were employed overall and in the target groups, and the welfare of the poorest workers and their families substantially improved. It is of course hard to say with certainty that these shifts are long-term and that they will survive a sustained economic downturn, but the effects in the short and medium term have been largely positive. It also seems that in certain respects the quality of work has improved and the rights of workers have been marginally enhanced. Policies on family leave and equal opportunity, for example, have been deemed largely successful. Here the key was not so much new British laws and programs as the importation of European standards. During its long period in opposition the Labour Party had faced a dilemma over its stance on the rights of unions and of workers more generally. The Thatcher government's industrial relations legislation was deeply resented by the trade unions but popular with voters. The party therefore needed to do something for the unions without alienating others. The solution was found in Europe: Labour decided to leave the Tories' legislative framework intact but to accept the Social Charter first proposed by Jacques Delors. The Tories, by contrast, opted out of that bit of the European bargain. The social rights outlined in the charter stood between the minimal rights accorded workers and unions in current British law and the much more extensive set of protections and immunities that unions had enjoyed in Britain up through 1979. The party managed to convince the trade unions that the European package was the best they could get; and on assuming office in 1997 the government opted in to its provisions. Unions and workers have benefited, more as individuals than collectively, and union membership, which declined precipitously in the 1980s and 1990s, has begun to recover, if only slightly (Howell 2004).

Public Services

If Labour inherited an improving economy in 1997, it also inherited a deteriorating array of public services. Nearly twenty years of Conservative government bequeathed a legacy of underinvestment in education, health, and transportation. Scholars have debated to what extent the Conservatives were able to roll back the welfare state, and it is clear that they were able to make only modest cuts in the National Health Services (NHS) and for the most part in education (Pierson 1994). It is nevertheless also widely agreed that rates of increase were cut, necessary improvements and maintenance were delayed, and pay and conditions for public sector employees declined or improved only marginally. There was thus a historic deficit of expenditures that the Labour government would want to make up.

That would almost have to happen, though finding the funds would not be simple. Doing so, and doing so with minimal tax increases or controversy, was Gordon Brown's primary achievement as chancellor. It took a couple of years for the government to begin increasing expenditures on public services, but over time it provided enormous sums. Indeed, it has been widely reported that the NHS was simply unable to spend all that it was receiving from the government. And there have been results: the recruitment of doctors and nurses went way up in the health services, waiting times came way down. Expenditures on health increased by 7.4% per year in real terms between 2002 and 2008, for example, and nearly as much was spent on education. Spending for transport also increased substantially.

Increased funding and better outcomes on a wide range of measures have nevertheless not brought happiness. Two reasons apparently account for this. First, taking responsibility for social provision makes any government, any agency, responsible for what goes wrong as well as for what works. Blair famously said that New Labour believes not in dogma but in "what works," but what works tends not to be noticed and so is taken for granted while failure attracts endless attention. Every botched diagnosis, every MRSA infection, every drop in exam results, every train failure is reported and someone is blamed, so it is very hard for any government to get proper credit for improved services. This enduring condition has been exacerbated by New Labour's approach to the public sector. Early on New Labour decided that increases in funding had to be accompanied by "reform," and reform was typically defined, controversially, as involving increases in competition and choice. The public sector, in New Labour's view, should be restructured according to the principles and practices of the market. In certain cases services should be provided directly by the private sector, even if that led to profit making at public expense. It also meant a shift in rhetoric, with public sector workers and their unions cast as opponents of reform, as "producer interests" that got in the way of the interests of consumers or patients or clients or passengers, and whose self-interested rigidities effectively reduced choice.

Why did New Labour choose this approach to the public sector? For some, it was because they really believed in choice and the superiority of market models. Evidently Blair really did think that competition and choice, whether in medicine or in education, would produce superior outcomes. For others, it was more a matter of expediency: getting the private sector to help finance new schools, hospitals, buses, and trains or to perform certain medical procedures would allow a more rapid expansion and improvement. Critics have of course pointed out that privately provided services and facilities are no cheaper or better than those done by and through public authorities, and sometimes have higher cost and lower quality, but that is not the point: the perceived need as of 1997 was for speed. There was also the issue of political expediency, in both the short and long term. Short-term, it was believed to be easier to sell increased public expenditure if that was going to produce not just more but better, more "reformed" services. Long-term, many within New Labour reckoned that the viability of the public sector depended on keeping the middle classes and the increasingly affluent working class within the system. The big threat to the public sector, it was argued, was the defection of people whose standards were rising and who could afford to go elsewhere. To keep them happy meant providing higher standards and more choice within the basic framework of public provision. This strategic argument is hard to prove or disprove, but it is not for that reason wrong, disingenuous, or unimportant. Labour's policies toward the public sector have as a result proved highly controversial, and disaffection within the ranks of public sector workers has prevented Labour from reaping the benefits that its record of increased expenditures might otherwise merit. Critics have claimed with some success that New Labour has eroded the "public service ethos" and in that sense violated its core principles.

This critique has been reinforced by the lack of interest that New Labour has shown in another core principle in its tradition: equality. The data here are frankly contradictory. Under Labour the fate of the poorest section of society has improved a great deal: child poverty in particular was lessened; the working poor became much better off; and the tax and benefit system became more redistributive. At the same time, inequality has slightly increased. How are these developments reconciled, in fact and in theory? It is clear that recent economic trends have been very regressive in their effects. Incomes have grown much faster for the middle and upper classes than for others, those with property and investments have fared much better than those without, and the ongoing shift away from industry and toward services has continued to reduce the number of high-paying manual jobs. In that context— as, it should be noted, in most other advanced countries—inequality steadily increases. In Britain, supporters of New Labour will argue, inequality has grown less and has to some extent been counteracted by government policy. The defense is compelling enough, but it is also true that in theory New Labour is not averse to increases in wealth or inequality. From the beginning New Labour asserted that it wanted to be pro-business and that it heartily approved of entrepreneurship and the accumulation of wealth. Labour professed to want "more millionaires," not fewer. And it is this attitude, particularly as and when it combines with the disparaging of the public sector and the constant hectoring to reform it, that has convinced at least some people that New Labour has truly "lost its soul."

The Constitution, Power, and Security

For most of its history the Labour Party has been about "the social." Of necessity it has had to develop a foreign policy, policies toward crime and the regulation of personal life, and a philosophy of how government should work, but it has typically not distinguished itself on these issues. The party has not fundamentally challenged the "Westminster model" of government but has sought instead to capture the model; it has been moderately liberal on matters of rights and social questions, but hardly in the forefront on these matters; and its foreign policy has not differed fundamentally from that of its rivals. Indeed before the advent of New Labour the Labour Party's greatest success had been in the 1940s, when it could claim to be the party which best represented the national interest rather than the interests of a particular class, and when it managed to portray its opponents as willing to sacrifice the national interest. Labour was at that moment the national party, not a sectional interest, and as such would do a better job of protecting the state, its institutions, and the "British way of life."

It is therefore ironic that in the decade after 1997 Labour brought into effect a series of far-reaching constitutional changes. The most important were devolution in Scotland and Wales, decisions with potentially transforming consequences for the shape and definition of the nation; reform of the judiciary and the House of Lords, a process that is far from completed; and the incorporation into British law of the European Convention on Human Rights and other EU laws which have in effect given Britain its first written constitution. In addition, there is peace and the beginnings of reconciliation and devolved government in Northern Ireland, a success in foreign policy with major constitutional ramifications. The full effects of these innovations will not be clear for a very long time, but they are likely to be profound.

Radical constitutional change was not something with which Labour had ever been identified, and it was not very high on Labour's list of priorities in 1997. It should not be surprising, therefore, that Labour has been given little credit for these initiatives. Instead it has suffered for its ambivalence toward these shifts even as it has overseen their implementation. It has appeared inconsistent and illiberal to advocates of constitutional reforms and so forfeited its place as the party most strongly committed to typically liberal reform. Labour has been vulnerable to the charge of illiberalism on several other fronts as well. Blair declared that Labour would be both "tough on crime, [and] tough on the causes of crime." The point was to take away the ability of the Tories to claim that Labour was "soft on crime" because of its concern with getting at its root "causes" rather than punishing criminals and protecting victims. Labour actually managed to get crime down, or at least the main measures of crime, and it adopted policies like the introduction of "anti-social behavior orders," or ASBOs, that allow it to claim to be decisively on the side of the victims of crime. The party's stances on immigration and asylum have been similar. Under Labour, Britain has had more generous policies on immigration and asylum than most other European countries, but the government has also worked assiduously to convince voters that both are under control. It has received little credit and considerable criticism for its specific mix of tough rhetoric and moderately open policy on these issues.

Assessing these policies is therefore especially difficult, partly because the issues and data are complex but mainly because it is difficult to know what standard to apply. Over a protracted period Labour has been a socially liberal party, although the Liberal Democrats (and the parties which merged to create them) have occasionally competed on these grounds. The architects of New Labour understood that the party needed to maintain that stance while also finding a way to compete for voters who were less socially liberal but might respond to other elements of the party's appeal. They chose in response to move toward what was regarded as the center on such issues as crime and immigration. To some extent this dilemma reflects the shifting social base of Labour. Like social democratic and liberal parties elsewhere, Labour now gets as many votes from the professional middle classes, especially in the public sector, as from the working class, and among these newer supporters social liberalism is quite important.[5] So too are economic issues like support for spending on public services, an area in which these voters very often work. By most accounts, however, working-class voters are less liberal or progressive on social issues. New Labour's strategy, both in opposition and in government, has been to try to satisfy both groups and find ways of maintaining the party's traditional liberalism while allaying voters' fears about crime, immigration, asylum, and most recently terrorism. It is a delicate balance, and probably the best that a party like Labour can do is adopt a series of compromises that will, with luck, keep the issues from becoming salient enough to rupture the coalition required for electoral success. Still, balancing of this sort gives further ammunition for those who wish to argue that Labour has "lost its soul."

Much the same dilemma confronts Labour regarding foreign policy, but on this issue the party has less control of what is and is not salient and when. Clearly, Iraq became far more salient than Blair or his colleagues ever dreamed, except perhaps in their worst nightmares. Just what an appropriate Labour foreign policy would look like is by no means obvious. After Blair's resignation and David Miliband's appointment as foreign secretary, the government chose to put somewhat less emphasis on the "special relationship" with the United States. It was also eager to be seen as more multilateral and more attentive to Europe than it seemed to be in the first years after 9/11, and to emphasize goals like development aid and climate change that command wide if perhaps shallow public support. It is not a distinctly new foreign policy, but a more agreeable one. It still leaves open, however, just what Labour's orientation should be, or should have been, toward the awkward questions of "humanitarian intervention," terrorism, and Britain's long-standing strategic posture as America's closest ally. The reason these are open questions is that despite Blair's activism and decisiveness and despite New Labour's efforts to rethink policy across a wide range of issues, the party as a whole has not engaged in any fundamental reassessment of foreign policy over the past quarter-century.

The roots of today's uncertainties within the Labour Party go back at least to the election of 1983, which Labour fought on a program of unilateral nuclear disarmament. Voters got to choose between Labour's antinuclear and implicitly anti-NATO stance and the Conservatives' far different policies— continued support for NATO and nuclear weapons and support for the United States regardless of the scary rhetoric of President Reagan's administration and the deployment of intermediate-range (Pershing and Cruise) missiles in Europe. Thatcher won a huge victory, aided in no small measure by Britain's recent triumph in the Falklands. In the aftermath Labour began to back off its unilateralist and non-nuclear positions, but it failed to do so effectively and the issue again cost votes in 1987. In the policy review that followed the defeat, one working group was commissioned to look at foreign and defense policy, but its members had great difficulty reaching a consensus until they took a trip to Moscow. Mikhail Gorbachev met the delegation and told them not to fret. The British nuclear deterrent was not a matter of great concern and besides, the United States and the USSR were in the process of agreeing to a package of major reductions in both intermediate and strategic weapons. The debate within the party was adjourned rather than resolved, and the issue dropped way down the list of party concerns as the cold war ended. The effect was to bequeath to New Labour a heritage of ambivalence in foreign and defense policy. Antiwar and antinuclear sentiments sat uneasily alongside the traditional Atlanticist and anticommunist record of the postwar Labour governments.

New Labour thus took office in 1997 with virtually no experience in foreign and defense matters, with few specific commitments and no clear vision. Once in power Labour opted for continuity: it reaffirmed support for the Atlantic alliance and came to share the basic policy orientation and preferences of President Clinton—free trade, the promotion of human rights and market-based democracies, the enlargement of organizations like the EU and NATO, and "engagement" with the UN and other multilateral institutions. New Labour also shared with the United States a determination to maintain Anglo-American military power at roughly the levels set at the end of the cold war. Blair and the shadow foreign secretary, Robin Cook, thus differed but minimally with their Tory predecessors, though in opposition they had sharply criticized the Tories' apparent indifference to the tragedy of Bosnia.[6] The Labour government would go on, largely at Blair's insistence, to emerge as a strong advocate for selective "humanitarian intervention," and Blair would personally push Clinton toward a more active policy in Kosovo. It was in the context of the debate over Kosovo that in April 1999 Blair gave his famous speech in Chicago on the "Doctrine of International Community" and made this position explicit (Blair 1999; Little and Wickham-Jones eds. 2000; Kampfner 2004; Rawnsley 2001; Coates and Krieger 2004; Freedman 2005).

That statement put Britain on record in support of aggressive action to respond to "rogue states" and humanitarian crises, a commitment that would facilitate the subsequent choice to invade first Afghanistan and then Iraq in the aftermath of 9/11. It was in that respect an important precedent, but it is clear that back in 1999 very few, including Blair, envisioned the world as it would become after 9/11 or the very different context in which foreign policy would be carried out in that world. Still, New Labour had cast its fate with the United States and the "special relationship," and with the principle of humanitarian intervention, and it would become very difficult to turn back. What made it especially difficult was that New Labour had no other coherent or convincing set of policies on which to draw. Debate over foreign policy had simply not been a priority in the party since the end of the cold war, and the New Labour project was a largely domestic affair: it did not encompass an alternative vision of Britain's role in the world. Nor, frankly, is it likely that a lengthy prior debate would have done much to prepare the party, or Britain more generally, for the difficulties presented by 9/11 and the rise of militant Islam. Knowing what they know now, neither Brown nor Miliband nor Jack Straw nor Blair himself would have been likely to argue for the invasion of Iraq, but even now the present lack of a clear alternative suggests that getting it right would have been very hard. And would the Americans have listened if they had succeeded?

Foreign policy matters, however, and Iraq matters because on this issue New Labour was seen very much to have lost its way and perhaps its very soul. That the Tories would undoubtedly have done the same thing as New Labour, and that the Liberal Democrats would never have had the opportunity to decide on the right or wrong strategy, does not make the loss of support, and of legitimacy, any less real for New Labour. Blair left in 2007, but his successor was not able to recoup the support that Blair lost because of Iraq. Again, that Brown's Conservative challenger failed to offer a fundamentally different policy did Labour no good, for it did not constitute a reason to come back to Labour. Nor was there an obvious set of domestic issues with which to lure voters back, for the Conservatives under David Cameron had moved to the center on most key issues and effectively stolen New Labour's rhetoric (Rentoul 2008). The effect of this curious conjuncture is that not only voters but also scholars, political leaders, analysts, and activists failed to appreciate the numerous and often quite successful innovations to which New Labour could rightly lay claim. New Labour thus became a model that voters chose to reject in May 2010. New Labour's history and its record may nevertheless contain lessons critical for the renewal and advance of the center-left everywhere but in Britain. If it is to play such a role elsewhere, or even regain a purchase on the allegiance of British voters, however, New Labour may well require new labels, new rhetoric, and new understandings. This will also not be easy. It has been claimed again and again that New Labour has offered no distinct vision, just clever rhetoric (Fairclough 2000). Perhaps, but not for lack of trying. When New Labour was still taking shape as a political force in the 1990s, there were in fact repeated efforts to outfit it with a discourse and rationale that would capture what was actually new and different about it. At least two big ideas were floated, along with a more modest argument from Blair, before New Labour settled on the ultimately unsatisfactory "Third Way." The first idea was community, or communitarianism. The reasoning was that the party needed a phrase that pointed to the same values or goals as socialism but avoided the assumption that the way to achieve them was through the state. Talk of community implied that citizens had duties as well as rights and that to some extent the two were interdependent; and it allowed the party to avoid charges that it was too soft or permissive. It fit especially well with the phrase, coined by Brown but used by Blair, "tough on crime, tough on the causes of crime."

The notion never quite caught on, perhaps because its inherent, and intended, illiberalism had little appeal within the party. The second concept that was aired and debated in the mid-1990s was that of "the stakeholder society" (Hutton 1995; Hutton 1997). Again, the purpose was to convey what was regarded as a key principle of socialism without using the word. All citizens had a stake in society and the economy, not just the owners of capital, and their interests should be taken into account in policymaking. It was precisely this meaning, however, which rendered the idea unviable: it was seen — allegedly by Gordon Brown, but surely by others as well — as too threatening to capital at a moment when Labour sought to reassure business of its intentions. The concept also lent itself to particular appropriation and use by trade unions, for if anyone besides owners could reasonably claim a stake in a firm, it was surely the organized workers. This too was a message that New Labour did not wish to send.

So both "community" and "the stakeholder society" were left to the side, as was an argument that Blair began to develop in his anniversary lecture on the election of 1945, published as Let Us Face the Future (1995). In it he made the controversial claim that what triumphed in 1945 was not socialism nor even social democracy, but a distinctly British type of progressive politics that combined socialism and liberalism. The model for Blair was thus less the Labour government elected in 1945 than the New Liberalism represented by the Liberal government elected in 1906. Blair insisted that the Labour Party should combine the virtues of both traditions. Once more, the obvious intention was to avoid the negative associations attached to socialism by instead proclaiming allegiance to the inheritance of liberalism in its reforming, socially concerned, and mildly collectivist variety of the early twentieth century.

This outpouring of argument, of theory, occurred at precisely the moment when New Labour was shedding its old image by abandoning clause IV of its constitution, and it was obviously directed at creating an effective substitute. None of these ideas succeeded in doing so, however, and by the time of the election of 1997 that seemed not to matter. New Labour won a decisive victory without having settled upon a big new idea or even an animating slogan. It was in this context that the party settled on the relatively vacuous notion of "the Third Way." As critics have cruelly pointed out, the Third Way has no intrinsic meaning at all: it is merely a way of saying that the Labour Party was neither this nor that, neither the hard-hearted Tories nor the dour and dirigiste socialists of the past. Its content was, at least at the beginning, negative and empty. Over time a cluster of quite thoughtful people—Anthony Giddens most prominently—would try very hard to fill in the vast conceptual space inside the Third Way (Giddens 1998; Giddens 2000; Giddens ed. 2001). The exercise was not without merit, for it provided the rubric under which quite useful debates were conducted on policy and on more fundamental questions about the relationship between markets and states, the individual and society, justice and equality, and the environment and the global economy. The work would continue in think tanks like the Policy Network, the Institute for Public Policy Research, the Foreign Policy Center, Demos, and others, and with considerable sophistication. Yet it was and still is an elite discourse—the Policy Network, for example, began as the Progressive Governance Network and included only the leaders of center-left governments—and its focus on policy did not and still does not easily translate into marketable slogans. There was probably never any real possibility that the concept of the Third Way could have inspired the kind of enthusiasm and loyalty which other terms—socialism, social democracy, or, in their own way, community or stakeholding—had done, or might have done, whatever the venue and style. In the event, talk of the Third Way inevitably died down and Labour in office was unable to come up with anything to take its place.

So long as the party kept winning elections, the absence of a big idea probably did not matter greatly. As the party's fortunes declined, gradually under Blair and then more seriously under Brown, the lack of a major unifying theme or vision came to be more acutely missed. Will Labour find one in opposition? Does it actually need any particular animating vision? There has recently been some renewed attention devoted to the possibility of combining the best of liberalism and of social democracy by crafting a new definition of citizenship which in one version would be anchored in a new constitution for Britain. There are also those who, in response to the weakening of New Labour, would prefer to revert to the old and reconnect with an older social democratic tradition emphasizing redistribution and an expanded role for the state. The issue is unlikely to be settled at the level of theory and will effectively be decided by the choices made by Gordon Brown's successors.

It was clear by early 2010 that the future of the Labour Party would hinge largely on the choice of leader, but also on the electoral performance of the party under Brown, on the manner and context of Brown's leaving, and on the character of the opposition that the party would face once Brown was replaced. The election of 6 May produced unexpected results on all three fronts. To begin, Labour performed better than predicted. During the election campaign the rapid rise of Nick Clegg and the Liberal Democrats—attributed most plausibly to the impact of television debates staged for the first time ever—raised the possibility that Labour would be pushed into third place behind the Tories and the Liberal Democrats. That did not happen: by election day "Cleggmania," as it was called, had faded and the party secured 23% of the votes and lost five seats in the House of Commons, for a modest total of 57; the Tories had failed to break through, getting just over 36% of the vote and a plurality (306) but not a majority of seats; and Labour had rallied to win 29% of the vote and 258 seats. The result was, or so it seemed, a hung parliament; and then, to the surprise of many, the Conservatives and the Liberal Democrats formed a coalition. In the process Gordon Brown made a dignified and gracious exit.

Critics of Labour, and especially of "New Labour," had anticipated a historic collapse, and the circumstances in which the election was fought were about as bad as one could imagine. Labour had been in power for thirteen years, and the enthusiasm generated way back in 1997 had long since dissipated. The party's achievements, which were many and substantial, were forgotten or taken for granted; its style—the tendency to "spin," its preference for increasing taxes and spending by "stealth," its sometimes vacuous rhetoric—had begun to grate; and many had never forgiven the party for the debacle in Iraq. Even more important, according to exit polls, was the state of the economy, for which Labour was forced to bear responsibility. Brown and his chancellor, Alastair Darling, had by all accounts responded effectively to the financial crisis, but the economy remained in terrible shape and the looming budget deficit seemed to guarantee an era of austerity which would erode much that Labour in power had wrought. In addition, there was the utter disaster of the expenses scandal, a phenomenon that affected both the major parties (and the Liberal Democrats rather less) and heightened the sense that something had to change. And finally there was Brown himself, with a "face made for radio" and an affect and personality that did not come across well in any medium, who was forced to compete on television with two younger and much better performers. Back in 1994, when Blair had persuaded Brown to step aside in the leadership contest, a key consideration was how much better Blair performed on television and in Parliament. Little had changed on that score by 2010.

Add these adverse conditions together and it is hard to imagine a party in power not losing many votes and seats. The party did lose on both measures in 2010, but no more and perhaps even less than they could and should have lost. Why? The short answer is that the architects of New Labour got it right and Labour's policies were more or less where they ought to have been. The Blairite embrace of the market may have been excessive, but only marginally so, and it was probably more effective than the alternative; the party may also have been too quick to "spin" rather than to explain, but in a world of instant communication and in a country with a press that feeds on controversy and scandal, to err in that way was surely better than to have erred in the direction of greater candor; constant talk of "reforming" public services and increasing choice may have alienated some of Labour's supporters in the trade unions and the public sector, but not enough to prevent the unions from bankrolling the party's election campaign; and in the desire to appear tough on crime and immigration and terrorism, the party may well have veered too far from its socially and politically liberal traditions, although its policies were less illiberal in practice than its rhetoric might have implied. And of course the Labour government's willingness to lend its support to the United States and its adventures was also profoundly controversial, but again, would the alternative have been more successful? The attack of 9/11 was truly an exceptional moment, and a reluctance to back the United States then would have been unthinkable. Once that backing was offered the options were limited; and New Labour had extremely bad luck in having to deal not with Bill Clinton or Barack Obama but with George W. Bush.

The argument that Labour, in its New Labour incarnation, had been sensible and effective gains at least some support, if not confirmation, by what has come to replace it. The Tories, it would seem, made gains by moving to the center and toward the mix of policies on welfare and the public sector favored by Labour (Bale 2010). If the heart of the Conservative Party remained Thatcherite, its head led Cameron and his allies to speak a different rhetoric, write a different manifesto, and run a different campaign. It may also be that the party did not do even better in the election because voters perceived this split between head and heart and feared a return to Thatcherism or something like it. If so, then the coalition with the Liberal Democrats was a brilliant move, for it allowed the Conservatives to ditch those policies that were most attractive to its Thatcherite wing and move much closer to the sort of centrist and socially liberal policies that can help them win elections.

If the coalition lasts—and the commitment by the two parties to stay together in government for a full five years should not be discounted—it will ironically represent the triumph of Labour's efforts to move Britain away from the Thatcherite settlement and toward the political center, toward something more humane and stable. It will also confront Labour with the need to differentiate itself from a discourse, a reality and a set of policies that it did much to create.

There is great irony, of course, in the fact that as the coalition speaks in the language of fairness, it has adopted a policy of extreme fiscal austerity and begun to blame Labour for running up deficits and leaving the country in dire straits. The cuts proposed by George Osborne seem to many to be the equivalent of the measures taken by Thatcher (McKibbin 2010). And yet both the total of cuts proposed, and many of the details, differ only marginally from what Labour had proposed or was prepared to do if it been reelected. This is surely why the initial resistance to the coalition's austerity measures was modest and restrained. That may change as the more controversial and draconian policies come into effect—especially if the protests over tuition fees are an indicator—but will Labour be able to offer a credible vision that is radically different? Will the new leader, Ed Miliband, succeed in crafting a credible Labour response? His politics are slightly less Blairite than those of his brother David, whom he defeated in the leadership election. Will that help or hurt in this process?

It seems unlikely, and the situation in which Labour finds itself would seem to argue more for continuity than for change, especially if change is conceived as a reversion to something that looks and sounds like "old Labour" and feels like the "winter of discontent." It would be foolish to keep talking about "New Labour" so long after its invention and so long after the phrase did its work in separating the party from those aspects of its past that were no longer popular. New slogans will by necessity emerge, and they ought to embody substantive new thinking about issues on which New Labour was most vulnerable. Still, a more fundamental break seems unlikely and indeed unwise, for a rejection of Labour's recent past would mean turning one's back on a record marked by considerable success and on a brand of politics that may well represent a viable future for center-left parties and movements in Britain and elsewhere.

Notes

1. For greater detail and more extensive documentation of this historical process see Cronin 2004.

2. Deciding who was the left, who was the center, and who was the right of the party was often tricky. A clear "right" had emerged in the late 1950s and early 1960s around the party leader, Hugh Gaitskell, and his ally, Tony Crosland, the main theoretician among the "revisionists." Leaders such as Callaghan were intellectually quite close to this camp, but their strong ties to the trade unions, or at least Callaghan's strong ties, were probably more important in determining his policies. He is probably better regarded as being in the center of the party. Harold Wilson's achievement was of course to bridge the factions, but at considerable cost; Tony Benn's later failure was to divide them and drive the right completely out of the party. Tracking the disputes and arguments within the party is entertaining; somewhat harder is figuring out the basis of coexistence. The best answer to the puzzle, I have argued, focuses on the term "labourism," an outlook that was genuinely shared and served to distinguish the party from its competitors in the United Kingdom and also from its sister parties on the continent. For an explanation see Cronin 2004, 7–10.

3. See the vigorous and engaging debate between Mark Wickham-Jones (1995) and Colin Hay (1997).

4. Stephen Gill (1995) used the phrase "disciplinary neoliberalism" to describe the Thatcher era and neoliberalism more broadly; it was revised to "compensatory neoliberalism" by Perry Anderson (2007).

5. See the essays by Gerassimos Moschonas and Ruy Teixeira in this volume.

6. Determining the right response to the post–cold war crisis in the former Yugoslavia was clearly not easy, but some people were demonstrably wrong. For a compelling argument on the deficiencies of the British response see Simms 2002.

Reluctantly Center-Left?

The French Case

Arthur Goldhammer and George Ross

Structuring the Puzzle

France today is often portrayed as a country uniquely refractory to reform. This is highly misleading. In the decades following the Second World War, which Jean Fourastié has referred to as les Trente Glorieuses, deep structural reform enabled France to achieve a rate of growth in per capita GDP that was among the highest in Europe.[1] The resources that made this remarkable performance possible—technologically advanced firms, superbly trained elites, highly productive workers, and a political will to remain competitive—remain in place. In recent times, however, France has been slow to respond to the challenges of the increasingly globalized economy. One reason for this has been that the French left has had serious difficulties functioning in this new environment.

Why has the French left had such difficulties? To answer this question we begin by underlining three persistent elements of the French political system that mark the period from the 1960s to the present. The first is chronic division. Unlike some other lefts, the French left has always been divided.[2] Communists and Socialists coexisted, often with smaller groups around them and frequently in conflict, for much of the twentieth century. The competitive games that these divisions created have complicated the tasks of devising the left's goals, programs, and policies, with powerful consequences for its identities and prospects. Next, partly because of these divisions, the left has been fixated on preserving a French social model. At the end of the Second World War elites agreed on the need for rapid economic modernization led by the state, together with an extensive welfare system under "paritary management," according to which social insurance programs (health, pension, unemployment) were administered not by the state but by employer associations, unions, and other organized "stakeholders." The left has increasingly defined itself as the defender of this distinctive "French model." The third element is presidentialism. The Constitution of the Fifth Republic endowed the presidency with vast powers, making it the linchpin of French political life, and diminishing the power of Parliament. Accompanying this, a two-round electoral system, intended to transform a multiparty system into a bipolar one, meant that a successful presidential candidate had to be able not only to unite his own party but also to appeal to centrist voters in the second round. These three structural elements have shaped the left's response to the challenges of the post-Keynesian era.

François Mitterrand Climbs the Summit

Since all power flowed from the presidency, the Socialists had to find a way to defy the old adage that "you can't win with the Communists and can't win without them." Mitterrand, leader of the Parti Socialiste (PS) since its reorganization in 1969–71, therefore struck a deal with the Parti Communiste Français (PCF), set out in the landmark "Common Program for a Government of the Left" (1972). The program, biased toward the PCF's reform proposals, advocated extensive new nationalizations, planning, energetic Keynesianism, expanded welfare programs, enhanced powers for unions and workers, and decentralization. With this compact Mitterrand came very close to defeating Valéry Giscard d'Estaing in 1974.

Giscard, intent upon building a new hegemonic center-right party, favored liberalizing social and economic reforms of which many Gaullists disapproved. The left began to argue that "liberalism," as practiced by Giscard and Raymond Barre, prime minister after 1976, marked a repudiation of the French postwar model and promised a "return to the model" if elected. The international situation had changed, however. In the English-speaking countries monetarism was becoming the new orthodoxy; price stability, even at the expense of employment, replaced Keynesian stimulus policies. In line with these trends Giscard and Chancellor Helmut Schmidt of Germany agreed to create a European Monetary System to limit the damage from floating exchange rates. Over time this system was likely to impose rigorous German monetary standards on the traditionally more lax French.[3]

The stage was thus set for the presidential elections in the spring of 1981, the critical moment for the French left. In the first round Mitterrand stood for the Socialists, Georges Marchais, secretary general of the PCF, for the Communists. On the right Giscard d'Estaing, the incumbent, faced a determined Jacques Chirac, the neo-Gaullist. Mitterrand (with 25.85%) decisively defeated Marchais (15.34%, down 6% from Jacques Duclos's share of the vote in 1979) and then Giscard in the second round. The PS also captured an absolute majority of seats in the National Assembly, leaving the Communists no choice but to join a left unity government under the new prime minister, Pierre Mauroy.[4] For a brief period the left's persistent division was overcome, therefore, and the first eighteen months of Mitterrand's experiment demonstrated that he was serious about restoring the French postwar model, with the state in a leading economic role. The government nationalized several key industrial firms and most banks.[5] Other key reforms included political decentralization, enhanced representation in the workplace, and stronger legal foundations for local unions, which led to greater flexibility in collective bargaining. The left also introduced a wealth tax on large fortunes (the Impôt de Solidarité sur la Fortune, or ISF), abolished the death penalty, and privatized television and radio networks.

The more immediate problem was high unemployment. To combat this, 170,000 new public sector jobs were created in 1981–82. The left also tried to stimulate consumption by raising the minimum wage, pensions, family allowances, and housing subsidies. A fifth week of vacation was added, the retirement age was reduced to sixty, and negotiations were begun to shorten the legal work week to thirty-nine hours. The effort failed, however. Unemployment rose by 300–400,000 in the first year, and high inflation led to exchange difficulties. Because France had attempted to reflate while other countries deflated, much of France's additional demand went to purchase cheaper foreign goods, creating the largest balance-of-payments deficit in French history. The franc came under pressure within the European Monetary System, and a first devaluation in the fall of 1981 failed to alleviate the problem. More generally, combining supply-side "progressive" technocratic statism with strong Keynesianism clearly did not work.

The U-Turn

The bills began to come due around June 1982, when the government retrenched with tough austerity measures, including a wage and price freeze, new restrictions on capital movements, de-indexing of wages, high interest rates, and draconian budget cuts. The new policies proved to be effective but not sufficient, and by the spring of 1983 the left faced a critical choice: either leave the EMS and float the franc, or stay and make basic domestic economic policy changes. After hesitating Mitterrand favored the second option, which led to the so-called U-turn. The government abruptly stopped using the public sector to maintain employment and turned instead to harsh industrial restructuring.

The shift affected diplomatic as well as economic policy. To Mitterrand, a staunch European, staying in the EMS meant renewed engagement with European integration. Austerity was unpopular, and Mitterrand needed a justification for his choice. Belt-tightening could be presented as a means to achieve noble European goals. The idea was to use European integration, which France strongly favored, to apply outside pressure in support of needed domestic policy changes in France. One result was the appointment of Jacques Delors as president of the European Commission.

In January 1985 Delors, Mitterrand's first finance minister and an architect of the policy shifts of 1982–83, launched a vast program to liberalize and deregulate the EC internal market. He would subsequently propose a new Economic and Monetary Union (EMU).[6] The French hoped thereby to seize some control over monetary policy from the German Bundesbank and thus reduce the bias toward price stability, at the cost of ceding French monetary policy prerogatives to European control.

The turn to austerity, the abandonment of key instruments of statist economic control, and the new European initiatives meant that important features of the French postwar model would be jettisoned. What remained was a French social model, without the full range of economic policy prerogatives that had kept it on track during les Trente Glorieuses. In the medium term there was perhaps vague hope that liberalization and Europeanization would rekindle growth and reduce unemployment. In the short run, however, the left needed to satisfy its electorate. The Socialist-governmental left had successfully coopted a part of the Communist-extragovernmental left's base, beginning the long, slow decline of the PCF. Yet without policies to satisfy the hopes that had been aroused in 1981, the PS could easily lose the new voters it had gained—voters who saw themselves as constituting a distinct left wing of the party, not always in solidarity with the increasingly center-left leadership and its very different social base.

Mitterrand won reelection in 1988, but the economic situation had worsened. Unemployment, 6% when the left won in 1981, had risen to over 11% by 1987. Earlier reforms, enacted in a more hopeful time, were now incorporated into a set of policies that have been described as the "social treatment of unemployment." A shorter work week, a fifth vacation week, and a reduced retirement age kept unemployment levels from rising even higher, albeit at the cost of lowering labor force participation rates. An ordinance in 1982 gave workers strong incentives to "pre-retire," or go half-time at fifty-five or even fifty (many were obliged to do so). In 1984 the government instituted further early retirement incentives to encourage industrial restructuring. New youth employment programs, usually involving temporary training positions, were added to the mix. More spending on education pushed a higher percentage of each age cohort into university and technical training, to similar effect.

Left governments were loath to change the standard labor contract (the CDI, or *contrat à durée indéterminée*). In contrast to countries with "flexicurity" arrangements—where law and social policy protect workers rather than jobs—the CDI protected particular jobs rather than workers. The CDI had been an important working-class victory, to be tampered with by left governments at great risk. But in a period of increasing economic uncertainty its persistence led French employers to avoid new CDI hires except in the most buoyant of economic circumstances. When the left tried to encourage new hiring, it therefore generally resorted to new, temporary, often heavily subsidized employment contracts. This made those who already had CDIs more defensive and those who did not more insecure. Older workers were likely to be better protected than younger ones. Younger workers with fewer educational credentials were worst off. Universalist republican rhetoric notwithstanding, differences between insider and outsider thus grew rapidly.

France's workforce and labor market changed dramatically in these years.[7] French society was becoming more "dualized": a part of the population held steady jobs at reasonable pay and enjoyed social protections; others lived more precarious lives. In the presidential campaign of 1988 Mitterrand responded to growing public concern about social exclusion by proposing the RMI (*revenu minimum d'insertion*).[8] In time, despite tight eligibility control, the "insertion" part of the RMI became less important than the "revenu," owing to the chronic absence of jobs.

The cost of French social policy therefore increased rapidly (from 19.2% of GDP in 1970, to 26% in 1981 and nearly 30% in 1995). Since payroll taxes paid for key welfare provisions, rising tax levels pushed France out of line with its European competitors. This prompted the creation of the *contribution sociale généralisée* (CSG) in December 1990. The CSG was a new flat tax on incomes dedicated to financing social programs, set initially at 1.1%. The idea was to broaden the tax base sustaining the French social model, a change justified in the name of "solidarity."

For the two most expensive social programs, pensions and healthcare, cost pressures increased. Pension costs rose in part because of changing demographics but also because the "social treatment of unemployment" removed older workers from the labor force by encouraging early retirement. In healthcare costs rose for the same reasons as everywhere else, including changing demographics and expensive technological progress. The French welfare state model contributed to these cost pressures. The model, it will be recalled, was built primarily on social insurance programs managed in a "paritary" way. Immediate stakeholders shaped policy decisions, with a tendency to offload costs on others. Yet paritary management and maintaining the stakeholders' voice were untouchable. Governments that pushed too hard to lower costs faced strikes and protests. Pension reform, for example, became a political third rail, while government efforts to reduce hospital costs (the one area of healthcare that it did control) prompted walkouts by nurses and physicians.

The government of Michel Rocard (1988–91) was as close to being "center-left" as French Socialists in the Mitterrand era came. Rocard benefited from the first serious upturn in the European and international economy since the 1970s, with GDP growth jumping to nearly 4% in 1988 and 1989. But France's structural economic problems remained. The economy was sluggish, the social treatment of unemployment was very expensive and compounded labor market rigidities, and chronic budgetary deficits obliged a constant chipping away at social costs.

The end of the Mitterrand years was also troublesome for the PS. The party was racked by scandal. With Mitterrand's second term expiring in 1995 and the president himself dying, struggles over leadership and potential presidential candidacies revived bitter factional disputes. One flashpoint occurred during the referendum campaign on the Maastricht Treaty in 1992. The PS and the Union pour la Démocratie Française (UDF), Giscard's center-right party, formed a united front to promote a "yes" vote, and they eventually prevailed, though barely. But parts of the PS, including the Centre d'Études et d'Éducation Socialistes (CERES) faction around Jean-Pierre Chevènement, campaigned for a "no." The episode showed that the decline of the PCF had not ended division on the left. Other "extragovernmental" political forces and social movements sought to occupy the spaces that the PCF had vacated. It was at this point, for example, that nationalist anti-globalization sentiment emerged, led by new groups, including the Association pour la Taxation des Transactions Financières et l'Aide aux Citoyens (ATTAC). These developments inevitably had repercussions inside the PS. Cowed by the renewed hard-left sentiment, all but a few center-left PS reformers muted their rhetoric.

The EMU that emerged from Maastricht was decisively "monetarist," despite the French aim of weakening German influence over European monetary policy. The new European Central Bank would be completely committed to price stability, while the treaty contained only vague language about coordinating macroeconomic policy and promoting growth. Maastricht also established strict convergence criteria for potential EMU members, including targets on national budget deficits (less than 3% of GDP), debt levels (less than 60% of GDP), interest, and inflation. In 1991 France was well placed to meet these targets, but this soon changed.

German post-unification policies helped fuel a European boomlet in 1991–92. When the Bundesbank tried to correct, it overshot, instigating a recession that hit France hard. Failing to meet convergence targets was not an option:

without France there could be no EMU, which would have been a disastrous defeat for the European integration that French statesmen had worked to promote. Yet the new policy constraints inevitably meant austerity, slow growth, and higher unemployment. The structural problems that had emerged in the 1980s would grow more serious over time. In the twilight of the Mitterrand years it fell to the right to deal with the consequences.

The Post-Mitterrand Era

The era of "historic compromise" à la française, which began with the Congress of Épinay in 1971, had thus reached its end. Mitterrand, the inscrutable master strategist and tactician (known by the sobriquet "Le Florentin," a tribute to his Machiavellian cunning), had been too clever by half. His seduction of the Communist Party ultimately sapped its sinews, leaving a large bloc of voters no longer firmly moored à gauche. Mitterrand had also taken various steps (such as the introduction of proportional representation for the legislative elections of 1986) to ensure that the Front National would emerge as a serious competitor to the "legitimate republican right," but had failed to foresee that the party of Le Pen would attract some of these now drifting voters (or their children). Alternative parties of the left—Trotskyites and Greens—competed for these votes as well, and after fourteen years of Mitterrandist rule and innumerable scandals, these groups were even less susceptible to the blandishments of power than they had been previously (doubts about the wisdom of becoming "parties of government" had never been extinguished in these quarters, even in the heyday of the Common Program). For these extra-governmental leftists, along with parts of the union movement, defending a French model that the Mitterrand years had undermined became a stock in trade.

As for the Socialists, with the president in decline no single voice could adequately represent the increasingly cacophonous party, once again divided into rival factions openly contending for the post-Mitterrandist succession. Although Lionel Jospin emerged as the dominant figure among the cohort of politico-technocrats with whom Mitterrand had surrounded himself, he had no shortage of rivals. All were experienced in a variety of ministerial and political roles, but none could claim Mitterrand's mastery of the art of politics. Hence small technocratic reforms took priority over more ambitious transformations. More and more voters came to feel alienated from political life and unrepresented at the national level.

In the wake of Maastricht the issue of whether to embrace or resist integration with the global economy loomed increasingly large. A deep fissure had developed in the Socialist Party. Internationalists—Delors, Rocard, Strauss-

Kahn—continued to support the transfer of many economic decision-making powers to the European level, but a distinct left wing of the party became increasingly skeptical of both Europe and reform. In this the Socialist left wing converged with the Gaullist right wing, although the issues were framed in rather different terms. If the goal of the socialist left was to protect the French social model by preserving the economic prerogatives of the French state, on the right it was to preserve French sovereignty and independence, which were seen as threatened not only by rival states but also by multinational corporations.[9]

Jacques Chirac, head of the Rassemblement pour la République (RPR), the largest party on the right, established his claim to become the right's presumptive presidential candidate in 1995 after leading his party to an overwhelming victory in the legislative elections of 1993. Meditating on his own experience under Mitterrand, who had persuaded him to become the first "cohabitation" prime minister in 1986 and then defeated him in the presidential election in 1988, Chirac prevailed on Édouard Balladur to accept the prime ministership. On the strength of strong opinion polls Balladur then decided to betray "his friend of thirty years" and challenge Chirac's claim.[10] The unions subsequently staged a series of actions to defend the social security system, in protest against Balladur's efforts to control the budget deficit through tax hikes and benefit reductions. Chirac, ever the political chameleon, entered the presidential arena armed with a new slogan: to "heal the social fracture."[11] He argued that the real "social fracture" was not between workers and employers but rather between insiders and outsiders and promised to reduce it as president. This was in part a ploy to finesse the divisions in his party and bridge the gap between pro-European neoliberals, indifferent, he implied, to the plight of the excluded, and anti-European "sovereignists," who scornfully dismissed the neoliberal "social Munich" but had nothing to offer insiders that would match the benefits accruing from participation in an increasingly globalized economy.

In effect the presidential election of 1995 endorsed a continuation of Mitterrand's equivocal economic policies: neither full liberalization and openness nor outright decoupling from Europe and the global economy. After Jacques Delors withdrew from the presidential race, Lionel Jospin easily disposed of the Socialist secretary general Henri Emmanuelli. The Socialist center-left thus gained ascendancy over the party's left. Chirac defeated Jospin in the second round, drawing votes from his right, which had nowhere else to go, as well as from the center. Chirac was elected with just under 53% of the vote.

Observers believed that Chirac came into office in a position of strength.

He had supplanted a tired Socialist regime, defeated a serious rival in his own camp, and enjoyed a majority of 80% in the National Assembly (as a result of the right's impressive victory in the legislative elections in 1993). He also controlled the Senate and most regional and departmental councils. Nevertheless Chirac, whose instinct was to err by excess of caution, had to be dragged into reform by his prime minister Alain Juppé, who forcefully pointed out that the problems Balladur had been trying to solve remained as obdurate as ever. In order to meet the requirements imposed by the EMU, Chirac would have to reduce the budget deficit. The problem had indeed grown to serious proportions: between 1990 and 1995 the social security deficit had more than quintupled, doubling as a share of the total deficit. Balladur had attempted to reduce the shortfall through privatizations, but one-time proceeds from the sale of national enterprises could do little to halt the rapid increase in outlays for medical care and retirement benefits. A more drastic overhaul was inevitable.

In short order Juppé had a plan. Its thoroughness, professionalism, and impeccable arithmetic drew wide admiration from intellectuals, editorialists, and much of the political class, including followers of the Socialist Michel Rocard and the CFDT trade union, eager to establish its reformist bona fides as a "modern" union that understood the trade-off between short-term wage restraint and long-term growth. The plan included a provision to require the parliament to vote each year on a social security financing plan (this was incorporated into the Constitution in February 1996). There were other significant innovations as well, such as the Contribution for the Reimbursement of the Social Debt (CRDS), a new tax set at 0.5% of revenue to pay off the accumulated social security deficit; a 1% increase in the Generalized Social Contribution, or CSG (described earlier); a 1.2% increase in health insurance payments by retired and unemployed workers; a one-time tax on the pharmaceutical industry; reduction of maternity benefits; a structural reform of the hospital system; and a host of lesser measures.[12]

The plan may have been technically seductive, but since it had been elaborated in secret and announced as a fait accompli, it proved politically disastrous. A perceived attack on railway workers, who enjoyed an especially favorable special retirement regime, led to a strike that brought the country to a standstill for several weeks, and many other categories of workers in both the public and private sectors supported the strikers because they felt that their own pensions were threatened.[13] Juppé, seriously weakened by the strikes, was forced to withdraw much of his reform program, although he hung onto his job for more than a year.

The social fracture rhetoric that had got Chirac elected thus found little translation into concrete policy. To be sure, modest health insurance reform was enacted, and "urban development zones" were established in the hope of reducing unemployment in the suburbs. In addition, the Contrat Initiatives Emploi (CIE) did create fifty thousand new jobs, but it cost twelve billion francs. Here was yet another stab at what had come to be called "social treatment of unemployment," by now a venerable tradition. The unemployment rate did begin to decline slowly, although critics claimed that the official statistics understated the real scope of the problem. By subsidizing entry-level jobs and protecting workers in uncompetitive firms, government policy discouraged long-term hires and the kind of deeper structural reform being tried elsewhere. Firms were encouraged to supply temporary labor needs with subsidized interim workers rather than invest in productivity-enhancing technology.

Chirac's master counterstroke, in reserve since the election, was to dissolve parliament in the spring of 1997. In his mind this maneuver would relegitimate his presidency and revive his mandate. The right-wing majority in the National Assembly, in place since 1993, had grown restive, and Chirac hoped that the maneuver would reestablish his control over his own party's deputies. Polls indicated that although the prime minister was unpopular, so was the left, and Chirac expected a new and reinforced majority to emerge from the early election (the next scheduled parliamentary election was not until 1998). He was wrong. Jospin, the last avatar of the Mitterrandist "Socialo-Communist" coalition scored 43% in the first round of voting, easily outstripping the RPR with 36.5 and the Front National with 15.

Thus Lionel Jospin became prime minister, and for the next five years Chirac would be obliged to "cohabit" with the man he had defeated for the presidency only two years before. Yet this stroke of good luck for the Socialists also inaugurated a period in which they sought to appease the extra-governmental left and their own left wing with policies in which they did not fully believe while at the same time hoping that the expanded European market, which they did not wholeheartedly embrace, would bring sufficient economic improvement to carry them through the next presidential election. It was not an unreasonable hope, because French growth had shown signs of recovery, with new jobs created and unemployment declining. Yet this temporary good news only allowed the party to postpone reconsideration of its core principles.

French Socialists had not been obliged to conquer power by adapting to a political landscape fundamentally reshaped by powerful conservative predecessors like Thatcher or Reagan. Instead they had power handed to them by the blunders of Chirac and Juppé. Once in power, the party therefore found itself saddled with a program even more incoherent than political programs generally are. The party platform for 1997 included a plank calling for a thirty-five-hour week. Dominique Strauss-Kahn, who had put it there, later said that he would not have done so if he had foreseen that the left might win. Unanticipated victory forced the government to make good on its promise. The chief burden of the change fell on smaller firms, which found the "flexibility" envisioned by the law difficult to achieve. This difficulty durably alienated a segment of the centrist electorate, especially middle managers and small business owners, whose support the Socialists would desperately need in future presidential elections. Some blue-collar workers also resented the loss of overtime opportunities.

The left also enacted the so-called Emploi-Jeunes or Youth Employment Act in 1997, creating a new type of state-subsidized five-year labor contract. The jobs were often with local government or charitable service agencies, and while the intention was to equip otherwise unemployable youths with "employment skills," again there was no stimulus to subsequent hiring by the private sector. Employment did increase toward the end of the 1990s, raising false hopes that these modest employment measures, together with continuing social security reforms similar to those already undertaken by the right, would soon set things right.

In more Eurocentric Socialist circles, there was considerable hope—and a certain naïveté—about the anticipated benefits from the post-Maastricht European Union. In an interview in 1997, Jean-Pierre Jouyet, Jacques Delors's chief of staff in Brussels before assuming responsibility for European affairs as a member of Jospin's staff,[14] envisioned the "political union of Europe through economic harmonization within ten years."[15] Optimism was buoyant and at first seemed justified, as temporary economic improvement led to Socialist success in the European Parliament elections of 1999, while Nicolas Sarkozy, who led the right-wing slate on a neoliberal platform, was beaten badly. But the incoherence of the left's program soon began to take its toll. Annual hours worked per capita dropped to one of the lowest levels in the OECD as the thirty-five-hour week took hold, social policy expenses grew, and subsidized low-end jobs weighed on the budget without increasing aggregate demand. The average retirement age fell. Workforce participation declined, especially for youths and seniors. All of this magnified the budget deficit, and when the economy turned downward after 2001, divisions within the left and the PS about the wisdom of "deepening" the European Union were exacerbated.

Jospin's government also moved on a second social front. In addition to shortening the work week it expanded and reformed medical insurance with the *couverture maladie universelle* (CMU, or universal health coverage), which was adopted on 27 July 1999.[16] The CMU not only expanded coverage but also made supplementary private insurance available to some five million people who could not otherwise afford it.

As the presidential election of 2002 approached, the disaffection from what the French call *la classe politique*—the established party leaderships of both the left and the right—was glaringly apparent despite extensive reforming since Chirac's election. In 1995 the abstention rate had been 20%, the highest in any presidential election in the Fifth Republic, and after seven years of confusion, in which the left and right had "cohabited" to pursue reforms that seemed to mirror one another, a substantial number of voters concluded that it hardly mattered who won. The smaller parties of the left, convinced that the Socialist Party had been taken over by technocrats, saw no particular utility in attempting to achieve unity in the pre-election period, and all contested Jospin's claim to represent the undivided opposition.

Lionel Jospin, on the other hand, had little taste for the hard-left rhetoric that Socialist leaders habitually mobilized to try to cement a coalition of the left in anticipation of an electoral test of strength with the right. As unemployment continued unabated, immigration and security became major issues. Inflation and stagnant wages (with a compressed wage spectrum owing to a high minimum wage and subsidized entry-level jobs) persuaded many workers that their standard of living was falling because of the EU and globalization. To top it all off, Jospin waged a singularly passionless and lackluster campaign. Disaster followed. Jean-Marie Le Pen narrowly outpolled Jospin in the first round of the election, 16.9% to 16.2. An anti-Le Pen coalition then gave Chirac more than 80% of the vote in the second round.

The verdict of the polls was harsh but not incomprehensible. The Socialists had demonstrated that they were no worse, and indeed probably better, at managing the market economy than their opponents. They had promised their voters something more, but had been unable to define clearly what this was or whether it aimed at success in the globalized economy or at some vaguely adumbrated "social market" alternative. They were at pains to deny that their approach to globalized capitalism had anything in common with any sort of "third way" compromise. Yet the policy package on offer from the left was similar to that on offer from the right: adjustment of the fiscal system to maintain social spending at a steady level while shifting the burden from payrolls to a broader citizen base; a variety of labor-market activation policies (job search assistance, job retraining, continuing education, benefit reform); and social security reform to take account of demographic changes. This policy convergence reduced the electoral contest to a battle over technical details: modifications to the legal work week (such as haggling over details of compensatory time, overtime pay, etc.), the precise package of retirement reforms, the mix of broad-based versus payroll taxes.

The left's policy package satisfied no one. Adherents of the "second left"— mainly university-educated "knowledge workers" whose politics had been forged in the anticolonial and cultural struggles of the 1960s and 1970s— were put off by what they saw as band-aid measures and rhetorical appeasement: subsidized McJobs (such as the Emplois-Jeunes), protectionism, and "economic patriotism" (denunciation of plant closings and investments by "Anglo-Saxon pension funds," predatory hedge funds, etc.). Workers and militant schoolteachers (who made up the rank and file in more than one Socialist Party federation) preferred the old class-against-class rhetoric and resented the dominance in the party leadership of graduates of elite schools such as Sciences Po and the École Nationale d'Administration (ENA). Much of the policy effort of this elite went into devising strategies to preserve the institutions of the French welfare state through small-scale reforms rather than understanding the profound transformation of the global economy. The idea that competition might require radical restructuring of the production process, quick response to exploit niche markets, and investment in productivity-enhancing high-technology back-office systems was too politically challenging to take on. Despite fitful efforts to revamp universities and promote closer cooperation between academic research and industrial R&D, the deepening fiscal crisis limited what might have been done even if more attention had been devoted to growth-enhancement policies.

From his peculiar if lopsided victory Chirac concluded that he could continue to muddle through, provided that he did nothing energetic enough to upset the applecart. In a conciliatory gesture that confirmed this strategy, he appointed Jean-Pierre Raffarin, a lackluster Giscardian centrist, as prime minister. The one undeniable success of his presidency—eight years after the debacle of the Juppé plan—was a partial overhaul of the retirement system for which his minister of social affairs, François Fillon, working closely with CFDT head François Chérèque, was chiefly responsible. By leaving the so-called special retirement regimes intact, Fillon and Chirac avoided a repetition of the paralysis of 1995, because transport workers remained untouched. In 2003 nature turned against Chirac, as a terrible heat wave led to fifteen hundred deaths, mainly of the elderly. The loss of life was probably compounded by shortages of personnel in hospital emergency rooms, due in part to cutbacks in the medical care budget, as well as by staff management problems that arose after reduction of the workweek.

If Europe and the EMU had been the undoing of Chirac's first term, it was again Europe that undid his second. Progress toward a European constitutional treaty, responsibility for which Chirac had assigned to his old nemesis Giscard, led the president, perhaps concerned as much with dividing the left as with the EU, to seek approval in a referendum in May 2005. Once again polls had indicated initially that the referendum course would be safe; majorities of up to 70% were predicted. In the event, however, the referendum went down to defeat by a margin of 55 to 45%. The Socialist Party remained split on the issue, while opposition within the UMP, though not inconsiderable, was tamped down by Nicolas Sarkozy, the erstwhile protégé first of Chirac and then of Balladur, who remained strongly pro-Europe.

Sacrificing Raffarin to atone for this gaffe, Chirac then made his second big blunder, appointing the impetuous Dominique de Villepin, his only remaining confidant and the architect of the ill-fated dissolution of parliament in 1997, to head the government. Villepin, who entertained presidential ambitions for 2007, had hoped to upstage his rival Sarkozy, but events intervened. In late 2005 riots erupted in a suburb of Paris after two youths died while attempting to evade the police. Then early in 2006 Villepin launched a new attack on the unemployment problem by proposing a "first hire contract" to encourage the employment of young workers—yet another half-measure in lieu of a comprehensive reform of labor laws. Students took to the streets in protest, universities were shut down by strikes, and there was sporadic violence. Villepin dug in and refused to withdraw the bill. The episode came to a comic conclusion when Chirac, bafflingly silent throughout the mounting unrest, finally decided to allow the bill to become law while promising at the same time that it would not be "promulgated," meaning that it would remain a dead letter. This effectively ended his presidency, though he would remain in office for another year, and it reduced Villepin's presidential aspirations to ashes. Sarkozy remained the only viable candidate on the right.

Meanwhile, the Socialist Party under the leadership of François Hollande had made no progress toward resolving its internal divisions. The center-left had its champion in Dominique Strauss-Kahn; Laurent Fabius, a centrist at heart who had opportunistically become a leader of the "no" camp in the EU constitutional referendum of 2005, proposed himself to lead the party's left wing. Hollande hoped to paper over the division between left and center-left with a new procedure to designate the presidential candidate, which he hoped would lead to a compromise candidate, perhaps himself. Membership of the party was thus opened up to anyone willing to pay a membership fee of 20 euros, with no obligation to attend meetings, serve the party, or participate in internal debates. All members could then vote in an internal party primary to name the candidate. In preparation there was unprecedented televised debate among the contenders, whose chances of success against Sarkozy were constantly monitored through opinion polls. Although many long-standing party members preferred one of the so-called éléphants—party stalwarts and courant leaders such as Dominique Strauss-Kahn, Laurent Fabius, or Jack Lang—it was ultimately not Hollande but his longtime companion and mother of his children, Ségolène Royal, who won. President of the Poitou-Charentes region, Royal was popular, telegenic, and well known because of service in Jospin's government as minister of the environment, among other roles. She routed her opponents, drawing over 60% in the party primary.

Yet Sarkozy, who in 2004 had assumed leadership of the Union pour un Mouvement Populaire (UMP), had a considerable head start, having had time to reshape the party into a support vehicle for his presidential ambitions. Though Sarkozy was a bitter foe of Chirac, the president had been unable to avoid appointing his popular young rival to various ministerial posts, and while at Interior, for example, Sarkozy had used his media skills to put various hot-button issues such as crime, immigration, and religion at the forefront of the political agenda. His strategy was clear: to woo Front National voters by taking a strong line on these divisive social issues while pushing for neoliberal reforms such as reduction of the wealth tax and estate tax, detaxation of overtime hours and other revisions of the thirty-five-hour week, reform of the special retirement regimes, labor-market activation, and employment contract reform that might appeal to a broad swath of center-right and even center-left voters disappointed with the Socialists' lack of clarity on economic policy. Although François Bayrou, the independent centrist candidate, made a strong showing in the first round, Royal survived only to be defeated by Sarkozy, who took 53% of the vote.

Sarkozy's approval rating immediately after the election rose to above 70%, a level scarcely seen in the history of the Fifth Republic, and the stage seemed set for quick enactment of his program. Although he did manage to enact reforms on a wide front with less opposition than might have been expected, by the end of 2007 his popularity had begun to plummet, and by February 2008 it had dropped below that of Chirac after the strikes of 1995. Widespread criticism of Sarkozy's presidential style and exposure of his turbulent private life contributed to this. With the increasingly unfavorable economic conjuncture in the wake of the American subprime debacle and subsequent global credit squeeze, anxiety about the future of the French social model resurfaced. Sarkozy, like Chirac before him, had been elected not to dismantle the welfare state but to introduce sufficient modifications to preserve it. What had seemed bold in May 2007 seemed a year later not to be enough, while

Sarkozy had apparently lost the ability to persuade his countrymen that confidence and energy alone are enough to overcome all obstacles. Any final judgment on his presidency, however, would be premature.

WE BEGAN BY claiming that the story of the French left since 1970 could best be understood by examining the lasting effects of three factors: persistent division on the left, firm adherence to the "French social model," and the central role of the presidency. These persistent influences continue to shape the French left today, but their surface manifestations have evolved considerably.

The fundamental cleavage on the left is no longer that which once separated the Socialist Party from the Communist Party. The PCF was never exactly a revolutionary party, despite unstinting support for Soviet interests, but its vocation had never really been to govern either. The Common Program of the 1970s transformed it into a party interested in governing but did not entirely dissipate the conviction of a part of the population (and of the PCF itself) that the best way to protect the interests of the "people of the left" was less to influence government policy than to oppose it. This sentiment, though less powerful than it once was, continues to motivate perhaps 10–15% of voters, who cast their votes for the parties of the extreme left, the extreme right, the Communist rump, and even the Greens, in the hope of demonstrating a disruptive potential sufficient to inhibit governments from pursuing reforms deemed to be aimed at dismantling the French social model.

The Socialist Party itself is divided internally, although the divisions were temporarily damped down by Mitterrand's leadership and success. Both had worn out by 1995, however, and since that date the PS's internal cleavages have become more important than those that divide the left more generally. In recent years these divisions have crystallized most visibly around the question of Europe. The referendum of 2005 on the European Constitutional Treaty made it clear that despite a substantial pro-Europe majority within the party, considerable anti-Europe sentiment persisted: 41% of militants wanted the party to oppose the proposed European constitution; 26 of 102 party federations turned out majorities in favor of a "no" vote.

The basis of this opposition is quite different from the negativism of the extra-governmental left. For the latter, which also opposed a strengthened "Europe," the French state, no matter who controls it, is helpless in the face of Europeanization and global capitalism. True political action can then take only two forms: using the electoral process as a "forum" to give voice to those hurt by neoliberal globalism, and resorting to extra-governmental activity (mobilization on the picket line, on the shop floor, and in the streets). Its aim must be defensive: to protect what remains of the French social model by blocking reform efforts decried as camouflaged destruction. For the left wing of the Socialist Party, by contrast, the political objective is rather to strengthen the state against supranational and transnational institutions believed to be intent on eroding the French social model. The state is supposed to stand between labor and capital, just as the king once stood (symbolically if not in reality) between the people and the nobility.

All Socialists thus see their part as very much a party of government, one whose raison d'être, unlike that of extra-governmental leftists, is to win elections and exercise power. Their version of the socialist project takes the form of policy prescriptions applicable to things as they are, not things as they might be if the rapport des forces were somehow different. Yet a division remains between those who have deeply internalized the U-turn of 1981–83 as a step in the right direction and those who look back on it as a mistake. The former like to describe themselves as modernizers, and since 1995 they have been touting the need for a "renovated" party. "Modernization" is of course a capacious word, invoked to justify political programs of both right and left since the Franco-Prussian War. In the present context, however, the central claim of center-left modernizers is that the scale of the capitalist system has changed; production, finance, and the supply of labor have all become globalized to a much greater degree since 1970 and especially since the mid-1980s. To maintain social protections, therefore, political and social actors must see the state that they wish to influence as part of a supranational institutional network. The political game therefore becomes multilevel and far more complex than in earlier periods.

The Socialist modernizers thus emphasize the international dimension of policy and especially the constraints imposed on domestic economic policy by France's implication in a global system. Acceptance of what might be called "center-left" outlooks—the importance of price stability, fiscal self-control, economic flexibility, and the need to innovate constantly—follows from this. Their opponents focus rather on the internal politics of the nation-state. For them the central problem is less to find optimal economic policies than to change the rapport des forces to give greater weight to the preferences of left-wing voters generally rather than those of left policy elites, which are often quite similar to the preferences of right policy elites. In sum, the left is now effectively tripartite: the extra-governmental left opposes both (statist) nationalists and (internationalist) modernizers. All three factions invoke preservation of the French social model, our second persistent influence, as the primary objective of politics. The problem is that their definitions of the core of the social model vary. In addition, each faction of the left believes that the others' preferred means of achieving the common goal will lead to disaster in the future as it has done in the past.

To win big elections, especially the all-important presidency, some kind

Table 1. Fragmentation of the French Left

	Extragovernmental Left	Socialist Left	Socialist Center
Strategic orientation	Obstructive	National-statist	International-multilevel
Policy preference	Defend social gains	Defend social gains, make governing institutions more representative, decentralize	Maintain productivity, reform universities, fund R&D
Europe	Oppose	Oppose	Support
Tactical orientation	Streets, shop floor, picket lines	Institutional reform	Economic governance

of political unity must be engineered out of division. Although the elements have changed, unity is no easier to achieve now than it was in the 1970s (table 1). Socialist modernizers have to conciliate nationalists and seduce extra-governmental parties and movements to have a chance of winning. Lionel Jospin refused to do this in 2002, instead campaigning as if only the second round runoff counted, and he failed disastrously. It is very likely that when modernizers do try to broaden their political base they will end up being bound to programmatic concessions and promises that they will have difficulty redeeming without sacrificing "modernizing" realism.

This reconfiguration of the left political contest parallels underlying economic and social changes. With the relative decline of heavy industry and mass production, the old armies of blue-clad factory workers have diminished in size and militancy. The unionization rate in France has fallen to the lowest level in Europe (7%). The workforce has become increasingly differentiated and better educated. Service and support workers outnumber skilled and semiskilled industrial workers. The patron of old—be he paternalistic guardian or Zolaesque taskmaster—is now buffered by squadrons of well-educated cadres versed in the techniques of human resource management. Older images of social conflict have partly given way to new images. Yet the older images sometimes resurface in misleading ways, as in the demonstrations against the first hire contract in 2006.

Again, the centrality of the presidency—and of Mitterrand's strategy for winning it, the only successful left strategy to date—cannot be ignored. The triumphant Common Program sustained an unnatural hybrid of a workers' party with a clientelist party built on the representation of a variety of local interests (including workers' interests) and competition among internal factions and grouplets. Neither party to the coalition had a clear agenda for national rule or a deep comprehension of the priorities that would need to be addressed after capturing the presidency. Mitterrand therefore called upon a cohort of technocrats to fill key positions in the government and administration. These people, creatures of Mitterrand and entirely beholden to him for their political careers, have dominated the party in the first decade of the twenty-first century: witness the contest to become the presidential candidate in 2007, which pitted Ségolène Royal against Dominique Strauss-Kahn and Laurent Fabius—all three énarques (graduates of ENA), all three former ministers, all three deeply imbued with a top-down, presidentialist vision of the political process.

Presidentialism has created a problem of credibility for the Socialists as the society has changed under them. A presidential campaign, if it is not to sink beneath a welter of tedious prescriptions for improvement *tous azimuts*, must articulate a clear and comprehensible transformative vision. For Mitterrand it was enough to give voice to the democratic desire for alternance. By 1981 voters who had never recognized themselves in Gaullism could be satisfied with the prospect of wielding power for the first time. But in the nearly thirty years since the Socialists' U-turn of 1983, the Socialists have become an established party of government. Like their opponents on the right they have pursued piecemeal reforms designed to shore up the welfare state, some of which have actually helped France face the future. Yet unlike the right, they have not been able to articulate a new transformative message to embellish their skillful technocratic management.

The center-left core of the Socialist Party has been struggling since 1995 to define what a "modernized and renovated" socialist program should look like. The result has been to cement old divisions and heighten mutual suspicion among party factions, albeit with new faces to represent them. In keeping with the training, predilections, and government experience of its key leaders, the center-left has emphasized the need for economic reform to maintain (insofar as possible) the productivity and competitiveness on which the welfare state depends. In many respects the reforms that it advocates resemble those favored by the center-right. The center-left's appeal to the median voter thus relies on trust: we advocate reforms similar to those proposed by the center-right, but we promise you a more favorable distribution of the expected fruits of growth. It is a vision predicated on centralized power, benevolent expertise, and a not-too-restive base. By contrast, the Socialist left wing is more responsive to the fears of its base that economic reforms represent a camouflaged attack on hard-won popular victories of the past. The quarrel is really over what constitutes the core of the French social model. Is it basically a bargain over the distribution of gains from economic growth, in which case the maintenance of growth is crucial? Or is it rather comparable to a military campaign, in which social gains are objectives which, once seized, must be held at all cost, to limit the strategic options of "the enemy?" To counter the institutional power of "the economists," the left wing advocates institutional change that would shift power away from the central administration and toward parliament, regions, and cities. Decentralization, it is hoped, will both multiply the range of voices in governing councils and definitively alter the priorities of policymaking.

The presidential candidacy of Ségolène Royal in 2007 can be viewed as an attempt to bridge these gaps. Some of her key advisors were from the Socialist left, and the candidate's emphasis on "citizen juries" and elimination of the *cumul des mandats* (holding of multiple offices) directly translated some of the left's platform planks for institutional reform. Yet she also signaled a readiness to accommodate the "economists" of the center-left by associating herself with Blairism, a conveniently vague portmanteau word standing for "Anglo-Saxon neoliberalism with a human face." More substantively, she signaled flexibility on reform of the thirty-five-hour week, labor contracts, and retirement benefits. Like others before it, this attempted reconciliation foundered on incomprehension and lack of trust. In this case, though, it was not the rank and file that feared betrayal by elite economists; it was rather the economists who feared that Royal, having spent her career without passing by way of the central posts of economic policymaking, could not be trusted to execute or even understand the nature of the necessary economic reforms.

Hostility to Royal was again evident in the selection of a new leader of the Socialist Party. The process of "renovation" launched immediately after the party's failure to capture the presidency in 2007 proved to be a muddled affair that ended in stalemate. Three challenges to Royal emerged from the center of the party, one led by Mayor Bertrand Delanoë of Paris, another by Pierre Moscovici, widely seen as a stalking horse for Dominique Strauss-Kahn, and a third by the mayor of Lille, Martine Aubry. A fourth challenge came from the left wing of the party, led by Benoît Hamon. Ultimately the three centrist factions united behind Aubry. In a first round Hamon took nearly 20% of the votes. In the runoff Aubry and Royal split the party down the middle. Aubry won with a plurality of 102 votes out of nearly 175,000 cast, but her victorious coalition was united by only one thing: hostility to Royal.

And there, for the time being, the French left remains stuck: divided into mutually suspicious factions, none capable by itself of putting forward the kind of comprehensible and comprehensive recipe for transformation that is needed to capture the presidency. The impasse is unlikely to be resolved by internal debate, which for twenty years has been largely a dialogue of the deaf. More likely it will take an external shock to push the factions together, or else to tear the left apart once and for all, as has begun to happen in a number of other EU countries (for example by the appearance of die Linke to the left of the German SPD). There might conceivably be a recomposition of the center, in which center-right and center-left join forces against radicalized extremes. But the presidentialist regime—our third persistent structural influence—tends to make this prospect unlikely.

Notes

The authors would like to thank James Cronin, Michael Löwy, and James Shoch for perceptive comments on an earlier draft.

1. See Fourastié 1979; Eichengreen 2007, 100.

2. This pattern of divisions also existed in trade union and mass organizational spheres.

3. Heisenberg 1999, chapter 3; Ludlow 1982.

4. Favier and Martin-Roland 1990, part I.

5. Becker 1998, 263–66.

6. Quatremer and Klau 1997.

7. CERC 2002, chapters 3, 4.

8. Becker 1998, part II, chapter 2. RMI was a means-tested guaranteed minimum "citizen's income," administered departmentally and tied to commitments to seek "insertion"—usually meaning training or work, a compromise between a guaranteed minimum income and "welfare to work."

9. Philippe Séguin and Charles Pasqua were the principal leaders of the Gaullist nationalists.

10. Chirac sought advice in a group named Phares et Balises, which was organized by the dissident Mitterrandist Régis Debray and the journalist Jean-Claude Guillebaud.

11. Palier 2002, 193.

12. Palier 2002, 195, 417.

13. The CFDT leadership's reluctance to endorse this popular uprising led eventually to the defection of a substantial portion of its membership, which joined the dissident union SUD.

14. In 2007 Jouyet joined Sarkozy's government as secretary of state for European affairs.

15. Victor 1999, 170.

16. Palier 2002, 252.

The Evolving Democratic Coalition

Prospects and Problems

Ruy Teixeira

After the presidential election of 2004, many on the center-left in the United States were strikingly pessimistic about the Democratic Party's future prospects. Retaking control of the Congress seemed out of reach given the advantages of incumbency and a Republican mobilization machine that was widely viewed as both more effective and more ruthless than that of the Democrats. Perhaps if the Democrats built up their strength and fought hard in the next round of reapportionment, retaking Congress might be possible in the next decade. But it was foolish to expect success much sooner than that.

As for the presidency, that seemed more possible, but Democrats worried that Republicans had a lock not just on the South but on a wide swath of culturally conservative states in the Plains, Southwest, Mountain West, and Midwest. The GOP's demonstrated ability to mobilize voters in these states with a conservatism that melded national security and cultural concerns was thought to offer the Democrats little chance of expanding the electoral map in their favor. The most that Democrats could hope for was to refight the battle of Ohio again in 2008 and hope that this time they would win.

But even at the time there were strong arguments to be made that this take on the Democrats' prospects was unduly pessimistic. An alternative line of analysis suggested that the Republicans' strength was vastly exaggerated, tied to an event (September 11, 2001) whose political salience would decline over time. This decline would eventually expose their weakness as a political party with a philosophy and program that were remarkably out of step with demographic and geographic shifts that had been transforming the American electorate.

The results of the midterm elections of 2006, in which the Democrats retook Congress and made significant gains in a wide range of swing and GOP-leaning states, seemed to suggest that the second line of analysis was more plausible and that the GOP was a party on the ropes while the Democrats were a party in ascendance. In the next election, of course, the political situation only worsened for the GOP and improved even more for the Democrats, as Barack Obama was decisively elected president and the Democrats expanded their majorities in both houses of Congress. However, the midterm elections of 2010, in which the Republicans regained control of the House of Representatives and picked up six Senate seats, restored at least temporary parity to the party system in Congress and clouded the immediate future of American politics.

In what follows, written mainly before the 2010 midterms, I describe the various trends that drove the Democrats' ascendance through 2008. I also much more briefly explain the contrasting 2010 results.

The Once and Future Democratic Majority

Racial and ethnic minorities are probably the single strongest element of the emerging Democratic coalition. In 2000 Al Gore carried the minority vote by 75–23, and even in John Kerry's losing effort in 2004 he still carried the minority vote by 71 to 27. In that election, according to the exit polls, minorities made up 23% of the overall vote. That compares to around 15% of voters in the early 1990s when Bill Clinton was first elected.[1]

And in 2006 and 2008 the Democrats did even better. In 2006 they carried the minority congressional vote by 77–22.[2] In 2008 the minority share of voters in the national exit poll reached 26% and the minority vote was an impressive 80–18 for Obama, a 62-point margin, significantly greater than Kerry's 44-point margin in 2004.

These minority gains figured greatly in many key states carried by the Democrats in 2008. In Ohio, for example, the minority share of voters rose from 14% to 17% and black voters supported Obama by a stunning 95-point margin (97 to 2), compared to Kerry's 68-point margin (84–16). In Nevada the minority share of voters rose by a full 8 points, from 23% to 31% of voters, with 95–4 black support for Obama (up from 86–13 in 2004) and 76–22 Hispanic support (up from 60–39 in 2004). And in Florida, while the minority share of voters did not increase, blacks supported Obama by the overwhelming margin of 96–4 compared to 86–13 support for Kerry, while Hispanics, whom Kerry had lost by 56–43, supported Obama by 57–42. The latter is truly a sign of change in Florida, as Hispanic voters, spearheaded by relatively conservative Cuban-Americans, have long been a key segment of the GOP coalition in the state.

It is worth stressing that the advantage accruing to Democrats from minority voters is going to continue growing. As mentioned, from 1988 to 2008 the proportion of minority voters increased from 15 to 26%. But that is just the beginning. People tend to think of 2050 as the year when America will become "majority minority." But the dates are closer than that: the latest census projections put them at 2042 for the entire population and at 2023 for the population under eighteen.[3] By 2050 the United States will actually be 54% minority: 30% Hispanic, 9% Asian, 13% black, and 2% other race.

Of course the minority community is not monolithic nor all growing at the same rate, so it is worth rehearsing some of the specifics of the black, Hispanic, and Asian vote.

Black voters are the most reliable Democratic constituency. In 2004 Kerry had a margin of 88 to 11 among blacks, down only slightly from the margin of 90 to 9 for Gore in 2000. In 2006 Democrats carried the black congressional vote by 89 to 10. Then in 2008 blacks voted by an amazing 95%–4% margin for Obama. Also in 2008 the share of black voters rose from 11% to 13%, hugely impressive for a group whose share of the overall population is growing very slowly.

Hispanic voters, while strong for Democrats, are not nearly as strong as blacks, and have famously been more volatile in their support. In 2004 it was initially reported that they gave Bush 44% of their vote. However, that initial exit poll figure is now widely acknowledged to have been flawed, and the generally accepted estimate is that Kerry carried Hispanics by 58 to 40.[4] Still, that represented a significant improvement of 5 points in Bush's support among Hispanics over 2000 and a substantial compression of the Democratic margin among this group.

There was much debate about the causes of this shift. Probably the best treatment of the issue was done by the political scientists Marisa Abrajano, Michael Alvarez, and Jonathan Nagler (2005), whose thorough analysis of exit poll data from 2004 indicates that for an unusually large proportion of Hispanic voters the pull of national security and moral values toward the GOP outweighed that of the economy, healthcare, and education toward the Democrats. This can be illustrated by the fact that Bush had an advantage of 13 points among Hispanics on being trusted to handle terrorism, while Kerry's advantage among Hispanics on being trusted to handle the economy was a more modest 5 points.[5] These figures underscore the extent to which Democratic appeals to Hispanics fell short in that election.

There was even more debate about the long-term significance of Bush's winning 40% of the vote among Hispanics. Abrajano, Alvarez, and Nagler found no evidence that a specific cultural issue like abortion was realigning Hispanics, nor did they find evidence for the "economic advancement" hypothesis: that Hispanics, particularly second- and third-generation Hispanics, are moving toward the GOP as they are becoming richer as a group.

It is also worth noting that the average level of Hispanic support for the Democrats was slightly higher in the two Bush elections of 2000 and 2004 than in the two Reagan elections of 1980 and 1984.[6] And in the next election following Reagan's relatively good performances among Hispanics—1988— the Hispanic presidential vote moved sharply Democratic, to 69%–30%.

Interestingly, the latter figures exactly match the Democrats' support among Hispanics in the congressional elections of 2006. And in 2008 Hispanics voted 67–31 for Obama, a 36-point margin that was double Kerry's margin in 2004. Though some observers speculated that racial frictions between Hispanics and blacks would prevent Hispanics from giving Obama wholehearted support, that most emphatically was not the case.

If Democrats can hold this group's support, demographic trends assure them of greater electoral benefits in years to come. The Hispanic population is growing rapidly, both in terms of absolute numbers and as a share of the United States population. Before 1980 the census did not even record Hispanic origin when it surveyed the country's residents. Today Hispanics have surpassed blacks as the nation's largest minority group, and census estimates indicate that there are about forty-five million Hispanics in the United States, 15% of the nation's population (Frey 2008).

This rapid increase in demographic importance will continue for decades. The Hispanic population has grown by 32% since 2000 and has accounted for about half of United States population growth in that period (Frey 2008). And as mentioned, census projections indicate that by about mid-century Hispanics will account for 30% of the United States population.

Of course it is true that the population strength of Hispanics is not currently matched by its voting strength, because of the large proportion of Hispanics who are not citizens and therefore cannot vote or are simply too young to vote. For example, of the 5.7 million Hispanics added to the United States population between 2000 and 2004, 1.7 million were under eighteen and 1.9 million were noncitizens. As a result, only 42% of Hispanics overall are eligible to vote, compared to 77% of non-Hispanic whites and 66% of African Americans (Suro, Fry, and Passel 2005; Frey 2009). Still, the proportion of Hispanics among the voting electorate has grown steadily and will continue to grow. Having made up only 2% of voters in the early 1990s, they rose to 9% in 2008 and within ten years will likely surpass the level of blacks as a proportion of actual voters.[7]

Asians over the last fifteen years or so have become a fairly solid Democratic constituency. In 2004 they supported Kerry over Bush by a margin of

56–44, similar to the margin they had given to Gore over Bush (55–41) in 2000. And in the Congressional election of 2002, when much of the electorate was going in the opposite direction, Asians increased their support dramatically for House Democrats, from 56–44 in 1998 to 66–34 in 2002. In 2006 Asians remained strong for the Democrats at 62–37.[8] And in 2008 Asians supported Obama by 62–35.

Asians' rate of growth was slightly higher than that of Hispanics in the 1990s. And since 2000 they have not been far behind (26%, versus 32% for Hispanics). Right now they account for 5% of the population and about 2% of voters.[9] Both figures will increase in the next ten years owing to this group's fast rate of growth, but because they start from a much smaller base than Hispanics, their impact on the population and voting pool will be far more limited.

Single, Working, and Highly Educated Women

As is well known, Democrats typically do better among women than men. But women voters are a vast group, and the true areas of strength for Democrats are among three subgroups: single, working, and highly educated women. In 2004 Kerry carried single women by 62–37, college-educated women by 54–45 (60–38 among those with a postgraduate education), and working women by 51–48.[10]

All of these margins, however, were smaller than they had been in 2000, particularly for working women, who gave Kerry a margin no greater than his margin among women as a whole. This was primarily attributable to his poor performance among *married* working women, part of the Democrats' general problem with married women voters in that election. Single working women, however, remained a very strong progressive constituency, with Democrats dominating by 65–35.[11] In 2006 Democrats generally did better among these constituencies, carrying single women by 66–33 and college-educated women by 57–42.[12] It is likely they also did better among working women, but since the exit polls did not ask respondents for their work status, this possibility could not be tested directly.

In 2008 single women voted Democratic by 70–29, a substantially larger margin than in 2004. And working women, who had voted Democratic by only 3 points in 2004, voted Democratic this time by an impressive margin of 60–39. Even married women with children, traditionally a difficult group for Democrats, supported Obama by 52–47.

While the balance of women relative to men is changing little, of course, trends within the female population are quite favorable to Democrats. Single women now make up almost half of adult women: 47%, up from 38% in 1970.[13] Their current size in the voter pool—more than a quarter of eligible voters—closely approximates the size of white evangelicals, the GOP's largest base group. And since the current growth rate of single women is so great—double that of married women—the proportion of single women in the voting pool will continue to increase (Greenberg Quinlan Rosner Research 2007).

And there is every expectation that this burgeoning population of single women will continue to be resolutely Democratic in its politics. Survey data consistently show this group to be unusually populist on economic issues and generally opposed to the conservative agenda on foreign policy and social issues (Women's Voices, Women Vote 2007).

Single working women tend to be a particularly progressive group among single women, as indicated by data cited earlier. They are also a rapidly growing group, increasing their share of the adult female population from 19% in 1970 to 29% today.[14] That is even faster than the growth rate among single women as a whole.

Finally, college-educated women are also a rapidly growing population group. Their share of the female population twenty-five and older has more than tripled since 1970, from just 8% to 28% today.[15]

Professionals

In the last fifteen to twenty years professionals have become a very strong Democratic constituency, something they decidedly were not in earlier eras. In the presidential election of 1960, for example, professionals supported Nixon over Kennedy by 61 to 38. But in presidential elections from 1988 to 2000, professionals supported the Democratic candidate by an average of 52 to 40. And in 2004 they moved still further in this direction, supporting Kerry over Bush by 63–37.[16] In 2006 exit poll data—using postgraduates as a proxy for professionals—suggest that professionals' support for Democrats was once again at record high levels.[17] And in 2008 Obama received 58–40 support from postgraduates. That figure included 54–44 support among white postgraduates.

Strong support from professionals is especially good for progressives because professionals are a rising group in American politics and society. In the 1950s they made up about 7% of the workforce. But as the United States has moved from a blue-collar, industrial economy toward a postindustrial one that produces ideas and services, the professional class has expanded. Today it constitutes just under 17% of the workforce. In another ten years they will be 18% to 19% of the workforce.[18]

Moreover, reflecting their very high turnout rates, they are an even larger percentage of voters—and not just of employed voters, but of voters as a whole. Nationally they account for about 21% of voters; in many Northeastern and Far Western states they form probably one-quarter of the electorate.[19]

The Millennial Generation

The Millennial generation is even larger than the Baby Boom generation. This is true no matter what definition we use. (A young generation often does not have a common name and clear start and end dates until a consensus emerges among demographers and social commentators over time.) For example, if we start Millennials in birth year 1978, after the "baby bust" (to which Generation X is typically linked) had ended and an era of steadily rising births had begun, and continue to 2000—as is common in market research—the size of this generation is truly staggering: 95 million (though only about half are adults) out of a population of 300 million, compared to 78 million Boomers. By 2018 Millennials, by this definition, will be 100 million strong and will all be old enough to vote. Even if we exclude noncitizens, there will still be 90 million citizen-eligible Millennial voters.[20]

And even if we use 1996 as the last birth year for the Millennials, so that the span of birth years covered by this generation (1978–96) is of the same length as that covered by the Baby Boom (1946–64), this generation is still larger than the Boomers: 80 million today and 83 million by 2016, when the members of the tail end of the generation vote in their first presidential election.

The Millennial generation is so large partly because many of its members are children of the Boomers (and make up the "echo boom"), while others are the children of immigrants, who settled in the United States in unprecedented numbers in the last several decades. The Millennials are the most diverse generation by far. According to census data published in March 2006, only 61% of Millennial adults were non-Hispanic whites, 18% were Hispanic, 14% were black, and 5% were Asian.

Like the Boomers, the Millennials are poised to have an impact on the country at every life stage and in myriad ways—but particularly in politics. By 2008 the number of citizen-eligible Millennial voters had neared fifty million. By the presidential election of 2016 Millennials will be 36% of the citizen-eligible electorate, and about a third of actual voters[21]—and this is making no assumptions about possible increased turnout rates among Millennials in the future, which could make their weight among actual voters higher. In addition, from that point on the Millennials' share of the electorate will rise steadily for several decades as more and more of the generation enter middle age.

On the level of sheer partisan politics, the increased number of Millennials in the voting pool is having substantial effects, since they have voted more heavily Democratic than other generations in their first few elections. For example, in 2006 voters aged eighteen to twenty-nine voted 60–38 Democratic for Congress, with the subgroup of voters aged eighteen to twenty-four going 58–37 Democratic (note how similar the strength of Democratic support is between the smaller group of Millennials and the larger group, implying that transition Millennials—those twenty-five to twenty-nine—did not vote much differently from their early Millennial counterparts). In 2004 voters aged eighteen to twenty-nine (dominated by the subgroup aged eighteen to twenty-six, who qualify as Millennials) voted 54–45 Democratic for president (55–44 for the House). But note here that the subgroup aged eighteen to twenty-four—Millennials all—voted 56–43 Democratic for president, while the older subgroup, twenty-five to twenty-nine—mostly *not* Millennials—voted only 51–48 Democratic. Even in 2002, a terrible Democratic year, voters aged eighteen to twenty-four (the first time Millennials constituted this group) still voted Democratic 49–47.[22]

But it was in 2008 that the Millennial vote had its largest effect. This is the first year that voters aged eighteen to twenty-nine belonged exclusively to the millennial generation (those born 1978 or later), and they gave Obama a 34-point margin, 66–32. This compares to only a 9-point margin for Kerry in 2004. The youth share of voters also increased across the two elections, from 17 to 18.

Obama's support among voters aged eighteen to twenty-nine was remarkably broad, extending across racial barriers. In that age group he carried not just Hispanics (76%–19%) and blacks (95–4) but also whites (54–44), a 10-point advantage that contrasts starkly with Obama's 15-point deficit among older whites.

Obama's huge overall margin among Millennials contributed mightily to his strong victory. Without voters aged eighteen to twenty-nine, Obama's popular vote margin would have been slightly under one percentage point. That figure means that 87% of Obama's popular vote victory was attributable to the support of Millennials between eighteen and twenty-nine. Indeed without these Millennial voters Obama would have been hard-pressed to claim much of a mandate from his election victory.

These results could hardly be more positive for the Democrats. And Millennials' influence on the electorate is certain to grow for the next several elections. There were about 48 million eligible Millennial voters in 2008, a figure that will rise to 64 million in 2012 and 81 million in 2016. That is a huge number of potential Democrats, given how this generation is leaning. In a Pew survey in early 2007, 48% of Millennials between eighteen and twenty-five identified with or leaned toward the Democratic Party, compared to just 35% who identified with or leaned toward the Republicans. The latter figure represents a huge crash in support for the Republicans among this age group: in the early 1990s voters in this age group, members of "Gen X," were identifying at a 55% rate with Republicans.

Gen Xers continue to be the most Republican generation today, while the Millennials are emerging as the most Democratic generation by a substantial margin. Other polls of Millennials and Millennial-dominated age groups confirm this solid Democratic lead in party identification. On election day in 2006 the exit polls showed the Democrats with a 12-point lead on party identification among voters aged eighteen to twenty-five.[23] And polls taken since then have continued to give the Democrats strong double-digit leads on party identification among this age group—Pew had the Democratic advantage at an astonishing 25 points in data covering the period from October 2007 to March 2008. Numerous political science studies confirm that party identification, once formed in a generation's twenties, tend to persist over a lifetime.

The Secular, the Less Observant, and the Non-Christian

It is a commonplace in American politics today that the highly observant—especially evangelical Christians—are a bedrock conservative constituency. Less well appreciated is the extent to which the secular, the less observant, and the non-Christian are a bedrock Democratic constituency. In 2004 Kerry carried those who attend religious services a few times a year by 54–45 and those who never attend by 62–36. And he carried all non-Christian groups by very wide margins: Jews (77–22), Muslims (74–25), those who profess some other religion (72–25), and those who profess no religion (67–31).[24] Democratic support among these groups was even stronger in 2006: those who attend religious services a few times a year (60–38), those who never attend (67–30), Jews (87–12), those who profess some other religion (71–25), and those who profess no religion (74–22).[25]

According to exit polls, the less observant made up 43% of voters in 2004 (the latter figure, incidentally, is exactly equal to the percentage of voters who were highly observant). That figure is likely to go up in the future. In the University of Chicago's General Social Survey (GSS), those who attend church *only once a year or less* is now 42% of adults, up from 29% in 1972.

Data from exit polls in 2008 suggest that attempts to inflame cultural issues in the election campaign were not successful. Democrats gained support throughout the religious spectrum. Consider first the vote broken down by how often people attend religious services. In the United States over the last couple of decades there has been a strong relationship between how often you attend services and how you vote, with those who attend most frequently being much more conservative than those who attend least often. This relationship was not broken in 2008, but it did become less strong.

For example, Obama ran the same relatively modest 12-point deficit among those who attend services more than once a week as he did among those who attend weekly. In fact, Obama's 17-point improvement from a 35–64 Democratic deficit among the most frequent attenders in 2004 to a 43–55 deficit in 2008 was his largest improvement among the different attendance groups in 2008. He also improved the Democratic margin by 8 points among those who attend a few times a month, by 10 points among those who attend a few times a year, and by 11 points among those who never attend.

In terms of religious affiliation, Obama improved the Democratic margin among Catholics by 14 points, from a 5-point deficit in 2004 to a 9-point advantage in 2008. He also reduced the Democratic deficit among Protestant and other Christian voters by 10 points, from 19 to 9. And he achieved enormous margins among Jews (78–21), members of other religions (73–22), and unaffiliated voters (75–23).

Speaking of unaffiliated—secular—voters, it is this group, not white evangelicals, who are the fastest-growing religious group in the United States. This, combined with racial and ethnic trends, will ensure that in very short order we will no longer be a white Christian nation. Even today only about 55% of adults are white Christians. By 2024 that figure will be down to 45%. This means that by the election of 2016 (or 2020 at the outside) white Christians will be in the minority. That will provide another long-range boost to Democratic prospects.

Union Household Voters

Union household voters have been a consistently strong constituency for progressives, and the election of 2004 was no exception. These voters supported Kerry by 59–40 and made up an impressive 24% of the voting pool.[26] In 2006 union households did even better for the Democrats, supporting them by 64–34, while making up a similarly high share (23%) of voters.[27] And in 2008 these voters supported Obama by 59 to 40, a margin essentially identical to Kerry's in 2004. Yet their representation among voters (21%) was 3 points less than in 2004. Even this 21% figure is impressive, however, given that union membership in the United States now stands at only 12% of workers. Clearly the union vote has little potential for growth and considerable potential for further decline without significant changes in labor law such as those proposed in the Employee Free Choice Act, which would make it easier for unions to organize workers. Given the progressive proclivities of union household voters, that would be of great benefit to the Democrats.

The White Working-Class Challenge

The key weakness of the emerging Democratic coalition can be summarized easily: very weak support among white working-class voters (defined here as whites without a four-year college degree). These voters, who are overwhelmingly of moderate to low income and, by definition, of modest credentials, should see their aspirations linked tightly to the political fate of the Democratic Party. But they do not. Instead the white working class, as it has declined in numbers, has shifted its allegiance from largely Democratic to largely Republican. Here is the story of that decline and political shift.

Let us start with basic numbers: the size of the white working class about the time of the the Second World War and today. Using the broad education-based definition above, America in 1940 was an overwhelmingly white working-class country. In that year 86% of adults twenty-five and over were whites without a four-year college degree. By 2007, with the dramatic rise in educational attainment and the decline in the white population, that proportion was down to 48%.[28] A similar trend can be seen if one uses a narrow education-based definition. In 1940 82% of adults twenty-five and over were whites with a high school diploma or less. By 2007 that figure was down to 29%. Or, using a broad occupation-based definition, in 1940 74% of employed workers were whites without professional or managerial jobs. By 2006 the steady climb in professional and managerial jobs, combined with the decline in the white population, had brought that proportion down to 43%.[29] A narrow occupation-based definition yields a decline of similar magnitude. In 1940 58% of workers were whites without professional, managerial, or clerical and sales jobs (or, looked at another way, whites who held manual, service, or farm jobs). By 2006 that figure had fallen to 25%.

The final class indicator to look at is income. Using a broad income-based definition of the white working class, 86% of American families in 1947 were white families with less than $60,000 in income (2005 dollars). With rising affluence—especially rapid in the period from 1947 to 1973—and the decline in the white population, that figure had declined to 33% by 2005.[30] Using a narrow income-based definition, 60% of families in 1947 were white families with less than $30,000 in income. That figure had dropped to 14% by 2005.

So each indicator that can be used to define the white working class, whether applied broadly or narrowly, shows huge declines from the Second World War era to today—declines roughly in the range of 30–50 percentage points. The income-based definitions show the sharpest declines and the occupation-based definitions the least, with the education-based definitions somewhere in between. And in each case these shifts have moved the white working class from being the solid and sometimes overwhelming majority of United States adults (or workers or families) to being a minority.

But the story of the white working class in the years following the Second World War is one of not just one sharp decline but also profound transformation. This is true no matter what indicator one uses to define the white working class. That is, whether one looks at white families with less than $60,000 income, whites who do not hold professional and managerial jobs, or whites without a four-year college degree, there have been dramatic shifts in the character and composition of the white working class.

Consider the following shifts among whites without a four-year college degree. In 1940 86% of these working-class whites had never graduated from high school (or even reached high school). But today just 14% of the white working class consists of high school dropouts. About two-fifths have some education beyond high school, with 13% having achieved an associate degree.[31] Note, however, that the economic situation of those with an associate degree is very similar to those with some college but no degree: the median household income of whites with an associate degree is only a few thousand dollars more than those with some college only (Teixeira and Rogers 2000, 16).

While the unavailability of data precludes a precise estimate, the economic situation of the white working class has altered dramatically. A reasonable guess is that median family income among the white working class rose from around $20,000 to $50,000 between 1947 and 2005, a 150% increase. And the jobs that the white working class holds have also altered dramatically. Today most white working-class jobs are not manual or blue-collar but low-level white-collar (technical, sales, clerical) and service occupations. And the blue-collar jobs that remain are increasingly likely to be skilled positions: only about a sixth of the white working class holds unskilled blue-collar jobs (even among white working-class *men*, the figure is less than one-quarter).[32]

Today only about a sixth of the white working class holds manufacturing jobs (even among men, the proportion is still less than one-quarter). In fact the entire goods-producing sector, which includes construction, mining, and agriculture as well as manufacturing, provides less than three in ten white working-class jobs. The remaining seven in ten are in the service sector, including government. There are about as many members of the white working class working in trade alone (especially retail) as there are in all goods-producing jobs.

Accompanying the decline and transformation of the white working class was a very significant shift in its political orientation, from pro-Democratic in most respects to pro-Republican, especially at the presidential level. The story of this shift away from the Democratic Party starts with the New Deal Democrats and their close relationship with the white working class. The New Deal Democratic worldview was based on a combination of the Democrats' historic populist commitment to the average working American and their experience in battling the Great Depression (and building their political coalition) through increased government spending and regulation and the promotion of labor unions. It was really a rather simple philosophy, even if the application of it was complex. Government should help the average person through vigorous government spending. Capitalism needs regulation to work properly. Labor unions are good. Putting money in the average person's pocket is more important than rarefied worries about the quality of life. Traditional morality is to be respected, not challenged. Racism and the like are bad, but not so bad that the party should depart from its main mission of material uplift for the average American.

That worldview had deep roots in an economy dominated by mass production industries and was politically based among the workers, overwhelmingly white, in those industries. And it helped make the Democrats the undisputed party of the white working class. Their dominance among these voters was the key to their political success. To be sure, there were important divisions among these voters—by country of origin (German, Scandinavian, Eastern European, English, Irish, Italian), religion (Protestants, Catholics), and region (South, North)—that greatly complicated the politics of this group, but New Deal Democrats mastered the complications and maintained a deep base among these voters.

Of course the New Deal coalition as originally forged did include most blacks and was certainly cross-class, especially among groups like Jews and southerners. But the prototypical member of the coalition was indeed an ethnic white worker—commonly visualized as working in a unionized factory, but in some cases not belonging to a union and in some cases working in a non-manufacturing blue-collar sector such as construction or transportation. It was these voters who provided the numbers for five consecutive Democratic election victories—four by FDR and one narrow one by Harry Truman in 1948—as well as political support for the emerging United States welfare state, its implicit social contract, and a greatly expanded role for government.

Even in the 1950s, with the Republican Dwight Eisenhower as president, the white working class continued to put Democrats in Congress and support the expansion of the welfare state, as a roaring United States economy delivered the goods and as government poured money into roads, science, schools, and whatever else seemed necessary to build up the country. This era, stretching back into the late 1940s and forward to the mid-1960s, created the first mass middle class in the world—a middle class that even factory workers could enter, since they could earn relatively comfortable livings even without high levels of education or professional skills—a middle class, in other words, that members of the white working class could reasonably aspire to join and frequently did.

So New Deal Democrats depended on the white working class for political support, and the white working class depended on the Democrats to run government and the economy in a way that kept that upward escalator to the middle class moving. Social and cultural issues were not particularly important to this mutually beneficial relationship; they had only a peripheral role in the uncomplicated progressivism that animated the Democratic Party of the 1930s, 1940s, and 1950s. But that arrangement and that uncomplicated progressivism could not and did not survive the decline of mass production industries and the rise of postindustrial capitalism.

First, there was the transformation of the white working class itself, discussed in detail previously. The white working class became richer, better educated, more white-collar, and less unionized. To get a sense of how important unionization was, consider that in the late 1940s unions claimed around 60% or more of the northern blue-collar workforce (Judis and Teixeira 2002, 63). Second, as this great transformation was changing the character of the white working class, reducing the size and influence of the Democrats' traditional blue-collar constituencies, the evolution of postindustrial capitalism was creating new constituencies and movements with new demands. These new constituencies and movements wanted more out of the welfare state than steady economic growth, copious infrastructure spending, and the opportunity to raise a family in the traditional manner.

During the 1960s these new demands on the welfare state came to a head. Americans' concern about their quality of life overflowed and their expectations increased: from a two-car garage to clean air and water and safe automobiles; from higher wages to government-guaranteed healthcare in old age; from access to jobs to equal opportunities for men and women and blacks and whites. Out of these concerns came the environmental, consumer, civil rights, and feminist movements of the 1960s. As Americans abandoned the older ideal of self-denial and the taboos that accompanied it, they embraced a libertarian ethic of personal life. Women asserted their sexual independence through the use of birth control pills and the right to have an abortion. Adolescents experimented with sex and courtship. Homosexuals "came out" and openly congregated in bars and neighborhoods.

Of these changes the one with most far-reaching political effects was the civil rights movement and its demands for equality and economic progress for black America. Democrats, both because of their traditional, if usually downplayed, antiracist ideology and their political relationship to the black community, had no choice but to respond to those demands. The result was a great victory for social justice, but one that created huge political difficulties for the Democrats among their white working-class supporters. Kevin Phillips captured these developments well in his book, *The Emerging Republican Majority* (1969): "The principal force which broke up the Democratic (New Deal) coalition is the Negro socioeconomic revolution and liberal Democratic ideological inability to cope with it. Democratic 'Great Society' programs aligned that party with many Negro demands, but the party was unable to defuse the racial tension sundering the nation. The South, the West, and the Catholic sidewalks of New York were the focus points of conservative opposition to the welfare liberalism of the federal government; however, the general opposition . . . came in large part from prospering Democrats who objected to Washington dissipating their tax dollars on programs which did them no good. The Democratic Party fell victim to the ideological impetus of a liberalism which had carried it beyond programs taxing the few for the benefit of the many . . . to programs taxing the many on behalf of the few."

But if race was the chief vehicle by which the New Deal coalition was torn apart, it was by no means the only one. White working-class voters also reacted poorly to the extremes with which the rest of the new social movements became identified. Feminism became identified with "bra burners," lesbians, and hostility to the nuclear family; the antiwar movement with appeasement of third world radicals and the Soviet Union; the environmental movement with a Luddite opposition to economic growth; and the move toward more personal freedom with a complete abdication of personal responsibility.

Thus the New Deal mainstream that dominated the Democratic Party was confronted with a challenge. The uncomplicated commitments to government spending, economic regulation, and labor unions that had defined the Democrats' progressivism for over thirty years suddenly provided little guidance for contending with an explosion of potential new constituencies for the party. Their demands for equality, and for a better as opposed to merely richer life, were starting to redefine what progressivism meant, and the Democrats had to struggle to catch up.

Initially Democratic politicians responded to these changes in the fashion of politicians since time immemorial: they sought to co-opt the new movements by absorbing many of their demands, while holding on to the party's basic ideology and style of governing. Thus Democratic politicians did not change their fundamental commitment to the New Deal welfare state, but grafted onto it support for all the various new constituencies and their key demands. After Lyndon Johnson signed the Civil Rights Act in 1964, the party moved over the next eight years to give prominent places within the party to the women's, antiwar, consumer, and environmental movements. This stance reflected both the politician's standard interest in capturing the votes of new constituencies and the broadening definition of what it meant to be a Democrat, particularly a progressive one.

But of course there was no guarantee that gains among these new constituencies would not be offset by losses among the older constituency—the white working class—which had little interest in revising what it meant to be a progressive and a Democrat. The conflict was brought to the fore in 1972 with the nomination and disastrous defeat of George McGovern, who enthusiastically embraced the new direction taken by the party. McGovern's commitment to the traditional Democratic welfare state was unmistakable. But so was his commitment to the various social movements and constituencies that were reshaping the party, whose demands were enshrined in McGovern's campaign platform. That made it easy for his Republican opponent, President Richard Nixon, to typecast McGovern as the candidate of "acid, amnesty and abortion." The white working class reacted accordingly and gave Nixon 70% of its votes (Judis and Teixeira 2002, 63).

Just how far the Democrats fell in the white working class's eyes over this period can be seen by comparing the average vote for Democrats of the white working class (whites without a four-year college degree) in 1960–64 (55%) to its average vote for Democrats in 1968–72 (35%) (Teixeira and Rogers 2000, 32). The Democrats were the party of the white working class no longer.

With the sharp economic recession and Nixon's scandals of 1973–74, the Democrats were able to develop enough political momentum to retake the White House in 1976, with Jimmy Carter's narrow defeat of Gerald Ford. But their political revival did not last long.

Carter did little to defuse white working-class hostility to the new social movements, especially the black liberation movement, and economic conditions in the late 1970s conspired to make that hostility even sharper. Stagflation—a vexing combination of high inflation and high unemployment with slow economic growth, including, critically, slow wage and income growth—had first appeared during the recession of 1973–75, but it persisted under

Carter and was peaking on the eve of the election of 1980. As the economy slid once more into recession, the inflation rate stood at 12.5%. Combined with an unemployment rate of 7.1%, it produced a "misery index" of nearly 20%. By that time white working-class voters had entered an economic world radically different from the one enjoyed by the preceding generation. Slow growth, declining wages, stagnating living standards, high inflation, and high interest rates were really battering them economically. The great postwar escalator to the middle class had drastically slowed down and for some even stopped.

These economic developments fed resentments about race—about high taxes for welfare (which were assumed to go primarily to minorities) and about affirmative action. But they also sowed doubts about Democrats' ability to manage the economy and made Republican and business explanations of stagflation—blaming it on government regulation, high taxes, and spending—more plausible. In 1978 white backlash and doubts about Democratic economic policies had helped to fuel a nationwide tax revolt. In 1980 these forces reinforced the massive exodus of white working-class voters from the Democratic tickets first seen in 1968 and 1972. In the presidential elections of 1980 and 1984 Ronald Reagan averaged 61% support among the white working class, compared to an average of 35% support for his Democratic opponents, Jimmy Carter and Walter Mondale (Judis and Teixeira 2002, 63; Teixeira and Rogers 2000, 32).

Such a thrashing, coming not that long after the debacle of the McGovern campaign, led many Democrats to form a new organization, the Democratic Leadership Council (DLC), to propose a reconfiguration of the Democratic approach. These "New Democrats" argued that in the late 1960s the liberalism of the New Deal had degenerated into a liberal fundamentalism, which, in the words of William Galston and Elaine Kamarck (1989), the public had "come to associate with tax and spending policies that contradict the interests of average families; with welfare policies that foster dependence rather than self-reliance; with softness toward the perpetrators of crime and indifference toward its victims; with ambivalence toward the assertion of American values and interests abroad; and with an adversarial stance toward mainstream moral and cultural values."

Galston, Kamarck, and the DLC advocated fiscal conservatism, welfare reform, increased spending on crime through the development of a police corps, tougher mandatory sentences, support for capital punishment, and policies that encouraged traditional families. This new approach did not really take off until it was embraced by the Democratic presidential candidate Bill Clinton in 1992, who synthesized these views with a moderate version of New Deal economic populism. It proved to be an electorally successful approach for Clinton both in 1992 and, thanks to some good economic times, in 1996 as well. But despite Clinton's electoral success, he did not receive a great deal of white working-class support: he averaged only 41% across his two election victories. But he did at least prevent these voters from siding with his Republican opponents in large numbers, eking out 1-point pluralities among the white working class in both elections (in each election a third-party candidacy was mounted by Ross Perot).[33]

Clinton's designated successor, Al Gore, was not so successful. He lost white working-class voters in the 2000 election by 17 points. And the next Democratic presidential candidate, John Kerry, did even worse, losing these voters by 23 points in 2004.[34] One could reasonably ascribe the worsening deficit for Democrats in 2004 to concerns about national security and terrorism after 9/11, but not so for the very sizable deficit in 2000. Apparently the successes of the Clinton years, which included a strong economy that delivered solid real wage growth for the first time since 1973, did not succeed in restoring the historic bond between the white working class and the Democrats.

Exit polls typically do not classify respondents by occupation, but they do classify by income as well as education. If one looks specifically at voters who seem to correspond most closely to one's intuitive sense of the heart of the white working class—white voters of moderate income who are not college-educated—one finds that these are precisely the voters among whom Democrats did most poorly. For example, among non-college-educated whites with a household income of $30,000–$50,000, Bush beat Kerry by 24 points (62–38); among college-educated whites at the same income level Kerry managed a 49–49 tie. And among non-college-educated whites with $50,000–$75,000 in household income, Bush beat Kerry by 41 points (70–29), while leading by only 5 points (52–47) among college-educated whites at the same income level.[35] Thus the more voters looked like hardcore members of the white working class, the less likely they were to vote for Kerry in 2004.

Clearly Democrats need to do better among white working-class voters if they are to capitalize on their burgeoning advantage among the constituencies enumerated earlier. And in 2006 and 2008 they were able to do so. In 2006 the Democrats dramatically improved their performance among white working-class voters, running only a 10-point deficit, down from a 20-point deficit in congressional voting in 2004. The Democrats also reduced their deficit from 32 to 21 points among non-college-educated whites with $50,000 to $75,000 in household income and completely eliminated their deficit among non-college-educated whites with $30,000–$50,000 in household income, going from 22 points down in 2004 to dead even.[36] In the election of 2008 the Democrats lost the white working class by 18 points, also an improvement over 2004 when they had lost them by 23 points, but worse than pre-election polls indicated they would do. As it turned out, Democrats were able to achieve a solid victory even with this large white working-class deficit. This is because minority turnout and support were at record highs and white college graduate support for the Democrats increased smartly as well. So an 18-point white working-class deficit was in the end adequate to produce a solid victory for the Democrats, rather than the squeaker that many, including myself, had expected. Indeed, if Obama had achieved a significantly lower deficit among these voters—say in the 10- to 12-point range—he would have won in a true landslide, given his support among other demographic groups. But Obama did not attain that: his white working-class deficit (18 points) was very similar to Al Gore's (17 points). It is also interesting to compare Michael Dukakis's performance in 1988 among white working-class and white college graduates to Obama's performance. In 1988 the Democratic deficit among these two groups was identical: 20 points. In 2008 the white working-class deficit was only a slight improvement (down 2 points), but the white college graduate deficit was just 4 points, a 16-point Democratic swing since 1988. This stubbornly high deficit for Democrats among white working-class voters is mitigated by the greatly diminished share of the voting pool. According to the exit polls, the proportion of white working-class voters is down 15 points since 1988, while the proportion of white college graduates is up 4 points and of minority voters up 11 points.

On the state level Obama did stunningly well among white working-class voters in four of the five highly competitive states that the Democrats won in 2000 and 2004 (Michigan, Minnesota, Oregon, and Wisconsin). The average white working-class deficit for Kerry in these states in 2004 was 8 points. In 2008 Obama had an average advantage in these states of 6 points, a pro-Democratic swing of 14 points. In Pennsylvania, however, the other highly competitive state that the Democrats won in 2000 and 2004, Obama did worse than Kerry, losing the white working class by 15 points as opposed to Kerry's 10 points. But college-educated whites in Pennsylvania swung Obama's way by 17 points, turning a 12-point deficit in 2004 into a 5-point advantage in 2008. The Democrats were also helped in Pennsylvania by the rapidly shifting distribution of voters. Since 1988 the share of white working-class voters has declined by 25 points, while the share of white college graduates has gone up 16 points and the minority share by 8 points.

In the highly competitive states that the Democrats lost in both 2000 and 2004 (Florida, Missouri, Nevada, and Ohio) the pattern was different. In 2004 the average Democratic white working-class deficit in these states was 13 points; in 2008 the average deficit was actually slightly worse (14 points).

But Obama made progress in other ways. Among white college graduates the Democrats improved their average margin by 9 points. And minority support went up substantially and in some cases spectacularly. Further, in each of these states one sees the same long-term trends in the distribution of voters: fewer white working-class voters, more white college-educated voters, and more minorities.

One factor that should favor the Democrats, albeit over the longer term, is that the decline of the white working class is likely to continue. First, there will be a continuing decline in the white population as a whole. By the presidential election of 2020, the Census Bureau projects that non-Hispanic whites will be down to around 60% of the population. By 2050 that share will have dropped to about 46%. Educational upgrading is also likely to continue, though it may slow. A working paper published by the Census Bureau (Day and Bauman 2000) predicts a 4–7 point increase in the high school completion rate, a 7–12 point increase in the college attendance rate (some college or higher), and a 4–5 point increase in the four-year-college completion rate by 2028.

Occupational upgrading will continue, though here too the rate may slow. According to occupational projections to 2016 by the Bureau of Labor Statistics, while professional (and service) jobs will grow at the fastest rate among major occupational groups, professional occupations will increase their *share* of jobs by only about a percentage point, a slowdown from the rate of share increase from 1950 to 2000 (changes in occupation coding make the comparison inexact). In addition, managerial occupations will grow at the second-fastest rate (though their share will remain flat).

Income upgrading should also continue, though the rate is very difficult to assess. Recall that median family income increased about 150% from 1947 to 2005. But most of that increase was in the twenty-six-year period between 1947 and 1973, when family income more than doubled, with an annual growth rate of 2.8%. In the thirty-two years between 1973 and 2005, income only went up 23%, an annual growth rate of 0.6%.[37] So how much income goes up in the future will depend very much on whether income growth follows the pre-1973 or post-1973 pattern, or something in between.

Since we do not know the answer to this question and recent history is inconclusive—there was a period of rapid growth in median family income from 1995 to 2000 (up 11%), followed by negative growth from 2000 to 2005 (down 2%)—one approach is to use the growth rate over the entire period 1947–2005 period (1.6%), which in effect averages the growth rates in the "good" (1947–73) and "bad" (1973–2005) periods. Applying this rate to median family income produces an estimate of $83,000 for the year 2030 (in

2005 dollars). Moreover, if one applies this rate to the fortieth percentile of the family income distribution, the fortieth percentile would move up to around $67,000 by 2030, meaning that roughly 65% of families in that year would have more than $60,000 in income. In 2005 the corresponding figure was about 47%.

The downward trajectory of the white working class therefore seems assured if its rate of decline is uncertain. As with the data since the Second World War reviewed at the beginning of this chapter, it appears likely that the future rate of decline will be fastest under an income-based definition, slowest under an occupation-based definition, and intermediate under an education-based definition. More precise statements about the projected population share of the white working class are difficult, but some educated guesses can be made.

Looking first at the broad education-based definition (whites without a four-year college degree), the rate of decline of the white working class since the Second World War has been 0.57 percentage points a year. Adjusting this rate downward a bit to allow for the expected slowdown in educational upgrading and projecting it forward to the presidential election of 2020 yields an estimate of 41% of adults in the white working class and perhaps a percentage point more of voters. Under the occupation-based definition (whites without a professional or managerial job), the rate of decline since the Second World War has been 0.47 percentage points a year. Adjusting the rate downward to allow for the projected slowdown in occupational upgrading and projecting forward to 2020 yields an estimate of 37% of workers in the white working class. Finally, under the income-based definition (white families under $60,000), the rate of decline since 1947 has been 0.91 percentage points a year. Keeping the rate the same and projecting forward to 2020 yields an estimate of 20% of families qualifying as white working class.[38]

These changes now make it possible for the Democrats to build majority support with smaller proportions of the white working class. Conversely, Republicans, who are dependent today on supermajorities of the white working-class vote to cobble together a majority coalition, will need ever larger majorities of the white working-class vote over time to sustain their coalition.

DESPITE THE SETBACK in the 2010 midterms, together the foregoing trends have put the Democrats in a position to eventually build a dominant center-left majority in the United States. Fundamental changes in the American electorate are more likely to favor them than the GOP for a considerable time to come. As recent events have demonstrated, however, the real challenge for the Democrats now is governance—and they entered office at a particularly challenging time, with the most serious economic crisis since the Second World War gripping the country. But with this crisis also came opportunity. It was far more feasible for Obama and the Democrats to attain passage of large-scale reforms with commensurate levels of spending than it would have been in more tranquil times.

Obama took advantage of this situation. Start with the $787 billion stimulus bill that included significant investments in education and clean energy. These expenditures, combined with extensive interventions to stabilize the banking system, pulled the United States economy back from the brink of a truly catastrophic meltdown and onto a growth path that while currently slow, should pick up considerably in the future.

And then there is healthcare reform, something that progressives in America have been trying to accomplish for nearly a century. It was a long, grueling process, but a healthcare reform bill was finally passed and signed into law by President Obama. It covers more than thirty million people who were previously uninsured, reforms the insurance market so that people with pre-existing conditions cannot be denied coverage, and much, much more. The details are byzantine, but the most important fact is this: for the first time, the principle that everyone in America should have access to affordable healthcare has been enshrined in law. The law will have to be extended and modified in the future, but the stunning nature of this accomplishment cannot be denied.

Obama also delivered on his promise to tackle climate change. Besides the investments in clean energy mentioned above, he pushed a cap-and-trade energy bill through the House of Representatives, although it unfortunately died in the Senate. And Obama traveled to Copenhagen, where he helped negotiate a preliminary agreement that may eventually lead to a binding international agreement on greenhouse gas emissions. The contrast could not be sharper with the Bush administration's lack of interest in fighting climate change. There is also a sharp contrast with the Bush administration's approach to international relations. Obama has thoroughly revamped the United States approach to working with other countries and international institutions, replacing Bush's unilateralism with an open, cooperative multilateralism.

Obama achieved one more important legislative goal: a regulatory reform bill for the financial sector, the most significant such legislation since the 1930s, establishing new federal regulatory powers to police financial markets and protect consumers and reining in the derivatives market that lay at the heart of the financial crisis. He promised to take bold action in this area during his campaign.

That is where we are on Obama's progressive agenda. But what of Obama's Democratic majority? Here the news is obviously not so good. Obama's approval rating peaked at 67% in the Gallup poll around the time of his inauguration in January 2009. Since then it has declined considerably, standing at about 47% across all polls in April 2011. His approval ratings are lower still on the economy, the budget deficit, and healthcare.

This declining public support for Obama and his policies contributed to the Republicans' 2010 midterm election victories. A few fundamental or "structural" factors explain this outcome: the poor state of the economy; the abnormally conservative composition of the midterm electorate; and the large number of vulnerable seats in conservative-leaning areas. Independent voters, white working-class voters, seniors, and men broke heavily against the Democrats because of the economy. Turnout levels were also unusually low among young and minority voters and unusually high among seniors, whites, and conservatives, thus contributing to a massively skewed midterm electorate. The Democrats therefore faced a predictable, and arguably unavoidable, convergence of forces (for a much more detailed discussion see Teixeira and Halpin 2010).

Although Obama and the Democrats lost support since the 2008 election among most demographic groups, the biggest decline was among the white working class. This makes sense for two reasons. First, this group is very sensitive to economic conditions, and those conditions have been terrible. Obama may have succeeded in averting an economic cataclysm, but he could not prevent a steady rise in the unemployment rate since his election (though it appears that that rise has finally abated). In November 2008 the unemployment rate stood at 6.8%. By the following November it was 10%, and a year later it was still 9.6%. Second, the white working class, even more than the American public as a whole, is inclined to be suspicious of government interventions and spending, of which there has been a considerable amount since the election. This hostility toward "big government" was bound to be inflamed by the perceived failure of these government actions (if we are spending so much money to fix things, why is the economy in such terrible shape?) and by the relentless attacks on Obama by the conservative opposition, ranging from the Republicans in Congress to "Tea Party" activists at the grassroots.

It is important to note, however, that although their loss of the House and the reduction of their Senate majority was a serious rebuke to the Democrats and the political status quo, it was not an endorsement of a conservative agenda. Data on voter opinions expressed in pre- and post-election polling confirms that the 2010 election was neither a mandate for antigovernment and Tea Party ideology nor an endorsement of GOP policies on taxes and regulation. Nor did the election turn on a repudiation of Obama's healthcare plan, despite staunch Republican opposition.

Given all this, looking ahead toward the presidential election of 2012, what is the prognosis for Obama's coalition? Better than one might expect in the wake of the recent midterms. In this regard the example of Ronald Reagan is instructive. Reagan had to contend with a severe recession, just like Obama—indeed for Reagan, unemployment peaked at 10.8%, higher than Obama has experienced. At about this point in Reagan's first term, his approval rating was actually lower than Obama's current rating, and his party wound up losing twenty-six House seats in the congressional election of 1982. But 1983 and 1984 were years of strong economic growth, and the unemployment rate declined over those years, reaching 7.2% by election day 1984. In that election Reagan won a landslide victory with 59% of the popular vote.

Obama's first term could well follow a similar trajectory. As noted above, his party lost seats in 2010, largely as a result of the poor economy and the historical tendency of incumbent parties to lose seats in midterm elections. But by 2012 the economic situation should be improved and unemployment lower—Obama's version of Reagan's "morning in America." Moreover, Obama will have the advantage of four more years of growth in his demographic coalition plus an election (presidential) in which that coalition is likely to turn out at high levels. The result, I believe, will be a victory for Obama in 2012 and the reemergence of the Democratic majority that we saw in the United States presidential election of 2008.

Notes

1. Author's analysis of data from Current Population Survey (CPS) and exit polls.
2. Author's analysis of 2006 exit polls from National Election Pool (NEP).
3. In 2009 the Census Bureau issued a set of projections that are "supplemental" to the 2008 projections. What this means is that even though the 2008 projections remain the recommended data series for general use, the 2009 supplemental projections can be used to assess the effects of different immigration scenarios on future population levels and distribution. Of the scenarios provided, the "low net international migration," or low NIM, which projects the number of immigrants per year to increase slowly to 2050, is fairly close to the original 2008 projections and quite similar to the projections produced by the demographers Jeffrey Passel and D'Vera Cohen for the Pew Research Center ("US Population Projections: 2005–2050," 11 February 2008), based on a constant *rate* of immigration relative to population size. The low NIM scenario puts the majority-minority crossover point at 2045. Some argue that the constant NIM scenario (under which the number of immigrants per year remains constant to the year

2050) should be preferred, since it corresponds well to the recent experience of the United States with immigrant flows (see William Frey, "Immigration and the Coming 'Majority Minority,'" Brookings Institution, 19 March 2010). The constant NIM scenario has a majority-minority crossover date of 2050, corresponding to the date frequently cited in popular accounts of rising diversity.

4. See Ruy Teixeira, http://www.emergingdemocraticmajorityweblog.com/donkey rising/archives/001234.php, for references and discussion.

5. Author's analysis of 2004 NEP national exit polls.

6. If you do an apples-to-apples comparison of data; see Ruy Teixeira, http://www .emergingdemocraticmajorityweblog.com/donkeyrising/archives/001227.php, for analysis and discussion.

7. Author's analysis of data from Current Population Survey (CPS) and exit polls.

8. Author's analysis of 2000–2006 exit polls.

9. Author's analysis of data from CPS and exit polls and Frey, "Immigration and the Coming 'Majority Minority.'"

10. Figures in this and next paragraph based on author's analysis of 2004 NEP exit polls.

11. Author's analysis of 2004 NEP exit polls.

12. Author's analysis of 2006 NEP exit polls.

13. Author's analysis of census data on marital status.

14. Ibid.

15. Author's analysis of census data on educational attainment.

16. Author's analysis of 1960–2004 National Election Study.

17. Author's analysis of 2006 NEP exit polls.

18. Bureau of Labor Statistics occupational projections.

19. Judis and Teixeira (2002); author's analysis of 2004 National Election Study.

20. All data in this and subsequent paragraph from author's analysis of census population projections.

21. Author's analysis of 2008 census national population projections, 2008 national NEP exit poll and 2004 Current Population Survey voter supplement data.

22. Author's analysis of 2002–2006 exit polls.

23. Author's analysis of 2006 NEP exit polls.

24. Author's analysis of 2004 NEP exit polls, except for the figure on Jews, which is taken from Mellman, Strauss, Greenberg, McCreesh, and Wald, "The Jewish Vote in 2004."

25. Author's analysis of data from 2006 NEP exit polls.

26. Author's analysis of 2004 NEP exit polls.

27. Author's analysis of 2006 NEP exit polls.

28. Data in this and following paragraph from author's analysis of 1940 census and 2007 Current Population Survey Annual Social and Economic Supplement.

29. This and following paragraph based on author's analysis of 1940 census and 2006 American Community Survey occupation data.

30. This and following paragraph based on author's analysis of 1947 and 2005 Current Population Survey Annual Social and Economic Supplement income data.

31. Author's analysis of 1940 census and 2007 Current Population Survey Annual Social and Economic Supplement education data.

32. Data in this and following paragraph are conservative extrapolations from Teixeira and Rogers 2000, 16–17.

33. Data in this paragraph from author's analysis of 1992 and 1996 Voter News Service (VNS) national exit polls.

34. Data in this paragraph from author's analysis of 2000 VNS and 2004 NEP national exit polls.

35. Data in this paragraph from author's analysis of 2004 NEP national exit polls.

36. All data in this paragraph from author's analysis of 2006 NEP national exit polls.

37. This and following paragraph based on author's analysis of 1947–2005 Current Population Survey Annual Social and Economic Supplement income data.

38. This paragraph based on author's analysis of 1940–2000 census data and 2007 Current Population Survey Annual Social and Economic Supplement education data; author's analysis of 1940 census data and 2006 American Community Survey occupation data; and author's analysis of 1947–2005 Current Population Survey Annual Social and Economic Supplement income data.

Party Politics and the
American Welfare State

Christopher Howard

Including the United States in this book may strike some readers as odd. If one aim is to chart the transformation of left parties into center-left parties, why study a polity that has never had much of a left? For years scholars have been analyzing the sources and symptoms of "American exceptionalism." Their central question, posed and answered in different ways, has involved the weakness of left-wing organizations and ideology (e.g., Kingdon 1999; Lipset and Marks 2000; Sombart 1976 [1906]). The best showing of any United States socialist party in national elections was a meager 6% of the vote—and that was way back in 1912. The power of organized labor was never great to begin with and declined throughout the second half of the twentieth century. The size of government, measured by public spending as a share of GDP, has consistently been smaller in the United States than in Europe. When socialism collapsed across Eastern Europe and the Soviet Union broke apart, the dominant reaction in the United States was a feeling of vindication, not loss. In the context of this book, it would seem to make more sense to focus on countries such as Sweden, Germany, France, and the United Kingdom, which several authors do.

Nevertheless, there are compelling reasons to investigate the American case. As the editors note in their introductory chapter, the United States is hardly sui generis. Lower union membership, the shift from manufacturing to services, the decline of Keynesianism and rise of neoliberalism, and new styles of political campaigns are evident on both sides of the Atlantic. The "new social risks" discussed by Jenson (this volume)—rooted in longer life expectancy, higher rates of female employment, and more single-parent families—affect millions of people in the United States as well as in the countries she analyzes. Policies long established in the United States, such as means-testing of benefits and the use of market mechanisms in healthcare, are becoming more common in Europe. As we shall see, recent trends in social spending, poverty, and inequality are also similar in the United States and Europe. In short, we should not exaggerate American exceptionalism.

In some respects the United States is a good choice for a case study. It is one thing to argue that certain forces have moved social democratic and labor parties toward the center. If those same forces affect the Democratic Party, which occupies the left in the United States but would be center-left almost anywhere in Europe, then they must be powerful indeed. Readers who wonder where the European left could be heading may consider the American experience a useful roadmap—or a cautionary tale.

The welfare state is a major component of the modern state, and how officials treat their welfare states tells us much about how they govern. In this chapter I will indicate how Democratic officials have changed their approach to the American welfare state in recent decades. When creating new programs Democrats have gravitated away from social insurance and toward tax expenditures and social regulations. While protecting some programs, especially those for the elderly, they have helped retrench programs for the poor. The net effect has been a bigger American welfare state. That is what a classic left-wing party is supposed to accomplish. And yet these changes have made it harder, not easier, to reduce poverty and inequality. "Doing more, achieving less" captures the current state of United States social policy.

To understand these developments we cannot focus solely on the Democrats. We also need to pay close attention to the Republican Party. When the American welfare state was established between the 1930s and 1960s, Republicans were clearly the minority party. Not anymore. Republicans have made important gains politically, winning five of the last eight presidential elections. Since 1980 they have controlled at least one house of Congress two-thirds of the time (Stanley and Niemi 2008). Without some cooperation from Republicans, the story would have been gridlock. Cooperation meant more than simple acquiescence; at times Republican leaders took the lead in enacting social programs and shifting the distribution of social benefits.

Because this book covers so much territory historically and geographically, readers may be unfamiliar with the specific details of individual countries. The beginning of this chapter presents, as quickly as possible, some of the significant moments and trends in United States social policy since 1975. This information will help readers to understand what happened before we consider how and why. The basic point is that the American welfare state is doing more but accomplishing less than it did in the immediate postwar era. This chapter then analyzes the role of Democrats and Republicans in reshaping United States social policy. Neither party acted in a vacuum; signals from the general public and from voters encouraged elected officials to find common ground.

The Contemporary American Welfare State

Scholars generally agree that the three decades following the Second World War were a golden age for welfare states. Across Europe and North America new social programs were enacted and existing programs expanded. Government social spending increased dramatically. Poverty and inequality diminished. At the same time, the power of left-wing political parties was relatively high, leading many scholars to link the remarkable growth of welfare states to the ascendance of these parties (Esping-Andersen 1985; Huber and Stephens 2001; Shalev 1983). The United States was no exception. Although Social Security was created in 1935, it did not become an important source of retirement income until the 1950s, and it experienced rapid growth in the 1960s and early 1970s. Disability insurance started in the 1950s; Medicare, Medicaid, and Food Stamps all originated in the 1960s. "Welfare," meaning income support for poor, single-parent families, grew rapidly in the 1960s and 1970s. The nation cut the poverty rate almost in half (from 22.2% to 12.3%) between 1960 and 1975.[1] Income inequality fell sharply around the time of the Second World War, and the share of national income controlled by the richest 1% dropped gradually in the 1950s and 1960s. This was an era when Democrats ruled Congress and Democratic presidents such as Lyndon Johnson made bold pronouncements about eradicating poverty and building a Great Society (Berkowitz 1991; DeNavas-Walt, Proctor, and Smith 2007; Derthick 1979; Howard 2007a; Piketty and Saez 2003).

Scholars sharply disagree over what has happened since the mid-1970s. At one end of the spectrum we find references to various crises of the welfare state—fiscal, political, ideological (Kotlikoff and Burns 2004; Mishra 1984; Offe 1984; Stoesz and Karger 1992). Less ominously, several studies find evidence of retrenchment as countries tightened eligibility for social programs, lowered benefits, and introduced forms of privatization (Allan and Scruggs 2004; Clayton and Pontusson 1998; Huber and Stephens 2001; Korpi and Palme 2003; Pontusson 2005a). Or retrenchment occurred indirectly as governments failed to address growing social needs (Hacker 2004; Taylor-Gooby ed. 2004). Other scholars are more optimistic and stress the resilience of modern welfare states. "Thus in most of the affluent democracies, the politics of social policy centers on the renegotiation, restructuring, and modernization of the terms of the post-war social contract rather than its dismantling" (Pierson 2002, 370; see also Brooks and Manza 2007; Pierson 1996; Wilensky 2002).[2]

While the American welfare state never reached the crisis stage, there certainly were episodes of retrenchment. The most prominent cutbacks came in 1996, when officials replaced Aid to Families with Dependent Children (AFDC), a core "welfare" program, with Temporary Assistance for Needy Families (TANF). This was not a simple one-for-one exchange: AFDC was a budgetary entitlement, but spending on TANF was capped; AFDC imposed no time limit on recipients, but TANF did. The goal was clearly to reduce government support for poor families with children. The current TANF caseload is less than half the size of the AFDC caseload circa 1996. This same bill included large cuts to the means-tested Food Stamps and Supplemental Security Income programs, most of them affecting recent immigrants. Other social programs were cut less dramatically. Officials increased the normal retirement age for Social Security from sixty-five to sixty-seven, which reduced the number of years that people can collect benefits. It became more difficult to qualify for disability insurance in the 1980s (Howard 2007a; Weaver 2000). The best example of outright termination occurred in 1981. As officials were cutting the budgets of several social programs, they completely eliminated public service employment (PSE). At its peak in the late 1970s PSE employed 725,000 people. Many of these people were teenagers and racial minorities who had great difficulty finding jobs in the private sector (Mucciaroni 1990).[3]

Nevertheless, for every cutback or termination there was at least one expansion. Social Security, Medicare, and Medicaid became three of the largest items in the national budget. All these programs benefited the elderly, which helps to explain why the poverty rate for senior citizens continued to decline after 1975 (DeNavas-Walt, Proctor, and Smith 2007). And the United States continued to create social programs. Several of these addressed the "new social risks" discussed by Jenson (this volume), such as the spread of low-wage work and the plight of children. The Earned Income Tax Credit (EITC), enacted in 1975, provides income support to millions of low-income Americans, especially those with dependent children. The primary objective of the EITC is to "make work pay" by providing subsidies to taxpayers who earn income from employment.[4] The Child Tax Credit (1997) benefits millions more families with children and is not means-tested. These two tax credits cost the United States government over $100 billion in forgone revenues and tax refunds in 2009 (U.S. Congress, Joint Committee on Taxation, 2010). To put this figure in perspective, it was greater than what the government spent on TANF, Food Stamps, and public housing combined. Another new policy designed to help parents balance work and family was the Family and Medical Leave Act (FMLA), enacted in 1993. The FMLA mandated twelve weeks of parental leave, a first for the nation.

With so many Americans uninsured or underinsured, the United States has had many opportunities to innovate in healthcare. The Consolidated Omnibus Budget Reconciliation Act (COBRA, 1986), was designed to make health insurance more portable for those who were between jobs. A second law, the Health Insurance Portability and Accountability Act (HIPAA, 1996), was supposed to make it harder for private insurers to deny coverage to people with preexisting medical conditions. The Emergency Medical Treatment and Labor Act (1986) compelled virtually every hospital to provide emergency care to all patients, even those without health insurance. In addition, new spending programs took root. The State Children's Health Insurance Program (SCHIP, later renamed CHIP) was enacted in 1997. The goal of this new block grant was to extend health insurance to low-income children, especially those from families with incomes too high for the existing Medicaid program. Congress approved a large prescription drug benefit for the elderly in 2003. Annual spending for this benefit is soon expected to exceed $50 billion (Henry J. Kaiser Family Foundation 2008; Howard 2007a).[5] These episodes lacked the drama of the attempted Clinton health plan, but they were clearly important. And then, of course, historic changes to health policy were enacted in 2010. Over time the ranks of the uninsured are expected to drop substantially (but not disappear), and costs are expected to rise more slowly. I will have more to say about this episode later in the chapter.

Apart from these new social programs, the other major breakthrough occurred in disability policy. The Americans with Disabilities Act (ADA) became law in 1990. It compelled innumerable public agencies and private businesses to make greater accommodations for their disabled customers and employees. As with COBRA, HIPAA, and the FMLA, the United States government tried to effect social change without spending taxpayers' dollars.

The net result of retrenchment and expansion has been growth. Measured by the number of social programs, the American welfare state is larger now than it was thirty years ago. Trends in social spending tell the same story. According to the Organisation for Economic Cooperation and Development (OECD), the United States devoted 13.1% of GDP to its welfare state in 1980. This is what most studies refer to as a nation's "welfare state effort," and it includes public spending at all levels of government. By 2005, the most recent year for which figures are available, that figure had risen to 15.9%. We see similar trends in other affluent democracies. The Canadian welfare state grew from 13.7% to 16.5% of GDP during this same era. The OECD average rose from 16.0% to 20.6% of GDP between 1980 and 2005 (OECD n.d.; OECD 2007a).[6]

These figures actually understate the true level of social spending because they omit a variety of tax expenditures, or what the OECD calls tax breaks for social purposes (TBSPs). Tax expenditures refer to a variety of exceptions to the normal tax code such as tax credits and tax deductions. Many countries have created special provisions in their tax codes to address a variety of social problems, and this indirect spending deserves to be counted just as much as traditional forms of direct spending do. Tax expenditures have been quite common in the United States. Besides the Earned Income Tax Credit and the Child Tax Credit, notable examples include tax breaks for employer-provided pensions and health insurance, and the home mortgage interest deduction. Since 1980 the largest of these tax expenditures have grown faster than traditional forms of social spending. Tax expenditures helped fuel the growth of the American welfare state (Adema and Ladaique 2005; Howard 2007b).

Such growth was impressive on several counts. It occurred even as the growth in overall government spending was negative or close to zero in many OECD countries. Thus the welfare state has accounted for a gradually increasing share of government spending in the United States and abroad. One might argue that this growth simply reflected greater social needs, particularly the aging of the population. Castles (2004) has calculated the ratio of social spending to dependents—defined as people over the age of sixty-five plus all working-age adults who are unemployed—and found that the United States spent more per dependent in 1998 than it did in 1980. If one creates a comparable ratio for social spending and the poverty population, the story remains the same: the ratio is larger now than it was a quarter-century ago. For the entire population, real social spending per capita has also increased substantially in the United States since 1980. Finally, one might ask whether the rapid growth in medical costs has been largely responsible for the growth in social spending. It certainly has played a part, but the public share of total health spending in the United States has grown too (OECD 2007b). Changes to Medicaid and the creation of SCHIP helped to increase the government's role in paying for medical care. The new drug benefit for the elderly will help sustain this trend.

Nevertheless, despite this growth the American welfare state has apparently lost its ability to fight poverty and inequality. Since the mid-1970s the poverty rate has fluctuated between 11% and 15%, depending on the economy. Although the rate was the same in 1975 and 2006, the United States economy was just pulling out of recession in 1975, whereas recovery from the 2001 recession was well under way by 2006. Severe poverty, meaning income of less than half the poverty line, increased from 3.7% to 5.2% of the population between 1975 and 2006. In addition, income inequality has been worsening. The most common indicator is the Gini coefficient, which ranges from 0 (total equality) to 1 (total inequality, i.e., one person has all the income). According to the Luxembourg Income Study, the Gini coefficient in the United States was 0.318 in 1974. By 2004 it had risen to 0.372. The U.S. Census Bureau, using a different methodology, calculated that the Gini coefficient moved from 0.395 to 0.470 during this period.[7] The richest one-fifth of the nation controlled 50% of national income in 2006, up from 44% in 1975. The richest of the rich saw their incomes grow even faster (DeNavas-Walt, Proctor, and Smith 2007; Luxembourg Income Study n.d.; Piketty and Saez 2003; U.S. Bureau of the Census n.d.).[8]

The United States has not been the only country experiencing difficulties. Income inequality has grown in Australia, Canada, Germany, Italy, Norway, Sweden, and the United Kingdom in recent decades. Poverty rates have remained constant or slightly increased in a number of wealthy democracies (Kenworthy 2008; Luxembourg Income Study n.d.). The combination of spending more on social welfare and achieving less has thus become more common among nations. This insight may help reconcile some of the conflicting judgments discussed earlier in this chapter. Crisis, retrenchment, and resilience may depend on which features of the welfare state are being studied.

It is quite possible that the American welfare state has been doing more and accomplishing less because the United States economy has been generating more poverty and inequality than it used to do. To test this argument we need to know how much money people had before taxes and government transfers, or what are sometimes referred to as "market poverty" and "market inequality." Market poverty rates have gradually increased and decreased in recent decades, with no clear upward trend. Market inequality, on the other hand, has definitely increased (Kenworthy 2008; U.S. Bureau of the Census 1992; U.S. Bureau of the Census 2001; U.S. Bureau of the Census 2007). We might conclude that changes in the United States economy have been widening the gap between rich and poor, and that public policy has been slow to adapt (Hacker 2004).

While true, and important, this conclusion leads us to focus on government inaction, and yet we know that the United States has been creating a number of new social programs and increasing social spending. Elected officials have not ignored the plight of citizens trying to afford healthcare and balance the demands of work and family. Officials have tried to help some of these people—particularly those in the middle and upper middle classes. Recent laws designed to shore up private health insurance (COBRA and HIPAA) have helped workers who have such insurance, who tend to be well-educated professionals, union members, and public employees. The Family and Medical Leave Act had a large exemption for small businesses, whose workers tend to have less education and lower incomes. Moreover, because the FMLA only required unpaid parental leave, it has provided more help to families that can afford to live without a paycheck. Similarly, families earning over $50,000 have been the main beneficiaries of the new Child Tax Credit (Howard 2007a; Howard 2007b; U.S. Congress, Joint Committee on Taxation, 2010). Such policies are a good way to expand a welfare state without making much progress against poverty or inequality.

A number of older social programs fit this same profile. The clearest evidence comes from the largest tax expenditures. The United States tax code has provided a huge and growing subsidy for private pensions (roughly $100 billion a year). On average, one-half of United States workers participated in some sort of tax-favored retirement plan in 2003. But averages can be deceiving. The participation rates ranged from 20% for workers earning less than $20,000 to 80% for workers earning over $120,000. Higher-income workers also contributed more to their plans and thus received a larger per capita subsidy from the government (Congressional Budget Office 2007). Sheils and Haught (2004) have calculated that tax breaks for private health insurance were worth ten times more to a family earning over $100,000 than to a family earning less than $20,000. Taxpayers earning over $100,000 claimed three-quarters of the value of the home mortgage interest deduction, the nation's largest housing program (U.S. Congress, Joint Committee on Taxation, 2010). Considering that homes are the largest single asset for many families, this tax break exacerbates inequalities in wealth.

Tax expenditures are sometimes criticized for redistributing income from poor to rich, but that is not entirely accurate. Few Americans earning less than $40,000 a year pay any income taxes. Whatever they owe is offset by the standard deduction, personal exemptions, and the Earned Income Tax Credit. Overwhelmingly, income taxes are paid by the upper middle class and the rich, people earning over $100,000 (U.S. Congress, Joint Committee on Taxation, 2010). The individual income tax is one of the more progressive taxes in the United States—certainly more progressive than payroll taxes or sales taxes. As a result, any deductions, exemptions, or credits are usually worth more to people in the higher tax brackets. Someone in the 28% tax bracket who puts $1,000 in a 401(k) pension plan will benefit more than someone in the 15% bracket who puts away the same amount of money. This example helps to explain why major tax expenditures for health, housing, and pensions are skewed toward the more affluent. Another reason for the skew is that these same people can afford to buy bigger homes and save more for retirement. Thus to the extent that tax expenditures redistribute income, most of the impact is limited to the upper half of the income distribution. Tax expenditures help the haves from falling farther behind the have-lots.

While social policy in recent decades has favored the middle and upper middle classes, less affluent Americans have not fared so well. The lives of low-income children hardly improved. True, they were helped by the expansion of Medicaid, the creation of SCHIP, and the remarkable growth of the Earned Income Tax Credit.[9] Greater access to public health insurance helped to offset the decline of private health insurance, but the rate of uninsured children was basically the same in 2001 as it had been in 1977 (Cunningham and Kirby 2004). The EITC helped millions of families among the working poor, and its expansion in the 1990s coincided with a meaningful decline in the child poverty rate. Still, the rate was essentially the same in 2005 as 1975 (DeNavas-Walt, Proctor, and Smith 2007). The nonworking poor have been the big losers. They were the ones who were kicked off welfare after 1996. They were the ones who watched the value of welfare and unemployment benefits gradually erode in the face of inflation.[10] They were the ones who could not qualify for unemployment benefits because they worked part-time or had been employed only a short time before being laid off (Graetz and Mashaw 1999). Recent immigrants also found it more difficult to get benefits. In many ways the United States safety net has been compromised. Little wonder that poverty stopped declining and severe poverty has been on the rise.

Party Politics and Social Policy

Since the 1970s divided government has been the norm in the United States. One might suspect that "doing more, achieving less" represented a compromise between the two parties: Democrats enacted new programs and increased social spending, while Republicans made sure that government expansion did little to reduce poverty or inequality. The reality turns out to be more complicated. Consider recent legislative milestones. The Clinton administration signed off on the Family and Medical Leave Act, new HIPAA regulations, and the Child Tax Credit, which was exactly what we would expect Democrats to do. But a number of social programs were enacted during Republican administrations. President Ford signed the Earned Income Tax Credit into law. The first President Bush and a number of congressional Republicans pushed for the Americans with Disabilities Act. After the ADA was enacted, Bush referred to it several times as one of the crowning achievements of his administration. An early version of the Child Tax Credit appeared in the GOP Contract with America. President George W. Bush was instrumental in passing the new drug benefit for senior citizens (Howard 2007a).[11] These programs were every bit as important as those passed under Clinton.

By the same token, Clinton's health plan went down to defeat even though Democrats controlled the White House and both houses of Congress. Although President Reagan cut or eliminated several means-tested programs in 1981, the welfare reform law signed by President Clinton in 1996 was arguably more severe. It was Clinton, after all, who promised to "end welfare as we know it." Republicans also defended certain social programs against cutbacks, especially the sizable tax breaks for health insurance, retirement pensions, and housing (Howard 1997; Howard 2007a). When Ronald Reagan signed the Tax Reform Act of 1986, which included the first major increase to the Earned Income Tax Credit, he publicly declared the EITC to be "the best antipoverty bill, the best profamily measure, and the best job-creation program ever to come out of the Congress."[12]

Trends in social spending have also been confusing. The nation's welfare state effort declined during the Reagan administration. That was no surprise. But it also declined under Clinton. Thank goodness for the Bush family. Social spending increased during the father's administration and the son's first term, and those gains more than offset what happened under Reagan and Clinton. Spending also grew during President Carter's time in office (OECD n.d.; OECD 1985; OECD 2007a).

Democratic administrations have performed somewhat better than their Republican counterparts on key social indicators. The poverty rate reached a lower point under Carter (11.4%) and Clinton (11.3%) than it ever did under Reagan (13.0%), George H. W. Bush (12.8%), or George W. Bush (11.7%). Of all these presidents only Clinton made any real progress against poverty. Analyzing the distribution of income between 1948 and 2001, Bartels (2004) has shown that inequality grew considerably faster when Republicans were in the White House. While this pattern held true for the entire postwar era, it was less pronounced after 1975. As measured by the Gini index, inequality was basically unchanged under Carter and actually increased a bit under Clinton (Democrats made a bigger dent in inequality under Presidents Kennedy and Johnson). Inequality has definitely grown under the three most recent Republican administrations (DeNavas-Walt, Proctor, and Smith 2007).

Thus it appears to be the responsibility of both political parties that the American welfare state is "doing more" and "achieving less." A closer look at public opinion and elections will help us to understand why the two parties converged enough to make meaningful changes to social policy. Over the last few decades opinion surveys have sent a clear and consistent message: Americans want their government to play a central role in social welfare, and in most cases that means spending more, not less. The main exceptions are welfare, which most Americans dislike, and unemployment benefits, which trigger mixed feelings. The biggest pieces of the welfare state—retirement pensions and healthcare—receive strong backing (Gilens 1999; Howard 2007a).

Although support has been stronger among self-identified Democrats, most Republicans also expect government to help the elderly, the sick, and the poor. When Republicans made history by capturing both houses of Congress in 1994, a large majority of people who called themselves strong Republicans said that current spending on Social Security was either too little (43%) or about right (44%). When President George W. Bush was reelected in 2004 Republican support for Social Security was, if anything, a little higher. Moreover, a majority of Republicans in 2004 said that too little was being spent on education and health. Only one of eight Republicans felt that too much was being spent to help the poor.[13] Republican officials may have wanted to slow the growth of the American welfare state, but they risked alienating their core supporters if they tried to shrink it.

Americans did not, however, want officials to expand the welfare state in any manner that they pleased. Most Americans, regardless of party affiliation, appeared to offer little support for redistributing income from rich to poor. And most Americans, regardless of party affiliation, did not trust their government very much. In this environment anyone pushing for a guaranteed income or national health insurance was going to be rebuffed. Relying on what are known as "tax expenditures" and social regulations was the better way to go. Tax expenditures usually relied on individuals and businesses to provide the desired goods and services and to complete the necessary forms. Social regulations likewise tried to harness the private sector to fulfill social objectives. Neither policy tool, as discussed above, did much to narrow the gap between rich and poor (Howard 2007a).

Of course public opinion in general may matter less than the views of those who actually vote. The American electorate does not, in fact, look like the American public. With turnout running between 55% and 60% in presidential elections, and around 40% in off-year elections, lots of Americans are not voting. They are disproportionately less educated and of lower income. In the election of 2004, for instance, almost three-fourths of college graduates reported voting, compared to only one-third of high school dropouts. People earning less than $15,000 represented 14% of the population but only 8% of actual voters (DeNavas-Walt, Proctor, and Smith 2007; Stanley and Niemi 2008).[14] Voting is not unique in this regard. Other indicators of political participation—campaigning, donating money, contacting officials, and belonging to interest groups—all increase with income, education, and age (Campbell 2003; Jacobs and Skocpol eds. 2005; Verba, Schlozman, and Brady 1995). Moreover, inequalities in political participation appear to be widening. According to data collected by National Election Studies, the gaps in voter turnout are growing larger between voters with high and low levels of education, and high and low incomes.[15]

During the late twentieth century and the early twenty-first, a period when the two parties were so evenly matched and control of government changed so frequently, Democrats and Republicans worked consistently to expand social benefits for the politically strong and periodically to retrench programs for the politically weak. Members of both parties protected tax breaks for housing, healthcare, and pensions, all of which were targeted at the more affluent members of society. Clinton wanted the Child Tax Credit to show middle- and upper-middle-class families that the Democratic Party had not forgotten them. Bush wanted the new drug benefit to show that Democrats were not the only ones who cared about senior citizens. Members of both parties pushed welfare reform to show middle-class voters that welfare dependence among the poor would no longer be tolerated. Democratic and Republican officials thus had similar reasons for expanding the American welfare state and for not pushing hard to reduce poverty and inequality. They had middle- and upper-middle-class constituents to satisfy. They could help those constituents pay for health insurance, save for retirement, purchase child care, and buy a home—in effect, to achieve the American Dream.[16] Other factors, specific to each party, also moved them in this direction.

Democrats

In several respects the Democratic vision of social policy has changed since the 1960s. More accurately, the views of many Democratic officials have moderated. The party is still so large and diverse that broad generalizations are hard to make; some contemporary Democrats would have been quite at home in the days of the New Deal and the Great Society. For the most part, though, the current generation of party leaders has stressed equality of opportunity over result, economic growth over redistribution, and work over welfare. They have preached fiscal discipline and become more concerned about deficits (Baer 2000; Pierson 1998; Shoch 2008).[17] One should not exaggerate the extent of change. The New Deal relied on a combination of work programs and cash relief. The Economic Opportunity Act of 1964 was one of the milestones of the Great Society.[18] In historical perspective, recent changes in the Democratic Party have been modest but meaningful.

One key change has been the choice of policy tools used to remedy social problems. During the New Deal and Great Society the main tools were social insurance, financed by payroll taxes, and grants, financed by general revenues. Democrats since the 1970s have shied away from payroll tax financing. Clinton officials used all kinds of mechanisms to fund health reform—higher tobacco taxes, administrative savings, contingent caps on insurance premiums, and a complicated set of charges on employers—but not payroll taxes (Skocpol 1996). More recently, while congressional Democrats objected to several features of Bush's proposed drug benefit for the elderly, few wanted to rely on payroll taxes rather than the combination of general revenues and monthly premiums that eventually passed. Faced with problems in existing social insurance programs, few Democrats proposed a general increase in payroll taxes. When the Social Security trust fund started to run dangerously low in the early 1980s, the main answer was to increase the retirement age. When Medicare experienced financial troubles, the main answer was to limit reimbursements to doctors and hospitals (Oberlander 2003).

This shift was part of a larger change in policy discourse (Campbell and Morgan 2005). Since the 1970s conservatives in the United States have been increasingly successful at focusing policy debates on the question of financing. "Who pays?" became just as salient a question as "Who benefits?" In this context liberals grew concerned about the regressive nature of existing payroll taxes and their impact on lower- and middle-income families. As a result, many Democratic officials came to view payroll taxes as unfair. The heavy focus on taxes obscured the impact of benefits, which in social insurance programs like Social Security clearly favor lower-income workers. With payroll taxes marginalized, "the American welfare state lost a major source of financing, stymieing redistributive initiatives for decades to come" (Campbell and Morgan, 2005, 180).

Instead Democrats embraced policy tools whose costs were less evident. Tax expenditures gained favor because they looked as much like tax cuts as spending. Democrats could (and did) say that the EITC and Child Tax Credit helped working families keep more of their hard-earned dollars. Tax expenditures have not figured prominently in official budget documents, a practice which obscures their cost. Social legislation such as the Americans with Disabilities Act and the Family and Medical Leave Act required businesses and individuals to change their behavior; their budgetary cost to the government was minimal. Instead of paying for parental leave the government told many employers to give their workers unpaid leave, and effectively told parents who wanted leave to find a way to live on less income. Instead of enacting national health insurance, the government tried to make private health insurance more widely available. As mentioned earlier in the chapter, many of these tax expenditures and social provisions benefited the haves more than the have-nots (Howard 2007a).

Democratic leaders also changed their approach to poverty. For one thing, their attention to the problem has diminished. Gerring (1998) analyzed Democratic presidential candidates' acceptance speeches and found that references to the poor and underprivileged peaked in the 1960s and then dropped off. Clinton's speech in 1992 barely mentioned poverty at all. In 1968 the official Democratic platform trumpeted the party's success in reducing poverty. It argued that the government's War on Poverty was working and should be expanded. The view from 1996 was far less sanguine: "Today's Democratic Party knows there is no greater gap between mainstream American values and modern American government than our failed welfare system. . . . Thanks to President Clinton and the Democrats, the new welfare bill imposes time limits and real work requirements—so anyone who *can* work, *does* work, and so that no one who can work can stay on welfare forever."[19] Tellingly, the discussion of welfare in 1996 appeared in the section of the platform titled "Responsibility," in which the Democrats also discussed crime and illegal immigration. Subsequent party platforms have reiterated the themes of work and individual responsibility when discussing poverty.

More than ever, Democrats came to believe that a strong economy was the best way to fight poverty. Democrats have wanted to keep unemployment low, interest rates low, and wages growing. Reducing the deficit was a key step in accomplishing these goals. Before President Clinton tried to reform healthcare or welfare, his first budget relied on a combination of tax increases and spending cuts to lower the deficit.

Nevertheless, Democratic officials knew that a rising economic tide would not lift all boats high enough or fast enough; targeted aid would still be needed. They proceeded to draw a bright line between the working poor, who would get additional money from the government, and the nonworking poor, who would get a stronger push to earn money. The Earned Income Tax Credit attracted considerable Democratic support and grew rapidly during the 1980s and 1990s. By definition the EITC benefits only those who work for wages. It now serves many more families than TANF and costs a lot more. At the same time, Democrats helped Republicans cut spending on traditional welfare programs, notably in 1981 and 1996. Democrats helped tighten eligibility rules and work requirements. They tried to collect more child support from absent parents. They shifted more spending away from income support and toward services such as childcare and transportation that would help welfare recipients find employment. The new measure of success was moving people off welfare, not out of poverty (Howard 2007a; Weaver 2000).

These changes were connected to the resurgence of the GOP and the emergence of the New Democrats (Baer 2000; Hale 1995). Republicans won both the presidency and the Senate in 1980, the first time in a generation that Democrats failed to control both houses of Congress. President Reagan won reelection in 1984 by a huge margin, capturing forty-nine states. In response a number of moderate and conservative Democrats joined forces to chart a new path. To become competitive again, these "New Democrats" wanted their party to shed its tax-and-spend image and promote a leaner, more efficient government. They wanted to shift responsibility away from Washington and toward lower levels of government, as well as toward businesses and individuals. New Democrats wanted to spend less time helping specific groups of disadvantaged citizens and more time helping the middle class, broadly defined. They talked often about the ability of economic growth to promote the American dream. This new vision would in theory appeal to a wider range of voters and enable the Democratic Party to win national elections more consistently. The creation of the Democratic Leadership Council and the Progressive Policy Institute gave New Democrats formal mechanisms for generating ideas and communicating with one another. Clinton's election and reelection gave them a president who shared many of their goals and managed to translate their vision into specific social programs. Al Gore and John Kerry did not depart from this vision when they campaigned for president in 2000 and 2004.[20]

Within Congress, however, were many traditional Democrats who still believed in the New Deal and Great Society. When Bill Clinton promised as a candidate to spend billions of additional dollars to improve the nation's infrastructure, these Democrats were hopeful. When Clinton as president failed to deliver, they were dismayed. Although Clinton felt that national health insurance along Canadian lines was a political non-starter, the liberal wing of his party disagreed and introduced single-payer legislation (Skocpol 1996). Traditional Democrats often viewed New Democrats with suspicion, if not hostility. The New Democrats, they argued, were turning their party into a watered-down version of the Republican Party.

Over the last few years the friction between new and old Democrats has diminished. Much of the credit belongs to George W. Bush, whose presidency helped Democrats realize that the differences among them were not nearly as important as the differences separating the two parties. To some degree, however, important elements of the New Democrats' creed have become accepted within the entire party. The Democrats now criticize the GOP for running deficits and expect new government programs to be deficit-neutral (except in a prolonged recession). After Democrats recaptured the House of Representatives in 2006, the incoming speaker, Nancy Pelosi, declared that "'Democrats understand the importance of a growing and vibrant economy.' . . . To be successful, 'you have to govern from the middle'" (Dunham 2006, 37; see also Scheiber 2007). The leading Democratic presidential candidates in 2008, Hillary Clinton and Barack Obama, proposed a number of new programs for healthcare, retirement pensions, housing, and education. Most of them relied to some degree on tax breaks. None of them qualified as social insurance.[21]

The Democrats' triumph in 2008 gave them united control over government for the first time since 1992. Obama had promised health reform on the campaign trail, and in his first year in office the new president started to deliver. He quickly approved a children's health insurance bill that President Bush had vetoed. He also expanded government's role in subsidizing health insurance for workers who had lost their jobs and their coverage. By far the biggest triumph came in 2010, as President Obama and congressional Democrats pushed through the largest changes to health policy since the Great Society. Given Republicans' unwillingness to cooperate, serious disagreements within the Democratic Party, and the loss of a key Senate seat after the death of Ted Kennedy (D-Mass.), failure was always a strong possibility. Nevertheless, the Democrats prevailed.

The health reform bill was as notable for what it did not do as what it did. The United States did not adopt a single-payer system similar to Canada's, and it did not even consider a national health service comparable to Great Britain's. It did not create a government insurance program to compete with private insurers, even though most liberal Democrats wanted this "public option." And it did not rely on any general increase in payroll taxes for funding. Instead health reform relied on a combination of regulations, tax breaks, and traditional spending to expand private and public health insurance. For example, it mandated that most individuals must buy health insurance, a step that some conservative think tanks and politicians had embraced years earlier. It prohibited insurers from denying coverage to people with preexisting medical conditions, or from imposing lifetime dollar limits on coverage. And it extended Medicaid to more low-income Americans. To pay for broader coverage the package relied on a variety of administrative reforms, limits on the growth of Medicare, new taxes on specific sectors in healthcare, and higher payroll taxes on the most affluent Americans (Kaiser Family Foundation 2010). According to the Congressional Budget Office, health reform should actually reduce the national deficit over the next decade, a feature that Democrats worked hard to achieve (Herszenhorn 2010). In all these ways the Democrats' approach to health reform in 2010 bore a stronger resemblance to President Clinton's plan than to President Johnson's.

Republicans

Hardly anyone is surprised to hear that President Reagan cut means-tested programs, or that congressional Republicans led by Newt Gingrich worked overtime to undermine Clinton's health plan and eliminate welfare as an entitlement. Republicans are supposed to be the party of limited government. The more interesting question is how the American welfare state managed to grow during a period when the Republican Party was strong and gaining power.

There were times when Republicans were simply outnumbered. For example, the first President Bush vetoed parental leave legislation twice. President Clinton made the issue one of his top priorities and, with the help of a Democratic Congress, enacted the Family and Medical Leave Act early in his administration. At other times, Republicans accepted measures to achieve modest expansion of the welfare state when they were coupled with other legislation that they strongly preferred; this is how the SCHIP health insurance program passed through a Republican Congress.

Nevertheless, as we have seen, Republican officials were important advocates of expansion on several occasions. In addition to the motives discussed previously, Republicans acted strategically. They expanded some parts of the American welfare state to keep other parts in check. The Earned Income Tax Credit was supposed to keep the poor off welfare and reduce pressure to increase the minimum wage. One of the primary motivations for the ADA was to make it easier for the disabled to work. In particular, the ADA would help people who could not meet the strict eligibility requirements of disability insurance yet clearly faced difficulties in the job market because of some handicap. Without the help of the ADA, many of these people might have had to rely on public assistance. Tax breaks for retirement pensions would slow the growth of Social Security. Tax breaks for employment-related health benefits, and government regulation of those benefits, would make national health insurance unnecessary (Howard 1997; Howard 2007a).

In short, many Republicans have been trying to build a different kind of welfare state, one focused heavily on work and benefits received through work. This goal has created opportunities for coalitions across party lines, especially with New Democrats. Those two groups could agree to block national health insurance, oppose increases in the minimum wage, abolish welfare "as we know it," slow (but not stop) the growth in entitlement spending, and use the tax code to make social policy. Nonetheless, that kind of welfare state was less capable of fighting poverty and inequality than one based more on social insurance and a reliable safety net.

Concluding Thoughts

This new bargain—do more, achieve less—may not strike readers as very desirable. True, the American welfare state does reduce poverty and inequality. It just does not do so as well as it did formerly, or as well as most other wealthy democracies do now. For policymakers here and abroad, the lesson may be to focus less on the level of social spending and more on the distribution of benefits. What this new bargain lacks in performance, however, it makes up for in political viability. Directing government aid to the middle and upper middle classes means helping the most active members of the polity. That is a smart strategy for practically any Democratic or Republican official.

Compared to other chapters in this book, my account emphasizes domestic influences on center-left parties. In the latter decades of the twentieth century Democratic officials changed their approach to social policy in response to election outcomes and public opinion. They largely abandoned social insurance, which has been the foundation of modern welfare states. Instead they embraced more indirect forms of assistance, especially tax expenditures and regulation, which required less obvious forms of government involvement than the old New Deal and Great Society model. They were more likely to declare war on welfare than war on poverty. This was neoliberalism American-style, and it often attracted support from Republicans.[22]

If history is any guide, the elections of 2008 mean that we should expect less poverty and inequality because Democrats are now in charge. The first two years of Obama's administration pointed in that direction. The American Recovery and Reinvestment Act of 2009 included a number of provisions aimed at lower- and middle-class citizens. This act expanded the scope of the Earned Income Tax Credit and increased its value; made the refundable part of the Child Tax Credit more widely available to poor families; exempted some unemployment benefits from income taxation; and created a Making Work Pay Tax Credit, designed to offset regressive payroll taxes. All these moves ran counter to the dominant trend in tax policy. They used the tax code to make social policy without directing most of the benefits to upper-income taxpayers. This same American Recovery and Reinvestment Act boosted traditional social spending as well, providing more money for unemployment benefits and Food Stamps. To a significant degree health reforms enacted in 2010 will use money from the rich to pay for health insurance for those with below-average incomes (Leonhardt 2010).

That said, we should not expect reductions in poverty and inequality to be immediate or large. Unemployment and poverty are again on the rise as the economy suffers its worst slump since the Great Depression. Income inequality remains high (DeNavas-Walt, Proctor, and Smith 2009). Much of what the Obama administration has accomplished will keep these problems from getting worse, but it is hard to expect more than a standoff in the near future. The president, for obvious reasons, is worried more about economic growth and unemployment, and so are ordinary Americans (Frank 2008, BU5).[23] Compounding these difficulties is a foreign policy agenda that is much more complicated—Afghanistan, Iraq, Libya, Iran, terrorism, international environmental agreements—than what President Clinton faced in the 1990s. Moreover, the electorate has not changed. Voters with above-average incomes divided their votes evenly between Obama and the Republican candidate, John McCain, in 2008; those with above-average incomes still made up the majority of voters in 2008. Those with below-average incomes voted Democratic by a 3:2 margin. The same basic patterns held for elections to the House of Representatives.[24]

The midterm elections of 2010 will make poverty and inequality even more difficult to address. Republicans took control of the House of Representatives and gained additional seats in the Senate. Their top priorities include preserving tax cuts for the rich, repealing parts or all of the 2008 health reform, and cutting social spending. As I write (December 2010), these Republicans seem less willing than their predecessors to compromise and less interested in creating alternative types of social programs. The differences between Democrats and Republicans, at least in Congress, will be stark. There have been periods of divided government in the United States when officials managed to make progress in fighting poverty and inequality; this does not appear to be one of them.

Notes

This is a revised version of a paper that I presented at the conference "What's Left of the Left? Liberalism and Social Democracy in a Globalized World" at the Center for European Studies, Harvard University, in May 2008. Many thanks to Andrea Campbell, Jim Cronin, Jane Jenson, Jonas Pontusson, and Jim Shoch for their helpful suggestions and comments.

   1. The postwar low was 11.1%, in 1973.

2. Considering that scholars differ about what happened in recent decades, it is not too surprising that they disagree about why as well. While some believe that political parties are still central to the development of welfare states (Allan and Scruggs 2004; Korpi and Palme 2003), others argue that interest groups (Pierson 1996), changes in the global economy (Mishra 1999), demographic pressures (Kotlikoff and Burns 2004), or public opinion (Brooks and Manza 2007) have become equally if not more significant.

3. This was not the first time that social programs had been terminated. A number of public jobs programs created during the New Deal, whose collective impact was far greater than PSE, were phased out in the 1940s (Amenta 1998).

4. The creation and expansion of the EITC might be considered evidence of the impact of globalization on United States social policy. Greater competition from firms overseas may have depressed wages and created more members of the working poor. Nevertheless, a large number of EITC recipients work in service industries (e.g., fast-food restaurants, hotels), which do not have much foreign competition. Moreover, policymakers linked the EITC to domestic issues such as escalating welfare rolls, increasing payroll taxes, and the minimum wage (Howard 1997; Howard 2007a).

5. Following Jenson (this volume), one might say that the addition of the Medicare drug benefit also qualifies as a "new social need," considering that prescription drugs were a growing expense for the elderly, driven by changes in medical treatment and longer life expectancies.

6. Although the OECD tracks social spending back to at least 1960, the categories used before 1980 are not entirely comparable with those after 1980 (OECD 1985).

7. Unless otherwise noted, all references to income inequality in this chapter are based on disposable income, after taxes and transfers.

8. While most of the debate over inequality has focused on income, differences in wealth have been much larger. The richest one-fifth of United States households controlled almost 85% of the nation's wealth in 2004, while the richest 1% controlled over one-third of all wealth. Like income, wealth has become more concentrated. The Gini coefficient for net worth was already an astonishing 0.799 in 1983, and it rose to 0.829 by 2004 (Wolff 2007).

9. The EITC is unusual among tax provisions in that eligibility is limited to low-income families and the benefits are refundable, meaning that taxpayers with zero tax liability can still benefit. It proves that tax expenditures do not have to benefit the more affluent.

10. Single-parent families are often considered a "new social need" in Europe. Such families have long been helped in the United States, dating back at least as far as Aid to Dependent Children (1935). Public policies helping two-parent families, such as the Earned Income Tax Credit and Child Tax Credit, are more recent.

11. Education is sometimes considered part of the welfare state and sometimes not. It is worth noting that President George W. Bush pushed for the No Child Left Behind Act partly because he felt that reducing educational inequalities would later reduce poverty and income inequality.

12. Reagan's comments can be viewed online at www.presidency.ucsb.edu/ws/index.php?pid=36629&st=&st1=.

13. These figures are based on responses to the General Social Survey, which can be accessed at http://sda.berkeley.edu/archive.htm.

14. For more evidence of the growing importance of professionals to the Democratic Party see the chapter by Teixeira in this volume.

15. See table 6A.2 ("Voter Turnout") at www.electionstudies.org/nesguide/nesguide.htm.

16. I am assuming that such concerns would be highly salient to voters, which would prompt the two parties, even if ideologically polarized, to work toward some compromise (see, e.g., Binder 2003).

17. While this chapter features general trends more than single events, it is worth noting that both Pierson (1998) and Shoch (2008) point to Ross Perot's impressive showing as an independent candidate in 1992 as a main reason why President Clinton and other Democrats became much more concerned about the deficit.

18. The act created Head Start and the Job Corps, designed to improve human capital and ultimately the performance of American workers.

19. Democratic Party platforms can be accessed at www.presidency.ucsb.edu/platforms.php.

20. Bertram (2007) shows that the conservative wing of the Democratic Party started to reshape antipoverty policies away from welfare and toward work starting in the early 1970s.

21. For a useful summary of the candidates' tax policies go to http://www.taxpolicycenter.org/tpccontent/tax_plan_matrix15a.pdf.

22. I agree with Huber and Stephens that globalization does not seem to have exerted a major influence on the American welfare state. As a general rule, countries that are more closely integrated into the world economy find themselves more vulnerable to unemployment (e.g., when demand for their exports drops). During the last decades of the twentieth century the authors "found that the immediate cause of welfare state retrenchment was a large and apparently permanent increase in unemployment. With more people dependent on welfare state transfers and fewer people paying taxes to support the welfare state, budget deficits ballooned and governments moved to control and then reduce deficits by cutting entitlements" (Huber and Stephens 2001, 2). The pattern in the United States has been the opposite: although unemployment declined during Reagan's and Clinton's administrations, so too did welfare state effort; as unemployment increased during the first Bush administration, so did welfare state effort. Moreover, spending cuts in the United States have been targeted at means-tested programs while the major entitlements have largely been spared. I am not saying that the impact of globalization should always be downplayed. There may well be policy domains in the United States (Shoch, this volume) or overseas (Ross, this volume) where changes in the global economy matter a great deal. But changes in major United States social programs do appear to have been driven more by domestic influences such as political parties and public opinion.

There is a long and large debate over the relationship between globalization and the welfare state. To learn more one might start with Brady, Beckfield, and Zhao (2007), Hays, Ehrlich, and Peinhardt (2005), and Iversen and Cusack (2000).

23. See, e.g., survey questions about the nation's most important problems at www .pollingreport.com/prioriti.htm.

24. For exit poll data from 2008 see www.cnn.com/ELECTION/2008/results/polls .main/.

Grappling with Globalization

The Democratic Party's Struggles
over International Market Integration

James Shoch

Europe versus America

In recent decades the American Democratic Party, like center-left parties everywhere, has confronted the challenge posed by economic globalization. But the Democrats' response to growing international market integration has differed from that of most European social democratic parties.

European parties—especially in the Nordic countries, characterized by small, open economies—have long recognized that trade liberalization raises aggregate national welfare by fostering exports, lower prices, and increased productivity and growth.[1] But these parties have also recognized that moves toward greater economic openness could be blocked by those suffering job and income losses related to globalization—especially less skilled workers in manufacturing industries that compete with imports, and more recently blue- and white-collar workers of all skill levels in industries engaged in off-shore outsourcing, as well as other workers partly competing in the same labor markets.[2] Thus since the 1930s and 1940s social democratic parties, again particularly in the Nordic countries, have built successful coalitions in support of open markets by arranging deals whereby globalization's "winners"—firms and more skilled workers in export-oriented and multinational sectors—agree to compensate the "losers" with extensive unemployment benefits, retraining, healthcare, pensions, and other welfare policies (Hays, Ehrlich, and Peinhardt 2005; Cameron and Kim 2006).

Moreover, since the early 1990s many of these same parties, grappling with the economic supply-side problems of the previous two decades, especially productivity shortfalls, have also backed greatly increased public investment in education, training, and technological research. These policies have increased overall economic productivity, thereby improving competitiveness, preserving jobs, and raising wages, while also creating well-paying new jobs in government and dynamic new industries. At the same time improved productivity has boosted tax revenues, helping to pay for public programs whose rising costs have at times eroded their popular support (Boix 1998; Benner 2003; Bernard and Boucher 2007; Becker 2007; Aiginger 2008).[3] All of this has again aided these parties in maintaining support for economic openness and broadening their coalitions among different sectors of the workforce.

Consequently, despite recent challenges from the nationalist and protectionist far right (Swank and Betz 2003; Burgoon 2009), by simultaneously pursuing open markets and compensatory social spending and public investment strategies, European social democratic parties—albeit more in the Nordic countries than on the continent (Einhorn and Logue 2010)—have successfully fostered growth, employment, social equality, and inclusion.[4]

The American Democratic Party has taken a different path. Historically the party of free trade, in the 1960s the party became much more equivocal in its support for that doctrine. Pressured by labor constituents battered by imports, many Democrats embraced protectionism and opposed further trade liberalization efforts. With a leap in the trade deficit, especially with Japan, and the political salience of trade during the presidencies of Ronald Reagan and his successor, George H. W. Bush, Democratic members of Congress and presidential candidates pushed bills first to curb imports and then to pry open closed markets, particularly Japan's. During his first term in office Bill Clinton also pressed Japan to open its markets.

Since the early 1990s, however, the United States has renewed its drive for further trade—and investment—liberalization.[5] Recent years have seen the approval of the North American Free Trade Agreement, a new General Agreement on Tariffs and Trade (GATT) treaty, permanent normal trade relations with China, and the Central American Free Trade Agreement, along with other bilateral deals. But whereas in Europe, as noted above, social democratic parties have been key supporters of trade liberalization, in the United States Democratic backing for liberalization has been much less reliable. In the American system of separated powers, movement toward freer trade has been due to the efforts of pro-trade presidents of both parties, allied with congressional Republicans and a substantial number of Senate Democrats, but only a minority, sometimes a small one, of House Democrats. For various reasons, above all pressure from the still powerful labor movement and wide public anxiety about globalization, the majority of House Democrats have opposed, sometimes overwhelmingly, almost all of these trade liberalization initiatives. During the 1990s their opposition led to the defeat of two important procedural measures, if not actual agreements.

More recently the entrance of the "BRIC" nations—Brazil, Russia, India, and China—onto the world economic stage has further heightened labor and public concern over globalization and trade. At the same time the ranks of congressional Democratic critics of free trade were expanded when the party regained control of the House and Senate in the midterm elections of 2006. The result was the blocking and delaying of new trade liberalization proposals in Congress, while the Democrats' presidential nominee and eventual victor in 2008, Barack Obama, also tilted, at least temporarily, against new free trade agreements and called for a more aggressive approach to China.

One reason for the Democrats' push for tougher trade policy and opposition to trade liberalization in recent decades has been their inability to win, or credibly promise, a substantial increase in compensatory social spending and public investment. That sort of increased spending might have reduced labor and popular objections to expanded trade as it has in much of Europe. Until recently, spending on the Trade Adjustment Assistance (TAA) program, intended to help workers dislocated by trade, had actually declined since 1980. Once a leader in publicly funded education, infrastructure, and technological research, after the 1960s the United States slipped in all three areas. With American industrial competitiveness eroding, in the early 1980s and again in the early 1990s the Democrats embraced first industrial policy and then increased public investment, along with certain compensatory social policies. But Democratic leaders soon backed off from these ideas, partly because of concerns fueled by the news media about budget deficits, and withering Republican and business criticism that the Democrats were advocating more "big government" and "tax-and-spend liberalism."

Again in the wake of the emergence of the BRICs and the Democrats' election victories in 2006, congressional Democrats renewed their efforts to increase TAA and public investment, while Obama backed similar policies during his campaign. But the scale of these proposals was again limited by deficit worries and Democratic fears of being politically tarred with the brush of fiscal irresponsibility. That is, until the global economic crisis struck in the fall of 2008.

That crisis for a time loosened constraints on government economic intervention. With Obama's victory and the expansion of the Democrats' congressional majorities in 2008, Obama and his congressional allies enacted a major economic stimulus package and a year later a historic healthcare reform bill that should eventually ease the dislocations caused by globalization and help build a more productive, competitive economy. In the short term, however, the economy remained weak while public skepticism toward the growth of government increased, leading to big Republican gains in the congressional elections of 2010. Had Obama and his party been able to produce policies that over time proved successful and thus popular, it is possible that opposition to trade liberalization from labor and the public at large might at some point have declined, allowing the Democrats' approach to globalization to draw closer to that of their European colleagues. But these prospects have now dimmed.

In this chapter, after presenting a very brief framework for understanding the determinants of party economic policy stances, I will explain the evolution of Democratic positions on trade, compensatory spending, and competitiveness policy, with a focus on the years since 1980.[6]

Parties and Economic Policymaking in the White House and Congress

As both the nation and his party's main economic policy actor, a newly elected president, assisted by his advisers, often tries to develop a new political-economic strategy and a corresponding policy program. Both strategy and program will be influenced by (1) the president's personal beliefs, including his normative values and his cognitive understanding of the causal dynamics of the economy; (2) the preferences of core party constituents, activists, and donors; swing voters; and powerful economic interests, especially business and labor; and (3) the anticipation of what Congress will accept (Spiliotes 2002; Dolan, Frendreis, and Tatalovich 2008). The president's program is almost never enacted without controversy and conflict. Members of the president's party in Congress usually benefit politically from his achievements and thus will be generally predisposed to back his proposals. But opposition party members have little interest in the president's success and will usually fight to change or replace them. Beyond this, congressional party members' positions on floor votes will also be determined by their own normative and cognitive beliefs, the preferences of their own core partisan and swing constituents, majority party members' desire to fashion an electorally valuable collective party record and minority party members' concern to prevent them from doing so, congressional party leaders' strategies and pressure, interest group lobbying and campaign contributions, presidential bargaining and persuasion, and the overall climate of interparty relations (Bond and Fleisher eds. 2000; Smith 2007; Lee 2009; Thurber ed. 2009).

Various cultural, political, and economic structures also influence the interests and preferences of contending political actors, constrain and enable their behavior, and condition the outcomes of their policy battles. Among these factors are (1) the nation's anti-statist political culture; (2) our distinctive electoral system and fragmented state institutions;[7] (3) configurations of institutional authority, including partisan control of the presidency and the partisan and ideological balance within both houses of Congress; (4) domestic and international socioeconomic structures;[8] and (5) international "regimes" and geopolitical relations.

Parties and Trade Policy from Roosevelt to Reagan

The Great Depression of the 1930s destroyed the old Republican political order and its dominant coalition of northern industry and labor. The successor Democratic or New Deal order and its underlying coalition—including unionized labor, urban ethnics, southerners, African Americans, middle-class liberals, and liberal business interests—emerged from the turmoil of the Depression and the Second World War. The new order rested on an economic base of "Fordist" mass production and consumption. It was institutionally stabilized by a new system of collective bargaining, new financial market regulations, a large military establishment, and a limited welfare state,[9] constrained in part by America's individualist and anti-statist political culture.[10] Democratic presidents employed a "Keynesian" political-economic strategy that relied on countercyclical fiscal and monetary policy to prevent another collapse of effective demand.

The New Deal era also saw the beginning of the dismantling of the prevailing system of tariff protection, which had sharply divided Republicans and Democrats since the mid-nineteenth century.[11] This system was erected and maintained mainly by the GOP, with the support of northern industries that competed with imports. It was mostly opposed by the low-tariff Democrats and their backers among southern agricultural export interests. In 1930 the Republicans, still dominant, responded to the onset of the Depression by enacting, in the face of united Democratic opposition, the Smoot-Hawley Tariff Act, which dramatically raised tariffs and may well have deepened the crisis.

In 1932 Franklin Roosevelt and the Democrats took unified control of government. Two years later, this time in the face of strong Republican opposition, they passed the Reciprocal Trade Agreements Act, which delegated to the president the authority to negotiate reciprocal, bilateral tariff reductions. After the Second World War, spurred in part by the beginning of the cold war, the Democratic administration of President Harry Truman took the lead in founding the GATT, under whose auspices tariffs were further reduced through several rounds of international negotiations.

The Democrats recognized that maintaining both economic openness and their own political support would require the protection of vulnerable domestic interests from trade-related economic distress. Thus was born the American version of the "compromise of embedded liberalism" (Ruggie 1982;

Ruggie ed. 2008; Hays 2009). In exchange for their support for openness, American companies and workers were cushioned against, or compensated for, exposure to foreign competition. Various devices were used to curb imports; hence trade would be "liberal" or "freer," rather than unqualifiedly "free." Certain limited social welfare and other spending policies were also employed, including TAA, passed in 1962, which provided unemployment benefits, relocation, retraining, and other assistance to help workers move into new jobs (Kapstein 1998).

Also important to the maintenance of the liberal postwar trading order was the eventual decline of partisanship surrounding the making of trade policy. This decline was due in part to the imperatives of the cold war, the influence of the GATT regime, and the operation of the embedded liberal compromise. But also important were the frequently cited "lessons" of Smoot-Hawley, sustained postwar prosperity, the still relatively closed nature of the United States economy, and the expansion of pro-trade export and multinational business interests. Thanks to all these factors, the political salience and divisiveness of trade issues gradually faded, and a bipartisan consensus in favor of liberal trade emerged by about 1960.

In the early 1960s, however, America's Fordist mass-production industries came under pressure from firms in Western Europe and Japan, whose economies had recovered from the devastation of the Second World War. These problems were soon compounded by a "crisis of Keynesianism," as the Democrats' postwar political-economic strategy of demand management now contributed to new supply-side cost and productivity problems that fueled inflation and cut into corporate profits and competitiveness. By 1971 the United States was running a trade deficit in manufactured goods for the first time since 1888.

Protectionist pressures, which had begun to gather in the 1950s, now intensified, while the organized labor movement, having obtained almost no aid through the TAA program, added its own demands for relief from imports. Partisan divisions over new trade liberalization measures also reemerged, at least in Congress, in the early 1970s, although the parties' historic positions were now reversed.

As noted above, before the 1930s the Democratic Party had been rooted mainly in the South, dependent on exports and hence pro-trade. But after the New Deal realignment of the 1930s the Democrats became more dependent on the votes, volunteers, and money of the increasingly protectionist labor movement in the Northeast and Midwest. Meanwhile the Republicans became more closely allied with export-oriented and multinational business interests that backed liberal trade.

Throughout the 1970s the dual crisis of Fordism and Keynesianism deepened, manifesting itself as "stagflation," a painful combination of high unemployment and high inflation that hastened a long, disruptive transition to "post-Fordism" involving several shifts: from mass production for mass markets to flexibly specialized production for niche markets; from basic manufacturing industries to new high-technology sectors; from a manufacturing-based industrial society to a service-oriented, postindustrial, or knowledge-based society; from a production-dominated international economy to a "financialized" global economy; and from a "Keynesian welfare state" focused on demand to a more supply-oriented "competition state" emphasizing cost cutting and productivity growth (Amin 1995; Castells 2000; Jessop 2002; Cerny 2000; Coriat, Petit, and Schmeder eds. 2006; Zysman and Newman eds. 2006).

Politically the crisis disrupted the New Deal coalition. Many white working-class voters, already alienated by the Democrats' identification with the social movements of the 1960s, now also turned away from the party for its failure to deliver continued prosperity. The transition to post-Fordism and post-industrialism simultaneously shrank this same blue-collar industrial working class while expanding the ranks of professionals, managers, and routine white-collar workers (Teixeira, this volume). Accordingly, leaders of both parties sought new political-economic strategies intended to facilitate, cushion, or in some cases slow the transition to post-Fordism, revive the economy, defend their core constituencies, and attract new constituencies (Blyth 2002; Collins 2000).

In 1980 Ronald Reagan, a staunch Republican proponent of "neoliberalism" or "market fundamentalism" and limited government, was elected president, inaugurating a new conservative political order. Reagan's victory was due mainly to voters' anger at Jimmy Carter's apparent mismanagement of the economy but also to a rightward shift in the public mood toward government (Stimson 2004). Reagan's conservative "supply-side" political-economic strategy included big corporate and personal tax cuts, reduced social spending, deregulation, restrictive monetary policy, and a commitment to liberal trade. Politically the strategy was intended to win the support of core middle-class Republicans; new middle- and working-class swing voters, including blue-collar "Reagan Democrats"; and big and small business interests, all of whom were weary of inflation and taxes (Blumenthal 1986, 55–86, 197–203). Soon after Reagan took office, though, the Federal Reserve's tight money policy drove interest rates and the value of the dollar up and the economy into what became the worst downturn since the Great Depression, while the United States budget and trade deficits ballooned.

Democrats Turn to Tougher Trade Policy and Competitiveness Initiatives

In response the Democrats intensified their search for a new political-economic strategy of their own. Their advocacy of demand stimulus policies was largely ruled out by the intellectual discrediting of Keynesianism, the more conservative public view of government, and the Democrats' embrace of fiscal discipline to score political points against "Reaganomics." Thus the Democrats instead launched what would become a decade-long attempt to make tougher trade policy a winning electoral issue for their party. The trade deficit with Japan was rising explosively, so the Democrats focused on curbing Japanese imports and then opening Japanese markets.

With imports battering the country's Fordist mass-production industries during his first term, Reagan, rather than strengthening the embedded liberal compromise, instead abandoned it. He only sparingly used the nation's trade remedy laws to stem the import tide. And along with cutting other welfare spending, he actually slashed TAA funding despite Democratic opposition. As a consequence many Democratic legislators from industrial states backed legislation and administrative action to curb imports—of cars, steel, and textiles—in the hopes of defending their embattled labor supporters, regaining lost working-class support, and perhaps even winning some support from business interests concerned about imports.

In the end, trade played little role in the presidential election of 1984. Nevertheless, at the beginning of Reagan's second term the Democrats sensed continued Republican vulnerability on the issue, now even among export interests. They thereupon turned toward efforts to break into closed foreign markets, again especially Japanese markets, through the tactic of "aggressive reciprocity." A long legislative process driven by Democrats culminated in the enactment of the Omnibus Trade and Competitiveness Act of 1988. The heart of the bill was the "Super 301" provision that threatened retaliation against unfair foreign traders who refused to open their markets to United States goods (Schwab 1994). The trade issue was again of little importance in the presidential race in 1988, but the Democrats kept the pressure on anyway. Four years later, in the middle of the next presidential contest, the House of Representatives, controlled by Democrats, passed another bill that would have reauthorized the expiring Super 301 law and imposed a cap on sales in the United States of Japanese cars, but the Senate failed to produce its own version of the bill.

Trade policy was not the Democrats' only foreign economic policy focus during the 1980s. Throughout the decade many Democrats, looking for an alternative to protectionism, supported different versions of a relatively low-cost supply-side or "competitiveness" strategy of their own, intended to both reverse the nation's apparent economic decline and revive Democratic political prospects (Hughes 2007). In the early 1980s, recalling both the short-lived planning experiments of the Depression and the Second World War and the apparent successes of the Japanese "statist" model of development, "old" liberals of the Rust Belt, backed by labor, called for an "industrial policy" to provide aid mainly to declining mass-production or "sunset" industries. At the same time, middle-class "neoliberals" from the suburbs and the Sun Belt,[12] facing the erosion of the Democrats' traditional blue-collar, working-class base, urged help for new, post-Fordist, high-technology or "sunrise" industries. Their hope was to expand their support among the growing ranks of post-industrial professionals and other white-collar workers, as well as among politically unaligned high-technology business interests (Graham 1992).

After several years of intense debate, by mid-1984 the Democrats had retreated from their advocacy of industrial policy for a number of reasons, including economic and administrative objections from Republicans, business, mainstream economists, and the news media. More fundamentally, the Democrats became convinced that industrial policy was bad politics. First, divisions between traditional liberals and neoliberals threatened to split the party. Second, the mass political appeal of industrial policy was undermined by its technical character and by the uncertain and long-term nature of its likely benefits. Third, the economic recovery of 1983–84 reduced the perceived political urgency of government action. Finally and most important, Democrats worried that intensified attacks on the concept by Republicans and other elites would further resonate with the public's long-standing anti-statist cultural sensibilities, branding the Democrats as the party of big government.

Although industrial policy had been driven from the political agenda by mid-1984, productivity growth and economic performance during the rest of the decade remained relatively lackluster, while after falling for several years, the United States trade deficit, especially with Japan, headed back up again. Concern for the apparent decline of American industry, now including high-technology firms, therefore also remained alive. Consequently, policy experts aligned with the Democrats developed new proposals for what was now termed expanded "public investment"—in education and training, infrastructure, and dynamic new technologies. Some proposals of this kind were included in the Trade Act of 1988 (which Democrats sponsored), were advanced by the Democratic presidential candidate Michael Dukakis that same year, and were subsequently introduced by congressional Democrats during George H. W. Bush's presidency.

The Clinton Years:
From Promoting Public Investment to Battling over Free Trade

Clinton's Public Investment Program and Its Demise

The Democratic presidential nominee in 1992 was Governor Bill Clinton of Arkansas. A self-proclaimed "New Democrat," Clinton had led the Democratic Leadership Council (DLC), a moderate group formed shortly after Ronald Reagan's reelection in 1984 to break the grip of labor and other "special interests" on the Democratic Party and pull it back to the political center. Making a new political-economic strategy central to his campaign, Clinton sought to facilitate the transition to a more internationally competitive post-Fordist economic order. But he also hoped to cushion the impact of this transition and to spread its benefits by reviving, albeit in more limited form, a version of the embedded liberal compromise.

Accordingly, in a plan released in June 1992, Clinton, like other New Democrats, embraced freer trade. But again influenced by public policy experiments during the Depression and the Second World War and by Japanese and European technology and labor market policies, he also called for increased public investment in physical and human capital.[13] Technology and manufacturing plans followed in September. This strategy was to be complemented by the establishment of a comprehensive new national health insurance system. At the same time, Clinton's plan called for halving the burgeoning federal budget deficit within four years.

Clinton's plan was therefore actually a hybrid of statist, social democratic, and neoliberal elements intended to appeal simultaneously to core Democratic constituencies, including labor and African-Americans; swing voters, including blue-collar "Reagan Democrats," middle-class suburbanites, and the socially diverse, deficit-conscious supporters of the independent presidential candidate Ross Perot; and various industrial and financial interests.

Yet by the time Clinton had become president and submitted his first economic plan to Congress in February 1993, his original public investment proposals had been cut in half in favor of a greater stress on deficit reduction. This shift of emphasis was due in part to the influence of the Federal Reserve chairman, Alan Greenspan, and Clinton's own economic advisors, who convinced him that the financial markets, averse to deficits and inflation, had to be further conciliated to bring down interest rates. Also important was Clinton's perceived need to secure reelection support from the backers of Perot, who had won a stunning 19% of the vote in the presidential race. In Congress Clinton's plan faced severe criticism from Republicans and business who saw it as a return to big government and "tax-and-spend liberalism." When these attacks appeared to resonate with voters' anti-statist cultural values, Democrats facing reelection, especially southern conservatives, voted to cut Clinton's investment program by half again to make room for still more deficit reduction. A year later Clinton's healthcare plan was similarly torpedoed by intense Republican and business opposition, which transformed initial public enthusiasm for the plan into opposition and again prompted leading congressional Democrats to back away from offering their own support.

After the Republicans captured control of Congress in the midterm elections of 1994, their opposition limited Clinton's subsequent public investment and social spending initiatives. But Clinton and his Democratic colleagues themselves continued to retreat from these ideas throughout the rest of his presidency. This was due to the subsequent economic recovery, which was attributed by the White House to the president's shift toward fiscal restraint; the election debacle, which was accurately perceived as being in part a reaction to Clinton's alleged tax-and-spend proclivities; and Clinton's reelection and modest Democratic congressional gains in 1996, which appeared to confirm for him and his party the political wisdom of his economic policy course adjustments.

The Intra-Democratic Struggle over Trade Liberalization

With the demise of his public investment strategy by the summer of 1993, Clinton turned to a two-pronged strategy of "export-led growth" to help revive the sluggish economy and improve his reelection chances. First, the White House escalated efforts begun by Reagan and Bush under Democratic pressure to open Japan's markets, concluding limited agreements with Tokyo in both 1993 and 1995. Second and more important, Clinton pursued a number of bilateral, regional, and multilateral free-trade agreements. By the early 1990s growing international economic integration had expanded the ranks of export-oriented and multinational firms, while interests threatened by imports had either been driven out of business or been forced to adjust to more competitive market conditions by technologically modernizing and moving production offshore. Together with the waning of Japanese economic strength, these changes produced a lasting reorientation of the objectives of American trade policy away from import limits and aggressive reciprocity and toward trade and investment liberalization.

Most presidents are free traders, because of their national electoral constituencies and their foreign policy responsibilities. But Clinton's concerted efforts to negotiate and win approval of these new trade deals were also consistent with his personal belief in open trade, and intended to win him the support of internationally oriented business interests and voters who were expected to benefit from export-related job growth. Conversely, Clinton was willing to risk provoking opposition from organized labor, many of whose members, absent any significant expansion of paltry existing compensation programs, were likely to be harmed by further trade liberalization.

The fate of Clinton's substantive and procedural free-trade initiatives was mixed. Congressional approval of the North American Free Trade Agreement (NAFTA) in the fall of 1993 was followed a year later by ratification of the "Uruguay Round" GATT treaty, which among other things established the new World Trade Organization (WTO). In both 1997 and 1998, however, trade liberalization ground to a halt, when the House of Representatives blocked legislation to extend Clinton's "fast-track" trade negotiating authority. Fast-track authority facilitates the negotiation of free-trade agreements by awarding them quick up-or-down votes in Congress without amendments that can unhinge the entire process. Clinton had hoped to use this renewed authority to strike new free-trade deals with Latin American and Asian nations. But two years later, in 2000, Congress approved legislation granting "permanent normal trade relations" status to the People's Republic of China.

This seesawing set of outcomes was decided mainly in the House, since Senate support for free trade was less problematic.[14] The variable and often very close House votes were determined principally by the shifting positions of House Democrats. By contrast, two-thirds to three-quarters of House Republicans consistently supported these measures, in large part because they represented mostly export-oriented and white-collar districts and were dependent on internationally oriented business donors.

During the Clinton years a deep split over trade opened in the Democratic Party, including within Congress. On one side were liberal, blue-collar, and labor-backed urban "old" Democrats from the Northeast and Midwest. The majority opposed free trade, not least because the demise of Clinton's public investment and healthcare plans left their working-class constituents heavily exposed to the dislocating pressures of the world economy. On the other side were moderate and conservative white-collar, business-supported, suburban "new" Democrats from the South and West, often aligned with the centrist DLC. Most supported free trade. The fluctuation in House Democratic voting on trade issues during these years can to a degree be explained by election-induced shifts in the relative strength of these two Democratic factions.

Other considerations were also important, including the varying intensity of the lobbying campaigns mounted by pro-trade business interests and by labor and other opponents of free trade, shifts in the relative dependence of House Democrats on business and labor campaign contributions,[15] the cohesiveness of the House Democratic leadership, and the effectiveness of the bargaining activities of Bill Clinton and other White House officials.

Trade Liberalization Advances: NAFTA and GATT

In November 1993 the first of Clinton's trade and investment liberalization deals, NAFTA, was ratified, thanks to a split in the House Democratic Caucus.[16] Hoping to appeal to both old and new Democratic constituencies, Clinton had endorsed NAFTA during his presidential campaign while also pledging to negotiate labor and environmental side agreements to allay the fears of unions and environmental groups of a "race to the bottom" by United States corporations looking to take advantage of Mexico's cheap labor and poorly enforced environmental laws.

Criticizing the agreements negotiated by the Clinton administration as too weak, organized labor and its allies waged an intense campaign against NAFTA, eventually leading 60% of House Democrats to oppose it. The other 40% of House Democrats had a number of reasons for voting in favor. First, a bloc of moderate and conservative, disproportionately southern Democrats backed the deal, encouraged by the DLC. Second, internationally oriented business interests organized a strong pro-NAFTA lobbying campaign, focused mainly on undecided Democrats. Third, the Democrats' dependence on business campaign contributions had increased since the early 1980s. Fourth, there was a deep split in the House Democratic leadership, reflecting rank-and-file differences. Finally, Clinton undertook furious efforts to persuade Congress and the public, which included both appeals to party loyalty and promises of selective import curbs and a new trade adjustment assistance program.[17]

In the following year the Uruguay Round GATT treaty was ratified by the House with considerably greater ease, as fully 65% of the Democratic caucus supported the accord. The key here was that labor expressed only token opposition to the deal, the effects of which seemed likely to be diffuse rather than focused on specific income groups; this made labor less concerned about the Uruguay Round than it had been about NAFTA, which the unions feared would produce a devastating flight of capital to Mexico (Baldwin and Magee 2000, 29, 42).

Trade Liberalization Stalled: The Fast-Track Battles

Three years later, in November 1997, the process of trade liberalization stalled when Clinton was forced to withdraw the "clean" fast-track proposal he had introduced (it contained no significant labor and environmental provisions). Principally dooming the proposal was the opposition of about 80% of House Democrats (Shoch 2000; Conley 1999; Schnietz and Nieman 1999; Bardwell 2000).

This pronounced shift in Democratic behavior had several causes. First, a substantial number of pro-trade Democrats retired or were defeated in the congressional elections of 1994 and 1996, while the latter year saw the election of a number of liberal and moderate Democrats from mostly northern districts where opposition to free trade was stronger. Second, the business campaign for fast-track authority was poorly organized and unenergetic, largely because fast-track was a procedural measure lacking concrete benefits, unlike the NAFTA accord, which contained many. Third, despite its secular decline labor waged a more intense and effective campaign against fast-track than it had done against NAFTA. In conjunction with the unions' success in turning out and influencing the labor vote in the congressional elections of 1996, this led most Democrats to oppose Clinton's bill in the hope of benefiting from a similar labor effort in the midterm elections in 1998 (Francia 2005). Fourth, after the elections in 1994 there was a shift of business campaign contributions from the Democrats to the now majority Republicans, as well as an increase in labor donations to Democratic candidates. This left the party, including even New Democrats, more dependent on labor money. Fifth, the House Democratic leadership undertook a more unified campaign against fast-track. Finally, Clinton's lobbying efforts were less concerted and effective than they had been on NAFTA. His "inside-the-beltway" strategy of promising concessions failed to sway Democrats alienated by his failure to deliver on retraining and other promises made during the NAFTA fight.

Hoping to mend relations with House Democrats, Clinton decided to hold off on sending another fast-track proposal to Congress until after the midterm congressional elections in November 1998. Instead, it was the Republican House speaker, Newt Gingrich, who in late June announced a fall vote on a new "clean" fast-track proposal. Gingrich hoped to use the bill in the elections against Democratic fast-track opponents from districts with concentrations of export-dependent agricultural interests (Shoch 2000; Biglaiser, Jackson, and Peake 2004).

In late September the House decisively defeated the GOP bill, as 86% of the chamber's Democrats voted against it. Democratic opposition to the bill was heightened by splits among businesses over the timing of the vote and the bill's poor prospects. Second, the unions waged another strong campaign against the bill. This again led both liberal and moderate Democrats to op- pose it in the hope of securing grassroots activism and campaign contribu- tions from unions in the upcoming elections. Third, Bill Clinton and many New Democrats refused to support the bill, which they saw as an obvious GOP attempt to embarrass and divide their party before the elections.

Trade Liberalization Resumed: PNTR with China

The final free-trade battle of the Clinton years was over permanent normal trade relations (PNTR) with China. PNTR status would have allowed Congress to abandon its annual vote on whether to grant "most favored nation" status to China, a cold war practice intended to pressure Beijing to improve human rights. Administration officials believed that awarding PNTR status to China was necessary if eager American firms were to receive the various market- opening and investment concessions that Beijing had made in an agreement struck with the United States in late 1999 to facilitate China's entry into the WTO. After yet another furious battle, the PNTR bill was approved by the House in May 2000. The key to the measure's passage was support from 35% of Democrats, up from the 20% and 14% of party members who had backed the fast-track bills in 1997 and 1998 (Hasnat and Callahan 2002).

This new turnaround in Democratic behavior was partly due to the vic- tory in 1998 of a number of young, pro-business, pro-trade moderate Demo- crats from affluent suburban districts, mainly in the Northeast. Organized labor, fearing the offshoring of United States production to China, had waged another strong campaign against PNTR. But that effort was weakened by support for the deal by some union locals representing workers in trade- dependent industries, and by fears that defeat of the measure would jeopar- dize the prospects in the forthcoming elections of the Democratic presiden- tial nominee, Al Gore, or the Democrats' hopes of recapturing control of the House. A third reason was that business interests saw vast market and in- vestment opportunities in the China deal and undertook a massive lobbying campaign on behalf of PNTR in Washington and at the grassroots, as they had not done when the procedural fast-track bill was being considered in 1997. Fourth, the 1999–2000 election cycle saw a new if limited shift of business campaign contributions back to the Democrats. Many corporate leaders, en- couraged by various New Democratic groups, recognized in the wake of the fast-track defeat in 1997 that in dramatically shifting their support to the Re- publicans after the midterms in 1994 they had lost influence with the Democrats, who had become more financially beholden to, and therefore more supportive of, organized labor. Fifth, that same election cycle saw the emergence of the internationally oriented high-technology sector as a major contributor to Democratic candidates, especially pro-trade New Democrats. Sixth, a new split opened among House Democratic leaders, some of whom, although opposed to PNTR, refrained from actively organizing against it to avoid offending existing and potential business donors. Finally, there were the reenergized lobbying efforts of Bill Clinton, who hoped that approval of PNTR would help to secure his legacy as a champion of free trade and lighten the stain of the House's vote to impeach him in 1998.

The Democrats and Trade Liberalization during the Bush Years

The dramatic presidential race of 2000 saw the election of George W. Bush, a Republican who pushed to complete the neoliberal "Reagan Revolution" with big new tax cuts. The process of trade liberalization also continued during Bush's presidency, but only after bruising fights, again mainly in the House. In the summer of 2002, after a series of extraordinarily close and partisan House votes, Congress gave Bush fast-track authority—now renamed "trade promotion authority" (TPA)—to help him negotiate a new international trade agreement under the auspices of the WTO and a Free Trade Agreement of the Americas. Finally, after another bitter, close, and partisan fight in the House, Congress approved the Central America Free Trade Agreement (CAFTA) in the summer of 2005.[18]

Whereas the positions of House Democrats on the several major trade liberalization measures of the Clinton years were quite variable, Democratic opposition to both TPA and CAFTA rose substantially. This was in part because the Democrats were no longer confronting a fellow Democratic president whose political fortunes they to a degree shared, but rather a staunchly conservative Republican one. But other factors discussed below were important too.

Bush's victories on both issues were thus due not to shifts in Democratic behavior but rather to increased GOP support for trade liberalization. Strong business lobbying and pressure from House Republican leaders and the White House played a role in this. Particularly important was the inclination of Republicans who might have opposed the trade liberalization proposals of a Democratic president to instead back TPA and CAFTA as the initiatives of a Republican president whose fate *they* in part shared.

The Trade Promotion Authority Battle

Despite the victory of PNTR, as George W. Bush took office in early 2001 pro-trade business leaders and policy experts remained concerned that presidential fast-track authority to facilitate the negotiation of new free-trade agreements had still not been renewed. Thereupon, in early October 2001 a trade promotion authority proposal sponsored by the GOP was introduced in the House. In the hope of winning at least some support from moderate New Democrats, the measure gave greater prominence to labor and environmental standards than previous bills had done. But to avoid GOP opposition, the bill was largely silent on enforcement mechanisms, which angered labor and environmental activists.

In early December, after a bitter fight, the bill passed by an excruciatingly close margin of 215–214 (Biglaiser, Jackson, and Peake 2004; Destler 2005, 290–98; Forgette 2004, 163–65). Six months later the House approved a motion to send the TPA bill to conference with the Senate—again, almost incredibly, by the margin of a single vote: 216–215. In a successful move to win more New Democratic support for the measure, a provision originated by Senate Democrats was added to expand the TAA program and provide a new healthcare tax credit and a wage insurance program for displaced workers. A month later the House narrowly passed a compromise conference bill by yet another extremely close vote, 215–212.

These were all not only close votes but also exceptionally partisan ones; the most partisan, in fact, of any congressional trade votes taken since the Second World War. Democratic opposition to TPA rose to 90% on the vote in December 2001 (up from 65% on PNTR), to 95% on the vote in June 2002 to send the House version of the bill to conference, and to 88% on the final conference bill. This would have been enough to defeat the measures had not Republican support for TPA on the three votes climbed to 89%, 93%, and 88%.

Opposition to TPA was strong among Democrats of all ideological orientations—including most moderate, usually pro-trade New Democrats—for a number of reasons. First, there was the perception that public anxiety over globalization was growing just as the economy was falling into recession. Second, a strong campaign was waged against the bill by environmental activists and especially organized labor, which was unimpressed by the limited TAA, healthcare, and wage insurance provisions included in the measure.[19] Labor's influence within the party had grown because of the unions' massive mobilization for Al Gore and other Democratic candidates in 2000 and the substantial union effort planned for the midterm elections of 2002, when low turnout was forecast. The decision by the AFL-CIO to endorse up to seventy-five moderate Republican candidates in those races also made it harder for the Democrats to take labor's support for granted. Third, there was the beginning of yet another shift of business campaign contributions back to the Republicans after Bush's victory and the GOP's success in retaining control of the House, which again left Democrats more dependent on labor money. Fourth, the collapse of the "dot-coms" and troubles throughout the high-technology sector hurt the New Democrats' fundraising, still further increasing their reliance on labor money. Fifth, because of a secular geographical and ideological realignment of the parties' electoral coalitions, the growing polarization of party activists, a combatively conservative Republican congressional leadership, and a divisive president playing to his base rather than to swing voters, the level of partisanship in Washington was extremely high, while both old and new Democrats were angry in particular at the way Bush and congressional Republicans tried to ram the TPA bill through the House. Finally, House Democratic leaders made determined efforts to rally their members against the TPA bill, which contrasted with their much more passive role in the PNTR fight.

The strong Democratic opposition to TPA would have been sufficient to sink the bill had it received a level of support from Republicans comparable to their support for free-trade measures of the previous decade. But for the reasons mentioned above, GOP support for TPA rose to new heights, making this the key to the bill's victory.

The Central America Free Trade Agreement

Buoyed by his narrow TPA victory, over the next several years George W. Bush used his new authority to negotiate and obtain the ratification of several uncontroversial bilateral trade agreements. In the summer of 2004, however, his administration also struck a much more contentious deal: the Central America Free Trade Agreement.[20] Central America was not a big market for United States goods. But the White House and business interests saw the approval of CAFTA as a stepping stone to the successful conclusion of the "Doha Round" of international trade negotiations, begun in Qatar in late 2001, and the negotiation of a Free Trade Agreement of the Americas.

As usual, the House battle over CAFTA in the spring and summer of 2005 was a bitter one, culminating in another nail-biting, highly partisan victory for the White House by a vote of 217–215. Democratic opposition to CAFTA reached 93%, which again would have sunk the pact had not 88% of Republicans supported it.

The unified Democratic opposition to CAFTA, which included most New

Democrats, again had multiple sources. First were the still growing fears that economic globalization was eroding the jobs and wages of United States workers, while there was also more specific disappointment with the results of NAFTA and of PNTR with China. Second, there was additional dismay that Bush had not delivered on training and education provisions of the TPA bill enacted in 2002. Third, labor undertook yet another energetic mobilization effort against the deal. Fourth, New Democrats, already inflamed by Republican hard-line conservatism and authoritarianism, were further angered by how they were treated during the CAFTA fight. House GOP leaders excluded the New Democrats from discussions of the CAFTA implementing legislation, goaded them to oppose a bill with weak labor and environmental provisions, and pressured corporate donors, including high-technology interests, to abandon their already diminished support for Democratic candidates. Fifth, a resulting further decline in business contributions left Democrats of all ideological stripes still more reliant on labor money. Finally, opposition to CAFTA was strong among House Democratic leaders.

As with TPA and for similar reasons, the key to CAFTA's passage in the face of strong Democratic opposition was the almost equally strong Republican backing for the deal.

Democratic Resurgence:
Trade, Compensatory Spending, and Competitiveness Policy

Despite CAFTA's approval, during the past six years popular concern over globalization has continued to mount, in part because of the emergence of four major new economic challengers, the "BRIC" nations—Brazil, Russia, and especially India and China—on the global economic stage. Organized labor, still a key Democratic constituency despite its long-term decline, remains resolutely opposed to new trade and investment liberalization measures. And the wider public is increasingly convinced that globalization, including expanded trade and now the offshore outsourcing of both blue- and white-collar jobs, has contributed to slow employment growth, stagnant wages, and eroding healthcare and retirement benefits.

The Democrats benefited from these sentiments in the congressional midterm elections of 2006. The party regained control of both houses of Congress for the first time since 1994, thanks in part to the victory of a significant number of "populist," labor-backed critics of free trade. During the next two years congressional Democrats refused to renew Bush's trade negotiating authority and blocked approval of a number of bilateral free-trade agreements, including, most controversially, one with Colombia (Destler 2007).

The Democrats' presidential nominee and eventual victor in 2008, Senator Barack Obama, was at heart a free trader. But during his campaign—and especially just before crucial primaries in heavily working-class Ohio and Pennsylvania—Obama called for a halt to the negotiation of new trade agreements without strong labor and environmental standards. He also pledged to revisit NAFTA. Finally, Obama also promised to get tough with China for unfairly subsidizing its exporters with cash, loans, and an undervalued currency. After his victory, however, freed from immediate election pressures, Obama softened his position on NAFTA and China, in the latter case for fear of provoking a sell-off of United States government debt held by the Chinese. He also hoped to win quick congressional approval of stalled trade agreements with Panama, Colombia, and South Korea and to finish negotiations on a global trade deal by the end of 2010 (Ashbee and Waddan 2010).

But with the victory of still more populist Democrats to Congress in the same election, and especially with the economy only slowly recovering from the worst recession since the 1930s, congressional Democrats continued their hardened approach to trade policy. Supported by labor and some manufacturers, in their big economic stimulus bill in early 2009 the Democrats included a controversial, albeit watered-down, "Buy American" provision. Later, strong congressional opposition, especially from House Democrats, led the White House to temporarily back off from its drive for new trade deals and to pledge instead to focus on more aggressively enforcing existing trade and labor rights rules, in the hope that doing so would eventually weaken opposition to further trade liberalization.[21]

In the late spring of 2010, however, along with an ambitious plan to spur job growth by doubling exports, Obama renewed his promise to push ahead on stalled and new free-trade agreements, including a new Trans Pacific Partnership.[22] A deal was subsequently reached in early November with South Korea that reduced barriers to United States auto and food exports to the country. The following April an "action plan" to improve labor rights in Colombia was negotiated to facilitate completion of the stalled free trade pact with the nation. Most of the labor movement, however, continues to oppose these agreements, which are still felt to lack sufficiently strong workplace and environmental standards. As a consequence, most congressional Democrats also remain opposed to these deals. Instead, about half of House Democrats are backing legislation that would require a wide-ranging review of NAFTA and other trade pacts and boost the role of Congress in negotiations over future deals. And in early October 2010 House Democrats, joined by many Republicans, passed a bill that would impose tariffs on imports from China should Beijing continue to manipulate the value of its currency. It is possible, though, that sufficient support for pending and future free trade agreements will eventually be found from Republicans and pro-trade Democrats to secure their approval.

With respect to compensatory spending, in November 2007 House Democrats passed a bill to expand and extend TAA benefits, but Senate Republicans blocked it. Democratic leaders suggested that approval of this measure and related unemployment, training, and other legislation was necessary before new trade deals with Colombia and other nations could be voted on. Obama likewise supported such compensatory policies during the presidential race. Both he and congressional Democrats also called for a major revamping of the United States healthcare system to expand access and lower costs.

Meanwhile, after fading away during Bill Clinton's second term and George W. Bush's first, the issues of competitiveness and public investment have recently returned to the United States political agenda with the rise of the BRICs. Building on the House Democrats' Innovation Agenda from 2006, in August 2007 Congress passed and George Bush signed the America Competes Act. The bill called for increased spending on various federal energy, science, technology, and research programs. Congressional Democrats also introduced legislation to modernize the nation's aging infrastructure. During his presidential campaign Obama had similarly promised to increase public investment in education and training, infrastructure, renewable energy sources, and technological research.

Then in the fall of 2008 came the dramatic worsening of the developing crisis of "financialized capitalism," the product of stagnant wages and rising consumer debt, an influx of foreign capital and loose monetary policy by the Federal Reserve, risky mortgage lending and derivatives trading, and lax financial regulation (Rajan 2010). Contributing to the demise of the Republican order and renewed Democratic control of the White House and Congress, the severe crisis also relaxed various constraints on greater government activism. Most important, as Obama took office in January 2009 the American public, traditionally hesitant about the economic role of government,[23] now backed a big economic stimulus package that included substantial new spending, even if it was expected to lead to bigger budget deficits.[24]

In addition, faced with collapsing consumer demand, frozen credit markets, growing unemployment, and the threat of deflation, as well as the seeming impotence of monetary expansion and lower interest rates to bring about recovery, usually deficit-wary economists, including veterans of Clinton's administration who were advising Obama, rediscovered the merits of Keynesian fiscal policy. Mainstream economists typically worry that big deficits will lead to inflation, a sell-off of government securities, a sagging dollar, the "crowding out" of private borrowing, and rising interest rates. But with economic resources lying idle, interest rates near zero, and domestic and foreign investors, including Chinese and other central bankers, nevertheless rushing to buy "safe" debt issued by the U.S. Treasury, most economists at least temporarily put aside their deficit fears and backed the major fiscal stimulus package and its big spending increases.

Accordingly, in mid-February Obama and Congress enacted a hefty $787 billion bill, the American Recovery and Reinvestment Act, with broad support from business, labor, and the public. Most of the bill consisted of personal tax relief and unemployment, healthcare, and other direct aid to individuals and fiscally strapped states. But there was also almost $270 billion in new public investment and about $30 billion in tax incentives intended to encourage both short- and long-term growth. Although the package was less than some liberals had hoped for, it was more than Clinton had been able to win in his entire eight years in office. The bill provided for tax credits and new and increased spending to promote infrastructure (roads, bridges, and mass transit), "green" investments (renewable energy sources, a new electric grid, and conservation), computerized medical records, rural broadband networks, scientific and technological research, education and training, and Trade Adjustment Assistance.[25]

Shorn in recent decades of most of their conservative southern wing, Democrats overwhelmingly supported the bill. Conversely, with the purge of moderate Republicans in the two previous elections, the legislation drew near unanimous GOP opposition, as party leaders again conjured well-worn images of pork, waste, deficits, big government, and even socialism. Nevertheless, the stimulus measure narrowly passed in a form that looked very much like Obama's original proposal.[26]

In late February Obama presented his budget proposal for fiscal 2010, which included hundreds of billions of dollars in additional spending on new energy projects (some of which were included in the climate and clean-energy bill passed by the House in June), high-speed rail, increased grants for college students, and most controversially a major healthcare expansion and reform plan. After another fierce battle, a final $3.4 billion budget resolution (or outline) passed both houses of Congress in late April without a single Republican vote.[27] The administration also provided tens of billions of dollars in loans and other assistance to bail out the beleaguered United States auto industry, even assuming a 60% ownership stake in General Motors, which had filed for bankruptcy.[28] Later in the summer Obama also proposed important new programs to improve the quality of K–12 and community college education. Bills backed by the president to establish a National Infrastructure Bank were introduced in both houses of Congress. Finally and most important, in the face of continued Republican intransigence and a public now increasingly concerned about the growth of big government, in March 2010 Obama and his congressional Democratic allies passed a historic ten-year healthcare reform bill with a cost of $940 billion (Howard, this volume).[29]

Obama and the Democrats' initiatives to date have been mainly designed to save and create jobs and reduce economic insecurity. But these measures should also help the country adjust to the challenges of globalization—by cushioning its impact on workers and communities, improving the competitiveness of existing industries, and fostering globally competitive new ones.

Conclusion: Toward a Revived Embedded Liberal Compromise?

In the past few years a number of prominent American policy intellectuals, including the former director of Obama's National Economic Council, Lawrence Summers, and even some business interests have called for reviving and strengthening the embedded liberal compromise (Shoch 2008; Schatz 2008). They propose a mildly social democratic approach to globalization that would combine open markets with substantial increases in compensatory social spending and public investment (Scheve and Slaughter 2007; Kuttner 2008a; Kuttner 2008b; Summers 2008; see also Pontusson 2005a and especially Hays 2009). This approach would involve learning from Europe, particularly from the Nordic countries, and a consequent degree of "hybridization" of American and European "social models" or "varieties of capitalism."[30]

Although not mainly intended as such a hybrid approach to globalization, Obama's economic and social program, even more than Clinton's ill-fated initiatives, embodies key elements of it, and the future of this approach depends in part on the success and popularity of Obama's overall program. What if Obama's and the Democrats' policies had contributed to a strong recovery and the beginning of a new era of growth while mitigating economic insecurity, including the trade-related dislocations experienced by workers in uncompetitive sectors? In addition to Obama's reelection and continued Democratic congressional dominance, this outcome might also have reduced labor and public opposition to further trade liberalization (Schatz 2008). That in turn might have encouraged Obama to conclude new trade deals containing strong labor and environmental standards, which congressional Democrats, together with pro-trade Republicans, might then have approved. In other words, we might have seen the emergence of a new embedded liberal compromise and a narrowing of the differences between the approaches to globalization taken by the Democratic Party and its European counterparts.

It does now appear that the "Great Recession" has bottomed out and that a recovery has begun, including in the labor market, thanks to an expansionary monetary policy but also to the stimulus bill, whose beneficial effects have not been widely recognized. It also appears, though, that absent another significant but politically unlikely stimulus package or a strong demand for exports, the recovery is likely to be a protracted and relatively "jobless" one—a "lost decade" like that endured by Japan is possible—because of the retrenchment of consumer spending, continued wage stagnation, employers' restructuring of their workforce, state and local government spending cuts, the tapering off of stimulus spending, and a reduction in bank lending and business investment in the face of weak effective demand. In addition, sustained, often deceptive Republican attacks on the stimulus program, government bailouts, and the healthcare bill, together with the perceived failure of these measures to strengthen the economy, have contributed during the past year to mounting public apprehension over the growth of government spending, deficits, and intrusiveness.

The struggling economy and negative sentiment toward their healthcare and other reform efforts cost the Democrats six Senate seats and control of the House of Representatives in the midterm elections in 2010. With the Republicans pressing for deep cuts in government spending, Obama's and the Democrats' programmatic achievements are now likely to be eroded rather than expanded. Even if Obama is reelected in 2012, the Republicans are likely to keep control of the House and even to regain control of the Senate, since 23 of the 33 seats to be contested are currently held by Democrats. This will doom any significant new Democratic compensatory and public investment spending initiatives, which in turn means that labor, popular, and Democratic opposition to trade liberalization will remain strong. Hopes for a revived, Democratic-led embedded liberal compromise will unfortunately go unfulfilled.

Notes

1. The commitment of these parties to trade liberalization has been further secured by the delegation of trade policymaking authority by member states first to the European Economic Community and later to the European Union (Katzenstein 1985; Hanson 1998; Young and Peterson 2006).

2. Here I am straddling Stolper-Samuelson and Ricardo-Viner, or "specific factors" models of individual trade policy preferences. The former theories, assuming that production factors are fully mobile across industries, argue that scarce factors (in advanced countries, unskilled labor) will support protection, while abundant factors (capital and skilled labor) will support free trade. The latter theories, assuming

that production factors are completely immobile, maintain instead that capital and labor in import-competing industries will support protection, while capital and labor in export-oriented and multinational sectors will support free trade. For recent empirical studies of public opinion on trade issues based on these two theories see Scheve and Slaughter 2006 and Hays, Ehrlich, and Peinhardt 2005. If instead, as others have argued (cf. Blonigen 2008), factor mobility varies over time and across countries, and production factors in the contemporary United States are partially mobile, then worker trade policy preferences may be influenced in the way I suggest. For additional recent discussion see Mansfield and Mutz 2009 and Jeong 2009.

3. It should be noted that a number of welfare state activities, especially "human capital" policies like education and training, have "productive" as well as "protective" functions. Thus, contra Esping-Andersen's well-known view (1990) that in "decommodifying" labor, politics work "against" markets, politics can also work "with" or "for" markets. See Room 2002; Andersen 2007; Hudson and Kuhner 2008; and Obinger, Starke, Moser, Bogedan, Obinger-Gindulis, and Leibfried 2010.

4. To briefly situate this discussion within current debates among comparative and international political economists, proponents of the "compensation" hypothesis see greater or increasing economic openness leading to a larger public sector, as winners compensate losers and often expand public investment to preserve open markets. Supporters of the contrasting "efficiency" hypothesis argue that globalization forces governments to cut spending and taxes in order to maintain national economic competitiveness and prevent capital flight. "Skeptics" find no causal link between globalization and the size of government, emphasizing instead the importance of domestic factors. For recent reviews of, and empirical evidence for, the competing positions see Busemeyer 2009, Potrafke 2009, Haupt 2010, Jensen 2010, and Walter 2010.

I would argue, following Carles Boix (2006), that the influence of globalization on government policy is contingently mediated by electoral politics, as parties struggle to construct winning political coalitions by deploying competing political-economic strategies. These strategies can include protectionism and opposition to further trade liberalization as an alternative to compensation and public investment or to fiscal conservatism.

5. Most of the free-trade deals of the past fifteen years have actually been intended more to open foreign countries to United States investors than to exporters. In this chapter I mostly use the shorter term "trade liberalization" for economy.

6. For a book-length version of much of the material contained in this chapter through Bill Clinton's presidency see Shoch 2001.

7. Including (1) winner-take-call, single-member district, two-stage, staggered, and separated presidential and congressional elections, and (2) the separation of powers, the presidential veto, bicameralism, the congressional party and committee systems, the Senate filibuster, federalism, and policy feedback effects.

8. Including prevailing macroeconomic conditions; the level of economic development; demographic, class, sectoral, and skill structures; the balance of social forces; the level of economic openness; the international division of labor; and the dependence of the state on globally mobile capital.

9. Critics of "American exceptionalism" argue that if socially oriented tax expenditures (Howard 2007a; Howard, in this volume) and employer-provided but
government-subsidized and regulated social benefits (Hacker 2002) are counted along
with direct government spending, the United States welfare state is actually comparable in size to the welfare states of Europe. This kind of concept "stretching" makes
it unclear why anything the government does that affects social welfare should not be
considered part of the welfare state (Hacker 2005).

10. On this "Lockean liberalism" and its policy consequences see Kingdon 1999 and
Lockhart 2003. Scholars of American political development have demonstrated that
there are actually "multiple traditions" or elements within this country's political culture. But as James Morone (2005) argues, in the narrower economic sphere the liberal
element is generally dominant.

In singling out the importance of political culture and mass public opinion in re-
straining the size of the American welfare state, I am reacting to analyses that neglect
these influences in favor of other limiting factors like the weakness of organized labor
or the strength of business, racial divisions and the power of southern Democrats in
Congress, this country's fragmented state and majoritarian electoral institutions, the
economy's dependence on general rather than specific skills, etc. (see also Zelizer 2003
and Schickler and Caughey 2010). For three recent comparative studies of the impact
of public opinion on the welfare state see Mehrtens 2004, Brooks and Manza 2007,
and Kang and Powell 2010.

11. On parties and trade policy in American history see Rattner 1972; Eckes 1995;
Keech and Pak 1995; Destler 2005; and Shoch 2001.

12. This label for moderate Democrats in the early 1980s should not be confused
with the more general term used above to designate a form of contemporary conservatism: "neoliberalism."

13. On the development of and the subsequent battle over Clinton's plan see Shoch
2008; Akard 1998; Weatherford and McDonnell 1996; and Pierson 1998.

14. The Senate is generally more supportive of free trade than the House is, for a
number of reasons. First, most senators represent fairly large, heterogeneous constituencies, including consumers and internationally oriented interests, that counterbal-
ance the views of domestically oriented interests opposed to free trade. Second, the
Senate overrepresents more agricultural, less unionized, and therefore more pro-trade
parts of the country. Third, senators have long terms, giving ideological free traders
considerable leeway to resist pressure from protectionist interests. Finally, senators
have broad foreign policy responsibilities that incline them to try to avoid trade conflicts with other nations. On the first two of these points see Wirls 1998.

15. Labor unions donate almost all their campaign money to Democrats in the hopes
of influencing which party controls the House. Conversely, some particularly ideological business interests give almost exclusively to Republican candidates. But most businesses are pragmatic, seeking instead to influence legislative decision making, which
leads them to support incumbents of both parties. These same business interests contribute additional money to candidates from the party in control of the House, or expected to win control of the House, as well as to candidates of either party who either

share or may be induced to share their positions on important issues. Consequently, to some degree business support for House candidates shifts with changes in (1) control of the chamber, either actual or anticipated, (2) party policy stances, and (3) the inclination of business donors to try to induce such changes in party positions (Fellowes and Wolf 2004; Stratman 2005).

16. The agreement was actually negotiated by George H. W. Bush's administration. For four excellent analyses of the politics of negotiating and approving NAFTA see Grayson 1995; Mayer 1998; Cameron and Tomlin 2000; and MacArthur 2000.

17. For a lengthy list of mostly quantitative analyses of the House vote see Shoch 2001, 344–45.

18. For a much more detailed analysis of the TPA and CAFTA fights see Shoch 2006.

19. Throughout the history of the program, organized labor has provided only weak support for TAA, choosing instead to focus on blocking trade agreements. From hard experience, labor knows that politicians, having secured the approval of free-trade deals, have often reneged on promises to deliver adjustment aid, which in any case is often ineffective and does little to save union jobs (Kapstein 1998; Burgoon and Hiscox 2000; Burgoon and Hiscox 2008; Davidson, Matusz, and Nelson 2007).

20. The CAFTA countries included the United States, El Salvador, Guatemala, Honduras, Costa Rica, Nicaragua, and the Dominican Republic.

21. Toward this end, and to preserve labor support for his healthcare reform effort, in September 2009 Obama announced a 35% tariff on Chinese tire imports and later imposed duties on Chinese steel pipe imports.

22. In which the United States would be joined by Australia, Brunei, Chile, New Zealand, Peru, Singapore, and Vietnam.

23. For the well-known argument that Americans are "ideologically conservative" but "operationally liberal," i.e., that they oppose government in the abstract but support the maintenance or expansion of most specific government programs, see Cantril and Cantril 1999. For a review of recent public opinion data on Americans' views of government taxing and spending see Shoch 2008.

24. For evidence of considerable public support for economic stimulus legislation see PollingReport.com 2009. Some polls did show that the public had concerns about overspending—concerns that would increase during the battle over healthcare reform—and preferred tax cuts to spending increases to boost the economy.

25. TAA benefits, previously reserved for manufacturing workers displaced by trade, were both increased and extended to service-sector workers whose jobs were lost to foreign imports or moved offshore.

26. House Democrats had wanted a bigger bill containing more spending and smaller tax cuts, but they were forced to make concessions in conference to a handful of moderate Senate Republicans and Democrats whose support was necessary to reach the sixty votes required to waive a budget point of order.

27. Later in the year Congress appropriated the funds for many of these initiatives.

28. Of course Obama, continuing efforts begun by George W. Bush, has also spent hundreds of billions of dollars to rescue the nation's banking system.

29. The bill also shored up the Pell Grant student loan program and allocated $2 billion for worker training programs at the nation's community colleges.

30. Adherents of the Varieties of Capitalism theory (Hall and Soskice 2001) see little likelihood of convergence or hybridization between what they call "liberal market economies" (LMEs) like the United States and the "coordinated market economies" (CMEs) of Europe, because of the presence within both types of economies of reinforcing "institutional complementarities" that prevent such change. I would suggest that more hybridization of different models is possible than this overly structuralist theory allows (Crouch 2005; Becker 2009; Campbell and Pedersen 2007). The structural and institutional complexes characteristic of the two (or more) varieties of capitalism are typically only loosely integrated and constraining. Consequently, a number of domestic political factors—including public opinion, the relative strength and influence of business and labor, party competition and conflict, and policymakers' ideas—can combine in various ways to produce a range of economically viable policies, including some borrowed from other capitalist models. Consistent with this view, Jonas Pontusson (2005a; and chapter in this volume) argues that LMEs can adopt quasi-Nordic social democratic *policies*—for example expanded education, healthcare, and other social welfare spending—even in the absence of social democratic *institutions*. But although LMEs *can* adopt certain social democratic policies, domestic political factors may instead prevent this. Thus Pontusson argues as well that without stronger unions, it will be very hard to move American economic and social policies in a social democratic direction. I will suggest below that additional domestic political influences are also likely to block the further growth of social and public investment spending in this country.

Part III
New Risks, New Challenges, New Possibilities

European Center-Left Parties and New Social Risks

Facing Up to New Policy Challenges

Jane Jenson

European center-left parties and the governments that they have formed or in which they have participated face a set of social policy challenges. Since the mid-1990s they have acted in an environment shaped by sociological and economic transformations that have put paid to many of the assumptions underlying the policy hopes of social democrats and the design of social policy during the years of postwar boom. In addition, the environment of these center-lefts has been profoundly altered by the neoliberal politics and enthusiasm for remaking the role of the state that swept through European societies in the 1980s and first half of the 1990s. While not all parties faced strong and avowedly neoliberal opponents, all had to live with ideological currents in their own societies and international organizations that worked to delegitimize some of the most cherished post-1945 victories of social democracy.

Social and economic transformations have generated what have come to be called "new social risks." Some changes are common to all societies. Population aging not only results in concerns about the sustainability of pension systems but also raises questions about social care. Who will, for example, provide—and pay for—care for the frail elderly as the ranks of the "oldest of the old" swell across European societies? Faced with this question, most European countries have instituted "cash for care," that is, benefits paid to elderly persons in need of services, but the conditions of access and amounts vary. Other changes are more challenging for some policy regimes than others. Where the postwar settlement included a strict gender division of labor for paid and unpaid work, policy adaptation to declining male earnings and rising numbers of single-parent families has been difficult, whereas there is less of a policy challenge around the balance of work and family where the dual-earner family has been the norm for decades. Finally, some policy choices made in the years of neoliberal hegemony have created greater stress than other choices on social policy design. Where income-security policies sustained attacks from neoliberals, the rates of child and family poverty are now much higher than where income transfers were redesigned rather than assaulted. As Christopher Howard (this volume) documents for the United States—and the situation is equally true for other liberal regimes[1] in Europe such as the United Kingdom and Ireland—poverty in general and child poverty in particular remains very high in international terms, and this despite significant policy attention to it over the last decade.[2]

The 1990s saw an increase in public social expenditure across Europe, just as it did in the United States.[3] It is important to emphasize from the beginning that the response to new social risks cannot be assessed simply by examining spending levels, which reveal little about the composition of spending.[4] Governments have shifted resources from one policy area to another and altered the mix of taxes, social transfers, and services. In general these reforms, even those promoted by center-left parties and governments, reflect ideas about the role of the state different from those that dominated in the years after 1945. The state was to be responsible for "social investments" in human capital—education, including early childhood education, and training—at least as much as for social "protection" against the risks of ill-health, job loss, and old age.[5]

After presenting the notion of new social risks and the challenges they present in more detail, this chapter examines the responses to them by three center-left parties: the Swedish Social Democratic Party, Britain's Labour Party, and the German Social Democratic Party. All three have recently been in government, and have therefore had the opportunity to shape public policy. The chapter describes their initiatives primarily as responses to "policy challenges" rather than as elements of political strategy.

The Policy Challenge of the New Social Risks

"Old social risks"—aging, illness, unemployment, and so on—have not disappeared. They remain both real in people's lives and on the agenda of governments. Nonetheless, attention has also turned to the risks resulting from income and service gaps in postindustrial labor markets as well as from demographic and social transformations. Labor market shifts associated with the emergence of knowledge-based as well as service-sector employment polarize skills and earning capabilities. Families with only one income have a substantially higher risk of being poor. Yet transformations in family life have brought a significant increase in single-parent families. There has been a decline in the fertility rate and an increase in life expectancy. The working-age population and several specific categories, such as single-parent families and those in need of social care, are more at risk of social exclusion as well as of low income.[6]

Policy challenges are of two broad types. One relates to the means of ensuring adequate income. If a single wage supported several adults and children fifty years ago, this is much less true today, both because of job losses in the industrial sector and because of the rise of the service sector, which traditionally has lower-paying jobs. More generally, the polarization of the post-industrial income structure in many countries has generated an increase in low-income rates among young families, whether single-parent or headed by couples: therefore the appearance of what has been termed "child poverty." These patterns are often also concentrated among minority ethnic groups and in cities. High unemployment and low employment rates also plague many economies. A second broad challenge is to social care arrangements. Across all types of welfare regimes there are now serious contradictions between the realities that families face in balancing work and family life and the assumptions used when European social protection systems were designed after 1945. For example, women's higher labor force participation means reduced availability for full-time family caring, while single-parent families have only one adult to provide both income and care. Aging populations mean more frail elderly in need of care and fewer family members at home to care for them.

Governments have reacted to the new structure of risk, albeit at different rates. One widely shared strategy is the deployment of labor market policies that seek to foster labor force participation by almost all working-age adults. These often focus on workers in declining sectors, on women, on youth, and on any category in need of skills training or updating. If active labor market policies (ALMP) have been widely used in Nordic countries since the 1950s (see Pontusson, this volume), they are now found in one form or another in all types of welfare regimes, within member states of the European Union and at the level of the EU itself.[7] As Tony Blair and Gerhard Schröder put it in their manifesto for "third way" politics (1999), "A welfare system that puts limits on an individual's ability to find a job must be reformed. Modern social democrats want to transform the safety net of entitlements into a springboard to personal responsibility."[8]

Blair and Schröder, like many other center-left thinkers, argued that achieving these ends would involve remodeling income-transfer programs. But they also understood the need for additional services for improving indi-

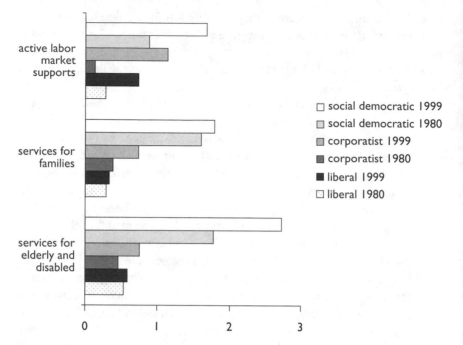

Figure 1. Spending on services for new social risks as percentage of gross domestic product in EU countries, by type of regime (developed from Taylor-Cooby 2004, 16).

viduals' employability and for social care. One example is the call for improved childcare services, including services that pay attention to the educational and developmental needs of children, which comes not only from advocates for gender equality and children's rights but also from long-time proponents of labor market activation strategies, such as the Organisation for Economic Cooperation and Development (OECD) (Mahon 2006).

We can see the results of responses to new social risks. Across all types of welfare regimes, services have gained ground in the expenditure mix. As figure 1 documents, the numbers for 1999 are all higher than those of 1980. In addition, the classic cross-regime patterns also continue to structure outcomes, with levels of spending varying in the usual way. They are highest in social democratic regimes and lowest in liberal ones.

Equally important is the timing and content of reforms, as shown by the detailed case studies discussed here. The social democratic welfare regimes altered several policy positions early on, so that the impact of new social risks was mitigated although not eliminated in the most recent decade. The continental European countries, in contrast, first reinforced traditional male breadwinner models under pressure from the social partners, but in the last decade have recognized the significance of the challenges and are undertaking redesign. The liberal regimes, as is their wont, relied on market solutions to welfare problems and found themselves faced with some severe manifestations of the costs of new social risks, especially in the form of high rates of poverty.

Center-Lefts Respond to New Social Risks: Three Welfare Regimes

Given these observations, this chapter concentrates on one case from each type of welfare regime: Sweden represents the social democratic type, Great Britain the liberal type, and Germany the continental-corporatist type.

A First Responder: New Social Risks and Sweden

Swedish Social Democrats: Platform 2006

Work for all is the most important goal for social democracy . . .

Justice and security are the core values of social democratic welfare policy . . .

Along side these primary goals the social democrats intend to carry through reforms in the coming parliament that provide the basis for a long term modernisation of our country:

1. A competitive Sweden with modern jobs . . .
2. Sweden, a model for the green turnaround . . .
3. The next step in welfare policy involves dental care . . .
4. Sweden will be the best of countries to grow up in . . .
5. Sweden will be the best of countries in which to grow old . . .
6. We all gain from supporting each other.[9]

If the new social risks are the result of labor market restructuring and new needs for social care, Sweden had a response to these risks well before the other two countries examined in detail in this chapter. Indeed Sweden had its own "third way" long before other countries were even thinking of one. During the heyday of international neoliberalism the Social Democratic governments (between 1982 and 1991), partly in response to the drop in the employers' enthusiasm for corporatism, promised a middle route between Thatcherism and Keynesianism (Ryner 1999, 60). But responses to new social risks predated even this precocious third way.

Sweden has a long tradition of active labor market policy. Indeed, as Jonas Pontusson argues (this volume), it has been a core ingredient of Swedish social democracy. Through the 1990s thinking about Swedish labor market policy was shaped by principles put forth at the end of the 1940s by the trade union economists Gösta Rehn and Rudolf Meidner. For them ALMP was a necessary ingredient in a policy mix designed to combine low inflation, full employment, and wage compression. Fearing unemployment in low-productivity sectors that would follow from anti-inflation measures, they recommended labor market retraining and other mobility-enhancing measures that would allow workers threatened by unemployment to transfer to high-productivity sectors, and thereby to relieve labor shortages there. While the original emphasis was on labor mobility, from the 1960s through the 1990s it gradually shifted toward holding down unemployment in general (Calmfors, Forslund, and Hemström 2002, 3–4).

The anti-unemployment objective was dominant by the 1990s, as Sweden entered its deepest postwar recession. Employment fell by 13% between 1990 and 1994, and as a result, placement of the unemployed in a labor market program served as the main short-run policy instrument to counteract the steep decline. Enrollment in a program became a mechanism of short-term income security, filling the gap when unemployment benefits ran out and as a means to regain entitlements.[10] As we will see below, exit from the recession also brought a redesign of ALMP.

Public provision of non-parental childcare developed early in Sweden in comparison to many other non-Nordic countries. By the mid-1960s the "sex role debate" was roiling through the Social Democratic Party and the major labor federation.[11] Led by feminists from left and liberal circles, it divided not only left from right but also the forces of the left itself. Eventually reaching a certain level of consensus by promising parents "choice" between work and care as well as about forms of non-parental care (center-based or family daycare), new investments in services brought a rapid increase in childcare spaces, from a modest 17,900 in 1965 to 224,900 a decade later. In the same years parental leaves were debated and introduced. In 1972 the Social Democratic Party opted for paid parental leaves, clearly rejecting the preference of the right-wing parties and some liberal feminists for a "care allowance" that would subsidize parental (stay-at-home mothers) as well as non-parental care.

This decision, which generated legislation two years later, alongside the commitment to public support for non-parental childcare, was decisive for the way that social care has been organized in Sweden. Its continuing influence shaped governments' decisions over the next decades to extend parental leave and childcare services. It also continues to be shaped by the Social Democratic Party's approach to gender and employment, which is that all Swedes enjoy "the right of being both an active parent and an active gainful employee."[12] As economic crisis shook Sweden in the 1990s, reliance on these policy instruments to organize social care were tested and debated but not abandoned. Electoral losses by the Social Democrats brought a revival of the care allowance proposal, and the center-right government of Carl Bildt introduced a "care wage," which was intended to reimburse partially the "lost wages" of parents who provided their own childcare. The same government, however, also introduced a guarantee of a childcare place for any child whose parent wanted one (something the Social Democrats had talked about for at least nine years) and a "father's month" as an incentive to fathers to share parental leaves. On their return to office in 1994 the Social Democrats rescinded the care allowance, while promising to institute a second father's month.

Social care for the elderly was launched on a generous high road in post-1945 decades, as services and housing were arranged in ways to maximize the possibilities for the elderly to live on their own, avoiding both residential care and dependence on their families, even when their health declined and their frailties increased. These early choices implied both improved housing and high levels of in-home services. Thus in the 1970s studies found that almost 40% of Swedes over eighty received home-help services, although another 30% were cared for in institutions (Sundstrom, Johansson, and Hassing 2002, 351). In contrast to childcare, the high point of coverage was reached in the 1970s, and it has declined since.

These policy instruments in the domains of ALMP and social care came under pressure as the new social risks structured the circumstances of more Swedes. The deep recession of the 1990s and subsequent restructuring hit several population categories particularly hard. The cutbacks in social spending instituted at the time were particularly costly for young people, single-parent families, recently arrived immigrants, and those poorly anchored in the labor market (Timonen 2004, 85). Three responses will be considered here: reconfiguring ALMP policies, addressing the needs of the elderly, and investing in children.

Swedish jobs rebounded somewhat after the 1990s, although not all the way back. Employment rates did not return to their previous highs, and dependence on public income transfers did not fall back to their previous lows (OECD 2007d, chapter 7). Precarious work, particularly in the form of part-time and limited-term contracts, has increased, and it affects women more than men. One policy response has been to provide better social protection to part-time workers with even very short hours. The emphasis on lifelong learning has also been intensified, with the Social Democrats proposing to create a new right to obtain it in their party program in 2001.

In a classic reading of the new social risks, the Swedish government also targeted youth and technological change. The "youth guarantee" program offers priority in receiving work, training, and education to workers aged twenty to twenty-four, and placement programs for youth were introduced and redesigned in the 1990s. Grants are also available to employers who hire the older long-term unemployed displaced by changing skill requirements. Computer training centers and other programs for new technologies were introduced over the 1990s. And an "activation guarantee" (*aktivitetsgarantie*) was instituted in 2000, targeted toward the long-term unemployed but also those working shorter hours than they wished (Timonen 2004, 96–97).[13]

In the same years awareness of population aging and an expansion of the number of frail elderly led to program adjustments. The proportion of older persons receiving publicly provided homecare has declined in Sweden in the last decades. A major reform by the center-right government in 1992 assigned responsibility for both residential care and home help to municipalities. As the number of elderly rose in Sweden, municipalities squeezed for funds maintained their coverage rate in residential care (that is the care used by the most frail and those without family support), but homecare coverage declined. Whereas in 1994 68% of seniors living alone and in need of help received some homecare from the municipality, by 2000 that number had fallen to 52%. The result was that almost half of frail seniors living alone and in need of help with everyday living relied on informal care from non-cohabiting family or friends. This was a big jump from the one-third who had found themselves in the same situation a decade earlier (Sundstrom, Johansson, and Hassing 2002, 353). Better-off seniors have moved into the private market to hire the help they need, and poorer seniors have returned to reliance on their families. There are also labor shortages in the social care field. Poor working conditions and better job prospects drain workers to other sectors. Municipalities, responsible for providing all public homecare services, face severe labor shortages (Timonen 2004, 89–92). These issues were addressed in the party platforms and program of the current decade; as noted in the passage quoted above, the Social Democrats promised to make Sweden "the best country in which to grow old." Yet in party documents attention to children and youth far outpaces that going to the elderly.[14] Significant gaps remain between needs and available services. With regard to these new social risks, Sweden is falling behind in comparison to its earlier record.[15]

Single-parent families constitute a paradigmatic location for new social risks. In Sweden the needs of this type of family have always been dealt with through standard labor market instruments as well as by providing generous family benefits to all families. In other words, mothers raising children alone have always been expected to be employed, and they have received the same family benefits as families headed by couples. In addition, the state guarantees a small monthly child maintenance payment if the non-custodial parent does not make his or her child support payments.

Child poverty has become an increasingly important topic in policy circles, and Sweden's single-parent families have not escaped the scourge (Kamerman, Neuman, Waldfogel, and Brooks-Gunn 2003, 6). In its pathbreaking study of child poverty in rich countries, UNICEF identified single parenthood as the overwhelmingly important factor in Swedish child poverty. Although Sweden has by far the lowest rate of child poverty overall (only 2.6% of children live in poverty after taxes and transfers are considered), the rate among single-parent families, which in Sweden are numerous, was almost five times greater than that of two-parent families (UNICEF 2000, 17, 19) [16] Policy changes have been proposed, such as replacing the housing allowances by a more generous income transfer. This proposal has been opposed quite widely, however. Therefore action falls back on the traditional strategy, and labor market policies are used to try to increase the employment of lone parents (Halleröd 2007, 26). Here performance lags. While Sweden is a strong performer in UNICEF's general "child poverty league tables," it is only in the middle-performing group with respect to rates of workless households, many of which are likely to be headed by one adult (UNICEF 2000, 17). These poor performance indicators result from the basic new social risk, which is the intransigence of new labor market structures in which young people in particular have so many difficulties finding employment, and especially good jobs.

Yet overall, much less attention is now paid to families than to children. This is a shift from the golden age of Swedish social democracy, when generous parental leaves and accessible childcare of high quality were promoted as policy instruments to achieve gender equality within the family and society. "[For] the development of pervasive, high quality and affordable public childcare in Sweden, starting in the 1960s . . . one motivation was just to allow gender equality in practice, by allowing women both to have children and to stay in employment and develop careers. Three particular landmarks are the 1976 law requiring municipalities to draw up ten year childcare expansion plans, the 1985 law giving all children aged eighteen months to seven years, with working or studying parents, or with special needs, a place in public childcare by 1991, and the 1995 law making it obligatory for municipalities to provide childcare on demand. The Family Policy Committee's 1972 Report also recommended buttressing the gender equity effects of the public childcare system by transforming maternity leave into a much longer and gender-neutral parental leave, subsequently introduced in 1974" (Ahlberg, Roman, and Duncan 2008, 83).

It was only with the reform of 1995 that access to childcare was clearly separated from parental labor market status. This was a turning point toward the child-centered social investment strategy that is now so prevalent.[17] This emphasis has been dominant for a decade now, shown by a simple quantitative indicator. The Social Democrats' election manifesto of 2006 mentioned families twice, parents twice, and children twenty-five times. Children had become the focus of policy interventions for combating poverty, achieving equality, and ensuring the future. The Social Democrats' program of 2001 had also devoted an extraordinary amount of attention to children. Thus the promise cited above that "Sweden would be the best of countries to grow up in" translated into promises to invest in services for children because, as the manifesto put it, "the choices made by children today will determine the future of Sweden." Children have become actors in their own right, and hold the future of the country in their little hands!

This shift to an emphasis on new social risks has not been without opposition. Trade unions and pensioners have used their solid organizational strength to defend earnings-related benefits and to launch campaigns to restore cuts to unemployment insurance. Nonetheless, new coalitions have also emerged, led by church and community-based groups, which present something of a challenge to the long-standing organization of Swedish politics around producer groups. These new coalitions promote the rights and advocate for the needs of groups such as immigrants and the working poor who have been most touched by the new social risks (Timonen 2004, 105). Therefore the full political consequences of the Swedish response to new social risks remain to be assessed.

Great Britain: New Labour Focuses on Child Poverty and Social Investment

> In our third term we will make public services safe for a generation. No going back to one-size-fits-all monolithic services. No going back to the Tory years of cuts and privatisation. Going forward instead to services free to all, personal to each: breaking once and for all the dropout culture in education and the waiting-list culture in health, by raising investment and driving innovation through diversity of provision and power in the hands of the patient, the parent and the citizen.
>
> In our third term we will cement a new social contract with rights matched by responsibilities. No going back to "no such thing as society." Going forward instead to power and resources in the hands of the law-abiding majority. A government committed both to abolishing child poverty and to putting the values of individual responsibility and duty at the very heart of policy.
>
> —Labour Party Manifesto 2005

The British center-left provides a classic example of a liberal welfare state's response to the new social risks. Out of power for a decade and a half while Margaret Thatcher's Conservative Party reshaped the social as well as economic landscape, Labour had ample time to reflect on ways to transform itself into *New* Labour. Eventually the social policy spotlight was shifted to new social risks, particularly worklessness and child poverty, and solutions were framed in terms of social investments.[18]

In the 1990s unemployment was high in the United Kingdom, as industrial restructuring slashed jobs from traditional industrial sectors and the service sector did not provide sufficient replacements. The recession at the beginning of the decade was severe, such that in 1994 21% of men aged fifteen to twenty-four and 14% of women were unemployed. Rates of economic inactivity were rising, and at 14.2% of all households, the rate of those that had no one in employment (that is, "workless" households) was the second-highest of the EU-15 (Taylor-Gooby and Larsen 2004, 58).

In large part because of this statistic, in a liberal welfare regime with little in the way of family benefits (in contrast to Sweden, for example), child poverty was also very high. Indeed "a fifth of Britain's children lived in poverty in the 1990s, a rate more than twice as high as in France or the Netherlands and five times higher than in Norway or Sweden. . . . And while child poverty has remained stable or risen only slightly in most industrial nations over the last 20 years [that is the 1980s and 1990s], it tripled in Britain" (UNICEF 2000, 21). The poverty rate was particularly high among single-parent families, in which the employment rate was significantly lower than elsewhere: 47% as compared to 59% across the EU as a whole (Taylor-Gooby and Larsen 2004, 58).

Given these patterns and under the pressure of successive electoral failures, the Labour leader John Smith established the Commission on Social Justice (CSJ) in 1992 to mark the fiftieth anniversary of the Beveridge Report, which underpinned the design of much British social policy after 1945. While rejecting any return to past policy habits, the commission's report called for, among other things, more "investments." This was a language that clearly distinguished it from the Conservatives' continuing reliance on the neoliberal goal of reducing the role of the state by cutting back. For example, "investing in skills, we raise people's capacity to add value to the economy, to take charge of their own lives, and to contribute to their families and communities" (CSJ 1994, 119–20). The report set out an argument for the advantages of spending on employability programs rather than welfare, on lifelong learning and on work for all. It made the point too that social justice is "an economic not merely a social necessity." The report also promoted concentrating on children for social investment: "the investment we make in babies and young children is wholly inadequate"; "children are not a private pleasure or a personal burden; they are 100 percent of the nation's future . . . the best indicator of the capacity of our economy tomorrow is the quality of our children today" (CSJ 1994, 122, 311). Finally, it concluded that "the best way to help the one in three children growing up in poverty is to help their parents get jobs" (CSJ 1994, 313).

Chosen as Labour's leader after Smith's early death, Tony Blair rarely acknowledged directly any debt to the CSJ. Yet the commission, housed in the Institute for Public Policy Research (IPPR), showed a skill for finding the middle ground within a divided party that identified a path for New Labour when it took office. Drafted by one of New Labour's rising stars, David Miliband, the commission's principles underpin the key values enunciated by Blair for New Labour. Reducing child poverty became one of the big policy ideas of the Labour government, and in 1999 Blair pledged to end it in a generation. For his part, Gordon Brown was in full agreement: "Our children are our future, and the most important investment we can make as a nation is in developing the potential of all our country's children. Together we can ensure that no child is left behind" (H.M. Treasury 2001, iii–iv). Child poverty, and the use of various benefits and services to lower the rate, were a major theme in Treasury documents for the decade before Brown succeeded Blair as Labour's leader. When he took over as prime minister on 28 June 2007, one of his three new creations was the Department of Children, Schools and Families.[19]

In contrast to the story of the Swedish Social Democratic Party, New Labour's is one of significant policy shifts in the mid-1990s (see Cronin, this volume). Whereas the Swedish Social Democrats could adjust to the economic crisis of the 1990s and the rise of new social risks by fine-tuning existing policies and programs such as parental leave, childcare, and homecare, New Labour struck out on new paths in several policy areas. In doing so it did not abandon its standard approach to designing policy within a liberal welfare regime (much of which had been built by "old" Labour after 1945). It remained true to the long-standing preference for market solutions to welfare problems, using instruments of income transfer and services targeted to the most in need. Nonetheless new programs were invented so as "to make work pay," with several built on work subsidies for families, in contrast to the previous Conservative governments (Seeleib-Kaiser and Fleckenstein 2007, 430).

In this way the focus on investing in children and ending child poverty came together in several initiatives with the issues of employment and combating worklessness. New Labour's commitment to increasing access to employment came in the form of several New Deals. "New Deal policies provided intensive training and work preparation programmes and slightly enhanced rates of benefit, and were targeted on specific groups of those out of work, most prominently young people and lone parents" (Taylor-Gooby and Larsen 2004, 68). The election manifesto of 1997 had promised that 250,000 young people would be moved into work by the next election, and the New Deal for Lone Parents set a target of 70% in work by 2010. Additional New Deals were then added for partners of the unemployed (in effect women), persons with disabilities, those over age fifty, and the long-term unemployed. The programs for youth and the long term unemployed were effectively workfare schemes, participation being compulsory in order to claim benefits (Taylor-Gooby and Larsen 2004, 69). The other programs were voluntary.

Learning has been a constant theme in international discussions of employability and was at the core of New Labour's approach to new social risks too. The green paper *The Learning Age: A Renaissance for a New Britain* (1998) encouraged workers to invest in their own training and learning throughout their lives, with some financial support from the state. Spending on learning would be an arm in the fight against childhood poverty, helping parents to upgrade skills and to ensure that children did not follow their parents along the low-skill road. Improving skills was closely linked to welfare reform. For example, single parents were targeted in the strategy Skills for Life, and basic skills counseling became part of their New Deal (Dobrowolsky and Jenson, 2005). While the New Deals offered some basic skill training, the major focus in this strand of the analysis is on learning by children. "The seed of inequality in adulthood is denial of opportunity in childhood. Education is the most important transmission mechanism—people with few skills and qualifications are much less likely to succeed in the labour market" (H.M. Treasury 1999, 7). Thus the "skills agenda" would include a heavy dose of investment in schooling.

Because Britain is a liberal welfare state, albeit a "modernizing" one, New Labour in its responses to the new social risks demonstrated a continuing preference for market solutions. Three kinds of important programs work at the margin of markets. The first set of programs was designed to "make work pay," and they operated at the margins of the labor market. These were of three types: increases in the minimum wage; policies holding down benefits for those out of work, to increase their incentives to seek work; and supplements to earned incomes.

With respect to linkages between unemployment programs and ALMP, Clasen and Clegg describe Britain as being no less forceful than Denmark in coordinating access to benefits and policy institutions, represented, for example, by the Jobcentres Plus that deal with both the unemployed and those in receipt of social assistance benefits. This effort to create a single point of entry is part of "the transition of UK labour market policy from an emphasis on unemployment to an increasing emphasis on 'worklessness'" (Clasen and Clegg 2006, 204). In large part the accent has been on reduced access to unemployment insurance, job searching, and some training, as noted above regarding the various New Deals.

The redesign and enrichment of benefits for the low-income employed and their families came in the form of various tax credits and benefits, some targeting low-income workers and some intended to help families with children. The Child Benefit and the Child Tax Benefit are available to adults caring for children, the latter being income-tested. In addition, some non-parental childcare costs are addressed by the Working Tax Credit. In other words, much of the redesigned social spending is work-tested, child-tested, or both. New Labour's Manifesto (2005) promised that "tailored help, especially for lone parents, is key, but we are also committed to making work pay—with a guaranteed income of at least £258 per week for those with children and in full-time work."

A second type of child-oriented program stressed improving access to childcare. Again the goal was market-shaping. Over the years of Labour government childcare has always been treated as a support for working parents.[20] On this issue the British government continued to be much less convinced than many other countries are that educational care of high quality—and more than part-time nursery school—is good for all children (Mahon 2006). New Labour always had clear ideas about the needs of children who are at risk of suffering from childhood poverty: they need superior publicly supported services to compensate for disadvantages at home. Sure Start, a neighborhood-based program targeting disadvantaged children, was the expression of this prong of the National Childcare Strategy launched in 1997. For the rest, however, the government continued to promise parental "choice." It preferred to "rely on private mechanisms through the expansion of childcare tax credits rather than the development of public childcare facilities" (Daguerre 2006, 222).

Third, New Labour innovated with a policy instrument for providing market access: asset building. Not long after the election of 2002 Blair described his vision of welfare reform. In a speech he saved his greatest enthusiasm and his most upbeat description of the future for one idea: "But if we are serious about transforming the welfare state, our strategy has to be about more than helping people into work and relieving poverty. To enable people to be independent and make their own choices, they need the back-up of having some savings in the bank or a nest-egg. Money put aside changes your horizons. It makes you plan, brings responsibility, offers protection and opportunity. And I want to ensure that those on lower incomes—and the next generation— can share those advantages" (Blair 2002).

Such notions about the wide range of benefits from fostering savings and the acquisition of assets are the purest expression of the social investment perspective. The Treasury had already been working on the idea, floated in the white paper *Savings and Assets for All* (2001). In presenting the white paper, Gordon Brown suggested that the initiatives had the potential of "creating a democracy where wealth ownership is genuinely open to all," and the first policy experiment was with the Child Trust Fund, a long-term savings and investment account. The government provides a lump sum to each child, and the package includes financial education for children, intended to create the "saving culture."

New Labour clearly responded to the new social risks. In doing so it arrived at rhetorical flourishes not all that different from those of the Swedish Social Democrats. Recalling the promise in 2005 that "Sweden will be the best of countries to grow up in," Labour's Children's Plan (2007) opens with the statement: "By 2020 we want England to be the best place in the world to grow up."[21] In contrast to both Sweden and, as we will see, Germany, much less attention has gone to the needs of the frail elderly.[22]

In postwar social policy, services for the frail elderly were provided by local authorities based on need and means testing. Under pressure from the disability rights movement, made up primarily of young activists who promoted independent living for the disabled, and seduced by the cost-control promises of in-home rather than residential care as well as by the discourses of "choice" so dear to neoliberalism, the Conservatives instituted a series of measures to enable care services in the home (Ungerson and Yeandle eds. 2007, 5, 188). In 1996 this basket of policies was expanded to include "cash-for-care," or direct payments to the disabled to allow them to assemble a care package themselves. Persons over sixty-five were excluded from this program until 2000, when the Labour government extended access to them, so that they could also receive direct payments in order to put together their preferred care packages (Ungerson and Yeandle eds. 2007, 115.) The benefits are needs tested and scaled to financial resources (LeBihan and Martin 2006, 42). Still, participation in the payments-for-care program remains low, and Britain does not shine internationally as a provider of care services for the frail elderly.

Instead, and in line with its driving theme of "social investment," the Labour Party in office concentrated on increasing employment through activation strategies and programs of human capital (from the early years through post-secondary education). Adults and their needs for training and retraining were a preoccupation, though one often justified as a means to ending child poverty, and in particular to increasing the employment rates of single parents. In contrast to Sweden, and somewhat unexpectedly for such a pure case of the social investment thematic, parents have not lost their place as policy targets. They remain linked to their children, who have become nonetheless political actors: "Children cannot be the forgotten constituency of politics; parents put their children first and they deserve support from government" (Labour Party Manifesto 2005, 79).

Germany: Rethinking the Risk Structure

> Our aim is to pursue a holistic policy for families, senior citizens, women and youth which promotes and reinforces solidarity between the generations and therefore of society as a whole. We want to encourage families to have more children, and we want a stronger role for the family in society. We want to make it clear that without children, Germany has no future.
> —Coalition Agreement 2005

Any analysis of the center-left's response to new social risks in Germany must take into account the strong structuring effects of previous policy choices, many of them initiated by left governments or grand coalitions in which the Social Democrats played a key role. As a policy process in which corporatist political relations as well as Bismarckian social insurance policy regimes have played a key role, the emphasis in studies of the German case is often on stability and blockages to change. Nonetheless, like other European countries Germany has experienced major changes in labor markets as well as in family and employment policy in the last decade. These reforms have been often instituted by the Social Democratic Party (SPD) in power, either in coalition with the Greens or, after 2005, with the Christian Democratic Union (CDU) and others in the Grand Coalition. One dimension of these changes has been a solid focus on demography, which has been shaping much social policy (thus the choice of quotation above).

In confronting one of the new social risks—social care for the frail elderly—Germany was an early innovator, though the innovations relied on the traditional policy instruments of social insurance. In 1994 the government, led by the CDU, instituted long-term care insurance, a proposal which had also been pushed by the SPD (Morel 2006, 233–34). In addition to relieving fiscal pressures in government finances, the goal of the new program was to promote family-based care by recognizing and subsidizing it (Ungerson and Yeandle eds. 2007, 138–39). Thus even in this innovation the difficulties that Germany has faced in moving away from the male breadwinner model, enshrined in so much of the German social architecture after 1945, are evident. But much of the deadlock has been recently removed by the actions of the current Grand Coalition government, headed by Angela Merkel since November 2005.

With a traditionally strong industrial sector, highly regulated labor markets, and low rates of women's employment, Germany has had an employment structure characterized by a large proportion of permanent, full-time employment. Nonetheless the industrial sector has shrunk, women have entered the labor market, and non-standard employment—particularly part-time employment—has increased. The result has been more "mini-jobs," low-skill employment, and working poor (Aust and Bönker 2004, 33–34). These changes have not gone unnoticed, of course, and they have been vigorously debated for two decades now. The controversy has turned on two issues: atypical employment and adjustments to the welfare state.[23] The center-left and trade unions were on the side of protecting long-term employment and opposed plans by Helmut Kohl's right-wing government to deemphasize fixed-term employment and accept even more mini-jobs. The consequences singled out for attention by the center-left were those for pensions in particular. With regard to the low-skilled, a lively debate within policy communities turned on whether to "make work pay" by supplementing (subsidizing) the earnings of low-waged jobs. Opposed by unions and some academic economists and supported by others, the center-left government after 1998 contented itself with a few pilot projects. The third prong of debate about labor market policy has been the interface between unemployment insurance and social assistance, with the center-left proposing a "modernized" welfare state that promotes activation (Seeleib-Kaiser and Fleckenstein 2007, 437).

Despite opposition from trade unions and state and local governments, the second government led by Schröder adopted measures that added up "to a substantial transformation of German labour market policy" (Aust and Bönker 2004, 46). Among these were "job centers" modeled on Britain's one-stop locations for job seekers (Seeleib-Kaiser and Fleckenstein 2007, 431–32). Social assistance and unemployment benefits were merged for many without jobs, thereby reducing the pool of unemployed who could count on replacement income; they received a much less generous benefit, similar in amount to the earlier social assistance rates.[24] One result was to widen the cleavage between insiders with jobs or full insurance benefits and the rest, whose access was to means-tested unemployment or job seeking assistance. Nonetheless, full-scale activation efforts of the Danish or British type were applied only to the unemployed under twenty-five. Social Democrats' hopes to do more were hampered by the constitutional division of powers, which assigns responsibility for "active" and "passive" measures to different levels of government (Clasen and Clegg 2006, 202).

In large part these policy stances adopted by the center-left reflect a long-term process of change in party philosophy. "Although intellectually the Social Democrats had recognised the limits of Keynesian policies in the mid-1970s, they more or less continued to follow the traditional Social Democratic policy path in terms of economic and employment policies until the mid-1990s" (Seeleib-Kaiser, van Dyk, and Roggenkamp 2005, 21). Thus change dates from the second half of the 1990s, just as in Britain. By 1998 the Social Democrats (and the Greens) were campaigning on the position that deficit-financed economic stimulation was impossible and social insurance contributions (the heart of a Bismarckian welfare regime) had to be limited, all to stay competitive in the global economy. The market was also rehabilitated as a social mechanism. As Blair's and Schröder's Third Way manifesto of 1999 put it, "we need to apply our politics within a new economic framework, modernised for today, where government does all it can to support enterprise but never believes it is a substitute for enterprise. The essential function of markets must be complemented and improved by political action, not hampered by it. We support a market economy, not a market society."[25]

If change has been slow but steady with respect to the new social risks of low-wage work and unemployment, the same is now less true of social care, both for the elderly and children. In both cases, though, it has been governments led by Christian Democrats that have brought about the most far-reaching reform.

In the Federal Republic of Germany the risk of long-term care until the 1990s was covered by a means-tested social assistance program of last resort and was a local government responsibility. But local authorities found it increasingly difficult to meet rising demand, and they turned to the central government to take responsibility for care of the frail elderly. There was also, as we have noted, some earlier mobilization for such a program by the Social Democrats. The Care Insurance Act (1994) is a compulsory insurance regime that provides basic benefits to those in need of care, as assessed by an expert team that includes doctors, nurses, and social workers. Benefits may be used in conjunction with personal resources or social assistance and may be taken in cash or in services. The incentive structure of the program is to increase reliance on home care and informal care. The recipient has full control over its disbursement.[26] The universal insurance scheme covers approximately 90% of the population (Morel 2006, 234).

The focus in the German scheme, in contrast to those of some Nordic countries (Jenson and Jacobzone 2000), was intended to satisfy the needs of the frail elderly, and much less attention was paid to informal caregivers (mostly female family members). While informal caregivers do receive some social security rights, the recipients' preference is by far for in-home care (71%) and within that for cash benefits (73%) rather than formal services (Morel 2006, 243). This means that the domestic economy of benefit sharing remains private and unknown.

Family policy is the other area of major change in Germany, which is finally moving away from the male breadwinner model and toward accepting the need for public intervention to ensure better reconciliation of work and family. Until well into the 1990s policy design had favored stay-at-home parents. A childcare allowance provided extended benefits to parents—read mothers—who remained out of the labor force for three years. The lack of non-parental childcare for infants and toddlers as well as school days that ended very early made it difficult to combine work and parenting even when children were of school age. The tax system penalized a move from part-time to full-time work (Gottfried and O'Reilly 2002, 44–45). Overall Germany was characterized by both low rates of female labor force participation and the third-lowest fertility rate in the EU-15.

In the election that brought the Red-Green coalition led by Gerhard Schröder to office in 1998, three of the four main themes in the SPD party platform had to do with macroeconomic and labor market policy; the fourth was improving family policies (Seeleib-Kaiser and Fleckenstein, 2007, 437). Parental leave was significantly reshaped in 2001 so as to increase flexibility. Both parents may take leave. They may do so at the same time, or they may split the leave in different combinations and at different times, until the child turns eight. Parents also gained the right to work part-time during the first two years after a child's birth. A second wave of reform in 2005 introduced an earnings-related parental benefit, providing a standard period of twelve months and 67% of the previous net income of the parent taking leave (capped at €1,800/month). By including two months of paid benefits with a "use it or lose it" provision, the design provides clear encouragement for the second parent (read fathers) to take some leave (Daly and Seeleib-Kaiser 2008, 5).

For a number of years the Social Democrats had advocated better supply of childcare, a stance in line with their preference for providing services rather than simply income transfers (Huster, Benz, and Boeckh 2008, 20). The Day Care Development Act of 2005 required municipalities to provide a childcare space for all children under the age of three whose parents were in work or in education or training. Then the Grand Coalition government in the spring of 2007 promised to increase publicly financed or subsidized care to fully meet demand by 2013. That year as well was targeted for introduction of an individual entitlement to childcare for every child. In other words the male breadwinner model had tumbled, and Germany's childcare guarantee mimics that of the child-centered Swedish model.

Short but well-paid parental leaves and generous childcare provision represent responses to new social risks. Much more than in Sweden or Britain, the German responses have been driven by fear of risk of declining fertility, as a report to the European Union on child poverty clearly reveals: "Under the guiding idea that Germany needs 'more children in the families and more families in society,' the federal government identifies three priorities with regard to children, youths and families for the current legislative period (2005–2009): support of young parents during the family formation phase (see the Day Care Development Act and the new Parental Benefit Act), strengthening the bond between the generations (see the new federal model program 'multigeneration facilities'), and more attention to be paid to children 'born on the dark side of life' (meaning children who grow up under difficult social and economic conditions)" (Huster, Benz, and Boeckh 2008, 18). Many analysts attribute the demographic challenge in Germany directly to the long-standing commitment in social policy design to the male breadwinner model and lack of attention until recently to reconciling work and family. Families were forced to choose between having two incomes and having children.

THESE THREE PATTERNS of response by center-lefts to new social risks, particularly family poverty and labor market exclusion, have been generated by the parties' understanding of the new social risks and their sometimes enthusiastic, sometimes reluctant embrace of the proposition that modernization of social policy is necessary. The second half of the 1990s was a key moment for all three parties, and indeed almost all European center-left parties. The harsh recession at the beginning of the decade and the political space offered by stumbling right-wing governments provided an opening for proclaiming their commitment to modernization. Sometimes the announcement was dramatic, as in Britain when Tony Blair declared that New Labour had arrived, or when he and Gerhard Schröder trumpeted their manifesto for a third way. Sometimes the rhetoric was more restrained, as center-left parties in Sweden and Germany attempted to reassure their long-time constituents and partners, especially in the unions, that change was necessary to maintain commitments to long-standing values.

There was therefore a political imperative to "modernize." But just as pressing was the policy challenge arising from recognition of the new social risks themselves. There was, it must be said, no significant political mobilization by those most affected by the new social risks.[27] Rather, sensitivity to the challenges came primarily from within social policy bureaucracies and the policy experts affiliated with center-left parties. What was to be done about the costs as well as the dwindling supply of social care? With women's employment essential to the modern service economy as well as an imperative of contemporary social relations, who would look after young children and the swelling ranks of the frail elderly? How could more working-age adults be brought into employment, and which activation models worked best?

This chapter has documented that in most cases answers to these questions were found within initial policy trajectories structured by left politics during the *trente glorieuses*. While it is hard to account for the responses to new social risks as the result of contemporary mobilization by the elderly, parents, or the poor, it is easy to see how the politics of the "old left" of the years since 1945 continues to influence the ways the new social risks are addressed. Choices about benefits and services frequently echoed those made in the 1950s and 1960s, in terms of generosity as well as policy design. Swedish Social Democrats' early response to what were "old risks" of labor market shortages and the need to encourage higher female employment rates helped to keep down some of the indicators of costly new social risks, because parental leaves and childcare services were already in place. Nonetheless the traditional solution of a job for everyone is less effective these days, as Sweden struggles with poverty and joblessness among single-parent families as well as young people. This problem is rising in importance and seems intractable to classic solutions. It blots the Swedish copybook, as does the foot dragging on care for the frail elderly. New Labour too continues its residualist tradition, with public programs filling gaps left by market failures for those at the margins of society. By dint of harping on social investments, New Labour managed to make a dent in child poverty, although many of the structural patterns of the new social risks—such as low wages and youth exclusion—remained in place. No more than the Swedish Social Democrats had New Labour found "the" solution to the new social risks.

One of the three cases does provide significant novelty. The German Social Democrats stonewalled before directly addressing the new social risks, caught as they were between their allies, their own ideology, and an imploding Bismarckian insurance-based regime. The result today is that first the Red-Green governments and now the Grand Coalition in which the Social Democrats participate have abandoned some of the fundamental principles of the post-1945 model concerning the male breadwinner family or the insurance-based provision of rights and benefits. Regarding the male bread-winner model, German family policy has drawn close to that of the social democrats. As for insurance-based rights and benefits, the movement seems to be in the direction of solutions favored by liberal welfare regimes and away from earned entitlements (Palier 2010). Center-lefts' responses to new social risks, in other words, may lead them down roads first mapped in the heyday of social democracy, but may also take them over quite unfamiliar terrain.

Notes

1. This chapter relies on the widely used concept of "welfare regime," first developed by Gøsta Esping-Andersen (1990). The United States as well as most of the other English-speaking countries fall into the liberal category, while the Nordic countries are classified as social democratic, and most of the continental European ones as corporatist, sometimes termed Bismarckian.

2. UNICEF 2007, 6, found that the ranking of children living in poverty in twenty-one countries placed the United States dead last, the United Kingdom second from the bottom, and Ireland in eighteenth place.

3. See the data reported by Howard (this volume) as well as the comparison of twenty-one OECD countries in Castles (2005, table 1, 416).

4. Even more problematic is that they mask an increasing reliance on policy instruments such as negative income taxes and "tax breaks for social purposes."

5. "Social protection" is the European term used to encompass everything from health to pensions, unemployment benefits, social assistance ("welfare" in American English), employment support and protections, maternity and parental benefits, and family allowances.

6. For studies relying on these definitions see Esping-Andersen, Gallie, Hemerijk, and Myles 2002; Jenson 2004; Bonoli 2005; and Bonoli 2006.

7. Goldhammer and Ross (this volume) describe, for example, French labor market activation policies, and Cronin (this volume) does the same for Britain. Ross (this volume) considers labor market policies in the EU. In their manifesto *Europe: The Third Way* (1999) Tony Blair and Gerhard Schröder included a chapter entitled "An Active Labour Market Policy for the Left" (on http://www.socialdemocrats.org/blairandschroeder6-8-99.html, consulted 15 July 2008).

8. The content and implications of this manifesto for a "third way" are discussed in detail in Green-Pedersen, van Kersbergen, and Hemerijk 2001 and Seeleib-Kaiser and Fleckenstein 2007, 438.

9. All the documents of the Swedish Social Democratic Party referred to here are available at http://www.socialdemokraterna.se/Internationellt/Other-languages.

10. "An important side objective of Swedish active labour market policy has always been to mitigate the moral hazard problems of a generous unemployment insurance:

by making payment of unemployment compensation conditional on accepting regular job offers or placement offers in ALMPs from the public employment offices, active labour market policy has been used as a work test for the recipients of unemployment compensation" (Calmfors, Forslund, and Hemström 2002, 4).

11. The analysis and details in the next two paragraphs are from Daune-Richard and Mahon 2001.

12. Party Program of the Social Democratic Party, adopted by the Party Congress in Västerås, 6 November 2001, 15.

13. For the long list of programs over time see Calmfors, Forslund, and Hemström 2002, 5–7.

14. Alongside two mentions of the "elderly" in SAP's program of 2001 were thirty-two going to children.

15. Because of the more generous benefits available in the "golden age" of its welfare regime, Sweden remains an example of a country in which access to services is still higher than, for example, in southern Europe or Britain (LeBihan and Martin 2006, 45).

16. According to UNICEF (2000), 21% of Swedish children live with one parent, the highest rate among the twenty-two countries it studied (the United States was at 16%).

17. Drawing on Esping-Andersen, Gallie, Hemerijk, and Myers (2002), Pontusson (this volume) identifies this child-centered social investment strategy as a core element of the current social democratic project. It is worth noting, however, that a policy focus on "investing in children" appeared in the mid-1990s in liberal welfare regimes as well (Jenson and Saint-Martin 2006).

18. In addition to the specific sources mentioned in this section, much of the analysis is from Dobrowolsky and Jenson 2005.

19. On his prime ministerial website the emphasis on children was clear: "Mr Brown sums his own beliefs up as: 'Every child should have the best start in life, that everybody should have the chance of a job, that nobody should be brought up suffering in poverty. I would call them the beliefs that you associate with civilisation and dignity.'" http://www.number10.gov.uk/output/Page12037.asp, consulted 17 July 2008.

20. For example, in the party's manifesto (2005), consideration of childcare is concentrated in the chapter "Families: Support at Work and at Home."

21. This document is "The Children's Plan. Building Brighter Futures" (December 2007), available from the Stationery Office and on http://www.dfes.gov.uk/publications/childrensplan/, consulted 19 July 2008. The quote is on page 15.

22. The election manifesto of 2001, for example, did mention the need to support caregivers, but the overwhelming focus on the needs of the elderly was with regard to pensions and income. The balance in the manifestos of 1997 and 2005 was the same.

23. The rest of this paragraph is from Aust and Bönker 2004, 42.

24. These reforms, known as Hartz IV, created a basic benefit which provides low-end security for jobseekers and the long-term unemployed. The changes are described and explained by Seeleib-Kaiser and Fleckenstein (2007) as the product of direct influence of British policy ideas and policy imitation.

25. See "Europe: The Third Way" on http://www.socialdemocrats.org/blairand schroeder6-8-99.html, consulted 15 July 2008.

26. For further details see Jenson and Jacobzone 2000 and Ungerson and Yeandle eds. 2007, 137–47.

27. This seeming political puzzle is identified by Bonoli (2005, 433).

Immigration and the European Left

Sofía A. Pérez

In altering the population of a state, immigration has consequences for many of the conditions that center-left governments have historically sought to address. Employment and competition in the labor market, the promotion of skills, and the achievement of greater income equality in a society are all likely to be affected by the arrival of a significant number of newcomers. Focusing on Western Europe, an area that has become a key destination for migrants from around the world in the past three decades, this chapter considers how center-left governments have responded to the political pressures created by large scale international migration since the cold war. It is hypothesized that the left faces distinct political dilemmas in dealing with immigration, dilemmas that reflect a potential conflict at the electoral level between the universalistic values that represent the left's main ideological appeal and its commitment to promote the interests of some of its core domestic constituencies. The move to restrict immigration in Europe during the last three decades, often under governments of the left, seems to lend support to this hypothesis. However, as will be discussed, the policies toward immigration under governments of the center-left in Europe have also varied substantially across countries, suggesting that the intensity of those electoral dilemmas may depend on other factors, such as the structure of national economies and the characteristics of different European welfare states.

We begin with a discussion of the particular political dilemmas that immigration presents for the left and then go on to a brief description of the major trends in the historical evolution of immigration in Europe over the last three decades. These trends can be linked to the three phenomena emphasized in this volume: the end of rapid post-war economic growth during the 1970s, the end of the cold war, and the intensification of globalization. Based on cross-country quantitative data, we find that, on average governments of the left have been at least as likely to restrict immigration in Europe as governments of the right. Nevertheless, we see very significant differences across countries, with center-left governments in some countries pursuing very expansive immigration policies while in others they have opted clearly to pursue policies that restrict immigration in practice. In the following pages we explore how the left, when in government, has responded to the phenomenon of large scale migration from outside the EU in four of the Union's largest member states: Germany, the United Kingdom, Italy, and Spain. One common trend that we see across these countries is that center-left governments have sought to recast the immigration debate by altering the bases on which foreigners are admitted to fit other national economic objectives, such as economic growth and the promotion of better skills. They have often counted on segments of businesss as an ally in this effort. Yet in some countries (notably Germany among our cases) they have encountered significant opposition from within their own ranks and ample segments of the electorate, while in others they have pursued very expansive immigration policies. The chapter concludes by offering a possible explanation for these differences in immigration policy and considers what they tell us about the wider implications of immigration for the European left.

Immigration and Left Partisanship

Unlike other aspects of globalization such as financial integration, trade competition, and the rise of the service economy, immigration is rarely considered an issue with clear partisan implications. Setting aside an important literature on the rise of the new radical right (e.g., Betz 1993; Kitschelt with McGann 1995), scholarship on the politics of immigration in Europe has tended to emphasize factors that apply equally across party lines. Based on her influential study of France and Britain, Jeannette Money, for instance, has argued that immigration is primarily a matter of local politics, proposing an "electoral geography" perspective according to which governments of whatever ideology will opt to curtail immigration whenever electoral districts in which native citizens compete economically with immigrants for jobs and public resources become crucial to the outcome of national elections (Money 1999). One implication that can be taken from her findings is that immigration is fundamentally neutral from a partisan perspective, with the exception of its possible contribution to the rise of the radical right. Other authors have further added to this view by noting that early efforts to restrict immigration in Europe during the 1960s and 1970s were promoted with equal intensity by politicians of both left and right. Thus Schain (2006) has documented how Communist Party politicians in France were among the first to promote efforts to restrict immigration, and Karapin (1999) points to anti-immigrant popular mobilization in key electoral districts in Britain and Germany to explain the decision by governments of both left and right to restrict immigration laws from the 1960s on.

To observe that both left and right governments have pushed for restricting immigration in Europe, or for that matter that immigration preferences tend to be specific to locality, does not obviate the possibility that parties of the left and of the mainstream right face fundamentally different political dilemmas in deciding upon policies involving immigration. Indeed, while arguments in defense of the rights of immigrants are commonly associated with the left, there are at least two reasons to believe that immigration creates particular electoral difficulties for the left and hence that governments of the left have particular incentives to restrict immigration. The first reason is that immigration has different economic impacts on different segments of the electorate upon which the left relies. As a number of political economists have pointed out, the costs and benefits of immigration accrue unequally to different income segments of the population. Immigration tends to weaken the labor market position of native low-skilled workers while improving that of high-skilled workers and professionals whose labor productivity and cost of living are improved by a larger supply of low-skilled and low-wage workers (Scheve and Slaughter 2001). Given that low-skilled workers also represent the prime beneficiaries of publicly subsidized housing, healthcare, and education, and that they are more likely to find themselves living in proximity to low-skilled immigrants, competition in jobs carries over to competition over such public resources and space. To the extent that voters view immigration in terms of their rational economic self-interest and that parties of the left must put together an electoral coalition spanning low-skilled workers, high-skilled workers, and professionals, the left is likely to face an electoral trade-off over immigration. Moreover other economic trends, such as the rise of the service economy and associated efforts to make labor markets more flexible (for instance the recent Hartz reforms in Germany) are likely to aggravate these electoral trade-offs by reducing traditional forms of labor market security for the working class in Europe.

In addition to the division over immigration policy that derives from the differing labor market positions of the center-left's potential electorate, political economists also postulate another way in which immigration can be expected to represent a particular problem for parties of the left. To the extent that the immigration of low-skilled workers (the primary recipients of social transfers) changes the income distribution so as to push former recipients up the relative income scale (turning them into median voters), the preference of the median voter may well move toward lower spending levels (Nannestad 2007). If so, immigration would represent a serious threat to the ability of the center-left to protect the European welfare state, and with it a centerpiece of its raison d'être.

While economists suggest that immigration is likely to divide the center-left's electorate along skill and income levels, these economic issues appear to divide the population of advanced industrialized countries along the same lines as the cultural cleavage between left-libertarian and authoritarian-populist values which appears to have emerged as a major feature of the electoral space in which center-left parties now operate (Kitschelt 1994; Kitschelt with McGann 1995). As Kitschelt's work suggests, labor market differences such as the new multiplicity of work experiences among the left's electorate (with male, manual workers threatened by globalization tending to fall in the new authoritarian camp and professionals with higher educational levels and communicative skills tending toward the left-libertarian camp) may translate into other issues of cultural identity and definition. The effect may be to harden antagonistic worldviews among the electorate to the point of rendering the actual individual economic impact of immigration a secondary matter. This cultural-identitarian dimension of immigration cannot be eluded by the left because any choice to restrict immigration (or the rights of immigrants) in order to address the impact on native workers requires some implicit or explicit justification for limiting social solidarity based on identity. Resort to such justification may undermine the perceived ideological coherence of the left, thus threatening one of its key tools in mobilizing voters: the appeal to universal values. At the very least, it is likely to alienate the left-libertarian segment of the center-left's electorate, contributing to partisan schisms such as that between Social Democrats and Greens in Germany or between the Socialist Party and alternative left candidacies seen in recent French presidential elections.[1]

Both economic analyses pointing to how immigration affects different sets of voters and cultural analyses of the attitudinal trends characterizing European electorates in the post-Fordist period thus suggest that the European left is likely to face considerable problems in defining its stance on immigration in the electoral space in which it operates. Given the possible tensions in immigration policy preferences among the center-left's electorate, how have center-left parties in practice addressed the question of immigration and immigration policy in Europe in the last decades?

Immigration and the Left in Europe: A Brief Periodization

Setting aside migratory moves due to postwar expulsions, the history of postwar immigration in Europe can be divided broadly into four periods. The first, lasting from the 1950s to the economic crisis of 1973, saw significant levels of immigration into the richer states of Western Europe through guest worker recruitment programs designed to alleviate labor shortages and Britain's and France's preferential treatment of former colonial subjects. The second period was marked by the abrupt ending of active worker recruitment schemes and the curtailment of lax citizenship provisions for former colonial subjects (the latter starting in Britain in the early 1960s). This left only two modalities of immigration into most states of Western Europe—family reunification and asylum laws—which were often defended by courts and public administrations in the face of government efforts to move to a de facto goal of zero immigration. The third period, beginning roughly with the end of the cold war in 1989, was marked by sharp increases in immigration through those two remaining avenues. It would end a decade later with a radical toughening of asylum laws across the EU. Led by Germany, EU-15 member states rescinded their acceptance of asylum petitions for those arriving through a "safe third country" (a condition that applied to virtually all arrivals into the EU-15 by land and many by air). Family reunification criteria were also toughened by several countries (including Germany), resulting in very low net immigration, or even a decline in the immigrant population in many countries. The most recent period has also been marked by the "securitization" of immigration policy following the September 11 attacks and a new emphasis on border control in the face of new, more organized forms of illegal immigration through EU's southern and eastern borders.

However, as figure 1 makes clear, the move to restrict immigration since 1989 has not been uniform across Western Europe. Some countries, including most strikingly Britain, Spain, and Italy, experienced very large inflows of immigrants from outside the EU until the world financial crisis in 2007.[2] Indeed, the EU-15 area as a whole is estimated to have seen an increase of new residents from outside the area.

What role, if any, have parties of the left had in this recent history of immigration in Europe and in the divergence we observe in the decades preceding the economic crisis? Considering the question from a historical perspective, the first observation is that early postwar immigration regimes across Western Europe did not seem to have had any particularly partisan character. Work-based immigration, or "guest-worker," programs that represented the main avenue for immigration into the richer states of continental Europe

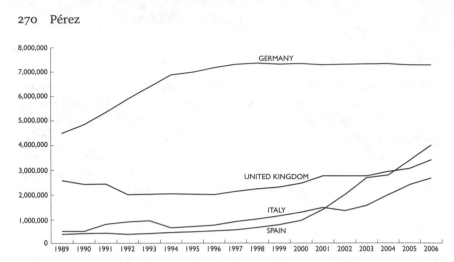

Figure 1. Number of foreign residents by country, 1989–2006 (figures from Eurostat).

during the 1950s and 1960s were instituted by Christian Democrats in Germany and the Netherlands, by Gaullists in France, and by Social Democrats in Sweden (Toro-Morn 2004). They were designed to recruit labor temporarily without offering a path to citizenship, and social democratic parties and labor unions alike were willing to go along with this notion of recruiting foreign workers who would not enjoy full social and political rights. On the other hand, in Britain both Labour and Conservative governments supported generous access for former British colonial subjects without tying it to work until 1962 (see Hansen 1999). And in France, where the left remained out of office throughout this period, governments dominated by the center-right embraced a similarly generous policy toward former colonial subjects from North Africa.

At the time of the oil shocks of the 1970s, the left was in a preeminent position across much of Europe. Social democratic governments in Sweden, Germany, and the Netherlands took the lead in ending worker recruitment schemes, often in direct response to pressure from labor unions.[3] Meanwhile, British Labour governments took measures to further tighten the restrictions on Commonwealth immigration that had first been introduced by the Conservatives in 1962.[4] Indeed, in the period after the oil shock immigration policy across most of Western Europe seemed to reflect a new consensus between center-left and mainstream right parties to stop the influx of foreigners and the transformation of European societies in a multicultural direction. No less an internationalist than Willy Brandt would declare in January 1973 that it had "become necessary to think carefully about when our society's ability to take up [foreigners] is exhausted, and when sense and responsibility require a halt."[5] With the exception of Britain, the consensus was reflected in what appears in hindsight to have been an unspoken agreement between mainstream left and right to end work-based immigration but not to politicize the broader question of Europe's increasingly multicultural character as a result of past immigration. In many parts of Europe, from France to Austria and Denmark, this modus vivendi was eventually challenged by the electoral rise of anti-immigrant parties in the 1980s, which led sections of the mainstream right to call for restrictions on immigrant rights, often in the language of law and order (France's "Peyrefitte law" of 1981 and the "Pasqua laws" of 1986 and 1993 are prime examples). In other places—notably Germany—the unspoken agreement appeared to hold until the asylum crisis of the early 1990s.

The sharp rise in asylum seekers that followed the outbreak of conflict in the Balkans as the cold war came to an end posed a challenge particularly to the European left. Many of its historic leaders regarded the right to asylum as a key guarantee against the kind of political persecution experienced during fascism. As a consequence, in places such as France and Germany left party politicians often sided with courts that blocked early restrictions imposed by governments of the right. In the end, however, the combined pressure of anti-immigrant popular mobilization and increased politicizing of the issue by the radical and later mainstream right led center-left governments to accept a radical curtailment of asylum rights, first in France during the 1980s, then in Germany in 1993, then in Germany's neighbor states. In 2005 the German principle of rejecting asylum seekers who had passed through a safe third country was finally adopted as the common guideline of EU member states.

To be sure, asylum was the most wrenching issue for parties of the left in Europe. Yet the record suggests that in practice, if not in discourse, the leadership of left parties in many European states also seconded a stance, most often enunciated by politicians on the right, of restricting net immigration to zero. Starting in the 1990s many European governments toughened requirements for family reunification visas, the last significant avenue for legal immigration into Europe after restrictions on asylum had been passed. The means of doing so varied from lowering the age up to which children could join their parents (to twelve by Germany, fifteen by Austria), to raising the age at which marriage takes place for a valid spousal application (to twenty-four by Denmark, twenty-one by the Netherlands), to increasing the sponsor's income or housing requirements, as was done in France and the Netherlands. In addition to these new legal restrictions, there is widespread agreement that immigration is highly susceptible to many policies that go well beyond the formal conditions for entry and residence in a country. These range from simple administrative delays in the processing of visas to the conditions under which foreigners are allowed to obtain employment, access to healthcare services, education, and other social services or benefits. Many, though not all, countries in the EU toughened these conditions during the 1990s and early 2000s.[6]

Given the many ways governments can seek to restrict immigration, it is difficult to assess the overall character of immigration policy pursued by a country under governments of different stripes by only looking at legal requirements for residency. One alternative way to consider the question is to compare levels of immigration under governments of the left and governments of the right. A simple test that pools annual figures available from Eurostat for eleven member states for 1989 through 2006 suggests that the average annual increase in the number of foreigners living in a country as a percentage of the population under governments of the left was just half of what it was under other regimes. When the data are adjusted by subtracting annual inflows of asylum seekers from the annual change in the number of foreigners, the results are similar: an average increase of 0.14% under governments of the left versus 0.23% under governments of the center or right. A more refined regression analysis of the impact of left government on the annual increase in immigrant proportion, controlling for key pull and push factors such as growth, unemployment, time-period (introduced to control for external events in countries of origin such as the Balkan crisis) and social spending, also shows left government to be associated with lower levels of immigration in Europe than governments not controlled by the left.[7]

However, as any visual analysis of developments within countries shows (see figure 1), in spite of these overall results there are clear differences in the extent to which governments have restricted immigration across Europe. In many countries (including Germany, France, and the smaller members of the EU-15) there has been a decisive trend to restrict immigration, and that trend appears more acute under governments of the left.[8] Indeed, it is this set of countries that are responsible for the overall results cited above. By contrast, in three European countries (Britain, Spain, and Italy) governments of the left allowed for large inflows of immigrants through 2006, and in one case (Britain) this represented a marked departure from the previous, right-wing governments. To explore what this might tell us about the politics of immigration in Europe, we next consider the experiences of these three countries alongside that of Germany, the country that arguably has taken the most restrictive turn in its immigration regime over the last decade, a period coinciding with the center-left's tenure in power.

Diverging Choices: Immigration Policy under the Center-Left in Germany, the United Kingdom, Italy, and Spain

Germany

Germany has long been one of the premier destinations for immigrants in Europe. At 12.9%, the proportion of its population that was foreign born in 2005 was equal to that of the United States and, until recently, the second-highest in the EU (only Austria, with a foreign-born population of 13.5%, had a higher percentage in 2005).[9] Nonetheless, immigration did not constitute a major point of contention between the postwar right and left until the 1980s. The German Social Democratic Party (SPD) showed few differences in its approach to immigration from the mainstream of the Christian Democratic Party (CDU) during Germany's economic miracle years. Both the CDU and the SPD backed the recruitment of foreign guest workers with limited rights of residence in the 1960s, and the CDU supported the ending of the program when the SPD declared a recruitment ban on foreign workers in 1973, thereby effectively ending work-based immigration. In the subsequent period the leadership of both the CDU and the SPD supported the view that Germany was "not a land of immigration" (a phrase most often associated with Helmut Kohl but previously deployed by Helmut Schmidt).[10] This was also reflected in both SPD and CDU governments' commitment to Germany's principle of *ius sanguinis* for citizenship status, which precluded large numbers of children of guest workers born in Germany from attaining citizenship. In all these ways Germany's postwar immigration policy reflected a consensus among the center-left and center-right that immigration was acceptable as an economic imperative but that there was a social limit on the extent to which Germany could integrate foreigners. This position appears to have reflected a strong fear on the part of the German political elite of the potential for xenophobic political mobilization among the German public (Karapin 1999).[11] Hence before the 1980s there was little politicizing of the issue at the national level (Zaslove 2007).

What would ultimately threaten this cross-elite consensus was the arrival, beginning in the late 1970s, of a significant number of political asylum seekers from places like Afghanistan, Ethiopia, Turkey, and Vietnam (Karapin 1999). Both the SPD and the FDP remained formally committed to Article 16 of Germany's Basic Law (1949), which allowed to asylum seekers whose applications had been rejected at the administrative level a strong right to appeal deportation through the German courts. Yet anti-immigrant mobilization by far-right groups in the Federal Republic's southern regions led segments of the CDU and the CSU to push for stricter asylum laws in the course of the national elections of 1980. In the run-up to the elections the regional government of Baden-Württemberg, then controlled by the CDU, and the CSU government of Bavaria announced their own restrictions on asylum seekers, a move later seconded by the SPD mayor of Essen. These decisions were inspired by local protests against the settlement of asylum seekers in particular localities and neighborhoods. The threat that such popular mobilization would spread led Schmidt's government to pass special visa requirements for citizens of Afghanistan, Ethiopia, and Sri Lanka just before the elections. However, stronger measures were for the time precluded by the constitutional status of Germany's asylum law, which could only be changed by a two-thirds majority vote in the Bundestag.

It would only be with the arrival of far larger numbers of asylum seekers in the early 1990s that the SPD would agree to give Kohl's government the necessary parliamentary support for such a constitutional reform. An amendment in 1993 of Article 16 voided the right of asylum for those having passed through a "safe third country" on their way to Germany—in practice, a vast majority of cases. At the same time asylum seekers, who had already been excluded from obtaining work in Germany, were shifted from the protection of the Federal Social Assistance Act to a separate social assistance regime that provided fewer cash benefits along with food vouchers, a measure that clearly stigmatized this part of the immigrant population. SPD support for such radical measures to restrict asylum applications appears to have been motivated by the extensive wave of anti-foreigner violence that occurred after German unification, which peaked with 3,365 attacks on foreigners in the first half of 1993, and the subsequent wave of intra-German migration (Human Rights Watch 1994; Karapin 1999). The virtual closure of the asylum route of immigration into Germany is reflected in the sharp curtailment of the previously rising number of foreigners residing in Germany from 1994 on (see figure 1).

After returning to power in 1998 the political left in Germany took two major steps intended to create a new immigration regime that would be politically more tenable. First, with the rate of net inflows of foreign residents slowing to a halt, and responding to growing concern over the integration of second-generation immigrants, the Red-Green coalition led by Gerhard Schröder campaigned on a promise to reform Germany's century-old law conferring citizenship only on the basis of ancestry rather than birth. The new law, adopted in 1999, made it possible for the children of immigrants born in Germany and meeting certain conditions to apply for German citizenship. Indeed, in its original proposals the government sought to make possible such applications without requiring applicants to renounce their existing citizenship, a matter crucial to the offspring of Turkish and Polish immigrants for whom abandoning their traditional nationality implied giving up inheritance rights in their parents' country of origin. In the end Schröder's government was dissuaded from insisting on the possibility of dual citizenship by the outcome of an election in Hesse, where the CDU successfully used the nationality law as a wedge issue to win control of the regional government.[12] The new citizenship law passed in 2000 nevertheless held great symbolic importance, for it shattered the principle that Germany was not a land of immigration. This alone was seen as a step forward in promoting the social absorption of second-generation immigrants. Yet because of the exclusion of dual citizenship, it resulted in citizenship applications by only a fraction of Germany's disenfranchised second-generation immigrants (around 750,000 of the original 3 million predicted by the government).[13]

Secondly, Schröder's government attempted to pass a new immigration law that would have reopened the door for work-based immigration, although only for highly skilled workers. The so-called Schily law (named after the coalition's interior minister, Otto Schily), aimed to alter the skill profile of immigrants by significantly toughening the standards for family reunification (the one remaining traditional avenue for immigrants) while replacing the ban on work-based immigration with a points system that would have allowed residence permits for highly qualified workers in areas in which German employers faced labor shortages.[14] The resumption of labor immigration was backed heavily by German business groups which put strong pressure on both the SPD and CDU in favor of the law (Ette 2003). On the other hand, a toughening of family reunification criteria (in particular a lowering of the age up to which children could join their parents from sixteen to twelve years) was advocated by both the SPD and the Christian Democratic opposition, which argued that the age should be lowered to ten years. Family reunification was held to be responsible for the low-skill profile of Germany's immigrant population because it necessarily built on the low-skill character of the earlier guest-worker policy and therefore largely perpetuated its results. The law also created new integration requirements in the form of language tests for the extension of residency permits.

Although the policy was legislated by the Red-Green government in 2002, it was successfully challenged in court on a procedural matter by the CDU, which argued adamantly against any reestablishment of work-based immigration and any expansion of the criteria for political asylum. The final version of the law, passed in 2004 with the support of the CDU in the upper house, excluded the SPD's centerpiece—the points-based system of labor immigration. It thus maintained the ban on work-based immigration, allowing only for three exclusions: one-year visas for foreign students after they finished their studies in Germany; permanent residence permits for top-level scientists and managers; and temporary residence permits for self-employed foreigners investing over one million Euros in designated economic activities (Münz 2004). As a concession to the Green Party, it did include gender- and non-state-based persecution as criteria for refugee status, although not political asylum.[15] The SPD government's major objective, to create an immigration policy regime that would alter the profile of immigrants from low-skilled to high-skilled was thus blocked, leaving simply an even more restrictive immigration regime than the one Germany had already adopted in 1993.

The United Kingdom

By contrast to Germany, Britain's initial postwar immigration regime was not driven primarily by economic considerations but by geopolitical ones. After the war Labour passed the British Nationality Act of 1948, which turned British subjecthood into British citizenship, giving a large number of former colonial subjects an automatic right to migrate to the United Kingdom. Yet far being from a partisan measure, this generous immigration policy represented a straight continuation of pre-war policy, which had aimed to protect Britain's preeminence within the Commonwealth in a postcolonial era through the creation of Commonwealth citizenship (Hansen 1999; Karatani and Goodwin-Gill 2003). The permissive stance toward Commonwealth immigration implied in Labour's nationality act thus enjoyed the full support of the Conservative Party, which in turn, after returning to power in the 1950s, would allow the arrival of many former colonial subjects for permanent settlement in the United Kingdom.

This liberal consensus on postcolonial immigration would be shattered by the outbreak of anti-foreigner, and specifically anti-black, violence at the end of the 1950s, which was seized upon by a populist wing of the Conservative Party, epitomized by Enoch Powell (Karapin 1999). In response to a large number of petitions for immigration controls from local party chapters, Harold Macmillan's government passed the first significant step toward immigration restriction with the first Commonwealth Immigration Act of 1962, which subjected the right to settle in Britain to government issuance of a skill-based work permit. Although Labour initially opposed the measure and then worked to have it protect the right of dependents to accompany holders of work permits, it engaged in a dramatic about-face on immigration policy after winning elections in 1964. The new government of Harold Wilson sharply restricted the number of work vouchers, entirely abolishing the category of unskilled labor and significantly reducing that of skilled workers in

1965. In 1968 it passed the second Commonwealth Immigration Act, with the aim of preventing the immigration of Kenyan Asians. The new act for the first time distinguished between "patrial" British citizens (those of British birth or descent) and other Commonwealth citizens, thereby bringing nonwhite immigration to Britain to a virtual end (Hansen 1999).[16] At the same time Wilson sought to balance this anti-liberal turn in immigration policy by introducing anti-discrimination legislation in the Race Relations Act (1968).

If British Labour, like center-left parties elsewhere in Europe, took a populist stance in restricting immigration during the 1970s, it has played a very different role over the last decade. As figure 1 illustrates, after more than a decade of sharp decline in the number of foreigners living in Britain during the Thatcher years (and only a modest reversal of this trend in the first half of the 1990s), the Labour victory of 1997 set the stage for a significant increase in immigration into Britain (most of it from non-EU states). Taking the view that immigration could be beneficial to Britain's economic modernization when and where it supported economic activity, the government of Tony Blair set out on a two-pronged strategy of expanding the issuance of new work permits for third-country foreigners while at the same time moving to deter asylum applicants whom it identified as a burden on Britain's purse. In a white paper titled "Fairer, Faster and Firmer: A Modern Approach to Immigration and Asylum" (1998) the new government decried "backlogs, inadequate control resources, and outdated procedures" in the existing system of asylum review, which made "it extremely difficult to deal firmly with those who have no right to be here" (Home Office 1998, paragraph 3.3). At the same time it began to increase the number of work permits granted for those seeking employment in key sectors. In 2002 Labour introduced the Highly Skilled Migrant Programme, arguing that legitimate, work-based immigration could bring "huge benefits: increased skills, enhanced levels of economic activity, cultural diversity and global links" (Home Office 2002, 9). It also increased visas for low-skilled, casual work. In the following year Blair promised to halve new asylum applications while moving Britain to a points-based system of immigration. "Operating at different ends of the employment spectrum," all of these initiatives were intended "to improve the supply of labour to the United Kingdom economy, to 'meet the challenge' of a globalizing environment" (Walters 2004, 239). The effect was a sharp upward turn in the number of foreign citizens residing in Britain, from just under 2 million in 1996 to almost 3.5 million in 2006, the overwhelming majority non-EU citizens (OECD 2007e).

Spain and Italy

Britain's move to managed, skill-based migration under Blair represents one of the major turns in European immigration policy in the last decades. Nonetheless, two other member states that in the past were major sources of emigration to the rest of Europe—Italy and Spain—account for a much greater share of the expansion in immigration that the EU has experienced over the last two decades. Italy's registered immigrant population rose in 1989–2006 from just under half a million to over two and a half million.[17] Spain's transformation has been even more spectacular. In just over a decade the country has seen immigration (measured in terms of resident foreign citizens) rise from marginal levels (under 400,000 in 1991) to the highest level in the EU in proportion to total population. By 2008 foreign citizens residing in Spain, at over five million, represented just over 11% of the population (*El País*, 20 June 2008).

This dramatic rise of immigration into the two southern member states is often attributed to the restrictive turn in other EU-15 states and to the difficulties that Spain and Italy have had in controlling illegal immigration because of shortcomings in border control and a lack of internal controls on the employment of illegal migrants. Scenes of boatloads of African migrants arriving in Lampedusa, the Canary Islands, or Spain's southern coast, and of the dramatic human tragedies often associated with their attempts, dominate press coverage of the phenomenon. Yet however dramatic and significant, illegal arrivals by sea represent a small fraction of immigration in the two countries (19,900 for Italy in 2007, 18,000 for Spain according to the UNHCR).[18] The dramatic increases in registered immigration in fact stem from clear choices on the part of the Spanish and Italian governments that have produced a far more liberal stance on immigration than what is now prevalent in the northern states of the EU-15. The key features of this liberal stance in the two countries have been (1) permissive family reunification rules, (2) generous terms for the issuance of work permits in sectors deemed to have particular labor needs, (3) the extension of social rights to both legal and irregular immigrants, and (4) repeated amnesties for irregular migrants who can show employment. While different in some significant ways (in particular with regard to the use of immigration amnesties), the immigration regimes developed and maintained by the two southern member states thus bear a significant resemblance to the more expansive work-based immigration regime introduced in Britain.

One way in which the Spanish and Italian cases nonetheless are different from the British is that the policies allowing for large-scale immigration in the two southern states have been carried out with almost equal intensity by governments of the left and the right. This is particularly striking in Italy, where governments of the right in the last two decades have included the Northern League, a party formation with an explicit stance against immigration whose leaders often engage in xenophobic appeals. When the right has been in power in Italy, its pattern has been to pass tough and even jarring "law and order" measures that make headlines (most recently the discriminatory treatment applied to Romanian gypsies), without actually restricting the overall levels of immigration. Thus Silvio Berlusconi's government of 2001 expanded the total yearly quota for third-country (non-EU) migrants from 89,000 in 2001 to 170,000 in 2006 (Cuttitta 2008).[19] And the Bossi-Fini law that it passed in 2002 (which required the expulsion of immigrants whose residence permits had not been renewed, and for the first time linked new residence permits to the prior attainment of work contracts) was accompanied by the largest immigration amnesty Italy had ever seen. It resulted in the legalization of almost all of the 700,000 immigrants who applied (Migration Policy Institute 2004). Meanwhile in Spain, the center-right Partido Popular passed its own amnesties for illegal immigrants in 1996, 2000, and 2001 and in the process approved approximately 400,000 applications (Maas 2006).

If governments of the right have thus been surprisingly liberal in their immigration policies in Italy and Spain, the left has generally gone further. In Italy the center-left in 2006 successfully ran on a platform of easing the immigration restrictions that had been imposed by the Bossi-Fini law. Romano Prodi's government subsequently adopted an open-door immigration policy, abolishing the requirement of prior work contracts for the granting of residence permits. And while Italy sparked controversy across the EU in 2007 when it legislated the expulsion of EU immigrants charged with violent crime (a measure taken in response to popular outcry over a spike in crime attributed to Romanian immigrants), its policies for granting residence and work permits to foreign applicants remained among the most liberal ever seen in the EU (Chaloff 2005). In Spain the Socialist government that took office in 2004 went on to pass Spain's most generous immigration legislation yet, granting full access to healthcare, education, and other social services to both legal and illegal immigrants, and passing an amnesty regularizing the status of over 600,000 further immigrant residents who could prove that they had employment.

Implications and Conclusions

As the cases discussed above suggest, there have been ample differences in the stances toward new immigration taken by governments of the left in Europe in the last two decades. Germany's SPD in 1993 went along with a constitutional revision that set the stage for a toughening of asylum rules not only in Germany but across the EU. Later, when in government, it attempted to shift to a selective, skills-based immigration regime that would have raised the skill profile of Germany's immigrant population (an attempt at which it failed owing to opposition from the Christian Democrats). And while the Red-Green coalition government sought to improve the integration of second-generation immigrants by changing German citizenship law, it also toughened criteria for family reunification, the principal remaining channel for low-skill immigration into Germany, and introduced new requirements for the renewal of residence permits. The result has been a virtual freeze on net immigration into Germany over the last decade.

In sharp contrast to this turn in Germany, New Labour in Britain opened the doors of the British labor market to new immigrants from outside the EU. At the same time, it shifted immigration into Britain from a rights-based system to a skills-based system that gave access to those types of migrants demanded by British business, both at the high and the lower ends of the skills spectrum. Under Blair's leadership the Labour government rejected the notion (which seemed to prevail in Germany) that there is a necessary trade-off between allowing more immigrants and achieving successful social integration; it opted instead to facilitate labor market access for the spouses and children of those workers recruited under the new points-based system, betting that this would also mean more successful integration. Only in the face of a worsening electoral outlook and heightened anger from labor unions at the large inflow of low-skilled workers did Gordon Brown's government choose to restrict the immigration of third-country nationals who fell outside the high skills category, promising 500,000 new "British jobs for British workers" just as the first signs of the world financial crisis appeared (*Guardian*, 10 September 2007).

Finally, in Italy and Spain, the two countries accounting for the largest increases of third-country immigration into the EU over the last decade, both left and right governments have chosen to allow high levels of immigration. While governments of the right (in particular in Italy) have sought to counteract the perception of this reality through headline-catching "law and order" measures, left parties have distinguished themselves primarily by extending social rights to immigrants, including non-regularized ones, as a way to promote integration. In both countries governments have made ample use of amnesties to bring illegal migrants into the formal economy, and in Spain the first government of José Luis Rodríguez Zapatero made healthcare available to all residents, regardless of their residency status. On the other hand, in both Italy and Spain as in Britain, governments of the left have been able to garner the support of both business and the labor unions for their immigration-friendly policies by basing the issuance of new work permits to immigrants on a selective system favoring those sectors facing labor short-ages, ranging from the low-skill construction and domestic work sectors to information technology.

If parties of the center-left can be expected to face similar electoral con-flicts over immigration policy on theoretical grounds, how are we to account for the observed differences in their immigration policy choices, in particu-lar as regards overall levels of immigration? One common explanation, the presence or absence of an electorally viable radical right, does not account for the variation among the four cases examined above: the radical right did not represent a serious electoral threat in national or even regional elections in Germany, whereas it does have significant electoral weight in Italy and even participates in government. Nor can the choices be attributed to the existing levels of the immigrant population, given that Germany's share of immigrants, while high, had been surpassed by that of Spain as early as 2004, when the Socialist government chose to pass yet another amnesty and expand the social rights of illegal immigrants.

A different and more convincing explanation of the contrast between the German SPD's choice in favor of immigration restriction and the more liberal stances of center-left governments in Britain, Spain, and Italy would focus on the ways immigrants are economically integrated in the different countries. Looking first at the labor market, one striking contrast between Germany and the other three countries is the wide range in their gaps between the unem-ployment rate for immigrants and the rate for the native population. In 2005 unemployment in Germany stood at 17.5% for foreign-born men and 10.6% for native-born men, and at 16% for foreign-born women and 10% for native-born women. In the United Kingdom and Spain these gaps were consider-ably smaller: in the United Kingdom there was a difference of only 2.8% for men and 3.4% for women; in Spain only 2.5% for men and 1.5% for women. In Italy the situation was slightly different: unemployment was a bit higher for native-born men (6.2%) than for foreign-born men (6%), though the rate for foreign-born women was somewhat lower than for native-born women. Still, the contrast with Germany is striking. Moreover, in both Spain and Italy the labor market participation rates of foreigners was considerably better than that of native-born citizens: in Italy, 81.6% compared to 69.4% for men, 46.7% compared to 45.3% for women; in Spain, 79.5% compared to 74.4% for men, 60.4% compared to 50% for women (OECD 2007e).

The reasons for this poor labor market performance of immigrants in Germany are complex. They seem to include obstacles to labor market integration by foreigners and their children that are created by German legislation, the low skill profile of the immigrant population compared to the native population (an inheritance from the low-skill focus of the guest-worker program), and the poor performance of the German economy, compared to the other three economies, at generating low-skill employment (Constant and Zimmermann 2005). The last of these features also implies that the left in Germany faces a particularly acute conflict between the interests of its low-skilled electorate and immigrants. Thus it is noteworthy that precisely when it introduced its first new immigration law, Schröder's government was seeking to reduce the high unemployment level among low-skilled workers through radical reforms of the labor market, including the introduction of more flexible employment contracts in the service sector and major cuts in unemployment pay. The so-called Hartz reforms were highly controversial, threatening the SPD's internal integrity. In this context slowing the inflow of new, low-skilled workers must have appeared as a good way to ease tensions in the labor market, and with it the potential electoral cost of the labor market reforms.

While all of this may explain why the center-left in Germany would be under particular pressure to restrict immigration, it does not explain why similar governments in the other three countries would not also act on such pressure. Here it must be said that Britain's managed migration policy, even before Brown's clampdown on low-skilled, third-country immigration, was structured so as to allow the government to keep a grip on the political tension that immigration might create among its voters. By limiting immigration to either high-growth or high-skill sectors, the managed migration policy also allowed the government to limit immigration in lower-growth sectors, where it might have had a more obvious impact on lower-skilled native workers.

An alternative explanation for Labour's original open-door policy may be the weakness of British labor unions, which were in a poor position to resist Blair's new open-door policy toward migrants in the face of consistent pressure from British business in favor of a more liberal immigration policy. Indeed, the outbreak of wildcat strikes protesting the hire of Italian and Portuguese workers in British oil refineries and energy companies in early 2009 illustrates the weakness of organized labor in influencing the Labour governments' immigration policy and the consequent sense of frustration among blue-collar workers. However, it would be difficult to make a similar case for Italy, where unions mobilized politically against the immigration restrictions imposed by the Bossi-Fini law, or Spain, where Zapatero's government has based immigration policy on tripartite agreements and where the unions participate in setting annual immigration quotas.[20] Looking at the actions of unions with regard to immigration policy in the latter two countries, it is noteworthy that their position on immigration has remained generally very favorable (Watts 2002).

There is another characteristic which the United Kingdom shares with Italy and Spain and which sets all three countries apart from Germany and other continental EU members: the United Kingdom's liberal welfare state is quite weak in the provision of services such as childcare and elder care (Ungerson 2003). And for different reasons, so are the Spanish and Italian welfare states.[21] Consequently, in all three countries there is high demand for cheap immigrant labor both from institutional employers such as nursing homes and hospitals and from private households. Comprehensive data on such employment are difficult to attain. Yet there is evidence in all three countries of the important role that immigrants play in providing these services. In the United Kingdom, for instance, a high proportion of nurses and elder care providers are from the Philippines (Lyon and Glucksman 2008). In Italy 34% of the almost 700,000 immigrants regularized during the amnesty of 2002 applied on the basis of employment in domestic work, and according to one report immigrants account for over 43% of domestic employment. And in Spain that figure is believed to be above 52% (Eiro Online 2006, 2007).

This role of (primarily female) immigration in the provision of key services is important because it suggests that significant segments of the center-left's electorate, including in particular median-income households which have become increasingly dependent on two incomes (which require external help with child or elder care in the absence of publicly provided care services) will have a very concrete personal interest in a liberal immigration regime. That the rise of female immigration has coincided with a rise of (native) female labor market participation rates in the two southern European countries attests to the importance that immigrant labor plays in the role of many two-income families (Chaloff 2005). In all three countries (Britain, Italy, and Spain) immigration thus compensates median-income households for the shortcomings of a residual-liberal or late and not fully developed welfare state. This tendency not only turns immigrants into a functional substitute for more comprehensive social provision. It also creates an infrastructure of personal contacts that is likely to counter anti-immigrant sentiment in the relatively affluent segment of the left's electorate—a segment that might otherwise turn to welfare chauvinism. By contrast, where care services are provided by the state either publicly or by allowing mothers to stay out of the job market through generous family allowances, this type of private stake in immigration is likely to be lacking.

These observations also speak to the broader relationship between immigration and welfare states. Whereas economists have tended to interpret lower levels of social spending and redistribution in countries such as the United States as a consequence of ethnic diversity—and hence a lack of social cohesion (Alesina, Glaeser, and Sacerdote 2001)—the recent experiences of Britain, Italy, and Spain suggest an opposite causal relationship: that higher immigration is encouraged by lower levels of social provision because it compensates for shortcomings in the welfare state. This relationship means that a correlation between lower social spending and ethnic diversification need not necessarily reflect any inherent conflict between multiculturalism and generous welfare spending but rather an effect of low social spending on rates of immigration. On the other hand, moves to restrict immigration in Germany and elsewhere among the corporatist welfare states of northern Europe may have more to do with the failure to integrate immigrant populations into the labor market, which in turn is more likely to turn them into welfare recipients. Restrictions on the acquisition of citizenship for the children of immigrants, limitations on family reunification, and restrictions on labor market access to family members who join legal immigrants—all represent barriers to labor market integration, and they may create the social dependence that is seen to spark welfare chauvinism in places such as Germany.

All this suggests that how immigration affects parties of the left is likely to depend on how immigrants are integrated into the labor market and on how the arrival of newcomers interacts with the characteristics of European welfare states (whether immigrants are rendered welfare state dependents by laws meant to discourage them from arriving in the first place, or whether they act as functional substitutes for citizens but without access to social policies). The environment will be shaped by the choices of parties on the right to politicize, or not to politicize, the immigration issue. But it will also be shaped by the politics of the welfare state (although in much more complex ways than simple theories of welfare chauvinism would have it), the characteristics of labor and product markets (both matters of government regulation), and past policies that have affected the characteristics of the immigrant population and its degree of economic and social integration. In this regard past German governments of both left and right, which have insisted on restricting long-term avenues of integration (including paths to citizenship for the children of immigrants and the ability of asylum seekers to obtain employment), seem to have created a climate in which it has been more difficult for the left to advance a new type of immigration policy in recent years—more so than for governments of the left in the other three countries.

This discussion of how the politics of immigration differ for center-left parties across Europe does not answer the question of whether large-scale immigration places the left at a consistent electoral disadvantage vis-à-vis parties of the right. The electoral tensions that immigration creates specifically for the left may mean that the issue can easily be exploited by parties on the right for electoral gain and at little political risk. In particular in countries where an anti-immigrant far right has emerged (such as Italy, discussed above, and France), it can be argued that the mainstream right has successfully exploited the issue to its advantage in the face of a left hamstrung by its internal tensions.[22] In Italy, for instance, mobilization of anti-immigrant sentiment played an important role in the right's return to power in 2001, even though Berlusconi went on to oversee a substantial increase in legal immigration levels while appeasing his populist partners through tougher deportation standards and new requirements for legal immigration enshrined in the Bossi-Fini law. Nicolas Sarkozy's victory over Ségolène Royal in 2007 has been at least partially attributed to his tough, often controversial stance on immigration and immigrants, or the children of immigrants.[23] And in Germany the staunch commitment of the CDU and the CSU to block plans for a new, skilled-based labor immigration policy has been credited with helping to bring about the Christian Democrats' sequence of regional electoral victories in Hesse in 1999 and then 2003, Lower Saxony in 2003, and, most importantly, North Rhine–Westphalia in 2005. The last of these brought down the last Red-Green state government and prompted the federal elections that brought an end to the left coalition government.[24]

However, while politicizing immigration may indeed create tensions for the left and thus tend to work predominantly in favor of the right in the short term, it is not costless or unproblematic for the mainstream right. An uncompromising stance on immigration, such as that pursued by segments of the CDU and CSU during the years of the Red-Green coalition, can result in ideological tensions within the right as well. Such tensions, both between different CDU regional leaders and between the party and church organizations, were evident during the prolonged negotiations of a compromise between Schröder's government and the CDU after the failure of the first Schily law.[25] Mainstream right parties face their own tensions over immigration because business, one of its key constituencies, typically favors more open immigration policies. This was evidenced both in Germany, where business organizations lobbied aggressively in favor of Schröder's efforts to reopen work-based immigration, and in Italy, where business opposed the requirement imposed by Bossi-Fini of prior work contracts for residence permits.[26] Tough talk on immigration by right-wing politicians is thus less likely to result in immigration restrictions during periods of right-wing government than the electoral rhetoric of the right might imply. And this may ease the political pressure on the left that political victories by the center-right in the context of increased global migration flows might otherwise produce.

The examples considered here suggest that although there is a real potential for the European right to mobilize anti-immigrant sentiment (note the electoral success of the Northern League in an area of Italy whose industrial economy depends greatly on immigrant labor), the left is not therefore locked into an inescapable choice between restricting immigration and permanent electoral defeat. In Spain (2008) and Britain (2001 and 2005) the left succeeded electorally after implementing very liberal immigration policies and running in the face of efforts by the right to politicize the issue. And in Italy the left won in 2006 after running on a promise to lift a measure imposed by the first Berlusconi government to require work contracts for the issuance of new residence permits. In Germany, on the other hand, the political pressure to restrict immigration appears largely to be a function of the low-skill profile of early immigrant labor recruitment policies coupled with the country's unique problems in creating jobs for low-skilled workers. And something similar may be true for France.

While we note these differences, it is also striking that in all four of the countries considered here governments of the left have actively sought to shape the profile of their immigrant populations in ways that fit the perceived needs of their economies, in particular by raising the skills level of the labor force. Indeed, while these efforts are now being copied by the right (for instance Sarkozy's government in France), the move to conform immigration policy to other economic policy goals (in particular the raising of the skills profile of the EU's labor force) is one in which governments of the center-left have played a leading role, two examples being Blair's "managed migration" model and Schröder's efforts to introduce a points-based system. One way to understand these initiatives is as an effort by the center-left to counteract the electoral dilemmas that immigration tends to create by reducing the extent to which immigration affects the most vulnerable in society.

Nonetheless, choosing this sort of pragmatism over a rights-based approach to immigration may be problematic in other respects. At the very least it poses a serious question as to how the European left will reconcile its definition of borders among peoples and its commitment to universal human rights. It also cannot be overlooked that the choice to promote high-skilled migration into the EU to ease electoral tensions and resolve Europe's demographic problems presents a serious moral dilemma. Any further efforts to draw human capital away from labor-exporting poorer countries are likely to have their own negative impact on precisely those areas of the world from which economic migrants in general seek to flee. Thus efforts to alter the politics of immigration in Europe by getting the "right" kinds of immigrants not only places left governments in an awkward moral position. It may also indirectly help to perpetuate the conditions in poorer countries that have produced large-scale immigration in the first place, along with the resulting dilemmas from which parties of the left are seeking to escape.

Notes

1. Inglehart (1971) links post-materialism to the emergence of a cosmopolitan political identity and sense of social solidarity.

2. After the last two EU enlargements, many of the traditional EU member states also experienced significant immigration from new EU member states, including Poland and Romania. The distinction here is drawn because intra-EU migration cannot be directly restricted beyond a transition period that follows a home country's accession to the EU. Most of the leeway for controlling immigration that EU governments have involves immigrants who are not citizens of other EU member states.

3. See for instance Hammar 1999, 174, on Sweden, Campbell ed. 1992, 451–56, on Switzerland, and Castles 1986.

4. The Commonwealth Immigrants Act (1962), passed by a Conservative government, made the right of abode for Commonwealth citizens contingent upon a government-issued work permit. After coming to power in 1964 Labour continued and intensified the Conservatives' move by drastically cutting work vouchers and passing the Commonwealth Immigrants Act (1968), which sought to halt the influx of migrants from African Commonwealth states.

5. *Regierungserklärung des zweiten Kabinetts Brandt/Scheel vom 18. January 1973* (Bonn: Presse- und Informationsamt der Bundesregierung, 1973), 46. Author's translation.

6. In Germany, for example, access to the labor market was eliminated for those seeking asylum decisions at the same time as cash benefits were cut. The immigration bill of 2002 (see more below) also required schools, doctors, and officials to pass on information about possibly illegal migrants, eliminated access to publicly funded healthcare for those overstaying their visa and their dependents, and even reduced legal immigrants' access to benefits such as child-rearing family allowances.

7. The results and methods are available in Pérez and Fernandez-Albertos 2009.

8. Annual figures for France are not available, but just a comparison of the census data on the number of foreigners residing legally in France every five years suggests that the trend there has been toward zero net growth in the number of foreigners re-

siding legally in France, and that this did not change during years of Socialist government.

9. The share of the population in Germany and Austria that was foreign born well outranked that of France (8.1%) and even Britain (9.7%) in 2005. See OECD 2007e.

10. See Maier-Braun 2006. Schmidt made the statement at a press conference on 11 November 1981.

11. The perception that German society would not be able to integrate Muslim immigrants in particular was often articulated by the chancellor, including in some of his later recollections of this period. See "Altkanzler Schmidt: Die Anwerbung von Gastarbeitern war falsch," *Frankfurter Allgemeine Zeitung*, 24 November 2004. See also "Helmut Schmidt: Multikulturelle Gesellschaft 'Illusion von Intellektuellen,'" *Die Zeit*, 22 April 2004.

12. Roger Cohen, "Schroeder's New Politics Tripped Up by Hesse Voters," *New York Times*, 8 February 1999.

13. This figure is calculated by subtracting the pre-2000 level of roughly 50,000 naturalizations per year from the higher figures in the six years following the new citizenship law before naturalization figures returned to their historical path.

14. For details on the course of the negotiations of the first Schily Law see the monthly EFMS (Europäisches Forum für Migrationsstudien) Migration Reports for October 2001 to June 2002.

15. The addition of these new criteria was also mandated by an EU directive. For more details on the second immigration law taking effect on 1 January 2005 see the EFMS Migration Report for July 2004.

16. The restrictive turn in Labour's stance on immigration is widely attributed to the lessons drawn from an unexpected defeat in the Labour stronghold district of Smethwick to a Conservative candidate running on an anti-immigrant platform in 1964 (see Karapin 1999). According to Hansen (1999) it also reflected "a triumph of Callaghan's strand of Labour ideology—nationalist, anti-intellectual, indifferent to international law and obligation and firmly in touch with the social conservatism of middle- and working-class Britain" (822).

17. Estimates of Italy's illegal immigrant population vary widely, from as few as 200,000 to one million (Jandl 2008).

18. "Mission by Sea over Illegal Migrants," *Economist*, 3 May 2008.

19. The number of permits issued consistently exceeds the quotas, which are used to negotiate controls on illegal immigration with sending countries.

20. In Italy the immigrant offices of the labor unions play an important role in facilitating the integration of immigrants; their work includes sanctioning the applications for residence permits of "self-employed" immigrants (see Veikou and Triandafyllidou 2004). In Spain annual quotas for work-based immigration are set after consultation with employers and unions.

21. Some authors attribute this to the "familial" underpinning of social policy in these countries. Yet this explanation seems to be contradicted by far higher levels of public daycare provision and by an important increase in Spain in recent years in pub-

lic spending on early childcare. Other explanations include the high level of spending on old-age pensions in Italy and the relatively late development of a comprehensive welfare state in Spain during a period of fiscal retrenchment.

22. I thank George Ross for putting this point to me.

23. See David Rieff, "Battle over the Banlieues," *New York Times Magazine*, 15 April 2007, and "Immigration: Malaise et surenchère," *Le Monde*, 20 March 2007.

24. Markus Deggerich, "Einwanderung: Die Angst der Parteien vor der Wahl," *Der Spiegel*, 30 January 2001.

25. See for instance *EFMS Migration Report*, January and February 2003; Ette 2003, 410–46; and Charles Hawley, "Letter from Berlin: German Conservatives Bicker over Integration (Again)," *Der Spiegel Online International*, 2 January 2008. Another prominent example is offered by the conflict between the French interior minister, Charles Pasqua, and the social affairs minister, Simone Weil, which resulted in a serious rift within Édouard Balladur's government in 1993. See Hollifield 1999.

26. *EFMS Migration Reports*, March 2001 and January 2002; Ette 2003; and *Migration News* (University of California, Davis) 8, no. 4 (October 2002).

The Central and Eastern European Left

A Political Family under Construction

Jean-Michel De Waele and Sorina Soare

The destruction of the Berlin Wall has had an influence well beyond the political boundaries of former "people's democracies," directly challenging left
and center-left parties all over the world. The most common forecast of the
early 1990s was that "socialism was dead and that none of its variants could
be revived" (Dahrendorf 1990, 38). Eastern Europe during the following years
thus rapidly became a breeding ground for neoliberal and pro-market ideas
and an endemic "allergy" to the left. The main dilemma that the new democracies faced was how to bolster the legitimacy of their new regimes. Anticommunist elites advocated total condemnation of the past, with "lustration
laws" to purge remnants and reminders of it that were based, it would seem,
on an underestimate of how completely Marxist ideologies had disappeared
(Hermet and Marcou 1998; Mink and Szurek 1998; Teitel 2000; Letki 2002;
Stan 2002; David 2003). An astute observation about Bulgaria works for the
entire region, save the Czech Republic: "None of [Marxism's] postulates, its
main policy recommendations such as central planning, completely admin-
istratively controlled prices, obligatory employment, state property, collec-
tivism, proletarian dominance through one-party rule, were left standing"
(Ganev 2005, 444). This was also, of course, a moment when the western left
faced its own crisis because of the end of Fordism, shifting class structures
and the weakening of class, changing voting trends, the coming of "postmaterialist" rivals, and the crisis of the welfare state (Callaghan and Tunney 2001, 63). Some scholars even argued that the end of the twentieth century could make traditional socialism and even social democracy impossible
everywhere (Przeworski and Sprague 1986).

The direction and extent of Eastern European transformations were also
much constrained by the prospect of joining the European Union. Democratic politics were essential for membership in the EU, and this obliged the

post-communist lefts to declare more or less complete allegiance to market-oriented programs in ways which disregarded traditional left concerns (Agh 2004). These constraints also seemed likely to prevent new lefts from emerging and to hasten the departure of older ones. Parties of the left and center-left in central and eastern Europe were thus left to transform themselves in an inhospitable environment, and very few observers or participants anticipated the resurrection of communist parties. Thus while in Romania the National Salvation Front (FSN) and in Bulgaria the Bulgarian Socialist Party (BSP), successor parties to the communists, managed to stay in power after 1989 and even win the first free elections, in most other places the past was brutally rejected. Successor parties in Poland, Hungary, and Czechoslovakia all lost their first electoral contests. Yet after starting as an endangered species, these successor parties would in fairly short order become stunning success stories.[1]

Democratization also brought traditional social democracy back to life after years in exile. Parties such as the Czech Social Democratic Party (ČSSD), the Romanian Social-Democratic Party (PSDR), and the Hungarian MSzDP were good examples. These parties had been repressed or forcibly incorporated into Soviet-sponsored communist parties after the Communists seized power in the late 1940s. Forty years later, in the first democratic elections, they seemed set for a political comeback. Their success proved limited, because weak organizations and inexperienced leaderships hampered their visibility and limited their electoral relevance (Waller 1995, 478). They were in most cases destined to disappear during the 1990s or merge with ex-Communist rivals. The exception was the Czech Social Democrats (ČSSD), which became one of the most stable center-left parties in the region. Another group of hybrid or highly specific and localized left parties emerged, like Smer in Slovakia, led by Robert Fico, a charismatic former reform-Communist. And some parties like the Communist Party of Bohemia and Moravia (KSČM), its Slovak counterpart the Party of the Democratic Left (SDL), and the Romanian Socialist Labor Party (PSM), chose not to drop their old ideology and instead made but minor programmatic revisions to fit the new democratic institutional framework. The Czech party has been the only success story in this category.

This chapter surveys the post-communist left or center-left spectrum in Bulgaria, the Czech Republic, Hungary, Poland, Romania, and Slovakia. Its main goal is to assess whether the evolution of these parties will be marked by a long and quiet path toward lasting success or rather enduring weakness, indicated by their current electoral problems. In light of these questions, the bulk of the chapter focuses on electoral results from the early 1990s through 2008. Later we shall consider internal and external stimuli leading to the reinvention of parties more generally in the region and reflect upon the likelihood of their long-term success.

Before we begin our analysis we need to clarify certain conceptual issues. At a comparative level we see a distinct evolutionary pattern. During the initial post-communist transition at the start of the 1990s, the political context blocked the emergence of parties, either left or right, with real ideologies that translated into programs and policies for well-defined electorates. Instead these were years of *high politics*, when debates were about the past, the large changes to be undertaken, and the positions of different countries in international affairs. In these conditions both right and left became stuck in rhetorical postures with few clear and realistic alternatives, and the region embraced a politics based on a superficial consensus in favor of democracy and Europe, in which most other problems became secondary.

In these circumstances left-of-center parties faced a threefold rebuilding task. Ex-communist parties first had to demonstrate acceptance of new democratic rules, including explicit renunciation of their earlier monopoly status and a willingness to live in a new multiparty world. Next they had to carry out organizational restructurings which included a massive loss of existing members, made more difficult by the emergence of a new generation of leaders whose presence did not help public visibility and recognition. Finally, the parties needed to rebuild their programs, abandoning the principles of Marxism-Leninism and importing ideological platforms from western European social democrats.

By the middle of the 1990s the return of left parties to power had demanded constructing a new image as "competent agents of change" that would distinguish them from parties of the right, using arguments that it was better to have "a steady hand at the wheel rather than inexperienced learner-drivers" (Hough 2005, 5). By this point their initial weak democratic legitimacy seemed for the moment overcome, and in all the countries we analyze, ex-communist parties had begun to demonstrate a political professionalism and organizational coherence that gave them substantial claims on electorates. Problems in the program persisted nonetheless. With a few exceptions the role of the government party constrained them to follow rhythms of reform coordinated by the EU and international creditor organizations. No matter what happened at elections, therefore, political agendas were dominated by needs to guarantee stabilization that necessitated policies of economic liberalization and privatization and brought extensive social costs.[2] In such a situation, "while there may be a clear social-democratic profile in programmatic documents and electoral campaigns, this does not necessarily have any bearing to the actual policies of a party in government" (Dauderstädt, Gerrits, and Markus [1999] as cited in Paterson and Sloam 2005, 37).

Thus however different parties' genealogies, social democracy often became an empty label. The parties were caught between their positions managing democratization and economic reform and historic affinities for taking care of those less well-off. These parties also came to contain numerous successful "red" millionaire entrepreneurs, and their policies often sacrificed social commitments for fiscal rectitude. Moreover, pro-European positions were often mainly electoral slogans, open to competing interpretations of the EU's policies and its future that were vague and slippery. In brief, with the exception of the Czech communists in the KSČM, the central characteristics of social democracy—its social values and its ties with trade unions and the working class—became at best elements in campaign rhetoric.[3] "Policy transfers" from western social democracy were typically superficial and meant mainly to establish credentials in the eyes of European allies. In this context it must be asked whether one is discussing a real political family, with organic links to the peoples, societies, and classes whose interests it purported to represent.[4]

The parties' genealogical patchwork does not in itself preclude a positive answer, but it does imply the likelihood of profound differences between these different social democrats operating in different national party systems.[5] Virtually all the successor parties quickly began to label themselves "center-left," with rather more weight placed on centrism. Ties to the broader social democratic family were nevertheless typically used to demonstrate democratic credentials and not to inform program or policy. Therefore the family in general was a heterogeneous group of parties who from the outset renounced commitments to equality and social justice in favor of pragmatism. Left-wing activism and a political culture oriented to the left were quite absent, and the parties came to be dominated more by charismatic leaders than by particular political appeals. The discourses traditionally associated with social democracy have for that reason turned out to be of little use in mobilizing supporters, particularly in the face of growing competition from populist parties claiming to defend the "rights of the poorest and weakest." Today's economic crisis has made even clearer this long pattern of convergence between the left and the populist and often nationalist parties, most notably on issues of guaranteeing minimum social standards.

Successor Parties: An Electorally Resistant Species?

In the aftermath of 1989 new competitive electoral markets boosted domestic and international confidence in the democratization process (Linz and Stepan 1996). Except in Romania and Bulgaria, during the first Central and Eastern European free elections, lefts—social democrats, successor parties,

Table 1. Percentage of Votes Cast in Parliamentary Elections, 1990–2007

		1990	1991	1992	1993	1994	1995	1996
Bulgaria	KPB		0.7			1.5		
	BSP	47.2	33.1			43.5[1]		
	EVROLEV							
Czech Republic	KSČM	13.2		14.0				10.3
	CSSD	4.1		6.5				26.4
Hungary	MSZP	10.9				32.6		
Poland	SLD		11.9		20.4			
	UP		2.1		7.2			
Romania	PSM			3.1				2.2
	PS							2.3
	PDSR/PSD	66.3		27.7				21.5
	PSDR	0.5		20.2 [2]				12.9 [3]
	PD			10.2				
Slovakia	KSS			0.8		2.7		
	SDL	13.3		14.7		10.4 [4]		
	SMER							

1. In coalition with the Bulgarian Agrarian People's Union, Alexander Stanboliski, and Ecoglasnost.

2. Part of the Democratic Convention, the PSDR obtains only ten deputies and one senator out of the sixty-two CDR mandates.

3. The Social Democratic Alliance unites the PD and the PSDR.

4. The Party of the Democratic Left is part of the coalition Common Choice, which also includes the Social Democratic Party of Slovakia, the Farmers movement, and other small political parties.

5. Starting with the 2001 elections the Coalition for Bulgaria unites the BSP and a number of smaller leftist formations such as the Party of Bulgarian Social Democrats, the Bulgarian Agrarian

and others—suffered severe electoral defeats, results that did not promise brilliant futures (table 1). Yet a brief few years later the defeated parties "took advantage of a . . . political environment where weak competitors systematically made strategic mistakes" (Hough 2005, 4). Left successor parties were geared toward power, ready to agree to programmatic compromises, and eager to occupy central roles in the new political game, which they soon proved able to do.

1997	1998	1999	2000	2001	2002	2003	2004	2005	2006	2007
1.3				17.2[2]				30.9[5]		
21.9 [1]										
5.6				0.9				1.3	12.8	
	11.0				18.5				32.3	
	32.3				30.2				43.2	
	32.9				42.0					
27.1				41.0				11.3		13.0 [6]
4.7								3.9		
			0.7				0.2			
			21.5[7]				36.6			
			7.0				31.5			
	2.8				6.3				3.9	
	14.7				1.4				29.1[8]	
					13.5					

People's Union "Aleksander Stambolijski," the Movement for Social Humanism, and the Bulgarian Communist Party.

6. During the 2007 elections the Left and Democrats coalition unites the Democratic Left Alliance, the Social Democracy of Poland, the Labour Union and the Democratic Party.

7. Initially part of the electoral alliance with the PSD, the PSDR merges with the PSD in 2001.

8. The Party of the Democratic Left merges with the Smer in 2005.

Source: www.europe-politique.eu, http://cdp.binghamton.edu/era/searchera.html, http://www.essex.ac.uk/elections.

Growth and Decline of the Polish Democratic Party

In chronological perspective, the Polish story began in the late 1980s with the Polish Round Table. Intricate negotiations between the Polish United Workers Party (PZPR), sponsored by the regime, and Solidarnosc were supposed to lead to partial liberalization and not wholesale democratic transition. Solidarnosc and opposition parties were allowed to run for 35% of the seats in Sejm, while voting for the upper chamber was completely open. Despite these precautionary measures "Solidarity's sweeping electoral success sounded the death knell of communism" (Millard 2003, 25). By the end of 1989 the Polish

Workers Party had been dissolved and Alexander Kwasniewski elected the leader of its successor, the Democratic Left Alliance (SLD), in parallel with the coming of a multiparty system and completely free elections in 1991. Owing to the lack of credibility of parties associated with the past and the predominance of pro-market discourses, voters then gave massive support to parties opposed to communism, with the SLD obtaining only 12%.

After the post-1989 coalitions fell apart, early elections were called in 1993. With functioning democratic institutions in place, political debate was centered around the introduction of property rights, the pace of economic reform, inflation, and unemployment. The SLD and the agrarian Polish People's Party (PSL), neither of which disputed the need for change, pledged gentler economic reforms that would be accompanied by increases in social spending. The elections, held under new electoral laws, thus led to severe losses for the other parliamentary parties, while the SLD, with 20%, came in first and formed a new government with the PSL. The defeat of the center-right was caused mainly by hardships tied to the reforms promoted under Leszek Balcerowicz, which had made voters impatient and desirous of less harsh reforms. One of the explicit goals of the Democratic Left, which drew its inspiration from the German SPD, was to build a welfare state and implement social programs robust enough to provide protection through the economic transition period (Buras 2005, 92). Likewise, the party distinguished itself from others in the party system by its secularist positions, like those defending the rights of women and sexual minorities.

It was not only economic problems that lay behind the electoral shift toward the ex-communists, for there was also a practical issue of credibility. The Democratic Left (SLD) was an organized party with professional elites energized by young leaders promoting secular values. The anticommunist parties, in contrast, had discredited themselves with nationalistic, pro-Catholic discourses and political amateurism. The "pro-SLD" *air du temps* continued into the presidential elections of 1995, which saw Lech Walesa, the historical leader of Solidarnosc, face off against the SLD leader Aleksander Kwasniewski, who won a surprising victory with 51% of the vote.

After this a pattern of regular electoral rotation seemed to take over. Despite continuous economic reforms and Poland's image as Eastern Europe's economic "tiger," the next elections in 1997 were won by Solidarity Electoral Action (AWS). Four years later, with 16% unemployment and very high budget deficits, voters focused on the ills of the Polish economy and turned sharply against the center-right coalition. The results were a limited victory for the reformed communists and the complete removal of the AWS from Parliament. The Democratic Left (SLD), in alliance with the small

Table 2. Membership of Central and Eastern European Left Parties

			Individual Membership	Total National Membership	Individual Membership as Percentage of National Membership
Bulgaria[1]	BSP	2002–2003	210,000	444,700	47.2
Czech Republic[2]	KSČM	1993	350,000	545,000	64.2
		1999	160,000	319,800	50
	CSSD	1993	13,000	545,000	2.4
		1999	18,000	319,800	5.6
Hungary[2]	MSZP	1993	59,000	165,300	35.7
		1999	39,000	173,600	22.5
Poland[2]	SLD	2000	87,000	326,500	26.7
	UP	2000	5,000	326,500	1.5
Romania[3]	PSD	2001	309,714	—	
		2003	300,000	1,735,430	17.3
		2002	699,431	—	
		2004	607,412	—	
	PD	1998	135,288	—	
		2002	117,000	1,735,430	6.7
Slovakia[2]	SDL	1994	27,600	127,500	21.7
		2000	21,223	165,277	12.9

Sources: 1. Spirova 2005, 606; 2. Mair and Van Biezen 2001, 17–18; 3. Soare and Preda 2008, 79.

center-left Labor Union and the People's Party, formed the new governing coalition.

Starting in the mid-1990s the SLD focused most on macro-policy issues and on reinforcing its organization under the leadership of Leszek Miller (Millard 2003, 36). For almost a decade no other party could match the SLD either in territorial strength or in membership (table 2). This pattern was not peculiar to Poland, and scholars have often pointed to ex-communist parties' superiority in membership, territorial organization, and material resources (Szczerbiak 1999; Szczerbiak 2001; Van Biezen 2003; Lewis 2003). Most new parties tended to be concentrated in urban areas and among a young and educated electorate, but the SLD had a socially broader and more widespread network. In its internal life the leader was the party's major cornerstone. In time, the party gradually consolidated an image of pragmatism that looked more to its voters than its members (Buras 2005, 88). In the longer run, however, the fragility and superficiality of its organizational structure and clientelistic relationships between leaders and members weakened the party's electoral grip. Corruption became systemic and a series of scandals rocked the party, inducing a hemorrhage of members and the creation of a splinter party, Polish Social Democracy (SdPl).

In 2005 the Democratic Left (SLD) was therefore moved to restate its official stance: "We want a Poland that is just, democratic, tolerant . . . . Poland must be a country for everyone, and not just for the chosen few. We want a strong and efficient state in equalizing opportunities for Poles, sensitive to human pain, exploitation and inequality. We want a Poland that is open, European and proud of its history, treated without falsification and concealment. We want a Poland that does not forget the achievements of 45 years of the People's Republic and without nationalistic, right-wing fictions."[6] Social policy proposals, Pro-Europeanism, and anti-nationalist arguments were thus central to the program. Electoral results nonetheless confirmed the relative decline of the SLD that had been identified in various pre-election surveys. The collapse of the coalition led by Jaroslaw Kaczynski led to early elections in 2007 and seemed to offer a chance for redemption to the SLD. The final competition was between the Law and Justice (PiS) and Civic Platform (PO) parties, while the SLD and other left-of-center parties formed a new grouping, the Left and Democrats (LiD), which to its dismay obtained merely 13.15% of the votes (fifty-five seats in the Sejm and none in the Senate).

More than twenty years after the Berlin Wall fell, the Polish left is at a crossroads in a political landscape where the right is now predominant. Populist parties have challenged the center-left's credibility, while internal conflicts and scandals have progressively undermined it. Despite efforts in 2007 to forge a coherent message and Kwasniewski's personal comeback, the LiD clearly needs both programmatic and organizational reshaping. The coalition and its constituent parties have had consistent problems creating an identity for themselves, even if they have continued to advertise their interest in policies tied to work and social rights, secularization, and building a social Europe.

The Hungarian Socialist Party: Constancy and Compromise

Hungary was the second communist state to breathe the air of democracy. Liberalization had started after the Budapest revolt of 1956 with the abandonment of Stalinist positions on social matters and the implementation of cautious economic reforms to enlarge and consolidate the legitimacy of the regime. Despite these changes, beneath the official consensus an opposition quickly organized, and by 1987 the monopoly of the Hungarian Socialist Workers' Party (MSzMP) had been broken. The Hungarian Democratic Forum (MDF) was created, followed by the Alliance of Free Democrats (SzDSz) and the Hungarian Civic Union (FIDESZ) (Pittaway 2003, 58). The Hungarian case is thus unusual because the reformed successor party "emerged *before* the collapse of the state socialism and not *after* . . . and played a very active and instrumental role in bringing down the former system" (Agh 1995, 492). By the end of the 1980s a widening gap had isolated hardliners among the communists (MSzMP), János Kádár had been removed from the leadership, and almost one-third of the Central Committee had been replaced.

Negotiations in June 1989 between the democratic opposition and the ruling Communist Party led to the first free elections in 1990. By September 1989 the Hungarian Socialist Party (MSzP) had become the successor to the Communist Party, carrying over a majority of the party elite, rank and file, and resources (Van Biezen 2003, 124). Continuity gave the party an important advantage in territorial network, financial assets, and real estate. But there was a break at the organizational level. The new MSzP adopted a flexible organizational model based on secret-ballot voting and decentralized selection procedures (Agh 1995, 493). Thus, "in line with the party's aspiration to bury the organizational model of the past . . . the MSzP was quite loosely organized and its organizational structure scarcely formalized" (Van Biezen 2003, 125). Membership was never the top priority of the new party (table 2), in part because only about 2% of the Hungarian electorate belongs to any party. The ironic effect was to make its membership relatively large, the typical member being "middle-aged, male, urban, and intellectual" (Agh 1995, 498). Programmatically the MSzP's prime concern at first was to advocate free-market policies and prove its loyalty to the new regime. Especially after its comeback in 1994 the Socialists (MSzP) were the promoters of market reforms based on austerity and rapid privatization. Their foreign policy from the beginning was open and internationalist, replete with anti-nationalistic and Europhile statements, and they worked to separate themselves from the nationalism regularly promoted by their opponents, mainly the Civic Union (FIDESZ).

Like other countries in the region, in the early 1990s Hungary experienced the perverse consequences of economic reform. Despite support by the Democratic Forum (MDF) for gradual economic transformation, the country's transition proved difficult. GDP declined and there was a deterioration in living standards. Conflicts inside the government and the amateurism of new, non-communist elites accentuated the climate of distrust. In the elections of 1994, held during an economic slump, the Socialist Party's organizational network and its renewed party elite attracted ordinary voters and even seduced its former enemy, the Alliance of Free Democrats (SzDSz). Like its Polish counterpart, the main successor party used its policymaking and administrative experience as key assets (Grzymala–Busse 2002, 138). But once back in power it was obliged by international lenders to cut social spending; and in the years that followed, Hungary had one of the highest unemployment rates in the entire post-communist region. During its time in power, allied with the liberals in SzDSz, the party thus became the advocate of austerity and worked to dismantle the institutions of the state economy.[7] These economic reforms eventually paid off, and by 1997 GDP had started to rise. The credibility of the MSzP government was nonetheless hurt by austerity and corruption scandals while, in parallel, the opposition had already begun to reorganize.

The electoral campaign in 1998 was dominated by the charisma and populism of Viktor Orbán, the leader of FIDESZ. Until a few weeks before the elections the Socialists seemed likely to be reelected, but the party won only 134 seats versus 148 for FIDESZ. The MSzP held on to 33% of the vote and its dominance in traditional industrialized districts, but opposition unity made the difference. Whereas in 1994 fragmentation of the right had helped the center-left, four years later a unified opposition blocked its reelection. In 2002 and again in 2006 FIDESZ, which was becoming a standard center-right party, and the MSzP progressively reinforced their electoral power while the other parties were falling apart.[8] In an almost bipolar electoral market in 2002, the MSzP in alliance with the Free Democrats (SzDSz) gathered a limited majority with 198 seats. The same formula worked in 2006, and the MSzP-SzDSz coalition won 210 seats in Parliament.

After the forced resignation of Prime Minister Peter Medgyessy, the Socialists installed the young businessman Ferenc Gyurcsany, one of the richest men in Hungary, as its leader. Under his stewardship the party adopted a Blairite "third way" agenda. The MSzP soon joined an exclusive club of post-communist parties to have won two successive elections while in government. Despite numerous scandals and riots in Budapest in 2006, the MSzP seems to be the healthiest left party in the region, despite organizational underdevelopment and an ambiguous programmatic posture between centrism and liberal policies.

The Hungarian Socialists (MSzP) have thus been in office for more than half of the two decades of post-communism, and they are one of the most pro-European parties in the region, with a history of compromise between an inherited left culture and an ambition to win elections. Still, the future remains in doubt. Confronted with one of the largest budget deficits in the region, especially after 2000, the party has been forced to shift policies so as to lower public spending, a policy that led to growing criticism among its supporters. This tense situation worsened after the crisis of 2006 and especially in 2009 under the new prime minister Gordon Bajnai, who was obliged to reduce wages, raise taxes, and cut social spending. In these conditions Jobbik (Movement for a Better Hungary), a right-wing nationalist party that had only been founded in 2002, became more and more important and registered a significant advance in the European elections of June 2009.

Common Origins and Divergent Paths: The Czechoslovakian Case

Czechoslovakia was the third country in Eastern and Central Europe to be swept up in the wave of democratization. Besides the challenges of the "double transitions" to democracy and free-market capitalism, the country also faced a serious nationality question (Kuzio 2001). After a "velvet revolution," the "velvet divorce" put an end to one of the most important states in the entire region (De Waele 1998, 49). Czechoslovakia has been regularly depicted as the region's only genuine democracy before communism, and ironically it was the one country where the Communist Party had been a relevant political force before 1948. It was known also for a strong social democratic tradition linked to the Czechoslovak Social Democratic Worker's Party (CSDSD) and Czechoslovak Social Democracy (CSD). In Slovakia, in contrast, a traditionally rural economy and the strength of the Catholic Church had prevented the emergence of a strong pre-war left party.

In 1946 the Czechoslovak Communist Party (KSČ) had won 38% of the votes and then occupied most ministerial posts. Despite this, in February 1948 the party chose to seize power in brutal fashion. Twenty years later troops from five Warsaw Pact countries repressed the Prague Spring and ended the party's and the nation's attempts to reform from within. The once well-rooted ruling party then experienced a progressive decrease in membership. The party had 1.79 million members in 1948–49, 1.38 million in the mid-1950s, and only 1.17 million by the 1970s, the lowest number since the coup of 1948. By 1987 party membership had gone back up to 1.61 million (Stolca 2005, 703), but despite this, strong demonstrations in 1988 culminated in six weeks of protest in November and December. In the same period the Slovak branch of the party developed a softer version of communism: "far away from both party supervision and decision-making, the then Young Turks from the Bratislava-based Institute of Marxism-Leninism, Peter Weiss and Pavol Kanis, had organized seminars to discuss the social and economic problems of society" and effectively created a reformed party (Haughton 2005, 179). These same young communist leaders would be in charge of the party after the Velvet Revolution. The bloodless overthrow of the communist regime initially gave power to the Civic Forum (OF) and the Public against Violence (VPN), while the former ruling party remained practically unchanged and "retained much of its orthodox profile in both ideological and organizational terms, with the hardliners within the party successfully withstanding pressure for change" (Van Biezen 2003, 136). The first free elections in June 1990 brought sweeping victory to movements and parties opposed to the old regime. At the same time divisions between Slovaks and Czechs deepened, and after the elections of 1992 leaders in Prague and Bratislava declared the dissolution of the former Czechoslovak Republic.

No fewer than twenty-two parties and movements registered for the first free elections. Despite everything in its past, the Communist Party finished second with almost 14% of the votes (table 2). The Social Democrats (ČSSD), who had been forcibly merged with the Communists but were now newly independent, failed at the national level to reach the 5% threshold required to win parliamentary representation in the country's proportional electoral system (Van Biezen 2003, 135). Initially hesitating between functioning within the Civic Forum and establishing an independent political organization, the ČSSD in the early 1990s was strongly divided. Those favoring collaboration with Civic Forum managed to win several seats under that label. Their opponents, led by Jiri Horák, controversially chose to collaborate with dissident communists expelled from the party in 1968. The effect was to cause turmoil in a party run by anticommunist dissidents. Still, Horák's openness to collaboration with other leftist leaders reinforced the party as an independent political force after Civic Forum broke apart in 1991 and allowed it to prosper.

The parliamentary campaign of 1992 was taken up by economic issues and disagreements about the future of the federation, whose breakdown they nourished. In the Czech half of the former country a coalition between the new Civic Democratic Party (ODS), led by the free-market enthusiast Vaclav Klaus, and the Christian Democratic Party (KDS) won thirty-seven seats. A left bloc led by the former communists (KSČM) won thirty-five and the Social Democrats (ČSSD) sixteen. In the Slovak half the elections were won by the successor party to the communists, the Party of the Democratic Left (SDL). At this point the former communists in the Czech half of the republic, the Communist Party of Bohemia and Moravia (KSČM), as it was known since 1989, came under internal pressure to change (De Waele 1998, 60). "Soft-liners," represented by the chairman Jiří Svoboda, were keen to promote a smooth transformation to the post-communist era, but strong reluctance from the base and hardliner control over the organization limited their attempts. Svoboda was forced to resign and the party held on to its orthodoxy under Miroslav Grebeníček (Handl 2005). In a subsequent document the KSČM publicly rejected the practices of former regimes but also put strong emphasis on its "aim to create a modern socialist society, which will guarantee real and lasting freedom and equality, regardless of property and social status. This concept is based on Marxism and an open dialogue with new ideas and experiences. Communists have always actively striven to defend and promote the interests of the exploited, the restricted, and the oppressed classes."[9] Thus while in the rest of the region Marxism seemed to have vanished, it remained alive in the Czech Republic. Organizationally the former communists preserved broad territorial coverage but rapidly lost membership—by 1991 they had about 750,000 members (Van Biezen 2003, 139), by 1999 about 130,000, and by 2008 only 77,115.[10] More than two decades after 1989 the party's core membership consists of male pensioners, with 15% active blue-collar workers. The majority of members have but a modest education, and only 10% have university degrees. Party statutes continue to emphasize the active involvement of ordinary party members: "Membership of the Czech Communist Party, moreover, is not restricted to activities in the public realm but also extends to the private and requires a dedication to personal and political involvement" (Van Biezen 2003, 142). The extent of this involvement has been considerable, a pattern also characteristic of the Social Democrats (ČSSD). Both parties' linkages with members and interest organizations have therefore been higher than for other Czech parties.[11]

After the "velvet divorce" took effect in 1993 it was clear that communists would maintain key positions in the Czech Republic, even if they were ostracized by other parties. In addition, the Social Democrats (ČSSD) began to gather increasing support. The leadership of the Social Democrats changed at its Congress of February 1993, and its new leaders emerged as strong opponents of the privatization by vouchers promoted by Vaclav Klaus, which aimed at rapid and massive redistribution of state property. The party also increased its credibility by unequivocally refusing to cooperate with the former communists (KSČM). By its promotion of gentler economic reforms, it was progressively recognized as a left alternative and thereby reinforced its electoral appeal.

In the mid-1990s Czech economic results were regarded as miraculous because of rapid privatization with low unemployment and inflation.[12] These achievements provided the setting for the elections of 1996, which produced a vote of confidence in Klaus's government and its call for a market economy inspired by Thatcherism (Orenstein 1995, 184). The government had been strongly shaken by the strikes of 1995, including actions by professors, doctors, and railway workers which served to garner support for the social policy positions of the Social Democrats (ČSSD) and to lend credence to the criticisms of the Communists (KSČM). The campaign of 1996 was thus dominated by such social and economic issues. The parties of the left were able to expand their electoral base, particularly in rural areas, but the right (ODS) was nonetheless able to hold on to its support in the cities and among retired voters.

Despite this favorable context the successor party's appeal remained limited, and it won only 10.3%. During this entire period the party adhered to its communist credo, including Pan-Slavism and Russophilia. It also advocated continued collaboration with what remained of the array of communist states—Cuba, China, and North Korea—and other opponents of "American imperialism" like Milosevic's Yugoslavia and Saddam Hussein's Iraq (Handl 2005, 126). The leaders and supporters of the not-so-former Communists (KSČM) were apparently nostalgic for the ancien régime and eager to protest and punish the compromises of the Social Democrats (ČSSD) (Handl 2003, 4). The party's biggest challenge remained its aging and shrinking electoral base, and despite some modest modernizing efforts, the organization attracted few voters in the election of 1996.[13]

The Social Democrats (ČSSD) won almost 27%, putting them just behind the Civic Democrats (ODS). But the economic situation then changed very quickly, and the Czech Republic fell into a deep recession. The unexpected resignation of Klaus, the ODS leader, who had been implicated in a financial scandal, deepened the political crisis. The Social Democrats won the elections in 1998 with 32.3% of the votes, while the communists won 11%. Refusing to collaborate with the successor party, the Social Democratic leader formed a minority government bolstered by an agreement guaranteeing opposition involvement in all major decisions. The party (ČSSD) maintained its strength in the elections of 2002, and its new leader, Vladimir Špidla, then formed a coalition government with the Christian Democrats and the Freedom Union, again refusing collaboration with the communists, who nevertheless won 18.5% and thereby increased their number of seats in the lower chamber from twenty-four to forty-one. During their extended period in office the Social Democrats (ČSSD) sought to consolidate their middle-class and public-sector supporters and progressively moved toward the center, a shift that became official under its new leadership. This repositioning nevertheless weakened the party in the presidential elections in 2003 and the European elections in 2004; now plagued by scandals and a blurred identity, the Social Democrats (ČSSD) lost in 2006, while the communist KSČM declined to 12.8%. Twenty years after the cold war's end the Czech political landscape remained deeply marked by the same ideological confrontation between Social Democrats and former and largely unreformed Communists that had emerged soon after the breakup of Czechoslovakia (Handl 2003, 7).

In Slovakia the Party of the Democratic Left (SDL) was the successor and heir to the once powerful Communist Party. Starting in the early 1990s it undertook a process of internal and programmatic reassessment. At the same time the Social-Democratic Party of Slovakia (SDSS), a historical party led by Dubček himself, was reborn. The more hardline Communist Party (KSS) briefly won several seats in Parliament, but from the outset the ability of the new Democratic Left (SDL) to adapt and the positive effects of its role in rural Slovakia reinforced its credibility. Moreover, the harsh economic reforms announced by President Václav Havel promised difficulty for what there was of Slovak industry; in consequence, "The pro-reform, anticommunist consensus was far less clear" in Slovakia than in the Czech Republic (Grzymala-Busse 2002, 151).

In the elections of 1992 the Democratic Left (SDL) obtained 14.7%, the hardliners (KSS) less than 1%. Both left parties were successfully challenged by the People's Party, or Movement for a Democratic Slovakia (HZDS), led by Vladimir Mečiar (Haughton 2005, 180). Initially a reaction against the right-leaning pronouncements of the government dominated by the Public Against Violence Party (VPN), the People's Party program was an eclectic blend of social policies, nationalism, and populism that directly challenged the Democratic Left (SDL) in its core constituencies (Williams 2003, 50). In the face of this challenge "the SDL saw its commitment to democracy as the main distinction between itself and the HZDS," and the key feature of its program became a formal and explicit commitment to democratic loyalty rather than a more typical social democratic identity (Grzymala-Busse 2002, 151). Like other successor parties the Democratic Left (SDL) "engaged in an acknowledged and deliberative emulation of programmatic and political ideas from Western social-democratic parties, the Socialist International and the Party of European Socialists" (Handl and Leška 2005, 106). As the party chairman Weiss declared, "we are for the market mechanisms and plural democracy . . . we do not want to be an ideological party" (Weiss, quoted by Grzymala-Busse 2002, 152). Yet the effort was largely superficial, for the party really saw itself as more liberal than the People's Party, while its free-market statements progressively distanced it from the trade unions that had been attracted to its populist discourse and program.

Aiming to broaden its electoral appeal, the Democratic Left (SDL) took part in the elections as the main member of the Common Choice coalition formed by the Greens, the Social Democrats, and the Farmers' Movement.

The coalition strategy backfired and obscured the party's visibility, "muddy-ing the party's image and program in the mind of the electorate" (Haughton 2005, 185). Common Choice won only 10.41% of the vote, while its populist rivals (HZDS) became the main party in the Slovak republic with 34.95%. The hardline KSS did worse, obtaining less than 3%. Typical voters for Com-mon Choice were young, urban, and highly educated, with a predominance of state employees.[14]

Four years later, in 1998 the People's Party (HZDS) obtained 27% of the votes, an unsatisfactory result for a party with limited coalitional potential. A centrist coalition—made up of the Democratic Union, the Christian Demo-cratic Movement, the Democratic Party, the Green Party, and the SDSS com-bined in the Slovak Democratic Coalition (SDK)—won 26.33%; the Demo-cratic Left SDL won just under 15% and the unreformed KSS less than 3%. The SDK leader became prime minister and the Democratic Left (SDL) joined in the government coalition, in which it promoted a series of aggressively pro-market reforms and thus alienated its traditional left electorate (Haugh-ton 2005, 185). The party was riven by debates between a "Third Way," with proposals for economic stabilization that its enemies claimed were inspired by the IMF and Milton Friedman, and more orthodox socialists who favored building a strong welfare state (Handl and Leška 2005, 114). This second posi-tion won out, but not without leaving deep scars. At the same time, during the coalition of 1998–2004 the party was plagued by scandals, something that seemed a common denominator in the entire post-communist political spec-trum. In this context one of the best-known party leaders, Robert Fico, left the SDL to form the Smer (Direction), whose original name included the phrase "Third Way," illustrating Fico's Blairite programmatic inspiration. Like New Labour, Smer sought a "modern" social democratic balance between equal opportunities and liberal economics.

In the elections of 2002 the Democratic Left (SDL) suffered a major de-feat, securing just 1.36% of the votes while the former communists in the KSS registered their highest score in the post-communist elections with 6.32%. These elections indicated how much the party had been marginalized, while the recently created Smer broke through with 13.46% of the vote (Handl and Leška 2005). Three years later Smer became the catalyst for a unification of the Slovak left, merging with the Democratic Left (SDL), the Social Demo-cratic Alternative and the historic Social Democrats (SDSS). In this format Smer won the elections of 2006, taking 50 of 150 seats. Surprisingly, the party then formed a coalition with the former ally on the right of the People's Party, the SNS, leading it to be suspended temporarily from the Party of European Socialists (PES), the EU-level social democratic organization.

"Once a Big Party":
The Rapid Decline of the Romanian Social Democratic Party

It is widely acknowledged that the annus mirabilis after the Wall fell had more limited effects in Romania than in the rest of the region, particularly since the Romanian Communist Party (PCR) continued in power. The successor National Salvation Front (FSN), under various appellations like FDSN (Democratic National Salvation Front), PDSR (Party of the Romanian Social-Democracy), and the current PSD (Social Democratic Party), was the undoubted winner of the events of December 1989. Enjoying organizational superiority and two charismatic leaders, Ion Iliescu and Petre Roman, the FSN won the first free elections with more than 66% of the vote against a motley collection of opposition parties—the agrarians (PNTCD), the liberals (PNL) and the historic social democrats—which together barely won 10%.

In this first part of its new existence the FSN proclaimed a revolutionary identity and until 1993 even refused to call itself a party, preferring instead the label of Front. This label, which had strong emotional connotations of official revolutionary origins, legitimized the FSN by reference "to the virtuous and unified people" (Soare 2004). The Front recalled the emotional solidarity of the early days of the "Revolution" and emphasized a direct link between the demos and the leaders, a quality reinforced by its leader Iliescu's paternalistic approach (Tismăneanu 2000, 11). The party's catch-all discourse guaranteed a broad electoral appeal, with particular penetration among a middle-aged electorate in rural areas outside the capital (Dătculescu 1994).

Benefiting directly from the former communists' organizational structures, the Salvation Front built a professional political apparatus to wrest control over state institutions and reinforce its territorial support and electoral strength, while encouraging broad membership as a substitute for credibility (table 2). For six years the FSN squashed its competitors and profited from its hegemony by deconstructing the wealthy communist state into a capillary system of patronage to reward those who supported its positions by giving them preferential access to the state's assets (Soare 2006).[15] Joining the FSN was thus not only an issue of status but also one of opportunity for economic and professional benefits. An unwritten rule has existed since then that whatever the turnover, rival parties would do similar things for their own benefit.

Immediately after the elections of 1990 tensions emerged within the quite heterogeneous Salvation Front (FSN). Opposition between hardliners and softliners echoed differences in perspectives within the governing party, as the visions of the party's two major leaders—Ion Iliescu and Petre Roman—clashed. The split was progressively institutionalized within FSN, and by 1992 two purportedly social democratic parties had emerged. In elections that year the parties together won nearly 40% of the vote, but the real winner was Iliescu's party, the FDSN (which soon became the Party of Social Democracy, or PDSR). Still, with fewer than 30% of the votes and the refusal of the Christian Democrats (CDR) to form an alliance, the party was left to soldier on in a minority government until it managed in 1994 to establish the so-called Red Quadrilateral Coalition with three right-wing parties: the Great Romania Party (PRM), the Party of the Romanians' National Unity (PUNR), and the small nationalist-socialist Socialist Party of Labor (PSM).

There were also traditional social democratic players during the first series of elections. Despite repeated electoral failures in the 1990s due to unwise strategic alliances, the historical Social Democrats (PSDR) succeeded in becoming a regular parliamentary party. In a landscape dominated by issues of "high politics," it was the only party interested in developing a coherent social democratic program. Its individual electoral weakness and coalitional missteps limited the impact and visibility of traditional left culture, however, and in 2001 the party merged with its larger rival, the Party of Social Democracy (PDSR) descended from the largest successor party.

Beginning in 1993 the FDSN/PDSR had begun a complex programmatic realignment. Symbolically it deemphasized its revolutionary claims and changed its name. This did not represent a fundamental break with the past, and the party's potential coalition partners were limited to other "outcast" parties. The second step of its strategy was a long campaign to join the Party of European Socialists and the Socialist International. By 2000, having been again renamed, as the Social Democratic Party (PSD), the party itself initiated its own, internally oriented campaign for change: it openly affirmed a social democratic identity, built greater linkages with trade unions and a more developed organization, and even introduced new mechanisms for designating electoral candidates.

From 1992 until 2005, of course, the party faced competition from a rival successor party. The Democratic Party (PD) was an alternative social democratic group that came together around the reformist leader Petre Roman. The party advertised itself as a new social democratic party inspired by western social democracy, and Roman's personal connections with leaders like Felipe González were used to open doors in the European family. But after electoral failure in 2000 and the election of a new leader, now president of Romania, the PD progressively distanced itself from international social democratic networks and also refused collaboration with the PSD, preferring instead to ally with center-right partners. In 2005, in a major programmatic shift, the PD became a people's party. Behind this shift lay a pragmatic strategy which had immediate results. Since the political disappearance of the Christian Democrats (PNTCD) in 2000, the EPP—the European alliance of Christian Democratic and Center-Right parties—did not have a major Romanian partner. This new connection was therefore extremely useful for both the EPP and the Romanian party. International visibility and EU parliamentary seats were prizes for which the new party—soon to be known as the Democratic Liberal Party and after 2007 as the Liberal Democratic Party—would gladly trade in its social democratic heritage and identity.

In spite of these strange moves the electoral results from 1990 through 2004 suggest that the Romanian social democratic family has been perhaps the most stable in the post-communist arena. Ever since the coming of a new democracy, at least one supposedly social democratic party has been in power. But the record of the Romanian social democratic family also draws attention to the strategic capacities of the parties for adapting to their environment. The Liberal Democratic (PD) realignment just discussed is one consequence of the persistent political marketing of post-communist social democratic parties and of a strategy that has indirectly been made easier by fluctuating societal cleavages. We have pointed out elsewhere that in Central and Eastern Europe major socioeconomic divisions have not been effectively tapped by parties, which instead have engaged in clientelistic trade-offs between parties and local leaders (Soare 2004). In Romania the fragmentation of the social democratic family—both branches of which profited organizationally from being successors to the communists—was determined more by personal and factional differences than by socioeconomic issues, and endemic clientelism has been inimical to the creation of strong parties. Partly in consequence, a "once big" party, the Social Democratic Party (PSD), is currently plagued by scandals and internal power struggles, while political patronage has in the long run been of limited utility as a substitute for organization to a party in opposition.

At the same time, beginning in 2000 the Social Democratic Party (PSD) did launch numerous programmatic documents focused on questions of equality and social justice. The party's position in government between 2000–2004 and 2008 limited the significance of these issues. It is significant, though, that the new program launched by the Social Democrats in 2006, "A Social Romania," proposed "equal chances and treatment for everyone regardless of their background; lifting the minimum salary to the level of the minimum pension so that the low-paid can meet day-to-day living costs; investing in the village economy; investing in the health system; improving the competitiveness of our economy; ensuring that income taxes are progressive; improving absorptive capacity of communitarian funds; and finally, significant investment in education" (Birchall 2007). But once back in power in 2008, and allied with their longtime rivals on the center-left, the Liberal Democrats, the party retreated from pursuing these policies.[16]

The Constancy of the Bulgarian Socialist Party

Influenced by perestroika and glasnost and pushed by the Bulgarian political elite, the Bulgarian Communist Party (BKP), led by Todor Zhivkov, had to open itself to change even before 1989. Beginning in the early 1980s young reformers inside the party quietly promoted a leadership change (Gallagher 2003). By 1987 the party had announced multiple-candidate regional elections as a sign of political liberalization. Then, in an apparently calm situation, during a European environmental conference in Sofia in October 1989 street protests led to a major mass demonstration in the capital city. Unable to control either the party or the situation, and under scrutiny from the international community, Zhivkov resigned and Bulgaria began its tortuous transition to democracy led by Mladenov, the former foreign minister. The BKP chose a social democratic path to political redemption, becoming the new Bulgarian Socialist Party (BSP), renouncing Marxism, and accepting the market economy. It then proved its loyalty to the new regime by accepting negotiations with the more anticommunist Union of the Democratic Forces (UDF in English, SDS in Bulgarian) and supporting the first post-communist free elections (Touykova 1997, 5).

As in Romania, the rigidity of the Bulgarian communist regime hampered the creation of effective alternative organizations. Noncommunist groups lacked the territorial organization and professional resources to compete with the successor party, the Socialists (BSP) (Spirova 2005, 602). Most of the forty-two organizations competing in the elections in 1990 were unknown and without widespread support (Karasimeneov 2004, quoted by Spirova 2005, 602). The campaign was monopolized by the issue of economic transition, and the Socialists endorsed gradual economic reform while also promoting the decollectivization of agriculture and reform of the banking system. With over 47% of the votes, they formed the first freely elected post-communist government in coalition with their strongest opponents.

In July 1991 a new basic law was adopted, and elections held in October were won by the Union of Democratic Forces (SDS) with 34.4% of the votes. The Socialists did almost as well—33.1%—but the party was at the moment politically ostracized and without possible coalition partners. The noncommunist coalition's victory was reinforced by the philosopher Zhelyu Zhelev's victory in presidential elections against a candidate from the Socialist Party

(BSP) in 1992. From this position of strength the SDS then launched deep economic reform, supported strongly by the international community. But as early as 1992 the first signs of serious social conflict had appeared in the form of regular strikes. The coalition government experienced conflicts between its dominant partner and the Movement for Rights and Freedom (DPS), while the Socialist Party continued its renewal and organizational rebuilding (Karasimeneov 1995, 579; Touykova 1997, 5). Statements in support of the EU and economic reform enhanced its national and international credibility, while its political visibility was enhanced by a functioning organization inherited from the Communists—350,000 members and an elite of political professionals (Spirova 2005, 603). The party maintained direct contact with its members through highly popular meetings like the annual May Day celebrations. The party's strategy was therefore to attempt to change and adapt to post-communist challenges while preserving continuity in its social base (Karasimeneov 1995, 581). And beyond a discursive commitment to promoting a market economy accompanied by equality and justice, it could easily be argued that in Bulgaria, as in Romania, "the declared interest . . . to enhance social protection was still not visible at the level of social expenditures" (Sotiropoulos, Neamţu, and Stoyanova 2003, 661).

By the mid-1990s the country was experiencing an economic crisis, and in the resulting political instability President Zhelev dissolved Parliament and called early elections for 1995. The Socialist Party then used its organization to advantage against an opponent plagued with internal dissension to win a huge victory: 43.5% of the votes and an absolute majority in Parliament. "The landslide victory of the BSP was," according to one analyst, "a vote of hope for change to more stability and security" (Karasimeneov 1995, 584). The hopes were soon undermined, for once in power the Socialists were forced to comply with IMF pressures for rapid economic reforms. By 1996 the Bulgarian economy faced a severe financial crisis with dramatic social costs, a shrinking GDP, high inflation, and a collapsing currency. The result was the calling of new early elections in 1997, at which point the Socialists were under fire both nationally and internally. Events had called the party's commitment to its "social" policies sharply into question, and an electorate nostalgic for the security of the old regime abandoned the party: the Socialist (BSP) vote dropped to 22.5%, while the liberal Union of Democratic Forces (SDS) won 137 seats in Parliament.

Stability proved elusive, and the elections of 2001 were dominated by a new populist party, the National Movement (NDSV), led by King Simeon II and campaigning under the motto "People Are the Wealth of Bulgaria."[17] Its discourse was a mixture of nationalistic appeals and simplistic solutions for the country and economic crisis. Claiming messianic legitimacy, King Simeon was strongly critical of traditional political parties and corrupt institutions. The result was that both the liberals (SDS) and the left (BSP) were roundly thrashed and the National Movement (NDSV) obtained 42.7% of the vote. Its success also proved short-lived, and just four years later the Left Coalition for Bulgaria, led by the Socialists, won the elections with almost 31%. In the process the Socialists confirmed their role as a regular government party and one of the most consistent socialist parties in the region, whose strong electoral results are facilitated by its stable organization and broad membership. Equally important, despite the fragmentation of the left and center-left after 1989, the Bulgarian Socialist Party has progressively become a trendsetter for the entire Bulgarian political arena (Spirova 2005). At the same time policy implementation lags. Even if party documents argue for raising living standards, improving social services, and enhancing the quality of healthcare and education, it is obvious that once again "this does not necessarily have any bearing to the actual policies of a party in government" (Dauderstädt).

Tortured Paths to Redemption and Incomplete Social Democratization

Told one after the other, these stories are fascinating. After 1989 the ex-communist parties were supposed to rapidly disappear, and scholars foresaw a crisis of the left in general once they did. Yet these parties have managed to survive and challenge scholarly predictions with their remarkable electoral consistency. Throughout the region successor parties, historical parties, new party formulas, and even orthodox communist parties have managed to survive initially grim situations. In most cases the successor parties monopolized the entire left spectrum, and "no significant social democratic alternatives arose where the successor parties could preempt their moderate leftist rhetoric. In contrast, where the communist parties failed to regenerate, other parties could take up the moderate left side of the political spectrum" (Grzymala-Busse 2002, 283). More recently, increasingly balanced political competition and increasingly stable party systems may have diminished the prominence of successor parties on the left as the region's only well-organized and more or less coherent political alternatives. For such parties, discredited by their past, the new regime required complicated changes (De Waele 1996). Following a classic assumption that "Parties don't just change," the last part of our chapter will focus on who and what gave left parties the motivation and resources to comply with the norms of the new political order (Harmel and Janda 1994).

The answer to *what* were the primary inputs of change is relatively simple.

First came the domino effect that brought down communist regimes and induced the rapid implosion of the USSR, which suddenly narrowed space for returning to the past. Overnight Moscow ceased to provide relevant political support, making loyalty to the new order the only pragmatic alternative. Next, despite the ostracism faced by formerly communist parties, the transition to democracy almost by definition meant that no political party, other than openly extreme groups, could be excluded from political competition. These circumstances effectively sealed the successor parties' commitment to the new order.

The transformation of the ex-communist parties has been quite fundamental, involving acceptance of multiparty competition and support for the market economy. Even so, it was eased considerably by the institutional framework. The transition process presented three main challenges: democratization, the creation of functioning markets, and the rebuilding of state institutions (Offe 1996). State change has been the paramount challenge for ex-communist parties, since the end of the cold war dismantled communist regimes and the states that embodied them. Under the ancien régime communist parties had an effective monopoly on legally acceptable political activity, and the state itself was deeply rooted in the parties. Throughout the entire region "the weakness of the communist state left its successor open to predation" during the early transition (Grzymala-Busse 2003, 1127). Post-communist institutional arrangements that characterized states run by parties with flexible identities and few principles allowed these groups to make these states compliant with the party in power. All around the region post-communist parties were able to penetrate new states and use public offices to their own advantage (Van Biezen and Kopecky 2007). Reformed communist parties benefited from a state model that was open to the influence of parties in power (Ganev 2001; Grzymala-Busse and Jones Loung 2002; Grzymala-Busse 2003). In other words, the political experience, know-how, professional capital, and broad territorial organization of ex-communists led new leaderships to seize the opportunities provided by fluid institutional frameworks.

The rapid strategic metamorphosis of ex-communist parties translated into well-disciplined, centralized, and efficient party organizations, and the process was further eased by their economic viability. They inherited financial capital from their predecessors at the start of the transition. The privatization process and their economic expertise then put the parties in a favorable position for doing business and balancing business and politics. A Romanian ex-cadre who had become a big-time entrepreneur explained the smooth transition: "Questioned about his miraculous transformation," his interlocutor explains, "he declared he sees no contradiction between his past and current career: 'On the contrary, I was a good communist and I'll be an even better capitalist!'" (Stoica 2004, 271). Of course other structural factors such as electoral systems have been significant as well. In most of the case studies, for example, proportional representation facilitated the comeback of left parties. But being the "successor" to the previous rulers was critical.

At the electoral level it is hard to construct an ideal picture of the base of left parties and to discern the typical voter at the regional level. The Romanian Social Democrats (PSD) and their Bulgarian counterparts (BSP) were better implanted in rural zones, where their voters were older and had minimal education. More recently the changing nature of party systems has challenged this profile and the two parties have lost these electoral fiefs, but they have also made inroads into urban areas. In this respect the victory of the Social Democratic candidate for mayor of Bucharest in the most recent local elections is significant. Hungarian socialist voters, in contrast, remain urban-based. The ways the recent economic crisis has hit Polish social democrats make identifying their typical voters more difficult. Urban voters are still the most important base in Czech and Slovak social democratic electorates. Yet in virtually all cases one finds parties appealing to voters over the heads of their own party members, a reflection perhaps of ideological weakness but also an explanation of membership decline.

Moving beyond this basic balance sheet, it is difficult to identify the precise trigger for change. The scholarly literature regularly emphasizes the inertia of big organizations as "a wall of resistance" to change, and one would expect even more resistance from highly centralized communist parties (Harmel and Janda 1994, 261). But in moments of great uncertainty the actions of leadership are strongly influenced by circumstances. The vanishing credibility of communist parties at a time of pervasive economic crisis and the powerful intuition that transition was unstoppable accentuated pressures for change. In most cases the communist parties also experienced a rapid and drastic erosion of their membership (table 2), which made breaking with the past less a choice than a necessity. The parties' organizational centralization nonetheless allowed elites to control the dimensions and pace of adaptation. Finally, the legacies of the past and the rigidity of communist regimes further enhanced the appeal of change. In Hungary, Poland, Bulgaria, and Slovakia the new communist leadership after 1989 consisted of younger party members keen for rapid transformation. In the Czech Republic, where old apparatchiks dominated, reformers had less visibility and space for maneuver. The Romanian case is unusual because the new leadership of "softliners" and promoters of moderate reformism were inspired more by perestroika than by democratization.

Twenty years is too short a time to reach definitive conclusions, so we must be tentative. We have told the story of an extremely resistant species. A historical and structural approach that favors legacy-based explanations for the evolution of the Central and Eastern European post-communist left is particularly relevant to account for the commonalities and divergences of the various political actors. Thus the reluctance of Czech communists (KSČM) to change and the longstanding political tradition of the Czech Social Democrats (ČSSD) offer a convincing argument for how historical legacies and national opportunities can be combined, and in this case explain how the Czech path diverged from paths taken elsewhere in the region. As for analyzing the shift from Marxism to capitalism by the descendants of the former ruling Communist parties, history reminds us that for the most part these parties had been imposed from abroad, and despite almost half a century in power, they had failed at building the socialism they preached. *Homo sovieticus* had been almost exclusively an issue of propaganda, while Václav Benda's theory of the "parallel polis" was closer to reality. In the end the successful transformation of the ex-communist parties thus attests to a paradox. Communist parties had been the only relevant political actors in the region for almost half a century. But except in the Czech Republic they all failed at direct continuation into the post-communist era. Symbolically, Marxism and its corollaries have been totally and effectively superseded by variants of liberal and pro-market theories. Yet the successor parties themselves often succeeded.

Historically driven explanations of the success of the left and center-left parties, and in particular of the ex-communists, focus mainly on their organizational advantages (De Waele 2002). Transformation of the communist parties was an organizational strategy without clear programmatic baggage. In the fluid political competition of the early 1990s, organizational continuity allowed these parties to preserve their influence and at least partially their skilled, experienced political elites. Their organizational resources contrasted sharply with those of the fledgling proto-parties that came to power immediately after the end of the old regime. While holding on to these resources, the successor parties also adopted a twofold strategy to achieve new legitimacy and respectability. They first gave full support to economic reforms, and in government these "social democrats," old and new, worked at "building capitalism." They then went on to embrace the EU and NATO.

Their concern for integration in the new capitalist system meant abrupt disengagement from traditional ideologies and at times traditional social bases. Successor parties and historical social democrats also neglected the development of a left or center-left political culture and outlook. Despite pervasive organization, the absence of such a political culture has eventually hampered these parties. Support for a market economy and regular stays in government have not been cost-free. All over the region populist parties have come to exploit this and in several cases have been able to find fertile breeding ground. In addition, traditional alliances between these parties and the trade unions, themselves operating at a disadvantage in the new era, have been weakened (Mudde 2004). In general the absence of intermediary organizations and committed social actors must be considered when reflecting on the limits of the center-left throughout the region. Domination of the political scene by parties, the weakness of civil society, and the alienation from politics regularly emphasized by surveys have blocked the emergence of a participatory culture. This participation deficit has progressively generated a real representation crisis, with a major impact on the center-left in particular.

The strong support for European and NATO integration has also created problems for center-left parties of whatever origin. The paradox is clear: "Social democrats have been the strongest advocates of accession in many countries . . . Why did social democrats support EU membership in spite of the costs and partial drawbacks for their own clientele?" (Agh 2004, 5). The reasons for this exaggerated Europeanism were the need for international credibility, pragmatism tied to a lack of alternatives, and perceived national diplomatic interests. Twenty years on, however, center-left parties are now progressively squeezed between EU requirements, national needs to comply with transition goals, and popular disenchantment due to the social costs of the new system. From the beginning the attempts of parties of the left to develop a coherent programmatic identity through the prism of national and local needs and social requirements have been neglected in favor of the choice for Europe. Despite a certain amount of electoral stability, the progressive shrinkage of the blue-collar working class and the appeal to the left's traditional working-class base of new right-wing populist parties have thus become very large challenges. In such new political circumstances, the center-left is on the defensive all around the region.

Twenty years after the fall of "peoples' democracies," the post-communist political landscape has changed fundamentally. The resurrection of old lefts in central Europe was helped by their political experience and organizational networks, and by the weakness and fragmentation of their opponents. But in time, their weaknesses in ideology, organization, and relationships with party members and voters, along with accusations of corruption, have become much more visible with the consolidation of the right and the emergence of new forms of populism. Thus the successes of the 1990s seem mainly to have obscured the Achilles' heel of these left parties, their ideological weakness. The ever greater convergence of social policies across different national party systems has also limited their margins of maneuver and progressively eaten away at their traditional electoral bases. Throughout the entire region the center-left thus remains trapped in a process of reconstruction which is made more difficult by outside pressures and a troubled past.

Notes

1. By successor parties we refer to those parties "that were formerly the governing party in the pre-1989 communist regime and which inherited the preponderance of the former ruling parties' resources and personnel" (Ishiyama 1998, 62).

2. Between 1991 and 1997 the Eurobarometer surveys measured high levels of dissatisfaction with the untoward consequences of democratization, in particular its social costs (Dauderstädt and Gerrits 2000, table 6).

3. Outside this divided family the KSČM looks to be the only large Communist party in the region continuing into post-communism, defining itself as "the only genuine Czech left party," whose goal remains "the transformation from capitalism to socialism" (Zprava, 5th Congress 1999, quoted in Handl 2003, 4). The KSČM may be related to the other parties, but it has become a separate case, following its own left social democratic paths while denouncing the "laxity" and loss of Marxist-Leninist political principles by others.

4. Even though the notion of the political family is a category of analysis often criticized as vague and based on common sense, it remains a useful tool in analyzing political parties, for it offers at the same time a "domain of identification" for party elites, members, and voters and a reference point in the "domain of competition" at the level of party systems (Mair and Mudde 1998; Sartori and Sani 1983).

5. On ideological groups and the link with structural cleavages see Lipset and Rokkan 1967.

6. "Democratic left alliance election manifesto 2005," www.sld.org.pl/index.php?view=1&art_id=7158&pid=18&ret_id=175&rsid=0.

7. The MSzP was to rapidly assume a central role in the rogue privatization of the public sector, which will allow the accumulation of capital in the hands of party leaders.

8. The MIÉP (Hungarian Justice and Life) fell short of the electoral threshold in 2002, the Independent Smallholders' Party (FKGP) collapsed after corruption scandals, the MDF (Democratic Forum) merged with the FIDESZ, and the SzDSz progressively shrank to 5% of the vote.

9. http://www.KSČM.cz/article.asp?thema=3247&item=28074.

10. According to an internal analysis, "the decline in KSČM membership oscillates at 6–7 percent a year, while the membership grows by 0.6 to 0.68 percent a year." "Czech Communist Party Membership Steadily Shrinking," 9 May 2008, www.praguemonitor.com/en/331/czech_politics/22449.

11. It is worth noting that all Czech parties experienced a steep decline in member-

ship starting in the early 1990s, with the ČSSD, whose numbers rose from 16,200 to 18,300, the only exception.

12. Significantly, the unemployment rate was much lower in the Czech Republic than elsewhere in the region. In 1995 unemployment stood at 2.9% in the Czech Republic, in contrast to 10.3% in Hungary and 14.7% in Poland. Similarly, the poverty rate was less than 1% in the Czech Republic, 2% in Hungary, and 31% in Poland (Graham 1998, 202).

13. Handl (2003, 5) observes: "During 1990–1998, 3289 new members entered the party. 67,3% party members are pensioners, 64% have only the elementary education" (based on Zpráva 5th Congress, 1999, 52–54).

14. http://slovakia.eunet.sk/slovakia/elections.html.

15. "Access to patronage typically provides party leaders with the means to build and maintain party organizations through the distribution of selective incentives to party supporters in exchange for organizational loyalty" (Van Biezen and Kopecky 2007, 241).

16. Elections pitting the two dominant parties, until recently in coalition, against each other were scheduled for late 2009.

17. www.ndsv.bg/content/531.html.

European Center-Lefts and the Mazes of European Integration

George Ross

The European Union (EU) has been called an "unidentified flying political object" because of its constantly changing objectives, scope, size, and institutions.[1] The European left, not an object at all, is many political formations varying nationally with each historical moment. Today's center-lefts are powerfully influenced by the EU, and vice versa, and our goal is to discuss how these things happen. We review the historic interaction of the EU and the left—until the Maastricht Treaty (1992), after the end of the cold war, and with the coming of globalization—and then look at the EU's present implications for lefts. The basic question that concerns us can be asked simply: Has European integration been friend or foe to European lefts?

The EU and Lefts to the Euro

The intertwined histories of the EU and European lefts before the Maastricht Treaty demonstrate the complexities of their interactions. European integration was not an idea that lefts warmly welcomed. But after a deep crisis in the 1970s sorely tested both the EU and national political economies, it was the French left which favored renewing European integration in ways which would promote a new market liberalism and challenge social market achievements. The EU's programs to complete the single market and economic and monetary union (EMU) undercut the autonomy of earlier national models. An argument can be made that these changes at the European level were central in transforming European lefts into the center-lefts we discuss today.

Lefts and the EU's Early Successes and Trials

The EU was started by six countries—France, the German Federal Republic, Italy, and the Benelux three—in the Rome Treaties (1957). Its first name, the

European Economic Community (EEC), and its colloquial name, "the Common Market," underlined its focus on economic matters. The Rome EEC Treaty set out great ambitions, including "ever closer union" among EEC members, but it was mainly devoted to creating a customs-free zone surrounded by a common external tariff within which barriers to trade in manufactured and agricultural goods were to be removed.

Institutionally the EEC copied its immediate ancestor, the European Coal and Steel Community (ECSC, 1952). It was basically intergovernmental—a council of (national) ministers decided key policy matters. But it also had a supranational European Commission given exclusive power to propose legislation. In addition there was a European Court of Justice (ECJ) to adjudicate and keep the EEC within its "treaty bases." Finally there was a "European Assembly" (precursor of today's European Parliament), whose members were appointed from national legislatures. The institutional model was chosen because the EEC's founders felt that supranational mechanisms like the commission and the court, purpose-built to promote intergovernmental cooperation, were needed to forestall the ineffective deals that would follow if governments were left to their own devices. They felt further that if this institutionally unique EEC could promote interstate cooperation in its initial economic-market purview, the linkages between economics and other policy areas could foster "spillover" and progressively broaden the scope of integration. Finally, they knew that European integration would work best in a fog of political stealth: if people knew too much, the processes might bog down.

The EEC began in Europe's postwar boom, when each member had its own national economic strategies, welfare states, and industrial relations systems. These national models placed limits on how far early Europeanization could go. Integration increased intra-EEC trade in manufactured goods, helping to stimulate national growth. A Common Agricultural Policy (CAP) prodded agricultural investment, cushioned difficult transitions from farming to factory work, and protected farmers. The external tariff was simultaneously a buffer against, and a subsystem within, the Bretton Woods trading system coordinated by the United States.

Postwar lefts composed of Socialist, Communist, and other parties represented groups—workers in the first instance—that were relatively new to democratic participation. Parties and party systems differed from place to place, much like the national models with which they worked. There were "mass" parties tied to organized labor like the German SPD that needed middle-class support to win elections. Communists, powerful in France and Italy, were also mass parties, but tied to the Soviet side of the cold war. French and Italian Socialists combined clientelism with a nineteenth-century brand of municipal socialism. In general it was rare for the EEC left to have exclusive representation over all left-leaning constituencies, even if the German SPD came close. More often lefts were divided, whether between Communists and Socialists, as in Italy and France, or by linguistic or religious differences, as in Belgium and the Netherlands, and these divisions created persistent strategic quarrels and electoral problems. That most lefts also competed within multiparty systems complicated strategic problems even more (Paterson and Thomas 1977).

Divided or not, EEC lefts were central in their national political economies, with stakes in expanding welfare states, labor rights, and state involvement in markets. But even here differences were striking. The German SPD lived in a "social market economy" which thrived on exports, wage restraint, and tough monetary policies. In direct contrast, center-right statism in France after 1958 assumed exaggerated proportions and marginalized a deeply divided left (Schonfield 1969). Belgium and the Netherlands lived within divisive pillar arrangements (Liphardt 1977; Visser and Hemerijk 1997). Italy was less developed and played catch-up in semi-statist ways which hid behind a clientelist center-right Christian Democratic regime, leaving behind the country's south, where economic conditions could resemble those of the third world, and marginalizing its largely Communist left (Hellman 2008, 249–81).[2] In general, if the first postwar decades are rightly associated with the construction of what some call "Keynesian welfare states," different lefts did not always have easy times.

The EEC itself was not a left project, mainly because lefts were focused on developing their national systems. Spaak, the Belgian minister who led the talks leading to the Rome Treaties, was a titular Socialist, but really more a Belgian national politician deeply molded by wartime experiences. Some left leaders of the French Fourth Republic (including Guy Mollet, head of the Section Française de l'Internationale Ouvrière, or SFIO, and François Mitterrand) were "Europeans," but entire swaths of the French left opposed integration (Featherstone 1988). German Social Democrats opposed integration initially but changed their minds after the mid-1950s when its economic advantages became clearer. The Italian left, socialist and communist, was more positive, as were Italian politicians more generally. But the EEC was really the product of an elite generation of politicians, often Christian Democrats, haunted by the Second World War.

Lefts had reasons to be apprehensive about the EEC. Trade liberalization could change comparative advantages and threaten national jobs.[3] The idea of "ever-closer union among the peoples of Europe" had federalist connotations which bothered leftists who saw national arenas as their best bets. The

Communist line was that the EEC was a plot sponsored by the United States to resurrect German power. The treaty's other explicit objectives, beyond the CAP, included common policies for transport, coordinating EEC economic policy, and an EEC antitrust regime, all readable by lefts as threatening. In addition, the treaty was a "framework agreement" that announced general goals and left practical substance for later in ways that implied future surprises.

The EEC's institutions prompted additional worries on the left. The European Commission was clearly meant to expand the EEC's mandate over time. This would be hard if the Council of (national) Ministers had the last word, giving governments a veto. But the treaty proposed that eventually the council would decide by "qualified majority vote" (QMV), in which votes by member states would be weighted by relative size, allowing member states to be outvoted. The ECJ could also be a threat because through its jurisprudence it could make European law that superseded national statutes. Yet the EEC institutions were empowered only in areas that the treaty specified, and this provided some comfort, in large part because social and tax policies remained national.

The early EEC thrived on buoyant economic conditions in a win-win game between it and national models. But things did not always run smoothly. President Charles de Gaulle, a center-right nationalist, spearheaded member states' resistance to the commission's attempt to acquire more power and to enlarging the community by extending membership to the United Kingdom.[4] Introducing QMV decision making was also postponed, making unanimity the norm well into the 1980s. De Gaulle spoke for France's specific French architectural stipulations about the EEC, but these concerns often reflected deeper realities. The Common Market had begun after each of its members had developed its own economic strategies and each had moved through the 1960s in its own ways.

The 1970s were a turning point (Eichengreen 2007, chapters 7, 8). In 1971 the United States renounced its Bretton Woods engagement to the convertibility of dollars and gold. Currencies floated, speculators shifted into high gear, and financial globalization began. The oil shocks of 1973 and 1979 sharply accelerated inflation, particularly in a Europe which had no oil. EC governments reacted in dispersed national order. The British Labour government and the Gaullist French tried austerity followed by Keynesian reflation, and the result was stagflation. Countries with effective wage restraint were less perturbed, although not immune—Germany, for example, which used tough monetary policies to maintain price stability. In general, though, lefts had difficult encounters with key constituencies and risky paths in the international economy.[5] During these years central bankers and Anglophone economists pronounced the death of Keynesianism. EC leaders, who at a summit in 1969 had proposed a list of changes including economic and monetary union, deeper foreign policy cooperation, and new social policies, had to abandon almost all of them. Floating exchange rates menaced EC trade and the CAP. In addition, changed economic circumstances had led member states toward using non-tariff barriers to protect themselves.

The European Monetary System (EMS), shepherded in 1978 by France and Germany, was one of the few innovations of this crisis period.[6] All EC members belonged to EMS, but its inner circle, the Exchange Rate Mechanism (ERM), included only those accepting stronger monetary constraints.[7] EMS was founded on a political equivocation. Stronger-currency EMS members used monetary policy to maintain price stability, following the German Bundesbank. Weaker-currency ones like France were more tolerant of inflation and devaluation.[8] French elites hoped that EMS would lead the Germans to constrain the profligate sides of French policies while the French won greater flexibility from the Germans. These differences were to provide a central thread in EC history through the 1990s.

EMS was no remedy for all EC problems. The British had done a bad deal when they joined in 1973, contributing more than they got back, and Prime Minister Thatcher made this issue a cause, insisting on a "rebate" while threatening to block anything else.[9] And after the collapse of southern European dictatorships in the later 1970s, the new democracies wanted to join the EC. But after Greece, governed by the Panellinio Sosialistiko Kinima, or PASOK, was admitted in 1981 it demanded serious development aid and threatened to prevent Spain and Portugal from joining until it got it. The EC was stuck.

The dramatic evolution of the French left got European integration unstuck. Out of power since 1958, the French Socialists and their Communist allies won a majority in 1981 after the presidential election of François Mitterrand. They brought with them a long list of pledges to reinvigorate France's dirigiste national model, including new nationalizations, planning, industrial relations reforms, decentralization, redistributive shifts of the welfare state, and strong Keynesian stimulation (Favier and Martin-Roland 1990). The "Mitterrand experiment" quickly ran into difficulties (Hall 1987). Pressures on the franc led to devaluations and retrenchment, and by the winter of 1983 the French faced a choice between leaving EMS, at high risk of isolation and failure, and staying in and making major policy changes.

Mitterrand's decision was providential for European integration. For France the new period started with deep austerity, budgetary constraints, liberalization including a rationalizing of the bloated public sector, privatization, industrial restructuring, and slow growth. It also brought deflation toward parity with the German DM and high interest rates that deepened the recession. France, of all EC countries, and a French left president, of all politi-cal animals, thus recognized the new international constraints, beginning a forced march for French Socialists from radical reformism toward "center-leftism."

Change was as decisive in foreign policy. Mitterrand, a "European" since the 1950s, recommitted France to Europe during the French EC presidency in 1984. Under his leadership leaders settled the "British check" issue and agreed on how to admit Spain and Portugal, ending the decision-making paralysis of the EC. Quite as important, Jacques Delors, former French min-ister of finances, became president of the European Commission. In January 1985 Delors announced a program to complete the single market. A commis-sion white paper soon followed, proposing massive EC legislation to remove all barriers to a single European economy and institute the free circulation of goods, capital, services, and people. The white paper prompted the Single European Act (SEA)—the first major EC treaty change since Rome in 1957—expanding EC prerogatives, changing decision rules, and granting the Euro-pean Parliament new powers (Ross 1995).

The next big EC push began in June 1988, when leaders appointed Delors to chair a top-level committee that would produce proposals for economic and monetary union (Quatremer and Klau 1997, 151–56). The French and other softer-currency countries wanted to get more control over monetary policy from the Bundesbank to construct a new basis for European monetary policy less biased toward price stability and more growth-friendly. The Ger-mans, with bargaining advantage from their financial power, set out strong preconditions: independent national central banks, an independent European central bank to produce price stability, stringent requirements for budgetary and economic policy convergence for EMU membership, and liberalization of capital markets (Dyson and Featherstone 1999). The drive to EMU culminated in the Maastricht Treaty on European Union. The EMU deal included the Ger-man priorities to price stability, national budgetary responsibility, and tough "convergence criteria."[10] Applicants had to lower annual budget deficits to 3% of GDP, squeeze longer-term debt to 60% of GDP, sustain low interest and inflation rates, and stabilize their currencies. EMU would begin fully on 1 January 1999, and only those who had met these criteria would be allowed to join.[11]

Stories in the Story: The French Left Makes Center-Leftism Obligatory?

European integration did not begin as a left affair, but it had been relaunched in the 1980s by Mitterrand, Delors, and Chancellor Helmut Kohl of Germany, the two French Socialist politicians in the lead. Relaunch was built on the single-market program and monetary integration, both deeply liberal economic initiatives. The relaunch would be one of the more important processes converting Europe to international market opening and post-Keynesian outlooks. To be sure, several EC member states had by then already opened up markets and abjured Keynesianism, but new European-level policies ensured that everyone would have to follow, including left parties and governments.

François Mitterrand was a complicated man. Europe was a traditional arena for French operations, the nexus of Franco-German relationships, and a key location for France to work indirectly on a global scale. On European issues Mitterrand followed long-standing Gaullist goals, promoting integration to make Europe more independent of American hegemony but eschewing supranationalism where possible. France also had foreign economic policy interests in decanting German market and monetary power into broader European vessels. Still, this does not fully explain France's dramatic shift in the 1980s. Mitterrand cared less about economic policy than about staying in power, and his high-visibility European initiatives intertwined with more mundane electoral concerns. Mitterrand needed exceptional reasons to justify abandoning the radical program upon which he had been elected. Presenting his about-face in terms of the sacrifices needed to help Europe flourish anew could put a different spin on things and perhaps cover up some of the left's deep failures. The new "option for Europe" plus day-to-day political prestidigitation helped Mitterrand win two terms, until 1995, making him the longest-serving president in the history of the Fifth Republic.

Jacques Delors was a different story. Mitterrand's outlooks fluctuated with his electoral prospects, but Delors had always been "center-left."[12] As finance minister after 1981, he had dragged his feet on renewing *dirigisme* and Keynesianism. The reformist strategy that Delors advanced as commission president was no surprise, therefore, because he believed in liberalization, ending inflationary spending, and serious structural reform. He also sensed the coming of globalization before most politicians did. But Delors was at heart a left Catholic corporatist who believed that key social groups should cooperate for the common good, and he felt strongly that new liberalization and monetary stability should be accompanied by social policy initiatives at the EC level. He thus invested considerable resources to promote "social dialogue" at the European level in the hope of stimulating Euro-level collective bargaining.[13] His Charter of Fundamental Social Rights (1989) sought new legislation in areas of social policy where the EC had legal prerogatives, in a not-so-hidden hope for spillover to new EC social policy powers.[14] Delors also successfully promoted redistributive EC-level development funding for poorer EC regions—what came to be called the "structural funds."

Delors's "social Europe" was a gamble, however. EC Europe worked on a consensus to which all Europeans, left or right, might subscribe that avoided partisan tones and spoke to common European interests. But in the real world of the EC the usual doctrinal struggles ground away. Big business and the political right wanted liberalization, deregulation, and sounder public finances, and they were happy to have the EU make them happen. They had little sympathy for social Europe proposals, regarding them as steps back into a past that they wanted to leave behind. Delors hoped to mobilize other groups, including unions, to Europeanize and reform European social models through social Europe. Business and neoliberal constituencies were strong, well organized, and able to shift resources easily to the European level. Those who might favor more social Europe, in contrast, were weaker, less well organized, and less mobile. Delors's social Europe enterprise was therefore a long shot. During the Delors years liberalization and monetarism went along with "upward harmonization" in workplace health and safety, equal opportunities, and environmental policy, in part because the relatively wealthy EC countries that counted most did not want a "race to the bottom." But momentum toward social Europe had stalled by the mid-1990s, far short of Delors's hopes.

What was most significant in the era of Delors and Mitterrand went unspoken. Shifting national sovereignty to the EC level was a high-stakes game that inevitably constrained EC members to change domestic policies. "Going European" was a prime way to circumvent national reluctance to reform. The single market program ruled out non-tariff barriers, state aids to industry, and pumping up industrial champions, methods that members of the French left, among others, had long taken for granted. EMU ruled out excessive inflation, high budget deficits, debt, periodic devaluations, and interest rates set for national purposes, all honored traditions in several EC member states. Thus whatever else they intended, the accomplishments of Mitterrand and Delors at the European level bound future national policies and practices and obliged European lefts to adapt.

The EU in Middle Age

The EU celebrated its fiftieth birthday in 2007, but the occasion was not very happy. The single market had not had the promised positive economic effects. EMU had become a corset constraining EU members, center-lefts with them, to limit economic growth. The end of the cold war had obliged EU members to undertake the complicated new tasks of enlarging to the east, necessitating a redesign of EU institutions for twenty-seven members. Amid these difficulties globalization had exploded, first financially, then in direct challenges to European manufacturing sectors. But the particular unfolding of EU policies, their impacts on EU citizens, and the ways the EU then responded created new puzzles. These responses also revealed how perplexing a terrain the EU and its institutions could be as a political arena to center-lefts.

The EU Tries Out European-Level Center-Leftism

EMU, designed during a good economic period, had to be prepared during a severe downturn after 1992.[15] Then, with a deadline of 1998 to decide EMU membership on the horizon the Germans, skeptical about eventual members like Italy and Spain, insisted on a new Stability and Growth Pact (SGP) that would bind Eurozone members to any convergence criteria decided in the future. The major troublesome issue has been that the European Central Bank (ECB) has emphasized price stability over anything else, growth included.[16] When countries get into difficulty the ECB holds them responsible for disciplining market actors and changing domestic policies (Martin and Ross eds. 2004). This has been difficult for both rights and lefts, but it has often been the best-organized constituencies of the center-left—like unions and welfare state stakeholders—that have been on the frontline of the pressures for change.

Criticism of the ECB and the retrenchment that it enjoined eventually targeted the Stability and Growth Pact. This was inevitable, since fully half of EMU members, including all the large continental countries and quite a few smaller ones, had violated the taboo against running annual budget deficits of more than 3% of GDP at one time or another after 2000. SGP reform in 2005 gave members slightly more room to confront ups and downs, in particular in the discounting costs of future-oriented policies for things like research and restructuring. In difficult circumstances EMU members thus could exceed the annual 3% deficit, but they were also enjoined to lower deficits when things went better.[17]

In 1993, after it had concluded that important EU economies faced serious longer-run problems in the run-up to EMU, the Delors Commission produced a new white paper, "Growth, Competitiveness, and Employment," which urged EU Europe to mobilize anew to confront the new monetary environment and globalization. Levels of European growth and investment had been shrinking over decades, it noted, and the EU's global competitive position was worsening. What followed was a manifesto that went well beyond Delors's early single-market, "social Europe" conceptualizations. The white paper asserted that "creating as favorable an environment as possible for company competitiveness" was essential, placing stress on innovation to push Europe toward an "information society" where new comparative advantage lay. It also called for more labor market flexibility, particularly through active labor market policies, plus substantial welfare state reform. The document was solidly "center-left." It began from recognition of new constraints from globalization and from the EU's own single-market and EMU policies, eschewed market fundamentalism, and aimed for the preservation of Europe's commitments to social market economies, but it also argued that Europeans should cooperate in the reforms that were needed to achieve that preservation. The white paper fell flat politically, however. EU members, facing severe domestic problems, were tired of constant Euro-level tension and refused its request for neo-Keynesian, employment-boosting loans.

The Lisbon Agenda (2000), promoted by a center-left Portuguese EU presidency and backed by Tony Blair, focused again on declining European global competitiveness and reformist preservation of the EU's social market economies. It declared that EU Europe should become the world's most advanced "knowledge economy" and restore full employment by 2010. It proposed a big increase in Euro-level research and development, greater coordination among research efforts by member states, training for new skills, new infrastructure, and environmental policies for sustainable development. It also focused on active labor market policies, increasing labor force participation, and removing disincentives to work that persisted in many national welfare states.

Delors's white paper and the Lisbon strategy were both couched in the EU's usual consensus rhetoric, and their goal was to reframe EU perspectives on general European economic goals. Their results have been mixed.[18] Most Lisbon policies fell within national prerogatives, meaning that the success of European policies and urging were dependent on voluntary national cooperation. To produce such cooperation Lisbon institutionalized an "Open Method of Coordination" (OMC). OMC began when the EU set out general guidelines, then encouraged member states to hold regular, open discussions about achieving them; identified national "best practices" and established indicators of progress; and finally, publicized successes and failures by naming and shaming from Brussels. OMC used soft law and exhortation because the EU lacked harder tools.[19] The hope was that they would help remodel overregulated labor markets and welfare state programs while preserving the "European social model." The center-right carved its own goals out of the consensual rhetoric of Lisbon, which it sought to use to push neoliberal structural reforms. By 2005, with the strategy far short of its goals, Lisbon was re-centered on narrower issues of structural reform and liberalization, and responsibilities were reassigned to national state governments in a retreat from OMC. Thereafter member states picked and chose what they wanted to do.

Delors's white paper and the Lisbon strategy were good examples of center-left thinking about economic and social reform applied at the EU level. They began proposing ideas, pleas, and programs to achieve new European competitiveness in globalizing circumstances. Since the EU could not legally oblige member states to follow, it could only hope to persuade them to cooperate in a decentralized, coordinated way. Would member states, each with special economic problems, political and partisan setups, and social models, cooperate enough voluntarily to make a difference? On a different plane, would OMC be seductive enough to wean labor movements and welfare state stakeholders, significant constituencies of the center-left, away from their deeply entrenched, often corporatist preferences? Or, in contrast, would it simply confuse them or, worse still, antagonize them?

As Lisbon moved toward the target year of 2010, it was hard not to conclude that the choices proposed by both Delors's white paper and Lisbon contained wishful center-left political thinking. The methods that they chose involved high-minded EU preaching to member states to produce national reform, "new modes of governance," and procedural innovations like OMC that covered up technocratic leadership, decentralization, and depoliticization. These approaches merged different issues and policy areas in untried ways and underplayed European and national disagreements. Today Lisbon has clearly not accomplished enough to live up to the hype surrounding it.[20] It is not at all clear, for example, whether it has helped to advance Europe toward greater competitiveness, its ostensible purpose (Buchs 2007; Buchs 2008). Further, in other quarters market fundamentalists have consistently derided original Lisbon formulations as ineffective, arguing that OMC approaches were too convoluted and that behind its consensual words Lisbon really sought to preserve the European social models that were the real barriers to new competitiveness. Center-left efforts at the European level to transcend the structures of older left worlds have not worked yet, or perhaps have not worked at all.

Troublesome EU Policies = Troubled EU Citizens

This lack of success correlated with rising public opposition to the EU and its policies. During its first decades EU leaders had been able to count on "permissive consensus" from citizens. This had left leaders free to use the European arena as long as they agreed to do nothing that caused too much national political grumbling. But in the decade prior to its fiftieth birthday, the EU dramatically lost favor with parts of public opinion. Its loss of popularity began as the Single Market broke the cocoons of national development models, EMU normalized an emerging international price stability regime, and Lisbon tried to "flexibilize" labor markets and welfare states. The Maastricht Treaty also increased EU power in areas like policing, immigration, and foreign and defense policy, and not everyone approved of this.[21] On another plane, Western European electorates were not fully persuaded that enlarging the EU to Central and Eastern European countries was wise, partly because leaders did not really explain the process and its goals. Enlargement and Maastricht's unfinished business also fed constant intergovernmental wrangling about adapting EU institutions and communicated directly to citizens the deep divisions about high EU politics. All this was presided over by a generation of national leaders preoccupied with national politics and relatively indifferent to the EU.

The most immediate explanation for the decline in EU popularity was the failure of the Single Market, EMU, and Lisbon Agenda to restore growth, limit unemployment, and respond effectively to globalization. Some EU countries fared better than others, but the problem of low growth and high unemployment persisted, and the worst performers were France, Germany, and Italy, among the largest EU countries, which together decide the EU's general economic fate. Eurobarometer polling showed that the EU remained valued in the abstract, but only 20% associated the EU with democracy and prosperity, while the same percentage associated it with bureaucracy and wasted money. It was globalization that worried EU citizens most: 42% felt that the EU might protect them from its negative effects, while 40% did not (Reynié 2008).

The most spectacular indicators of weakening public support for the EU came in national referenda. In 1992 the Danes fired the first warning shot by refusing to ratify Maastricht in 1992, while the French barely voted yes the same year. The Irish refused the Nice Treaty in 2002. The French and Dutch refused the European Constitutional Treaty in 2005. Most recently the Irish refused the Lisbon Treaty in June 2008. The trends revealed in these votes were worrisome for anyone invested in European integration. They were doubly so to European lefts, for it was constituencies most likely to support left parties—workers, the poor, and social movement activists—who demonstrated the least enthusiasm. The problem was complicated by the more favorable disposition toward the EU of the new middle-class groups that the center-left also needed to attract, making coalition building a perplexing task (Fligstein 2008).

For center-lefts to have influence on EU-level policies they had to be able to play at the EU level, and for this they needed to win national elections and mobilize national support behind what they wanted the EU to do. This was a real challenge. EU market liberalization breached the borders around the relatively self-contained national development models upon which most lefts had long depended.[22] Globalization then obliged everyone to squeeze down inflation and avoid deficits and debt, with EMU and the SGP intensifying the squeezing. Newly mobile financial markets limited tax policymaking and wage growth and put new pressure on labor markets and social programs. Manufacturing successes of lower-wage areas of the world compressed the wages and benefits of European manufacturing workers and added to employment insecurity.

These changes coincided with the end of socialist dreams, meaning that center-lefts had to find new grounds to win the electoral support they needed to assert influence at the EU level. The saga surrounding the white paper and Lisbon marked perhaps the Euro-level center-left's best effort to do this, and it did not work, or at least has not yet worked. Persuading traditional left constituencies and stakeholders to hear and accept new reformist strategies was difficult when they faced growing economic insecurity and had strong incentives to hold on to positions that the left had helped them win in the postwar period. To make things even harder, new radical forces were emerging, particularly from the new middle classes, mobilized around very different dreams: things like environmental change, stopping globalization, and anti-immigrant populism. The European world of center-lefts had become an uncertain place.

Fragmented Center-Lefts, Biased Policy Agendas, and Confusing Institutions

The importance of the EU in its members' domestic politics and lives has grown enormously in the last two decades, to different degrees in different countries. The single market and EMU increased employment insecurity, constrained public finances, and compressed growth, making it more difficult for lefts to reward traditional constituencies. Center-left national governments have had to trim spending, remodel welfare states, restrain wages, and introduce new flexibility into labor markets, policies that have often run counter to the expectations of center-left supporters. In the meantime deindustrialization had reduced the number of blue-collar workers, undercutting unions and service workers, and "new middle class" groups have grown, complicating coalitional and electoral problems.

In the abstract it makes sense for center-lefts to work more effectively at the EU level for the changes and reforms they seek. The kinds of policies proposed in the white paper in 1993 and reposed in the Lisbon Agenda ought to be seen as examples of this, while the problems that the center-lefts have faced underline the problems of doing so. The EU is a tricky place for center-lefts to work. One reason is that the deep historic trajectories of the EU asymmetrically favor the center-right. The backbone of what the EU does, grounded in international treaties, has been market liberalization and budgetary restraint through EMU, things which the center-right has most often favored. The center-left has often advocated Euro-policies for "re-regulating" markets and redistributing resources, but the EU has always been much better at de- than re-regulating, and even when the EU has re-regulated it has done so in more economically liberal ways than most center-lefts have desired. Beyond this, the treaties have granted to the EU only limited powers to effect redistribution, because most social and tax policy matters remain national. This is no accident: member states and national parties have preferred to keep resources at home rather than donate them to others.

The EU's policy asymmetry is complemented by the workings of EU institutions. Even if it has serious mechanisms to promote binding cooperation among members, the EU remains made up of states which evolve in different ways and whose national politics vary greatly. When translated into different national interests at the EU level, this is one reason why European integration has proceeded by fits and starts, punctuated by crises. Moreover, at any moment the EU is likely to be inhabited by both left and right governments. Except in extraordinary circumstances, therefore, not much can happen at the EU level unless a consensus can be reached among member governments, right and left. Because decisions built on complicated intergovernmental negotiations must be compromises between national interests, the EU's processes are slow, sometimes too much so to reach appropriate decisions in time to solve important problems effectively.

The institutional problems of reaching consensus have grown with the enlargement of the EU since 1995 from twelve to twenty-seven members.[23] The political mathematics of this are simple. The more EU members there are, the greater the likelihood of a divergence of preferences about issues and decisions, and of blocking coalitions. When compared to national political processes, in which majorities and minorities are derived from electoral results, it will be harder to do things at the European level. All else being equal, this creates a bias in favor of slow forward movement and frequent decision-making problems. This makes it difficult to achieve the reforms that are the center-left's stock in trade.

Irrespective of the limits imposed by EU institutions on the left's influence, to have influence European lefts need to agree on what they want to do together. Here is where the largest problems for center-lefts arise. Today's center-lefts are as diverse as their countries, for several reasons. However realistic center-left elites might be about European and international constraints, they have first to win power nationally. The primacy of this task shapes their outlooks by path-dependent national histories, policy legacies, institutions, organizations, and coalitional patterns.[24] And European-level policies will affect each country differently. It also follows that when working in European arenas center-left governments will pursue national interests that go beyond and probably dilute partisanship. The resulting puzzle is difficult for any center-left to solve. More importantly, different national outlooks will limit the capacities of center-left parties to cooperate on Euro-level policy goals, if only because the degree to which they agree to cooperate on these goals may limit their capacities to succeed nationally.

By now center-lefts have all accepted new constraints on what they can do nationally, but this has not appreciably narrowed differences between them, as a few examples should demonstrate.[25] All the members added when the EU was enlarged in 1995—the Scandinavian neutrals except Norway, plus Austria—were wealthy and had extensive experience with budgetary and wage restraint, employment flexibility, and participation in open international markets, making their adaptation to post-EMU EU constraints relatively easy. British New Labour had been prepared by Thatcherite deconstruction of the old Labour world, which left public finances in order and growth prospects good. New Labour, with openings for domestic social policy initiatives of an "activating" kind, could adapt easily (Cronin 2004). Continental lefts were the main problem cases, often because of corporatist rejection of labor market and social policy reforms and growing electoral problems. The position of the French Parti Socialiste was complicated by chronic left pluralism. The German SPD, leading a Red-Green coalition from 1998 to 2005, faced post-unification difficulties and had to enact unpopular labor market reforms which helped create die Linke, a new rival to its left. Italy had divided left coalitions that were chronically unable to face its intractable problems. Of the left parties in big continental EU members only the Spanish PSOE, helped by Europeanization and EMU, has flourished. Lefts in the smaller continental countries struggled and to varying degrees declined. The new Central and Eastern European lefts, involved in democratic transitions, were center-left from the beginning and constrained by the requirements of joining the EU, but loath to give up any more of their new and hard-won sovereignty. There were center-lefts and center-lefts, in other words, each profoundly national and each affected in different ways by what the EU did.

What this differentiation implied for left cooperation at the European level can be gleaned from one of the rare occasions when several center-left governments held power at the same time. In the later 1990s New Labour, the "plural left" around the PS in France, a center-left coalition in Italy, and the Red-Green coalition in Germany governed four of the largest EU member states, while eleven of fifteen EU governments leaned leftward more generally. The effect was to impart a leftish tinge to EU-level politics, leading in particular to the European Employment Strategy (EES), an immediate precursor of the Lisbon Agenda. The EES combined ideas from socialists in the European parliament, the Delors white paper of 1993, the commission's directorate-general for employment and social affairs (then led by a very clever Swedish Social Democrat), and New Labour "Third Way" prescriptions about employability (Aust 2004). Its goals included more active and flexible labor markets, social programs sustaining commitments to existing social models, and increasing labor force participation. But because labor market and social policy realms remained national, the EES used OMC methods. The results, seen in EES and the Lisbon Agenda, have been uneven and ambiguous. EU member states could choose to cooperate more or less depending on their national situations. Changes are ongoing, but are most rigorously pursued in those countries that were already committed to such things before the EES and Lisbon were devised. In other places, particularly on the continent, opposition to protect the status quo has been strong (Pochet and Zeitlin eds. 2005; de la Porte 2008).

The episode surrounding the EES and Lisbon illustrates just how weak agreement and cooperation between different EU member state lefts can be. New Labour under Tony Blair, more pro-EU than any British government in history, remained Euro-skeptical in key areas—participation in EMU and EU social policies among them.[26] The French "Plural Left" government under Lionel Jospin, cool toward the EU in general, was neo-Keynesian, dead set against Blairite commitments, and preoccupied with domestic work-sharing reforms of which most other center-lefts disapproved. The German SPD chancellor Schröder, preoccupied with domestic concerns, was cynical about the EU and the willingness of German unions to undertake changes that might jeopardize their domestic positions. The Italian left had usually been pro-European—it played a key role in allowing Italy to join EMU—but the government of the time was an unruly multiparty coalition which on matters of EES and Lisbon domestic reforms was at the mercy of refractory neocommunists. The Danish, Swedish, and Austrian center-lefts, deeply social democratic and in favor of reforms of the sort embodied in EES, were Euro-skeptical, in keeping with traditional perspectives of "don't touch our intricate and successful domestic arrangements."[27] Further, in virtually every case national trade union movements, whose cooperation in labor market reforms were essential, stood behind their national governments' varying EU positions, despite the hard work of the transnational European Trade Union Confederation. The larger story was that even when center-lefts had a political edge at the EU level and might have weighed heavily on EU decisions, they had difficulty agreeing on what the EU might do and on carrying out the EU's proposals.

EU institutions also make it difficult to achieve cooperation between Euro-reformists and the left.[28] Center-lefts are now well organized in a transnational Party of European Socialists, for example, but the European Parliament as an institution restricts what they can do.[29] Unlike national parliaments it cannot initiate legislation, because the European Commission has exclusive right to this power. But to exercise this power effectively the commission must solicit cooperation among member states. Thus it cannot act like a government or party leader, and can propose only after carefully gauging what national governments are willing to accept.[30] Proposals for legislation are thus the product of consensus across national differences and party lines. The European Parliament has usually shared this consensus-oriented outlook and often proceeded on agreement between center-left and center-right. Without power of initiative, the EP's work mainly lies in scrutinizing those commission proposals that it gets, which it does in committees rather than in partisan debate on the EP floor. In addition, the European Parliament is only a co-legislator in the EU system. To reach any decisions it must negotiate compromise with an intergovernmental Council of Ministers.

EU institutions in general, like the commission and Parliament, are purpose-built to promote and facilitate transnational cooperation, and therefore speak in consensual, pan-European languages. The institutions have thus more often than not turned potentially partisan issues into technocratic ones. These forms of expression have helped make the EU distant from citizens. The intergovernmental dimensions of EU-level governance, the European Council, which also talks in consensus language, and the Council of Ministers, which continues to meet in diplomatic secret, do little to translate EU matters into national vocabularies. The European Parliament is the most likely translator of Euro-level politics into national political dialects, but it has not yet replicated national left-right cleavages in readable ways and its concerns have rarely penetrated national agendas (Franklin 2006). For these and other reasons elections to the EP have had low participation and national issues have predominated in election campaigning. Thus if EU policies have profound effects, the EU itself has so far not been able to Europeanize the pertinent political lives of center-lefts.

Conclusions: Center-Lefts in Chilly European Climates?

The EU is today in a difficult situation. Exhausting and complicated debate about the institutional change needed for enlargement to twenty-seven members, interspersed with French and Dutch no votes on the "constitutional treaty" in 2005 and the Irish no to its successor, the Lisbon Treaty, in 2008, underline chronic problems that ordinary citizens have in making sense of the EU. It is common to talk of an EU "democratic deficit," even if it can be argued that EU institutions meet reasonable constitutional standards for democracy.[31] Whatever one calls the EU's political dilemmas, however, the European Union has serious problems of legitimacy and credibility.

EU institutions suffer from serious "readability" problems as well. Citizens are accustomed to the structures, cultures, and politics of the countries which have first claim on their loyalties and identities. Adding another layer of very different institutions at the EU level and expecting citizens to understand and identify with them may be overoptimistic. The European Commission is thus easy to demonize as a distant and irresponsible "Brussels bureaucracy" whose roles are mysterious except to insiders aware that it is designed to prevent strong member states from running the EU show and ensure that governments honor their commitments. Some citizens know that their leaders get together as the EU Council of Ministers and that this makes a difference, but they get precious little information about how the council works. To this mixture one must also consider what the EU actually does. It is not a state, and is unlikely to become one. Yet it does some things that states do, shares in the doing of other things with these states that they used to do by themselves, and can have strong indirect impacts in areas where citizens have every reason to expect national leaders to be able to act on their own. The Parliament, as just noted, does not resemble anyone's "real" parliament. On top of all this there is no EU "we the people," but rather twenty-seven different peoples with different histories, cultures, and languages.

All this places the EU at a distance from most of its citizens, whether on the left or the right, and when the EU touches matters that are perceived as fundamental to the daily lives of citizens it is bound to stir up controversy. Given that daily lives are organized differently from one EU country to another, controversies will take on different forms. And since these days, thanks in part to center-leftish programs like the Lisbon Agenda, it can look as if the EU is bent on shaping up its member states for liberal globalization, the EU is likely to be controversial to wary and uncertain "peoples of the left." The EU's base of support, such as it is, is found among the better educated and better off. The lower one goes down the social ladder, the more the EU arouses opposition.

The center-left's traditional constituencies are those likely to be skeptical. A more complex problem is that center-lefts must also find ways to appeal to higher pro-European strata.[32]

In fact "real" European politics happens largely in national arenas, built on what national governments want to share with other EU members and what they prefer to keep out of EU hands. There exists little European political culture except among elites. There are no European news media—despite the claims to pan-European status of Anglophone sources like the *Economist* and the *Financial Times*—just nationally based media that interpret EU events through national lenses. National parliamentary discussions rarely place European issues squarely before the public, while elections to the European Parliament remain tightly linked to national political debates. With few exceptions—Denmark, for example—national parties have barely begun to embrace European matters. The gap between the thickness of national democratic deliberative practice and its thinness at the European level is evident. This is important to center-lefts, whose political bases may be conflicted about the EU but whose leaders must also have strategies to work at EU levels if they win power.

All this has tended to make European center-lefts more takers than makers of European-level policies. The EU decides and center-lefts integrate the consequences into their diverse national arenas, like it or not. In the EU's earlier years, when European integration was handmaiden to national development models and EU members had a national veto, this was less of a burden. It has become a much larger one with the EU opening economic and other borders, running a monetary union, and engaging in "mission creep" into broader areas like policing, immigration control, civil law, education and research policy, environmental and energy policy, and foreign and defense policy. Also, today's EU of twenty-seven members includes practically all the peoples on the European continent, adding to complex diversity.

In policy terms things have not worked quite as planned. The EU has liberalized extensively and EMU works in technical terms. But encroaching globalization has meant that economic growth and prosperity have returned only for those who were already well prepared, for national reasons, to grow. Those center-lefts that inherited flexible, muscular economic and social policy systems and learned to function without Keynesianism and with non-accommodating monetary policies have done best. Other center-lefts, particularly on the European continent, face constituents who resist the national imposition of center-left policy formulas and insistently worry whether today's EU is a cushion to ease them into a globalized world or, in contrast, an agent of neoliberal globalization. This is where things now stand.

That European center-lefts have been takers rather than makers of Euro-level politics does not mean that they should be seen as persistent victims of EU policies. EU Europe has historically been an open arena for debating re-formist changes and sometimes has even led the implementation of changes.[33] While there has been much of bureaucrats talking to other bureaucrats and a few Members of the European Parliament, with small groups of academics and lobbyists listening, some of the discussion must be taken seriously, as historical record shows. When new members have joined the EU they have been expected to accept what is called the *acquis communautaire*, the EU's accumulated institutional rules and processes, and this acceptance has enhanced their commitment to human rights, good governance, and social, environmental, and other policies. Moreover, the European power of northern European "social market" societies has meant that European-level policies have usually involved "upward harmonization" rather than races to the bottom. Environmental policies are an important case in point, but there are others, such as equal opportunities between men and women in the workplace, and workplace health and safety. And even when the EU has few explicit treaty powers it can also try to promote reformist change through decentralized "soft law" techniques like those used in OMC and the Lisbon strategy.

What does this all come to? That EU Europe is an obstacle course for center-leftists does not mean that the EU is a paradise for the neoliberal forces: they too have found EU-level politics frustrating. One reason is that today's EU works badly. It must function ideologically according to the presumed consensus, or at least the presumed common interest, of Europeans—500 million individual citizens, different localities, regions, civil societies, and nation-states, and, yes, EU officials and leaders. Any such EU consensus is bound to be a vague common denominator of the huge variety of interests living under and around the EU's big tent. The lack of clarity that results is not comforting for everyone.

The handicaps of working with such a vague European consensus are not the same as those of winning the policy struggles whose content is often obscured by the EU's veils of consensus and difficult-to-fathom institutional life. It is hard to underestimate the significance of recent EU battles between neoliberals and the advocates of something that might be called social market economies. Lefts and their center-left successors have been present and active in these battles, which are far from over. As we write, EU efforts to liberalize service markets and recent ECJ decisions about freedom of business movement across borders threaten social and labor protection programs underlying national social contracts. Center-lefts cannot stand aside on such matters any more than on other battles about Europe's place in global competition and the desirable shape of globalization itself. It is nonetheless clear that the center-lefts have not been nearly as effective as they might have been in these and other EU skirmishes. The EU demands that center-lefts answer vitally important questions, but it is not terribly helpful in providing them with answers.

Notes

1. The official title changes over time. Until 1965 it was the European Economic Community (EEC). After a merger treaty in 1965 bundling the ECSC, Euratom, and the EEC it became the European Communities, or EC. After the Maastricht Treaty was ratified it became the European Union, or EU.

2. The variety grew when one looked at the EEC's near neighborhoods. Scandinavian lefts built densely organized egalitarian social democratic systems where social actors internalized national cooperation for international economic success. The British, determined but ineffective saboteurs at the start of the EEC, had a strong workerist Labour Party and a Labour-created public sector and welfare state stalled by bad economic policies, a flawed industrial relations system, and a collapsing empire.

3. The Rome EEC Treaty also proposed abolishing "obstacles to freedom of movement for persons, services and capital," a reform which, were it actually done, might pose an even bigger threat to national jobs than open trade in manufacturing.

4. When the commission proposed a very liberal Common Agricultural Policy (CAP) that threatened French agricultural subsidy systems, it was shot down, replaced by a costly scheme of administered price supports that protected EEC farmers internationally.

5. Perhaps the best example came when British Labour's failed "Social Contracts" led to the election of Margaret Thatcher in 1979.

6. They also took the lead in promoting direct elections to the European Parliament and creating the European Council, which held institutionalized summits of member state leaders.

7. ERM members committed to keeping their currencies within a "narrow band" of exchange rates as compared to a basket of currencies tied to the dollar, as well as to market intervention to buoy threatened currencies and negotiations to revalue when needed. Revaluation occurred twenty-six times between 1979 and 1999.

8. This endowed EMS with a rhythm. When weaker currencies ran up against the "narrow band" barrier, central banks had to intervene. Stabilization was often temporary, however, and the troubled country might then have to negotiate a revaluation, often entailing change in its economic policies.

9. Wall 2008, chapters 1–3, provides a British insider's account.

10. See Dyson and Featherstone 1999 for EMU negotiations.

11. The French wanted an "economic government" to set EMU macroeconomic policy, but the Germans refused, insisting instead on a completely independent European Central Bank statutorily committed to price stability.

12. Delors 2004 is an indispensable source.

13. He managed to persuade the EU to invest heavily in this, getting a clause dedicated to its pursuit included in the SEA and then pumping up the finances of the theretofore weak European Trade Union Confederation to allow it to play more significantly at the EU level. Martin and Ross eds. 1999, chapter 8.

14. The Social Charter played a role in the domestic politics of a number of EC countries. In the United Kingdom, for example, it convinced the Trade Union Congress, battered by Thatcherism, of the importance of Europe.

15. Inflation in Germany fed by the unification of West and East put pressure on EMS currencies and prompted a severe response from the Bundesbank. Realigning currencies might have ended the problems, but few wanted to try realignment in the middle of a French referendum campaign to ratify Maastricht. The first result was "Black Wednesday," 16 September 1992, when the British pound left ERM, followed by wild currency fluctuations elsewhere. The EMS crisis contributed to lowered growth and rising unemployment—to over 10% in the larger continental economies, and made EMU convergence a major burden.

16. In January 1999 the Euro was valued at $1.18, by autumn 2000 at $0.80, and by early 2008 at $1.60.

17. The "policy mix" between federalized monetary policies and decentralized macroeconomic policies has often been suboptimal. The "Eurogroup" of EMU members has tried to promote coherence through "broad economic policy guidelines," but member states have not been obliged to harmonize macroeconomic policies.

18. Liberalizing services was a centerpiece, but resistance to a commission proposal in 2004 watered down the directive. Financial services and energy market liberalization are incomplete. Brussels has moved on chemicals regulation (REACH) and climate change, and talked about lightening its regulatory hand, with limited results.

19. It had been pioneered in the EU Employment Policy, begun after the Amsterdam Treaty in 1997 and then extended to social policy areas like "social inclusion" (poverty policy) and pension reforms.

20. Lisbon has certainly helped the professional profiles of the progressive democrats who have waxed eloquently in—often scholarly—journals about the virtues of OMC as "directly deliberative polyarchy," a substitute for representative parliamentarism.

21. The EU's rocky foreign policy start did not help. The EU was impotent in its Yugoslavian backyard, leaving American help as the only recourse.

22. Stein Rokkan's work on shifting borders and nation building in Europe has been resurrected recently in discussions of European integration (Bartolini 2005; Kriesi et al. 2008).

23. New CEEC members have just regained sovereignty and are unlikely to want to give up much of it to the EU. In addition, their development models are often different from those of Western Europe (Zielonka 2006).

24. Schmidt 2006 hints at this story, alas only part, in trying to analyze the effects of the EU on "simple" versus "compound" polities.

25. This chapter does not attempt to discuss how EU constraints on national center-lefts actually alter the structures and functioning of these national parties, a topic that remains badly underresearched and probably underconceptualized. For a critical introduction see Gombert 2008.

26. EES and Lisbon demonstrated an aggressive New Labour line that liberalizing reforms of welfare states and industrial relations systems was the only road to future successes. For a taste of aggressive Third Way proselytizing on labor market and social policy see Giddens 2007.

27. See the essays by Pekarinnen, Aylott, Haaher, and Veiden in Notermans ed. 2001. Chapter 12 in Gaffney ed. 1996 reviews the Scandinavian cases.

28. Center-rights vary in similar ways, but lesser commitments to re-regulating and redistributing at the Euro level and the EU's liberal bias lessen their coordination difficulties.

29. Some experts, like Simon Hix, see this, plus growing right-left divisions in the EP, as nourishing stronger "Euro" dimensions in national center-lefts. See Hix 2007. There are good reasons to think that this effect will be limited and slow, however. On the European Socialist Party see Ladrech 2003 and Moschonas 2007.

30. This is true even if in recent years commissions have been appointed in the wake of European Parliament elections to reflect the partisan balance in the Parliament.

31. See Moravscik 2002.

32. Moschonas 2008b provides a different argument, complementary to what follows.

33. At the time of writing, for example, EU officials had begun an extensive debate on the EU's "social agenda" by circulating an important document on "Europe's Social Reality." See European Commission 2008 for details.

Conclusion

Progressive Politics in Tough Times

James Cronin, George Ross, and James Shoch

The stories told here are all about the fate of the center-left in tough times. What made the times so tough for social democrats and liberals were the three critical events noted at the beginning of this volume: the end of capitalism's "golden age" and the loss of faith in the Keynesian policies that guided it; the end of communism and its disenchanting effects; and the globalization of the economy. All this made for a much less hospitable environment for the center-left. So too did the acceleration of the trend toward postindustrial employment and the shifts in social structure and demography that accompanied the transition. These forces were of course compounded by the legacies that liberal and social democratic parties brought into the new era. In some cases the center-left was clearly uncomfortable with the managed capitalism of the postwar period and had trouble reconciling its transformative goals with a more prosaic, if also more prosperous and democratic and equitable, reality. In other cases parties of the moderate left had become rather too comfortable in the mixed economy, too thoroughly enmeshed in its corporatist institutions and in the compromises they represented, and so unable to think beyond the time when those arrangements would cease to work. In all cases adapting to an era of slower growth and tighter budgets, greater technological change, and a more demanding and competitive world economy in which markets were seen as more useful than the state was a serious challenge. The main work of this book has been to chart and assess this adaptation. Here, roughly, is what we have found.

Center-Lefts Have Been Successful

Center-lefts were historically central in building, explaining, consolidating, and lately defending the modern welfare states and employment relations systems which have protected workers and citizens in Europe, North America, and elsewhere from the risks and uncertainties of capitalism. These innovations have taught us that peoples' lives need not be completely subject to the cycles of markets, the inequalities that markets produce, or the capriciousness that owners of capital might otherwise demonstrate. They have thus smoothed and humanized what would have been much rougher lives for hundreds of millions of people. Our first conclusion, therefore, is that these innovations are still solidly in place notwithstanding the tough times and substantial challenges, social changes, and outright attacks. To be sure, other actors have contributed to this result, and different center-lefts have played their roles in different ways to make this happen. But absent these historic victories and the efforts of center-lefts to maintain them, which during the tough times beginning in the late 1970s have often required difficult reforms, today's globalizing world would not have models to emulate for those who would democratize capitalism. This achievement has meant that neoliberalism has not won the decisive victory that three decades of political dominance might have led one to expect.

Center Lefts Vary Greatly

The second major conclusion to emerge from this book is that there is no single, universally agreed model either for democratized capitalism or for the center-left itself. Some center-lefts have obviously been more successful than others. Moreover, the special nature of each center-left has created a wide range of organizations, policy practices, and goals. Untangling these variants and the political economies within which they have arisen and worked has been one of our most important tasks.

The greatest center-left successes, which provide the most widely admired models for many center-lefts, are found in Scandinavia, and the reasons for this are elaborated in the chapter by Jonas Pontusson. In this region are several small, very well-organized societies where organizations, social groups, citizens, and politicians cooperate at a high level to maintain international competitiveness and domestic welfare. Here are highly coordinated market economies with unusual adaptive capacities and policy creativity which do very well on most performance criteria: growth, employment, innovation, per capita income, productivity, education, social security, gender equality, and reconciling work and family. The Swedish system, promoted as a viable "third way" before anyone had ever heard of Tony Blair, is the envy of center-leftists everywhere. What the Danes call "flexicurity" has recently been held up as a workable and humane policy response to a globalized and highly competitive economy. Norway continues to impress, albeit while benefiting from oil resources, and Finland's ability to shift gears after the cold war toward a growth model led by high technology has been truly extraordinary. Successful labor market reforms in the Netherlands may also have made the Dutch into honorary Scandinavians.

Scandinavian center-lefts are unique. They all emerged from very small economies and largely homogeneous societies which could only grow in conditions of trade openness to which they had to learn to adapt. To avoid the social disruptions and inequalities that could have followed their adaptation, they also had to find ways to help their citizens manage life transitions. Often they did so through institutions that simultaneously obliged employers to innovate and helped employees to move from declining to growing sectors. Many social democratic formations drew strong distinctions between industrial workers and other citizens. Most Scandinavian parties, by contrast, sought to promote equality among citizens, as Sheri Berman underlines, through policies of wage compression, redistribution through taxation, and universal access to a wide range of social programs and services, including retraining to facilitate job transitions. This has turned out to be a fundamental distinction.

Scandinavian center-left approaches have had one additional consequence. Their combination of well-coordinated, competitive market economies able to make supply-side adaptations in the face of industrial change with commitments to equal socioeconomic citizenship have been difficult for opponents to dislodge, because practically everyone has become a stakeholder. This helps to explain a recent paradox: the systems have held on despite the electoral and organizational weakening of center-left political parties. In Sweden social democrats can still effectively dominate policymaking, even if they are in opposition. Norwegian social democrats remain—barely—in control of broad coalitions, but the model persists. Elsewhere Scandinavian center-lefts today are part of broad coalitions whose precise directions they often cannot control, or in some places, like Denmark, have been in opposition for some time, but again the framework remains intact. Scandinavian political economies thus seem durable, even if center-left political hegemony is not.[1]

Center-lefts on the European continent, particularly in France and Germany, the most important members of the European Union, have evolved in a different fashion. In the postwar period both France and Germany chose export-led development models, but in very different ways. In both countries social democracy came with a focus on industrial workers rather than on equal citizenship for all. This focus fed strong concerns about redressing workers' conditions (which in Germany meant primarily male workers), leading to compromise with Bismarckian and Christian-Democratic social insurance approaches, in which benefits reflected wage inequalities, and strong measures to protect industrial workers in the labor market. In the reconstruction years of high postwar growth and full employment, virtually everyone was a "worker," however, which obscured potential problems.

Germany chose corporatist approaches according to which welfare state programs and labor market protection were built mainly on private deals between employers and unions. One result was that Germany's perennially successful export firms built job security, retraining, in-house flexibility, and a degree of redistribution into their company practices, often accompanied by *Mitbestimmung*, which gave workers a say in corporate choices. The French model had similar aims but used different techniques. Starting from behind, France under de Gaulle chose statist techniques to build national champion exporters alongside its Bismarckian, corporatist welfare state programs and legislated labor market protection (both strategies were informed by the goals of a broad Resistance coalition that included Christian Democrats but was premised upon an ideology of Republicanism). Neither the German nor the French model has weathered recent tough times well, though for different reasons.

Large problems appeared first in France. As Goldhammer and Ross show, French statist strategies were stymied by the international changes that began in the 1970s. Mass unemployment followed, uncovering large categories of citizens who were not "workers" in the traditional sense and so suffered from a range of exclusions. The center-left, in power during much of this period, devised innovative reforms to combat surging poverty while also deliberately removing large numbers from the workforce and promoting work sharing among those who remained in it. This policy contravened the conventional wisdom of the moment, which instead advocated new supply-side activation and more flexible labor markets; it also contributed to growing divisions between outsiders and insiders, often the remnants of weak French unionism, who used their influence to protect their advantages. The French center-left suffered greatly as a result. The French political system, in which the presidency is the key to governance, places a premium on forming and managing multiparty coalitions. The Socialist Party—which has not won an important national election since 1997—has had great difficulty doing so, in large part because of widening diversity in the left's electorate, which has aggravated intractable internal problems.

The German story is different. Germany withstood new challenges after the 1970s because of its successful pursuit of monetary stability and its continuing adeptness at competing in export markets. But unification of West and East Germany proved costly and contributed to a slow unraveling of collective bargaining, greater unemployment, and rising social policy expenditures. If Germany's export sector was to continue to conquer international markets as long as they remained buoyant, to do so it needed strong productivity gains, leading it to shed more and more labor. One result has been that Germany's once-powerful union movement has fallen into serious if largely unacknowledged decline, as unemployment and the growing costs of pensions, healthcare, and unemployment compensation have posed new problems for German governments. The Red-Green coalition (1998–2005) led by Gerhard Schröder finally confronted some of these problems in ways that have since proven costly among social democratic voters, while at the same time Germany has created its own growing insider-outsider labor market problem. The SPD now finds itself in a situation where sustaining its traditional working-class base, and by implication the German export sector, runs counter to reforms that might attenuate the problems of outsiders. The consequence has been a steep decline in SPD electoral performance—to 23% in the parliamentary elections of 2009, its lowest score since 1945. It now has severe problems in claiming political leadership and preventing the rise of electoral competitors, and faces new and difficult coalition-building tasks.

"Southern" European center-lefts, whose electoral fortunes are discussed by Gerassimos Moschonas, have had different histories from both the Scandinavians and the continentals. Portugal, Spain, and Greece, less developed than northern European countries, all suffered under unpleasant and protectionist dictatorships during the postwar period. When the dictators all fell in the 1970s, the long complicity of right-wing parties with them gave center-lefts significant political advantages. The center-lefts then chose strategies of catch-up modernization and Europeanization, and when in power, which they have very often been, they opened and remodeled their economies, joined the EU and received helpful development aid from it, improved national institutions, and revamped social and labor market regimes. What is most significant in these stories is the difference in political timing from the European North. From the 1980s northerners struggled to adapt over-rigid and costly postwar structures, while southern center-lefts embarked on a modernizing trajectory that presented opportunities to build electoral strength, win elections, and govern.[2] Yet there are signs that this southern trajectory may be running down, mainly because the benefits accruing from being on the right side of history are dissipating, while economic growth has become harder to engineer and financial stability increasingly difficult to maintain.

A particular goal of this book has been to give appropriate attention to center-lefts in the "liberal market economics" in the United Kingdom and the

United States. The two cases are historically rather different. In the United Kingdom postwar development toward what might have resembled a continental model was quite advanced by the 1970s, but it abruptly stopped in 1979 after the electoral victory of a Conservative Party that under Margaret Thatcher had rediscovered the virtues of markets. The consequences for Labour, as elaborated by James Cronin, have been dramatic. Thatcherism worked such fundamental economic and social changes that Labour was forced to adapt, since it could persist in or return to pre-1979 politics only at the risk of electoral irrelevancy. The Labour Party eventually made basic changes in outlook and strategy. These were embodied in Blairite "third way" politics whose starting point was a broad acceptance of the more market-oriented policy frameworks that Thatcher had left behind. The thrust of Labour's new strategy was thus to promote economic management for balanced growth within these frameworks and then, once economic success was obtained, to use the fruits of growth to initiate reforms that would reinforce safety nets, attenuate the extreme inequalities left by the Thatcher era, and rebuild public services on new grounds. New Labour's record of success at most of these endeavors was considerable. One important index was a substantial reduction after 1997 in the dramatic income inequality that Thatcherism had wrought.[3] But after Labour had been in office for more than a decade, support began to ebb. Labour began to look tired and exhausted, it was stuck with an uncharismatic leader in Gordon Brown whose grip on the highest office was nevertheless tenacious, and its record looked decidedly less impressive as the economy was hit by the financial crisis of 2008. As the nation and Conservatives looked forward to a Tory victory in 2010—and got something different but close enough—the key question became how much a new government would move away from the policies of New Labour. Labour had effectively re-centered the political settlement left in place by Thatcher, moving it toward the left by making it more humane and restoring public services and according to government a greater role in society. Would the Tories under David Cameron move back to the right, hewing to their Thatcherite heritage, or would they obey the logic of electoral competition and fight on the more centrist ground occupied by Labour (Cronin 2009; McKibbin 2009)? The unusual outcome of the election of May 2010 seemed to give at least an indirect answer: the Tories, in coalition with the Liberal Democrats, would be required to adopt a rhetoric and style of politics that would distinguish their policies from the still toxic past evoked by the name of Margaret Thatcher. To this extent the settlement brokered by New Labour would not be quickly or easily undone while Labour's fortunes, ironically, might not easily be revived against rivals with which it did not seem to differ greatly. The issue remains very much in doubt, however, for the austerity policies proposed by the coalition are harsh and contain more than a whiff of Thatcherism.

The American case, discussed from different angles by Ruy Teixeira, Christopher Howard, and James Shoch, also begins with a "liberal" market context that is quite different from that of Europe and a history different from that of Britain. The United States, which during the New Deal in the 1930s made a strong start toward what might have been a welfare state and an industrial relations system along European lines, stalled far short of completion in the immediate postwar period. Among other New Deal beginnings were a Bismarckian pension system, the groundwork for strong labor market regulation in the Wagner Act, and initiation of a discussion of national health insurance. But despite active Keynesian economic management and the perpetuation of the New Deal political coalition, reformist momentum slowed, sometimes in historically ironic ways. The development of trade unions led to collective bargaining for privately provided health insurance and supplementary pensions in ways that benefited insiders at the expense of outsiders, and blunted the political thrust behind campaigns for more universal programs. The successful civil rights movement and disastrous Vietnam War of the 1960s and economic problems in the 1970s tore apart the New Deal coalition and opened the door to a powerful neoliberal offensive marked by a strident anti-statism, a strong reassertion of individualism, and a determination to weaken the social programs and labor protections created by the New Deal and Great Society programs of the 1960s. In critical respects this thrust lasted longer than Thatcherism, encompassing twelve years after 1980, interrupted by the two-term presidency of Bill Clinton, during much of which Republicans controlled both houses of Congress, and then, until 2009, the two-term presidency of George W. Bush. During that extended period the entire American political spectrum was moved dramatically to the right, bringing with it a large increase in inequality and an exaggerated insider-outsider society in which the lowest-paid and least secure were kept going, more or less, by harsh workfare policies (Wilentz 2008). The victory of Barack Obama in 2008 appeared to have revived center-left reformism, but Obama was compelled to start from a very low baseline. The economic stimulus bill, healthcare reform, and new financial regulations were all important achievements. But in the face of intransigent Republican opposition, an ambivalent public, and significant institutional obstacles, progress has been difficult and, after the Republicans' big gains in the 2010 congressional midterm elections, will become even harder. Further advance, if it occurs, will demand extraordinary strategic skills on the part of the center-left, and the results are likely to be different from those in Europe.

The post–cold war center-lefts in Central and Eastern Europe, discussed by De Waele and Soare, provide yet another trajectory. After 1989 there was no possibility of reforming the socioeconomic order established by Soviet domination, and strong incentives existed instead for moving decisively toward market-based democracies. In the years immediately following the end of communism, this was the path taken throughout the region. Initially the lead was taken by anticommunist reformers, but in many places they were quickly supplanted by parties that were technically "center-left" but had been hastily built around the vertebrae of older communist parties whose leaders had converted to markets and democratic institutions. The secret of this odd success story was the ability of ex-communist leaders and parties to shift political and organizational resources from the old regime to new purposes, while competitors had no comparable resources at hand. These "successor party" center-lefts faced contradictions. Once in power they had to pursue liberalizing reforms that displeased their supporters and undercut their prospects. Predictions about the future in this region are hazardous, of course, because the period since the early 1990s is so brief and the outcomes of transition remain uncertain.

Center-Lefts Are a Family That Often Disagrees, Even about Its Models for Society

The record surveyed here leads to several further conclusions. One is that even if center-lefts may have had broadly similar outlooks and have faced similar challenges in the tough times we examine, their responses have been divergent, and they have often disagreed profoundly on day-to-day matters. In brief, center-lefts, given the variety of their situations, have had different strategies and goals. This is mainly because their actions have been constrained by different political economies which have opened quite different "paths" upon which they became "dependent." These paths, together with significant institutional variations, have also created widely varying electoral equations. To illustrate, let us take the issue that has perhaps loomed largest for center-lefts in recent years: the need to introduce supply-side flexibility into postwar social and employment policy systems.

The Scandinavians have been able to "flexibilize" with relative ease, even though they have had to make serious changes, because of their long experience with international openness and existing practices of supply-side flexibility. The "continentals," in contrast, have had a rockier time because changing activation and flexibility policies has meant changing benefit systems and protective regulations, eliciting strong resistance from entrenched interests. The result has been reluctant, spasmodic, and weak supply-side reforms whose economic effects have been modest but which have nevertheless contributed to a loss of political support. "Southerners" have faced similarly entrenched corporatist interests, but they have often been able to limit the damages through their broader modernizing strategies. Center-lefts in "liberal" environments—the United Kingdom and the United States in our volume—had to work with the consequences of conservative policies to open markets, make labor markets more flexible, and weaken unions, regulation, and social protection. These changes left a legacy of flexibility with a harsh, almost Darwinian edge. Center-lefts could then propose new policies to limit the harshness. In the new market democracies of Central and Eastern Europe, center-lefts faced yet again different choices. With little choice but to slash and burn earlier protective arrangements which had guaranteed social services and jobs (not always good ones) for practically everyone, center-lefts created "activated" and often much harsher labor markets and social policies. Economic growth cushioned these processes somewhat, although better-skilled and better-organized center-rights have already emerged to challenge these center-lefts.

There are many more examples of the differences between center-lefts. Despite a general commitment to greater social security and justice, center-lefts have had widely varying approaches to the new social policy challenges surrounding what Jane Jenson labels "new social investment," particularly in the areas of "care" and poverty policy. And while most center-lefts have become vulnerable to rightist anti-immigrant populism, they have responded in very different ways—often successfully—as Pérez shows. In the light of such persistent differences in approach, there is little mystery in the difficulty that European center-lefts have had in finding common ground on EU-level policies, as George Ross suggests.

Center-Lefts Face Common Challenges

Despite these differences, a common set of problems confronts center-lefts almost everywhere. The most important is electoral erosion, which is happening in different places at different rates, with the one significant but only partial and not necessarily lasting exception of the United States. In his wide-ranging essay Gerassimos Moschonas notes that this erosion has been slow and that it affects major center-right parties as well, although to a lesser degree. Deep sociological causes undoubtedly explain a great deal. Traditional lefts were usually built on a projection that industrial workers—with common situations, identities, needs, interests, and goals—would come to dominate politically. But service-sector work and salaried "new middle class" work has grown much more rapidly than traditional working-class occupations. In addition, those who do these "new middle class" jobs have often developed outlooks quite different from those of workers, sometimes joining single-issue parties, social movements, and lobbies which disagree with parts of what center-lefts advocate.

Another reason for the slow electoral erosion is that the basic programmatic and utopian projects that lefts developed over more than a century are now largely exhausted. The goal of "democratizing capitalism" has largely been achieved. Programs to take democratization further or in new directions do not mobilize in the ways they once did. Today's center-lefts are often confronted with the apparent need to "modernize" and reform what they have largely put in place, a much less glamorous, less inspiring, and also more divisive project than before. "Transcending capitalism," the early left's utopian goal, could in the past connect day-to-day reformism to a grander vision for a new and dramatically different society. This utopia is no longer politically plausible. Markets are here for the duration, and everyone knows it.

In the earlier "imaginary," the goal of transcending capitalism and the reformism that came with it promised successive redistributions that would reach an end state in which privileged capitalists would no longer exist. Center-left reformism, no longer backed by the socialist dream, today lives in a reality which seems to demand policies that would reconfigure and fine-tune social protections and supports, and redistribute income and opportunity from some parts of "the people" to others. The goal could be restated in terms of "equality." Older lefts could at least pretend to be engaged in a quest to create nearly absolute equality among citizens by positing and proposing to fight a zero-sum redistributive game with capitalists. Today's center-lefts, while they may still focus on reducing excessive wealth, in particular because of the substantial recent increase in high-end incomes, are aware that the concentration of wealth is only a small part of the "equality puzzle" they face. In many places large insider-outsider gaps have opened in which relatively secure salaried employees and unionized workers coexist with badly paid, insecure workers who face much harsher labor market and living conditions. The need to respond to these gaps is now a central issue, and since doing so often requires shifting resources from one part of the center-left's potential base toward another, solutions are not easy. Still, the alternative is to allow a caste-like, dualistic social order to emerge. Pledging to increase "equality of opportunity," as practically everyone has been doing for some time, may be electorally successful on occasion, but center-lefts stand to lose if the pledges turn out to be hollow, as they very often have been in the past.

Center-Lefts Have Had Trouble Combining Management and Reform

It is also clear from our analysis that center-lefts with serious claims on governmental power have long had to strike delicate balances between managing markets and reforming them. Finding the right combination has been difficult, as was amply demonstrated throughout the Keynesian postwar era. It may be that in some places electoral decline has been tied to an overemphasis on the part of center-lefts on management and a move away from serious reformism, a reflex that would be understandable in response to brutal neoliberal offensives and the inroads of globalization. Given new social patterns and coalitional difficulties, the challenges of creative reformism have undoubtedly got much larger, while the tasks of management and governing have not become any easier. It may also be that the temptation to run by proving superior management skills alone has grown among center-left parties. Have at least some center-lefts shifted their visions too much from creative reforming to managing the complexities of ever more powerful markets? This is at least what the former French foreign minister and socialist elder statesman Hubert Védrine thinks. He found "incomprehensible" the miserable results of center-lefts in elections to the European parliament in 2009: "Perhaps it is because so much of social democracy over the last thirty years wanted so much to free itself of the absurdities of communism and hard left ideas that they have shifted too far in the other direction. As a result ideologically they've wrong-footed themselves. They bought into the market economy, which they believed to be well-regulated along the lines of 'the Rhine capitalist model' and instead they woke up in some kind of jungle" (Védrine 2009).

The more "managerial" that center-lefts become at the expense of proposing distinctive reformist programs, the more likely it is that center-left and center-right appeals will become difficult for citizens to distinguish. Historically lefts led reformist crusades, but as reform has succeeded, the crusading spirit has ebbed. Though differences of emphasis remain, in recent times the center-lefts in many countries appear to stand for programs and policies quite similar to those of their rivals on the center-right. In this new context at least some voters will look for parties that do have real crusades on offer, while others will try to judge dispassionately between the comparable platforms of the major contenders on the basis of which is more likely to be a better manager. Still others will vote to throw out incumbents because of perceived performance failures or simple boredom.

The narrowing of programs and identities between center-lefts and center-rights has occurred not only because of growing managerialism on the left.

Social changes toward what many call post-industrialism have transformed center-left parties into broad cross-class or "catch-all" parties oriented toward the much-discussed median (or swing) voter. Together with the advent of modern polling and other campaign techniques, this transformation has helped to erode or blur left-right partisan distinctions and reduce the importance of issues altogether, in favor of an emphasis on candidates' personal characteristics and other non-policy factors. This point should not be overstated, since incentives remain for parties to remain attentive to their informed and engaged core constituencies, even in majoritarian electoral systems like those of the United States and the United Kingdom where the pursuit of the median voter is more likely than in systems based on proportional representation (PR). In PR systems the formation of center-left electoral strategy is more complex. To win and govern effectively, successful parties must appeal to the political center, but they must also build strong and stable coalitions with other parties—usually Greens, liberals, or groups further to the left. This task, easier when the key center-left party is dominant on the left side of the political spectrum, becomes more complicated when the center-left is less dominant and smaller parties see it as a promising source of more support for themselves. In such situations, which appear to be becoming more typical, the bidding process for votes on the left may make it much more difficult for center-lefts to appeal to critical median voters. Too exclusive a focus on centrist median voters, of course, can lead traditional center-left supporters to defect to smaller parties to the left.

Many European center-lefts are thus likely to face more difficult strategic circumstances in the electoral "tough times" to come than they have done in the period we have reviewed. There are good recent examples of this. In the presidential elections of 2002 the French socialists failed to qualify for the runoff round when the far-right National Front got slightly more votes. Analysts attributed this failure to the campaign strategy of the Socialist candidate Lionel Jospin, who focused on median voters with the runoff in mind (which polls indicated he might well have won had he got through the primary) rather than attending to coalitional issues on the left. In Germany's general elections in 2009 the Social Democrats, threatened with a loss of votes to die Linke on its left, chose not to move left. Instead they decided to market governmental competence against a Christian Democratic chancellor who could and did outbid them on these grounds. Italy presents yet a different variant: there a motley collection of different left-leaning parties—hard-line leftists, left liberals, Greens, and a relatively strong ex-Communist party which has become center-left—has on occasion been able to win elections but not to stick together on important policy matters thereafter. As might be expected, recurring bouts of failure in government have had disastrous effects on the electoral fortunes of the center-left. Dilemmas of this sort present themselves across Europe, and they seem to be getting more serious, while effective answers have proved illusive and at best temporary.

Center Lefts in the Great Recession

Lefts and center-lefts have always had to confront new situations, changing realities, and emerging problems. The onset of the global financial crisis in 2007–8 and the protracted downturn that ensued meant that center-left parties and movements which had barely and not always effectively adapted to the post-Keynesian and post-communist era found themselves at yet another historic crossroads. Are the stances arrived at after thirty years of debate and experimentation likely to persist, or will the new Great Recession lead to another effort at rethinking and yet another shift in orientation and practice?

The Great Recession is the largest disruption of capitalism to occur since the Great Depression of the 1930s. The expanded economic role of governments in the immediate response to the crisis was initially interpreted as a rebirth of Keynesianism which could redound to the political benefit of the center-left.[4] The reappearance of government and the return of Keynes proved superficial and short-lived, however, and three years into the crisis, center-left parties have profited little from the onset of hard times. Worse still, small but significant groups of voters in Europe, including some who earlier may have been on the left, have opted to support xenophobic anti-immigrant parties in ways that have shifted electoral balances further to the right. Such has been the case in Sweden, Denmark, the Netherlands, Belgium, Austria, France, Italy, and several Central European countries. And even where there were historical and institutional barriers to this, as in Germany and the United Kingdom, there have been indirect effects of a similar kind.[5] In the United States, where Obama's victory raised the hopes of center-leftists everywhere, the rightward shift has had a slightly different shape, but has been quite as great.

The Great Recession began in the United States, where loose monetary policies and unregulated financial practices stimulated an extraordinary housing bubble, which then burst disastrously. The resulting shock waves shook the global financial world. Stock markets dropped, losses decimated private savings, credit dried up, and governments and central banks were forced to bail out financial institutions because the functioning of the "real economy" depended on their ability to provide credit. Different emergency efforts across the transatlantic area gradually brought about a semblance of stability, and by mid-2009 the initial financial panic had subsided and it appeared that the downward spiral toward depression had been limited by various stimulus measures.

Yet the Great Recession was not so easily overcome, as events in the Eurozone then confirmed (Dadush et al. 2010). Initial crisis coordination within the EU followed the transnational scenario of bailouts, stimulus plans, and reregulation of the financial sector. There was one puzzling early European indicator—a North-South divergence in interest rate spreads on Eurozone government bonds—that was duly noted and then filed away. The bond spread issue exploded in the spring of 2010, however, threatening to push the global financial order again into chaos and cut short a still anemic economic recovery. The initial cause was Greek national insolvency, which spurred intense market speculation, but similar debt problems affected Ireland, Spain, Portugal, and even Italy. To save the Greeks and then the Irish, devising new anti-crisis measures became obligatory for richer EU members, but they disagreed about what to do and took months to find compromises, during which the financial markets chipped away at the EU's financial credibility. Eventually a large bailout fund was put in place by the EU and the International Monetary Fund (IMF), but not before much damage was done to Europe's economy and to the EU as an institution.

The acute phase of the crisis, when global economic catastrophe threatened, would have been much worse had governments not acted as they did. But even with these actions, the economic downturn that followed was protracted and painful. By late 2009 the drive for further government intervention had stalled. Government intervention helped ease the crisis, but it was also apparent that the resilience of neoclassical economics and opposition from business, parties of the right, and fearful voters to major systemic reforms were great. The result for center-lefts was a new and even more complicated situation.

Center-Left Prospects

Our authors have gone to great lengths in examining the kinds of reforms to existing social programs and the kinds of new programs that center-lefts could promote to ensure the maintenance and continued viability of humanized democratic societies in today's challenging globalizing environment. As they have noted, it was heartening that the easiest successes in these areas, ensuring the provision of basic security and opportunity needs for entire populations, had been won in most places, although not all, as the experience of the United States shows. There existed a viable social model that center-lefts had done much to put in place. Reforming successful programs and devising new programs to meet new problems are demanding tasks, but not at all impossible, the authors believe. Who but center-left thinkers, movements, and parties will devise paths to more genuine equal opportunity? Who but the center-left will put in place the new flexibility that market societies need by giving people the educational and employment resources that will allow them to maximize their personal capacities and confront the frequent life and occupational transitions that are already becoming the norm? Who but those nurtured in the social democratic tradition are best placed to promote genuine social inclusion? Who but those long committed to an egalitarian society can struggle effectively against deepening inequalities in income and wealth?

The center-left has not gained much in the new century, however, whether in the "normal times" before 2007–8 or since the Great Recession. Before the crisis center-right parties in countries like Germany, France, Denmark, and Sweden had already won power, although often in coalition, by promising to administer and reform the welfare state, to make it work efficiently in the face of new constraints induced by globalization, rather than roll it back. Sometimes they also capitalized on growing anti-immigrant sentiments. More recently center-lefts across Europe suffered major losses in the European parliamentary elections of June 2009, and in September of the same year the German Social Democrats had their worst national election vote since the end of the Second World War. Next Labour lost the British general election of May 2010 and the Swedish Social Democrats failed to regain power in September of the same year. The Greek, Norwegian, and Portuguese social democrats did manage, barely, to win at the polls, and the Spanish left managed to cling to power. But who would now want to be in government in Greece, Portugal, or Spain in the aftermath of the Eurozone crisis? With Obama's victory in 2008 the United States appeared to be an important exception to the lack of center-left political success in the Great Recession. It now seems, however, that Obama's election was more a reaction to the noxious policies of George W. Bush and the shock of economic crisis itself than any announcement of a growing movement for change.[6]

To put it simply, the characteristic twentieth-century pattern of enduring and largely class-based political mobilization has given way to a more fluid and unstable environment. This context, whose maturation was a key feature of the era covered by this book, means that no party can be expected to achieve the sort of sustained political dominance premised on a "hegemonic project" or "bloc" that once seemed possible. Success in the new world of politics is more temporary and precarious. The resurgence of center-left parties in Europe during the late 1990s did not last, and not simply because of the mistakes of its leaders. Obama's victory in the United States has been even more fleeting, and there is no certainty that the few reforms it won will result in durable gains for the party. There is thus little certainty either in Europe or the United States that the political payoff for reengineering relations between state and society and creating a more just and humane social model will be either large or permanent.

The predominance of center-right parties that we see today faces an analogous mix of uncertainties. Just as center-left parties long relied on a big, solid phalanx of working-class votes which is no longer so big nor so solid, parties of the right long relied on the backing of a solid alliance of the upper, middle, and lower middle classes that is no longer so coherent and effective. That coalition—brought together by fear of the left and resistance to high taxes and union power, and consolidated by the cold war—has also begun to fragment. Anticommunism no longer holds the amalgam together, while the growth of the professions, the state, and services throws up a highly educated new middle class more open to some of the appeals of the center-left, especially on social issues. Party allegiance on the center-right has therefore also weakened, bringing a politics based on ad hoc alignments, "wedge" issues, and personalities.

The medium-term evolution of politics and policy on both sides of the Atlantic could thus converge around a pattern in which the center-left remains an important and essential player in a political universe without dominant parties. The implications of living in this universe, which have become clearer in recent years, are that center-left victories, when they come, are modest, while defeats, when kept within bounds and understood for what they are, need not be crippling. This is not an argument for complacency, for we must not forget that center-lefts will still have important contributions to make in ensuring that global capitalism does not develop unopposed and that its progress does not undermine the security and quality of life that parties and movements of the center-left have done so much to bring about. It is nevertheless a counsel for patience and for looking to the long term.

Still, the prospects of parties of the left will be enhanced precisely to the extent that they can provide effective responses to the challenges of the present era. Before the financial crisis the major challenge was to generate sustained growth in a highly competitive global economy while preserving and making more effective the essential supports that will make it possible for ordinary people to live and compete in that world successfully and with security and dignity. Post–Great Recession conditions add new challenges. To be sure, the economic crisis has underlined how much today's globalization cries out for intelligent new governance and new regulatory initiatives both nationally and internationally, which center-lefts, because they are more likely to believe that such things are needed, could provide. But post–Great Recession circumstances are likely to make success considerably more difficult to attain. This is because staving off the worst in the global financial crisis has turned into a long-term and very costly enterprise.

As in any recession, tax revenues declined because of reduced growth and consumption, while outlays for social programs rose considerably. Beyond this, when governments entered the scene as lenders of last resort to shore up credit, employment, and consumption, national budget deficit and debt levels shot up. Rare indeed in Europe and North America are countries whose annual budget shortfalls after 2007 have been less than 10% annually and whose national debts have not ballooned. We should not forget, however, that the Great Recession was the first financial disaster of the era of globalization, and this has made an ironic difference. The financial markets that caused the crisis were quickly called upon to finance the new national debts that the crisis produced. Investors had to be repaid, of course, and this meant that the markets had to evaluate the quality of the debt instruments that were issued, leading to the differential interest rate spreads that among other things underlay the Eurozone imbroglio. This, perhaps more than anything, limited how much stimulus different countries could enact, and quickly created large new concerns about budgetary stability.

One consequence was that an armada of international authorities (the G-20, OECD, IMF, EU, and ECB, among others) urged a massive turn to austerity. Such a turn, already begun in Europe and pressed by ascendant Republicans and conservative Democrats in the United States despite persistent low growth and high unemployment in both regions, greatly complicates the strategic situation for all political forces. The level of austerity imposed on the economically and fiscally weaker European states could be lessened were the stronger states, especially Germany, to engage in more fiscal expansion, thus boosting exports, growth, and tax revenues in the more vulnerable nations. But the continuing hegemony of orthodox economic thinking prevents this.

Consequently, devising medium-term austerity politics on the scale that will be needed challenges everyone. It may be less of a problem for center-rights, however, to the degree that they are less committed to social programs involving redistribution. Cuts in existing welfare programs, educational systems, healthcare, and pensions, like those that the recently elected British coalition of Conservatives and Liberal Democrats is already implementing, may be easier to make in the heat of crisis and "in the interests of all" than they would ordinarily be. Indeed, post-crisis conditions may provide a more propitious moment for center-rights to work basic change in social programs, perhaps to undercut their universality, for example, than they have seen in some time (Vis 2010). That right-wing populist explosions on both sides of the Atlantic are moving political discourses and repertoires rightward may also facilitate neoliberal declensions of austerity.

The situation presents formidable new challenges to center-lefts. The few center-lefts actually in power, in Greece, Spain, and Portugal, for example, now have little choice but to propose and administer harsh austerity and to do so without dismantling past achievements. This demands strategic intelligence that few of these parties possess. Where center-lefts are now in opposition they first have to reflect on how to take advantage of the decline in center-right popularity that is likely to follow attacks on longstanding social programs. This could lead them into a political minefield, however. They will inevitably be drawn toward struggles to defend such programs, but excessive reliance on defensiveness will allow opponents to label them as irresponsible naysayers in national crusades to survive. To avoid this they will have to summon unusual creativity in proposing redesigns of programs that will also save money, an almost impossible task. At the same time, they will also have to position themselves as better and more innovative managers of austerity than center-rights. The risk is that center-lefts will come to look programmatically very much like the center-rights whose draconian measures they oppose. These are not altogether new strategic dilemmas, but they have become much more difficult to resolve in Great Recession conditions. The center-left's future will very much depend on whether it is able to resolve them.

Notes

1. Volatile new forces of the right, mobilized against immigrants, could sap even more center-left electoral support. Managing coalitions may therefore turn out to be more complicated than fending off neoliberalism.

2. We should recall here the Italian case, briefly discussed in the Introduction. Italy's center-left probably falls into its own category, somewhere between the other "southern" cases and what we have referred to as the continentals, even though comparative European politics textbooks often discuss Italy with northern countries. Italy had no dictators after the Second World War, but it was politically dominated most of the time by the Christian Democrats, whose power was based on Catholicism, cold war fears of both the internal and the external left (Italy had one of the most powerful and skillful communist parties in the world), old-fashioned clientelistic patronage politics, and considerable corruption. The country thus modernized in an unusual way, its northern half to levels of development and wealth comparable to those in northern Europe, its southern regions as poor as the poorest parts of Latin Europe, its institu-

tions and welfare state a mixture of clientelism and modernity. Once the center-left was able to make claims on governing after both Christian Democracy and the cold war collapsed in the 1990s, it suffered from serious multipartisan pluralism. It was able to win and sometimes, as in the mid-1990s, able to work significant change, but eventually its coalitions would collapse in acrimony, recently giving way to the odd, sometimes clownish, charismatic politics of Silvio Berlusconi.

3. See the OECD's recent report *Growing Unequal?* (2008e).

4. On the revival of Keynes see Skidelsky 2009.

5. It is almost as if contemporary successors of the crisis-shaped electoral movements of the early 1930s, which were often protectionist, are now xenophobic. Students of electoral politics may soon be able to explain this better than we can now, but the answer may lie in political economy: it may be that broad-scale protectionists movements have been more or less ruled out by economic globalization, which has greatly increased the strength of elites and domestic interests with stakes in open international markets. Instead, the sentiments that once rallied behind protectionism and restrictions on the movement of goods are now turned against the international migration of persons.

6. Obama's presidency managed to pass a major reform of American healthcare and the financial sector over fierce Republican opposition in Congress, but at the cost of many of the other changes that it had initially promised, after which it was stymied politically. Worse still, a confluence of different anti statist, populist, and conservative oppositions accusing Obama of a multiplicity of alleged sins, including a desire to install "European-style socialism," helped Republicans win a massive victory in the 2010 midterm elections. The question for the American center-left then became whether it would be able to find enough support in 2012 to reelect Obama rather more than how to pursue any new progressive agenda.

Bibliography

Abrajano, Marisa, Michael Alvarez, and Jonathan Nagler. 2005. "The Hispanic Vote in the 2004 Presidential Election: Insecurity and Moral Concerns." *Journal of Politics* 70, no. 2 (April), 368–82.

Adema, Willem, and Maxime Ladaique. 2005. *Net Social Expenditure*. Paris: OECD.

Agh, Attila. 1995. "The Case of the Hungarian Socialist Party." *Party Politics* 1, no. 4 (October), 491–514.

———. 2004. "The Europeanization of Social Democracy in East Central Europe." *Europäische Politik* 4 (August), 1–9.

Ahlberg, Jenny, Christine Roman, and Simon Duncan. 2008. "Actualizing the 'Democratic Family'? Swedish Policy Rhetoric versus Family Practices." *Social Politics: International Studies in Gender, State and Society* 15, no. 1 (spring), 79–100.

Aiginger, Karl. 2008. "New Challenges for the European Model and How to Cope with It." *Growth versus Security: Old and New EU Members' Quest for a New Economic and Social Model*, ed. Wojciech Bienkowski, Josef C. Brada, and Mariusz-Jan Radlo. Basingstoke: Palgrave Macmillan.

Akard, Patrick. 1998. "Where Are All the Democrats? The Limits of Economic Policy Reform." *Social Policy and the Conservative Agenda*, ed. Clarence Y. H. Lo and Michael Schwartz, 187–209. Malden, Mass.: Blackwell.

Alesina, Alberto F., Edward L. Glaeser, and Bruce Sacerdote. 2001. "Why Doesn't the US Have a European-Style Welfare System?" NBER Working Paper W8524.

Allan, James P., and Lyle Scruggs. 2004. "Political Partisanship and Welfare State Reform in Advanced Industrial Societies." *American Journal of Political Science* 48, no. 3 (July), 496–512.

Allen, Christopher. 2009. "'Empty Nets': Social Democracy and the 'Catch-All Party Thesis' in Germany and Sweden." *Party Politics* 15, no. 5 (September), 635–53.

Amenta, Edwin. 1998. *Bold Relief: Institutional Politics and the Origins of Modern American Social Policy*. Princeton: Princeton University Press.

Amin, Ash, ed. 1995. *Post-Fordism: A Reader*. Malden, Mass.: Wiley-Blackwell.

Andersen, Jorgen Goul. 2007. "The Danish Welfare State as 'Politics for Markets': Combining Equality and Competitiveness in a Global Economy." *New Political Economy* 12, no. 1 (March), 71–78.

Anderson, Perry. 2007. "Jottings on the Conjuncture." *New Left Review* 48 (November–December).

Anderson, Perry, and Patrick Camiller. 1994. *Mapping the West European Left*. London: Verso.

Armstrong, Philip, Andrew Glyn, and John Harrison. 1991. *Capitalism since 1945*. New York: Basil Blackwell.

Arter, David. 2003. "Scandinavia: What's Left Is the Social Democratic Welfare Consensus." *Parliamentary Affairs* 56, no. 1 (January), 75–98.

Ashbee, Edward, and Alex Wadden. 2010. "The Obama Administration and United States Trade Policy." *Political Quarterly* 81, no. 2 (April–June), 253–62.

Aust, Andreas. 2004. "From 'Eurokeynesianism' to the 'Third Way': The Party of European Socialists (PES) and European Employment Policies." *Social Democratic Party Policies in Contemporary Europe*, ed. Giuliano Bonoli and Martin Powell. London: Routledge.

Aust, Andreas, and Frank Bönker. 2004. "New Social Risks in a Conservative Welfare State." *New Risks, New Welfare: The Transformation of the European Welfare State*, ed. Peter Taylor-Gooby, 29–54. Oxford: Oxford University Press.

Aylott, Nicholas. 2001. "The Swedish Social Democratic Party." *Social Democracy and Monetary Union*, ed. Ton Notermans. New York: Berghahn.

Aylott, Nicholas, and Niklas Bolin. 2007. "Towards a Two-Party System? The Swedish Parliamentary Election of September 2006." *West European Politics* 30, no. 3 (May), 621–33.

Baer, Kenneth S. 2000. *Reinventing Democrats: The Politics of Liberalism from Reagan to Clinton*. Lawrence: University Press of Kansas.

Bailey, David. 2009a. *The Political Economy of European Social Democracy: A Critical Realist Approach*. New York: Routledge.

———. 2009b. "A Critical Explanation of the 'New' Social Democratic Turn to 'Social Europe': (Not Quite) Reconciling Some Real Contradictions." Paper presented at the annual conference of the Political Studies Association, Manchester, England, 7–9 April.

Baldwin, Peter. 2009. *The Narcissism of Minor Differences: How American and Europe Are Alike*. New York: Oxford University Press.

Baldwin, Robert E., and Christopher S. Magee. 2000. *Congressional Trade Votes: From NAFTA Approval to Fast-Track Defeat*. Washington: Institute for International Economics.

Bale, Tim. 2010. *The Conservative Party: From Thatcher to Cameron*. Cambridge: Polity.

Bardwell, Kedron. 2000. "The Puzzling Decline in House Support for Free Trade: Was Fast Track a Referendum on NAFTA?" *Legislative Studies Quarterly* 25, no. 4 (November), 591–610.

Bartels, Larry M. 2004. "Partisan Politics and the U.S. Income Distribution." http://www.princeton.edu/~bartels/income.pdf.

Bartolini, Stefano. 2005. *Restructuring Europe*. Cambridge: Cambridge University Press.

———. 2007. *The Political Mobilization of the European Left, 1860–1980: The Class Cleavage*. New York: Cambridge University Press.

Becker, Frans, and René Cuperus. 2007. "The Political Centre under Pressure: Elections in the Netherlands." Netherlands Policy Network, www.policy-network.net.

Becker, Jean-Jacques. 1998. *Crises et alternances, 1974–1995*. Paris: Le Seuil.

Becker, Uwe. 2007. "The Scandinavian Model: Still an Example for Europe?" *Internationale Politik und Gesellschaft online / International Politics and Society* no. 4, 41–57.

———. 2009. *Open Varieties of Capitalism: Continuity, Change and Performances*. New York: Palgrave Macmillan.

Benner, Mats. 2003. "The Scandinavian Challenge: The Future of Advanced Welfare States in the Knowledge Economy." *Acta sociologica* 46, no. 2 (June), 132–49.

Berger, Stefan. 2004. "Nothing but Doom and Gloom in the House of Social Democracy? An Upbeat Assessment of European Social Democracy's Future." *Labour History Review* 69, no. 1.

Bergh, Anders, and Gissur Erlingsson. 2009. "Liberalization without Retrenchment." *Scandinavian Political Studies* 32, no. 1 (March), 71–93.

Bergounioux, Alain, and Gérard Grunberg. 1996. *L'utopie à l'épreuve, le socialisme européen au XXe siècle*. Paris: Fallois.

Berkowitz, Edward D. 1991. *America's Welfare State: From Roosevelt to Reagan*. Baltimore: Johns Hopkins University Press.

Berman, Sheri. 2006. *The Primacy of Politics: Social Democracy and the Making of Europe's Twentieth Century*. New York: Cambridge University Press.

———. 2009. "Unheralded Battle: Capitalism, the Left, Social Democracy, and Democratic Socialism." *Dissent* (winter).

Bernard, Paul, and Guillaume Boucher. 2007. "Institutional Competitiveness, Social Investment, and Welfare Regimes." *Regulation and Governance* 1, no. 3 (September), 213–29.

Bernstein, Eduard. 1898. "The Struggle for Social Democracy and the Social Revolution." *Neue Zeit*, 19 January.

Bertram, Eva C. 2007. "The Institutional Origins of 'Workfarist' Social Policy." *Studies in American Political Development* 21, no. 2 (October), 203–29.

Betz, Hans-Georg. 1993. "The New Politics of Resentment: Radical Right-Wing Populist Parties in Western Europe." *Comparative Politics* 25, no. 4, 413–28.

Biglaiser, Glen, David J. Jackson, and Jeffrey S. Peake. 2004. "Back on Track: Support for Presidential Trade Authority in the House of Representatives." *American Politics Research* 32, no. 6 (November), 679–97.

Binder, Sarah A. 2003. *Stalemate: Causes and Consequences of Legislative Gridlock*. Washington: Brookings Institution.

Birchall, Ana. 2007. "Education: Cornerstone of the Romanian Social Model," http://www.policy-network.net/publications/articles.aspx?id=1080.

Blair, Tony. 1999. "Doctrine of the International Community." London: Prime Minister's Office, 24 April, http://www.number10.gov.uk/Page1297.

———. 2002. "PM Speech on Welfare Reform," 10 June.

Blair, Tony, and Gerhard Schröder. 1999. *The Third Way / Die neue Mitte*. London: Labour Party, www.pmo.gov.uk/output/Page1716.asp.

Blau, Francine, and Lawrence Kahn. 2005. "Do Cognitive Test Scores Explain Higher U.S. Wage Inequality?" *Review of Economics and Statistics* 87, no. 1 (February), 184–93.

Blonigen, Bruce. 2008. "New Evidence on the Formation of Trade Policy Preferences." NBER Working Paper 14627, December.

Blumenthal, Sidney. 1986. *The Rise of the Counterestablishment: From Conservative Ideology to Political Power*. New York: Times Books.

Blyth, Mark. 2002. *Great Transformations: Economic Ideas and Institutional Change in
the Twentieth Century*. New York: Cambridge University Press.

Boix, Carles. 1998. *Political Parties, Growth and Equality: Conservative and Social
Democratic Economic Strategies in the World Economy*. New York: Cambridge University Press.

———. 2001. "European Monetary Union and the Spanish Left." *Social Democracy
and Monetary Union*, ed. Ton Notermans. New York: Berghahn.

———. 2006. "Between Redistribution and Trade: The Political Economy of Protectionism and Domestic Compensation." *Globalization and Egalitarian Redistribution*,
ed. Pranab Bardhan, Samuel Bowles, and Michael Wallerstein, 192–216. Princeton:
Princeton University Press.

Bond, Jon R., and Richard Fleisher, eds. 2000. *Polarized Politics: Congress and the
President in a Partisan Era*. Washington: CQ Press.

Bonoli, Giuliano. 2004. "Social Democratic Party Policies in Europe, towards a Third
Way?" *Social Democratic Party Policies in Contemporary Europe*, ed. Giuliano
Bonoli and Martin Powell, 197–213. London: Routledge.

———. 2005. "The Politics of the New Social Policies: Providing Coverage against
New Social Risks in Mature Welfare States." *Policy and Politics* 33, no. 3 (July),
431–49.

———. 2006. "New Social Risks and the Politics of Post-Industrial Social Policies."
The Politics of Post-Industrial Welfare Society, ed. Klaus Armingeon and Giuliano
Bonoli, 3–26. New York: Routledge.

Bonoli, Giuliano, and Martin Powell, eds. 2004. *Social Democratic Party Policies in
Contemporary Europe*. London: Routledge.

Brady, David, Jason Beckfield, and Wei Zhao. 2007. "The Consequences of Economic
Globalization for Affluent Democracies." *Annual Review of Sociology* 33, 313–34.

Braunthal, Gerard. 1994. *The German Social Democrats since 1969*. Boulder: Westview.

Braunthal, Julius. 1967. *History of the International, 1864–1914*. New York: Praeger.

Brooks, Clem, and Jeff Manza. 2007. *Why Welfare States Persist: The Importance of
Public Opinion in Democracies*. Chicago: University of Chicago Press.

Buchs, Milena. 2007. *New Governance in European Social Policy: The Open Method of
Co-ordination*. Basingstoke: Palgrave.

———. 2008. "How Legitimate Is the Open Method of Coordination?" *Journal of
Common Market Studies* 46, no. 4 (September), 765–86.

Buras, Piotr. 2005. "Polish Social Democracy, Policy Transfer and Programmatic
Change." *Journal of Communist Studies and Transition Politics* 21, no. 1 (March),
84–104.

Burgoon, Brian. 2009. "Globalization and Backlash: Polanyi's Revenge?" *Review of
International Political Economy* 16, no. 2, 145–77.

Burgoon, Brian, and Michael J. Hiscox. 2000. "Trade Openness and Political Compensation: Labor Demands for Adjustment Assistance." Paper presented at the annual meeting of the American Political Science Association, Washington.

———. 2008. "Who's Afraid of Trade Adjustment Assistance? Individual Attitudes to Trade-Targeted Adjustment Assistance in the United States." Paper presented at the annual meeting of the American Political Science Association, Boston.

Burk, Kathleen, and Alec Cairncross. 1982. *"Goodbye, Great Britain": The 1976 IMF Crisis.* New Haven: Yale University Press.

Busemeyer, Marius. 2009. "From Myth to Reality: Globalization and Public Spending in OECD Countries Revisited." *European Journal of Political Research* 48, no. 4 (June), 455–82.

Callaghan, John. 2000. "The Rise and Fall of the Alternative Economic Strategy: From the Internationalisation of Capital to 'Globalisation.'" *Contemporary British History* 14, no. 3 (autumn), 105–30.

———. 2002. "Social Democracy and Globalisation: The Limits of Social Democracy in Historical Perspective." *British Journal of Politics and International Relations* 4, no. 3 (October), 429–51.

Callaghan, John, and Sean Tunney. 2001. "The End of Social Democracy?" *Politics* 21, no. 1 (February), 63–72.

Calmfors, Lars, Anders Forslund, and Maria Hemström. 2002. "Does Active Labour Market Policy Work? Lessons from the Swedish Experiences." CESifo Working Paper 675, no. 4.

Cameron, David R., and Soo Yeon Kim. 2006. "Trade, Political Institutions, and the Size of Government." *Globalization and Self-Determination: Is the Nation-State under Siege?*, ed. David R. Cameron, Gustav Ranis, and Annalisa Zinn, 15–50. London: Routledge.

Cameron, Maxwell A., and Brian W. Tomlin. 2000. *The Making of NAFTA: How the Deal Was Done.* Ithaca: Cornell University Press.

Campbell, Andrea Louise. 2003. *How Policies Make Citizens: Senior Political Activism and the American Welfare State.* Princeton: Princeton University Press.

Campbell, Andrea Louise, and Kimberley J. Morgan. 2005. "Financing the Welfare State: Elite Politics and the Decline of the Social Insurance Model in America." *Studies in American Political Development* 19, no. 2 (October), 173–95.

Campbell, Joan, ed. 1992. *European Labor Unions.* New York: Greenwood.

Campbell, John L., and Ove K. Pedersen. 2007. "Institutional Competitiveness in the Global Economy: Denmark, the United States, and the Varieties of Capitalism." *Regulation and Governance* 1, no. 3 (September), 230–46.

Cantril, Albert H., and Susan Davis Cantril. 1999. *Reading Mixed Signals: Ambivalence in American Public Opinion about Government.* Washington: Woodrow Wilson Center Press.

Carr, William. 1987. "German Social Democracy since 1945." *Bernstein to Brandt: A Short History of German Social Democracy*, ed. Roger Fletcher. London: Edward Arnold.

Castells, Manuel. 2000. *The Rise of the Network Society*, 2nd edn. Malden, Mass.: Blackwell.

Castles, Francis. 1978. *The Social Democratic Image of Society*. London: Routledge.
————. 2004. *The Future of the Welfare State: Crisis Myths and Crisis Realities*. Oxford: Oxford University Press.
————. 2005. "Social Expenditures in the 1990s: Data and Determinants." *Policy and Politics* 33, no. 3 (July), 411–30.
Castles, Stephen. 1986. "The Guest-Worker in Western Europe: An Obituary." *International Migration Review* 20, no. 4 (winter), 761–78 [special issue: Temporary Worker Programs: Mechanisms, Conditions, Consequences].
Cautrès, Bruno, and Anthony Heath. 1996. "Déclin du 'vote de classe?' une analyse comparative en France et en Grande-Bretagne." *Revue internationale de politique comparée* 3, no. 3, 566–68.
CERC (Conseil Emploi Revenus Cohésion Sociale). 2002. *La longue route vers l'Euro*. Paris: Documentation Française.
Cerny, Philip G. 2000. "Political Globalization and the Competition State." *Political Economy and the Changing Global Order*, 2nd edn, ed. Richard Stubbs and Geoffrey R. D. Underhill, 300–309. New York: Oxford University Press.
Chaloff, Jonathan. 2005. "Italy." *Immigration as a Labor Market Strategy: European and North American Perspectives*, ed. Jan Niessen and Yongmi Schiebel. Brussels: Migration Policy Group.
Clark, Colin. 1940. *Conditions of Economic Progress*. London: Macmillan.
Clasen, Jochen, and Daniel Clegg. 2006. "New Labour Market Risks and the Revision of Unemployment Protection Systems in Europe." *The Politics of Post-Industrial Welfare Society*, ed. Klaus Armingeon and Giuliano Bonoli, 192–210. New York: Routledge.
Clayton, Richard, and Jonas Pontusson. 1998. "Welfare-State Retrenchment Revisited: Entitlement Cuts, Public Sector Restructuring, and Inegalitarian Trends in Advanced Capitalist Societies." *World Politics* 51, no. 1 (October), 67–98.
Coalition Agreement. 2005. www.spd.de/show/1683399/Koalitionsvertrag2005_engl .pdf.
Coates, David, and Joel Krieger. 2004. *Blair's War*. Cambridge: Polity.
Cohen, G. A. 1999. *If You're an Egalitarian, How Come You're So Rich?* Cambridge: Harvard University Press.
Colarizi, Simona. 1996. "Socialist Constraints following the War." *Italian Socialism*, ed. Spencer Di Scala. Amherst: University of Massachusetts Press.
Collins, Robert M. 2000. *More: The Politics of Economic Growth in Postwar America*. New York: Oxford University Press.
Colton, Joel. 1966. *Léon Blum*. New York: Alfred A. Knopf.
Congressional Budget Office. 2007. *Utilization of Tax Incentives for Retirement Saving: Update to 2003*. Washington: Congressional Budget Office.
Conley, Richard S. 1999. "Derailing Presidential Fast-Track Authority: The Impact of Constituency Pressures and Political Ideology on Trade Policy in Congress." *Political Research Quarterly* 52, no. 4 (December), 785–99.
Constant, Amelie, and Klaus F. Zimmermann. 2005. "Immigrant Performance and Selective Immigration Policy: A European Perspective." *National Institute Economic Review* 194, no. 1 (October), 94–105.

Coriat, Benjamin, Pascal Petit, and Genevieve Schmeder, eds. 2006. *The Hardship of Nations: Exploring the Paths of Modern Capitalism*. Northampton, Mass.: Edward Elgar.

Cronin, James. 2004. *New Labour's Pasts: The Labour Party and Its Discontents*. London: Pearson Longman.

———. 2006. "New Labour's Escape from Class Politics." *Journal of the Historical Society* 6, no. 1 (March), 47–68.

———. 2009. "Converging at the Center in Britain." *Current History* 108, no. 716 (March), 110–16.

Crosland, C. A. R. 1967. *The Future of Socialism*. London: Fletcher and Son.

Crouch, Colin. 2005. *Capitalist Diversity and Change: Recombinant Governance and Institutional Entrepreneurs*. New York: Oxford University Press.

CSJ (Commission on Social Justice). 1994. *Social Justice: Strategies for National Renewal: Report of the Commission on Social Justice*. London: Vintage.

Cunningham, Peter, and James Kirby. 2004. "Children's Health Coverage: A Quarter-Century of Change." *Health Affairs* 23, no. 5 (September–October), 27–38.

Cuperus, René. 2007. "Populism against Globalisation: A New European Revolt." *The Challenge of Immigration and Social Integration in Western Societies*. Pamphlet of Policy Network and the Friedrich Ebert Stiftung, www.policy-network .net.

Cuperus, René, Karl Duffek, and Johannes Kandel. 2001. "European Social Democracy: A Story of Multiple Third Ways: An Introduction." *Multiple Third Ways*. Amsterdam: Wardi Beckman.

Cuperus, René, and Johannes Kandel. 1998. "The Magical Return of Social Democracy." *Social Democracy: Transformation in Progress*, ed. R. Cuperus and J. Kandel. Amsterdam: Wardi Beckman / Friedrich Ebert Stiftung.

Curtice, John. 2007. "Elections and Public Opinion." *Blair's Britain, 1997–2007*, ed. Anthony Seldon, 35–53. Cambridge: Cambridge University Press.

Cuttitta, Paolo. 2008. "Yearly Quotas and Country-Reserved Shares in Italian Immigration Policy." *Migration Letters* 5, no. 1 (April), 41–51.

Dadush, Uri, et al. 2010. *Paradigm Lost: The Euro in Crisis*. Washington: Carnegie Endowment for International Peace.

Daguerre, Anne. 2006. "Childcare Policies in Diverse European Welfare States: Switzerland, Sweden, France and Britain." *The Politics of Post-industrial Welfare Society*, ed. Klaus Armingeon and Giuliano Bonoli, 211–26. New York: Routledge.

Dahrendorf, Ralf. 1990. *Reflections on the Revolution in Europe*. London: Chatto.

Daly, Mary, and Martin Seeleib-Kaiser. 2008. "Emerging Family Policy Models in Germany and the UK." Paper presented at the Conference of Europeanists, Chicago, March.

Dătculescu, Petru. 1994. "Cum a votat România: O analiza a alegerilor generale si prezidentiale de la 27 Septembrie 1992." *Revista de Cercetari Sociale* 1, 43–61.

Dauderstädt, Michael, and Andre W. M. Gerrits. 2000. "Democratisation after Communism: Progress, Problems, Promotion." *Internationale Politik und Gesellschaft Online / International Politics and Society*, no. 4, 361–76, http://www.fes.de/ipg/ipg4_2000/daudiopti2.htm.

Dauderstädt, Michael, Andre W. M. Gerrits, and György G. Markus. 1999. *How Social Democrats, after the Collapse of Communism, Face the Task of Constructing Capitalism.* Bonn: Friedrich Ebert Stiftung.

Daune-Richard, Anne-Marie, and Rianne Mahon. 2001. "Sweden: Models in Crisis." *Who Cares? Women's Work, Childcare, and Welfare State Redesign,* ed. Jane Jenson and Mariette Sineau, 146–76. Toronto: University of Toronto Press.

David, Roman. 2003. "Lustration Laws in Action: The Motives and Evaluation of Lustration Policies in the Czech Republic and Poland." *Law and Social Inquiry* 28, no. 2 (April), 387–439.

Davidson, Carl, Steven J. Matusz, and Douglas R. Nelson. 2007. "Can Compensation Save Free Trade?" *Journal of International Economics* 71, no. 1 (March), 167–86.

Day, Jennifer Cheeseman, and Kurt J. Bauman. 2000. "Have We Reached the Top? Educational Attainment Projections of the U.S. Population." U.S. Bureau of the Census, Population Division, Working Paper 43.

De Grand, Alexander. 1989. *The Italian Left in the Twentieth Century.* Indianapolis: Indiana University Press.

de la Porte, Caroline. 2008. "The European Level Development and National Level Influence of the Open Method of Coordination: The Cases of Employment and Social Inclusion." PhD diss., European University Institute, Florence.

Delors, Jacques. 2004. *Mémoires.* Paris: Plon.

Déloye, Yves, and Michael Bruter, eds. 2007. *Encyclopedia of European Elections.* London: Palgrave Macmillan.

Delwit, Pascal. 2005. "Electoral Developments in European Social Democracy." *Social Democracy in Europe,* ed. Pascal Delwit. Brussels: Éditions de l'Université Libre de Bruxelles.

———. 2007. "Les partis socialistes d'Europe du sud: Des organisations performantes?" *Pôle sud* 27, 21–43.

DeNavas-Walt, Carmen, Bernadette D. Proctor, and Jessica Smith. 2007. *Income, Poverty, and Health Insurance Coverage in the United States: 2006.* Washington: U.S. Government Printing Office.

———. 2009. *Income, Poverty, and Health Insurance Coverage in the United States: 2008.* Washington: U.S. Government Printing Office.

Derthick, Martha. 1979. *Policymaking for Social Security.* Washington: Brookings Institution.

Destler, I. M. 2005. *American Trade Politics.* 4th edn. Washington: Institute for International Economics.

———. 2007. "American Trade Politics in 2007: Building Bipartisan Compromise." Washington: Peterson Institute for International Economics. Policy Brief PB07-5, May.

De Waele, Jean-Michel. 1996. "Les partis sociaux démocrates à l'est: Sociale-démocratie ou 'nouvelle gauche.'" *La gauche en Europe depuis 1945: Invariants et mutations du socialisme européen,* ed. Marc Lazar, 679–95. Paris: Presses Universitaires de France.

———. 1998. *L'émergence des partis politiques en Europe centrale.* Brussels: Université de Bruxelles.

———. 2002. *Partis politiques et démocratie en Europe centrale et orientale.* Brussels: Éditions de l'Université de Bruxelles. Collection Sociologie Politique.

Dinan, Desmond. 2004. *Europe Recast.* Boulder: Lynne Rienner.

Di Scala, Spencer. 1996. *Italian Socialism.* Amherst: University of Massachusetts Press.

———. 1998. *Italy from Revolution to Republic.* Boulder: Westview.

Dobrowolsky, Alexandra, and Jane Jenson. 2005. "Social Investment Perspectives and Practices: A Decade in British Politics." *Social Policy Review 17: Analysis and Debate in Social Policy, 2005,* ed. Martin Powell, Linda Bauld, and Karen Clarke, 203–30. Bristol: Policy Press.

Dolan, Chris, John Frendreis, and Raymond Tatalovich. 2008. *The Presidency and Economic Policy.* Lanham, Md.: Rowman and Littlefield.

Dølvik, Jon-Erik. 2008. "The Negotiated Nordic Labour Markets: From Bust to Boom." Paper presented at the conference "The Nordic Models," Minda de Gunzburg Center for European Studies, Harvard University, 9–10 May.

Duncan, Fraser. 2006. "A Decade of Christian Democratic Decline: The Dilemmas of the CDU, OVP and CDA in the 1990s." *Government and Opposition* 45, no. 4 (October), 469–90.

Dunham, Richard S. 2006. "Who's Afraid of Charlie Rangel?" *Business Week,* 13 November, 37.

Dyson, Kenneth, and Keith Featherstone. 1999. *The Road to Maastricht.* Oxford: Oxford University Press.

Eckes, Alfred E., Jr. 1995. *Opening America's Market: U.S. Foreign Trade Policy since 1776.* Chapel Hill: University of North Carolina Press.

Eichengreen, Barry. 2007. *The European Economy since 1945: Coordinated Capitalism and Beyond.* Princeton: Princeton University Press.

Einhorn, Eric, and John Logue. 2010. "Can Welfare States Be Sustained in a Global Economy? Lessons from Scandinavia." *Political Science Quarterly* 125, no. 1 (spring), 1–29.

Eiro Online. 2006. "Spain: Role of Immigrant Women in the Domestic Services Sector." 27 June.

———. 2007. "Employment and Working Conditions of Migrant Workers: Italy." 31 May.

Eley, Geoff. 2002. *Forging Democracy: The History of the Left in Europe, 1850–2000.* New York: Oxford University Press.

Engels, Friedrich. 1962. *Anti-Dühring.* Moscow: International Publishers.

Esping-Andersen, Gøsta. 1985. *Politics against Markets: The Social Democratic Road to Power.* Princeton: Princeton University Press.

———. 1990. *The Three Worlds of Welfare Capitalism.* Cambridge: Polity.

Esping-Andersen, Gøsta, Duncan Gallie, Anton Hemerijk, and John Myers. 2002. *Why We Need a New Welfare State.* New York: Oxford University Press.

Estevez-Abe, Margarita, Torben Iversen, and David Soskice. 2001. "Social Protection and the Formation of Skills." *Varieties of Capitalism,* ed. Peter Hall and David Soskice, 145–83. Oxford: Oxford University Press.

Ette, Andreas. 2003. "Germany's Immigration Policy, 2000–2002: Understanding

Policy Change with a Political Process Approach." Bremen: Center on Migration, Citizenship and Development (COMCAD). Working Paper 3/2003.

European Commission. 2008. *Communication from the Commission, the Social Agenda and European Commission: A Consultation Paper from the Bureau of European Policy Advisers, Europe's Social Reality.* Brussels: Comm. 33 Final.

Fairclough, Norman. 2000. *New Labour, New Language.* London. Routledge.

Favier, Pierre, and Michel Martin-Roland. 1990. *La décennie Mitterrand 1: les ruptures.* Paris: Le Seuil.

Favretto, Ilaria. 2006. "Resisting the 'Pervasiveness of Capitalist Ideals'? The Italian Left and the Challenge of Affluent Society since 1945." *Transitions in Social Democracy: Cultural and Ideological Problems of the Golden Age,* ed. J. Callaghan and I. Favretto. Manchester: Manchester University Press.

Fay, Stephen, and Hugo Young. 1978. *The Day the £ Nearly Died.* London: Sunday Times Publications.

Featherstone, Kevin. 1988. *Socialist Parties and European Integration: A Comparative History.* New York: St. Martin's.

Feinstein, Charles. 1999. "Structural Change in the Developed Countries during the Twentieth Century." *Oxford Review of Economic Policy* 15, no. 4 (winter), 35–55.

Fellowes, Matthew C., and Patrick J. Wolf. 2004. "Funding Mechanisms and Policy Instruments: How Business Campaign Contributions Influence Congressional Votes." *Political Research Quarterly* 57, no. 2 (June), 315–24.

Ferrera, Maurizio, Anton Hemerijk, and Martin Rhodes, eds. 2006. *The Future of European Welfare States: Recasting Welfare for a New Century.* New York: Oxford University Press.

Fitzmaurice, John. 1999. "The Luxembourg Socialist Workers' Party." *Social Democratic Parties in the European Union,* ed. R. Ladrech and P. Marlière. Hampshire: Macmillan.

Fletcher, Roger, ed. 1987. *Bernstein to Brandt: A Short History of German Social Democracy.* London: Edward Arnold.

Fligstein, Neil. 2008. *European Clash.* Oxford: Oxford University Press.

Fondation Robert Schuman. 2008. *L'opinion européenne en 2008.* Paris: Lignes et Repères.

Forgette, Richard G. 2004. *Congress, Parties, and Puzzles.* New York: Peter Lang.

Fourastié, Jean. 1979. *Trente glorieuses.* Paris: Fayard.

Francia, Peter. 2005. "Protecting America's Workers in Hostile Territory: Unions and the Republican Congress." *The Interest Group Connection: Electioneering, Lobbying, and Policymaking in Washington,* 2nd edn, ed. Paul S. Herrnson, Ronald G. Shaiko, and Clyde Wilcox, 212–28. Washington: CQ Press.

Frank, Robert H. 2008. "Why Wait to Repeal Tax Cuts for the Rich?" *New York Times,* 7 December.

Franklin, Mark. 2006. "European Elections and the European Voter." *European Union: Power and Policy-Making,* 3rd edn, ed. Jeremy Richardson. London: Routledge.

Freedman, Lawrence. 2005. "The Age of Liberal Wars." *Review of International Studies* 31, 93–107.

Freeman, Richard B. 2003. "What Do Unions Do. . . . to Voting?" NBER Working Paper 9992.

Freeman, Richard, Birgitta Swedenborg, and Robert Topel, eds. 2006. *NBER rapporten II: Att reformera välfärdsstaten*. Stockholm: SNS.

Frey, William H. 2008. "Race, Immigration and America's Changing Electorate." Paper presented at Brookings–American Enterprise Institute conference "The Future of Red, Blue and Purple America," Washington, 28 February.

———. 2009. "How Did Race Affect the 2008 Presidential Election?" University of Michigan, Population Studies Research Center, September.

Friedman, Benjamin. 2004. *The Moral Consequences of Economic Growth*. New York: Vintage.

Friedman, Thomas. 1999. *The Lexus and the Olive Tree: Understanding Globalization*. New York: Farrar, Straus and Giroux.

Gaffney, John, ed. 1996. *Political Parties and The European Union*. London: Routledge.

Gallagher, Tom. 2003. "The Balkans since 1989: The Winding Retreat from National Communism." *Developments in Central and East European Politics*, ed. Stephen White, Judy Batt, and Paul G. Lewis, 74–91. New York: Palgrave Macmillan.

Galston, William, and Elaine Kamarck. 1989. "The Politics of Evasion." Washington: Progressive Policy Institute.

Ganev, Venelin I. 2001. "Postcommunism as a Historical Episode of a State-Building: A Reversed Tillyan Perspective." Paper presented at the 12th International Conference of Europeanists, Chicago. Working Paper 289, http://kellogg.nd.edu/publications/workingpapers/WPS/289.pdf.

———. 2005. "Where Has Marxism Gone? Gauging the Impact of Alternative Ideas in Transition Bulgaria." *East European Politics and Societies* 19, no. 3 (summer), 443–62.

Garrett, Geoffrey. 1998. *Partisan Politics in the Global Economy*. Cambridge: Cambridge University Press.

Gerring, John. 1998. *Party Ideologies in America, 1828–1996*. New York: Cambridge University Press.

Giddens, Anthony. 1998. *The Third Way: The Renewal of Social Democracy*. Oxford: Friedrich Ebert Stiftung.

———. 2000. *The Third Way and Its Critics*. Cambridge: Polity.

———. 2007. *Europe in the Global Age*. Cambridge: Polity.

———, ed. 2001. *The Global Third Way Debate*. Cambridge: Polity.

Giddens, Anthony, Patrick Diamond, and Roger Liddle, eds. 2006. *Global Europe, Social Europe*. Oxford: Polity.

Gilens, Martin. 1999. *Why Americans Hate Welfare: Race, Media, and the Politics of Antipoverty Policy*. Chicago: University of Chicago Press.

Gill, Stephen. 1995. "Globalisation, Market Civilisation and Disciplinary Neoliberalism." *Millennium* 24, no. 3, 399–423.

Glatzer, Miguel, and Dietrich Rueschemeyer, eds. 2005. *Globalization and the Future of the Welfare State*. Pittsburgh: University of Pittsburgh Press.

Glyn, Andrew, ed. 2001. *Social Democracy in Neoliberal Times: The Left and Economic Policy since 1980*. New York: Oxford University Press.

———. 2006. *Capitalism Unleashed: Finance, Globalization, and Welfare.* Oxford: Oxford University Press.

Gombert, Sylvain. 2008. "Basically Unaffected? Revising the Domestic Party Politics of European Integration through Political Sociology." Unpublished paper for ECPR, Rennes.

Gorski, Philip, and Andrei Markovits. 1993. *The German Left: Red, Green, and Beyond.* New York: Oxford University Press.

Gottfried, Heidi, and Jacqueline O'Reilly. 2002. "Reregulating Breadwinner Models in Socially Conservative Systems: Comparing Germany and Japan." *Social Politics: International Studies in Gender, State and Society* 9, no. 1 (spring), 29–59.

Gouldner, Alvin. 1980. *The Two Marxisms.* New York: Seabury.

Graetz, Michael J., and Jerry L. Mashaw. 1999. *True Security: Rethinking American Social Insurance.* New Haven: Yale University Press.

Graham, Bruce. 1994. *Choice and Democratic Order: The French Socialist Party, 1937–1950.* New York: Cambridge University Press.

Graham, Carol. 1998. *Private Markets for Public Goods: Raising the Stakes in Economic Reform.* Washington: Brookings Institution.

Graham, Otis L., Jr. 1992. *Losing Time: The Industrial Policy Debate.* Cambridge: Harvard University Press.

Grayson, George W. 1995. *The North American Free Trade Agreement: Regional Community and the New World Order.* Lanham, Md.: University Press of North America.

Greenberg Quinlan Rosner Research. 2007. "A New America: Unmarrieds Drive Political and Social Change."

Green-Pedersen, Christoffer, Kees van Kersbergen, and Anton Hemerijk. 2001. "Neoliberalism, the 'Third Way' or What? Recent Social Democratic Welfare Policies in Denmark and the Netherlands." *Journal of European Public Policy* 8, no. 2 (April), 307–25.

Grunberg, Gérard, and Gerassimos Moschonas. 2005. "Le vote socialiste: Les bénéfices du vote-sanction dans une élection de 'second' ordre." *Le vote européen, 2004–2005: De l'élargissement au référendum français,* ed. P. Perrineau. Paris: Presses de Sciences Po.

Grzymala-Busse, Anna Maria. 2002. *Redeeming the Communist Past: The Regeneration of Communist Parties in East Central Europe.* Cambridge: Cambridge University Press.

———. 2003. "Political Competition and the Politicization of the State in East Central Europe." *Comparative Political Studies* 36, no. 10 (December), 1123–47.

Grzymala-Busse, Anna Maria, and Pauline Jones Loung. 2002. "Reconceptualizing the State: Lessons from Postcommunism." *Politics and Society* 30, no. 4 (December), 529–54.

Hacker, Jacob S. 2002. *The Divided Welfare State: The Battle over Public and Private Social Benefits in the United States.* New York: Cambridge University Press.

———. 2004. "Privatizing Risk without Privatizing the Welfare State: The Hidden Politics of Social Policy Retrenchment in the United States." *American Political Science Review* 98, no. 2 (May), 243–60.

———. 2005. "Bringing the Welfare State Back In: The Promises (and Perils) of the

New Social Welfare History." *New Directions in Policy History*, ed. Julian Zelizer. University Park: Pennsylvania State University Press.

Hale, Jon F. 1995. "The Making of the New Democrats." *Political Science Quarterly* 110, no. 2, 207–32.

Hall, Peter. 1987. "The Evolution of Economic Policy under Mitterrand." *The Mitterrand Experiment*, ed. George Ross, Stanley Hoffmann, and Sylvia Malzacher. Cambridge: Polity.

———, ed. 1989. *The Political Power of Economic Ideas: Keynesianism across Nations*. Princeton: Princeton University Press.

Hall, Peter, and David Soskice. 2001. "An Introduction to Varieties of Capitalism." *Varieties of Capitalism: The Institutional Foundations of Comparative Advantage*, 1–70. Oxford: Oxford University Press.

———, eds. 2001. Varieties of Capitalism: The Institutional Foundations of Comparative Advantage. Oxford: Oxford University Press.

Halleröd, Björn. 2007. *Sweden: Tackling Child Poverty and Promoting the Social Inclusion of Children*. Brussels: DG Employment, Social Affairs and Equal Opportunities, www.peer-review-social-inclusion.net.

Halperin, William. 1946. "Léon Blum and Contemporary French Socialism." *Journal of Modern History* 18, no. 3 (September), 241–50.

Hammar, Tomas. 1999. "Closing the Doors of the Swedish Welfare State." *Mechanisms of Immigration Control: A Comparative Analysis of European Regulation Policies*, ed. Grete Brochmann and Tomas Hammar. Oxford: Berg.

Handl, Vladimir. 2003. "'Hard Left' and 'Soft Left' Antagonism? The Transformation of the Communist Party of Bohemia and Moravia and Its Relations to the Social Democrats." Paper presented at the 4th European Conference of the Rosa Luxemburg Foundation, Warsaw.

———. 2005. "Choosing between China and Europe? Virtual Inspiration and Policy Transfer in the Programmatic Development of the Czech Communist Party." *Journal of Communist Studies and Transition Politics* 21, no. 1 (March), 123–41.

Handl, Vladimir, and Vladimir Leška. 2005. "Between Emulation and Adjustment: External Influences on Programmatic Change in the Slovak SDL." *Journal of Communist Studies and Transition Politics* 21, no. 1 (March), 105–22.

Hansen, Randall. 1999. "The Politics of Citizenship in 1940s Britain: The British Nationality Act." *20th Century British History* 10, no. 1, 67–95.

Hanson, Brian T. 1998. "What Happened to Fortress Europe? External Trade Policy in the European Union." *International Organization* 52, no. 1 (January), 55–85.

Hansson, Per Albin. 1982 [1928]. "Speech in the Reichstag." *Från fram till folkhemmet: Per Albin Hansson som tidningsman och talare*, ed. Anna Lisa Berkling. Stockholm: Metodica.

Harmel, Robert, and Kenneth Janda. 1994. "An Integrated Theory of Party Goals and Party Change." *Journal of Theoretical Politics* 6, no. 3 (July), 259–87.

Hasnat, Baban, and Charles Callahan III. 2002. "A Political Economic Analysis of Congressional Voting on Permanent Normal Trade Relations of China." *Applied Economics Letters* 9, no. 7 (June), 465–68.

Haughton, Tim. 2005. *Constraints and Opportunities of Leadership in Post-communist Europe*. Burlington, Vt.: Ashgate.

Haupt, Andrea B. 2010. "Parties' Responses to Economic Globalization." *Party Politics* 16, no. 1 (January), 5–27.

Häusermann, Silja. 2010. *The Politics of Welfare State Reform in Continental Europe*. New York: Cambridge University Press.

Hay, Colin. 1997. "Anticipating Accommodations, Accommodating Anticipations: The Appeasement of Capital in the 'Modernization' of the British Labour Party, 1987–1992." *Politics and Society* 25, no. 2 (June), 234–56.

Hays, Jude C. 2009. *Globalization, Domestic Institutions, and the New Politics of Embedded Liberalism*. New York: Oxford University Press.

Hays, Jude C., Sean D. Ehrlich, and Clinton Peinhardt. 2005. "Government Spending and Public Support for Trade in the OECD: An Empirical Test of the Embedded Liberalism Thesis." *International Organization* 59, no. 2 (April), 473–94.

Heisenberg, Dorothee. 1999. *The Mark of the Bundesbank: Germany's Role in European Monetary Cooperation*. Boulder: Lynne Rienner.

Hellman, Stephen. 2008. "Italy." *European Politics in Transition*, 6th edn, ed. Mark Kesselman and Joel Krieger. Boston: Houghton Mifflin.

Henjak, Andrija. 2003. "New Social Divisions and Party System Developments." Paper presented at the ECPR Joint Sessions Workshop "Cleavage Development: Causes and Consequences," Edinburgh.

Henrekson, Magnus, and Ulf Jakobsson. 2005. "The Swedish Model of Corporate Ownership and Control in Transition." *Who Will Own Europe?*, ed. Harry Huizinga and Lars Jonung. Cambridge: Cambridge University Press.

Henry J. Kaiser Family Foundation. 2008. "The Medicare Prescription Drug Benefit," http://www.kff.org/medicare/upload/7044_08.pdf.

———. 2010. "Summary of New Health Reform Law," http://www.kff.org/health reform/upload/8061.pdf.

Hermet, Guy, and Lili Marcou. 1998. *Des partis comme les autres? Les anciens communistes en Europe de l'est*. Brussels: Éditions Complexes.

Herszenhorn, David M. 2010. "Fine-Tuning Led to Health Bill's $940 Billion Price Tag." *New York Times*, 18 March, § A, 16.

Hibbs, Douglas. 1993. *Solidarity or Egoism?* Aarhus: Aarhus University Press.

Hicks, Alexander. 2000. *Social Democracy and Welfare Capitalism: A Century of Income Security Politics*. Ithaca: Cornell University Press.

Hinnfors, Jonas. 2006. *Reinterpreting Social Democracy*. Manchester: Manchester University Press.

Hirschman, Alfred O. 1981. *Essays in Trespassing: Economics to Politics and Beyond*. Cambridge: Cambridge University Press.

Hix, Simon. 2007. *What's Wrong with the European Union and How to Fix It*. Cambridge: Polity.

H.M. Treasury. 1999. *Tackling Poverty and Extending Opportunity*. The Modernisation of Britain's Tax and Benefit System, vol. 4. London: H.M. Treasury.

———. 2001. *Tackling Child Poverty: Giving Every Child the Best Possible Start in Life: A Pre-Budget Document*. London: H.M. Treasury.

Hobsbawm, Eric. 1978. "The Forward March of Labour Halted?" *Marxism Today*, September.

———. 1981. "The Forward March of Labour Halted?" *The Forward March of Labour Halted*, ed. Martin Jacques and Francis Mulhern, 1–18. London: Verso.

Hollifield, James F. 1999. "Ideas, Institutions, and Civil Society: On the Limits of Immigration Control in France." *Beiträge* [Institut für Migrationsforschung und interkulturelle Studien] 10 (January), 57–90.

Home Office. 1998. "Fairer, Faster and Firmer: A Modern Approach to Immigration and Asylum." Presented to Parliament by the Secretary of State for the Home Department by Command of Her Majesty, July 1998. London: Stationery Office.

———. 2002. "Secure Borders, Safe Haven: Integration with Diversity in Modern Britain." Presented to Parliament by the Secretary of State for the Home Department by Command of Her Majesty, February 2002. London: Stationery Office.

Horn, Gerd-Rainer. 2007. *The Spirit of '68: Rebellion in Western Europe and North America, 1956–1976*. Oxford: Oxford University Press.

Hough, Dan. 2005. "Learning from the West: Policy Transfer and Programmatic Change in Communist Successor Parties of Eastern and Central Europe." *Journal of Communist Studies and Transition Politics* 21, no. 1 (March), 1–15.

Howard, Christopher. 1997. *The Hidden Welfare State: Tax Expenditures and Social Policy in the United States*. Princeton: Princeton University Press.

———. 2007a. *The Welfare State Nobody Knows: Debunking Myths about U.S. Social Policy*. Princeton: Princeton University Press.

———. 2007b. "The Haves and the Have-Lots." *Democracy: A Journal of Ideas* 4 (spring), 48–58.

Howell, Chris. 2004. "Is There a Third Way for Industrial Relations?" *British Journal of Industrial Relations* 42, no. 1 (March), 1–22.

Howell, Chris, and Rebecca Kolins Givan. 2009. "Rethinking Institutional Change in European Industrial Relations." *British Journal of Industrial Relations*, forthcoming.

Huber, Evelyne, and John D. Stephens. 2001. *Development and Crisis of the Welfare State: Parties and Policies in Global Markets*. Chicago: University of Chicago Press.

Hudson, John, and Stefan Kuhner. 2009. "Towards Productive Welfare: A Comparative Analysis of 23 OECD Countries." *Journal of European Social Policy* 19, no. 1 (February), 34–46.

Hughes, Kent H. 2005. *Building the Next American Century: The Past and Future of American Economic Competitiveness*. Baltimore: Johns Hopkins University Press.

Hughes, Stuart. 1977. *Consciousness and Society: The Reorientation of European Social Thought, 1890–1930*. New York: Vintage.

Human Rights Watch. 1994. "Germany." *Human Rights Watch World Report, 1994*. New Haven: Yale University Press.

Huo, Jingjing. 2009. *Third Way Reforms: Social Democracy after the Golden Age*. New York: Cambridge University Press.

Huster, Ernst-Ulrich, Benjamin Benz, and Jürgen Boeckh. 2007. *Germany: Tackling Child Poverty and Promoting the Social Inclusion of Children*. Brussels: DG Employment, Social Affairs and Equal Opportunities, www.peer-review-social-inclusion.net.

Hutton, Will. 1995. *The State We're In*. London: Cape.

———. 1997. *Stakeholding and Its Critics*. London: Institute of Economic Affairs.

Inglehart, Ronald. 1971. "The Silent Revolution." *American Political Science Review* 65, no. 4 (December), 991–1017.

———. 1977. *The Silent Revolution: Changing Values and Political Styles among Western Publics*. Princeton: Princeton University Press.

———. 1990. *Culture Shifts in Advanced Industrial Society*. Princeton: Princeton University Press.

Ishiyama, John T. 1998. "Strange Bedfellows: Explaining Political Cooperation between Communist Successor Parties and Nationalists in Eastern Europe." *Nations and Nationalism* 4, no. 1 (January), 61–85.

Iversen, Torben. 2005. *Capitalism, Democracy, and Welfare*. New York: Cambridge University Press.

———. 2009. "Dualism and Political Coalitions." Paper presented at the annual meeting of the American Political Science Association, Toronto, 3–6 September.

Iversen, Torben, and Thomas R. Cusack. 2000. "The Causes of Welfare State Expansion: Deindustrialization or Globalization?" *World Politics* 52, no. 3 (April), 313–49.

Iversen, Torben, and John Stephens. 2008. "Partisan Politics, the Welfare State and Three Worlds of Human Capital Formation." *Comparative Political Studies* 41, nos. 4–5 (April), 600–637.

Iversen, Torben, and Anne Wren. 1998. "Equality, Employment, and Budgetary Restraint." *World Politics* 50, no. 4 (July), 507–46.

Jacobs, Lawrence R., and Theda Skocpol, eds. 2005. *Inequality and American Democracy: What We Know and What We Need to Learn*. New York: Russell Sage Foundation.

Jacobs, Michael. 2002. "Reason to Believe." *Prospect*, October.

Jacques, Martin, and Francis Mulhern, eds. 1981. *The Forward March of Labour Halted*. London: Verso.

Jandl, Michael. 2008. "Methodologies for the Estimation of Stocks of Irregular Migrants." Paper presented at the joint UNECE/EURSTAT/UNFPA/MEDSTAT II Work Session on Migration Statistics, Geneva, 3–5 March.

Jensen, Carsten. 2011. "Conditional Contraction: Globalisation and Capitalist Systems." *European Journal of Political Research* 50, no. 2 (March), 168–89.

Jenson, Jane. 2004. *Canada's New Social Risks: Directions for a New Social Architecture*. Ottawa: CPRN. Report F43, www.cprn.org.

Jenson, Jane, and Stephane Jacobzone. 2000. *Care Allowances for the Frail Elderly and Their Impact on Women Care-Givers*. Paris: OECD. OECD Labour Market and Social Policy Occasional Papers 41.

Jenson, Jane, and Denis Saint-Martin. 2006. "Building Blocks for a New Social Architecture: The LEGO™ Paradigm of an Active Society." *Policy and Politics* 34, no. 3 (July), 429–51.

Jeong, Guyung-Ho. 2009. "Constituent Influence on International Trade Policy in the United States, 1987–2006." *International Studies Quarterly* 53, no. 2 (June), 519–40.

Jessop, Bob. 2002. *The Future of the Capitalist State*. Cambridge: Polity.

Judis, John B., and Ruy Teixeira. 2002. *The Emerging Democratic Majority*. New York: Scribner.

Kalyvas, Stathis. 2003. "Unsecular Politics and Religious Mobilization: Beyond Christian Democracy." *European Christian Democracy: Historical Legacies and Comparative Perspectives*, ed. Thomas Kselman and Joseph A. Buttigieg. Notre Dame: University of Notre Dame Press.

Kamerman, Sheila B., Michelle Neuman, Jane Waldfogel, and Jeanne Brooks-Gunn. 2003. *Social Policies, Family Types, and Child Outcomes in Selected OECD Countries*. Paris: OECD. OECD Social, Employment, and Migration Working Papers 6.

Kampfner, John. 2004. *Blair's Wars*. London: Free Press.

Kang, Shin-Goo, and G. Bingham Powell Jr. 2010. "Representation and Policy Responsiveness: The Median Voter, Election Rules, and Redistributive Welfare Spending." *Journal of Politics* 72, no. 4 (October), 1014–28.

Kapstein, Ethan. 1998. "Trade Liberalization and the Politics of Trade Adjustment Assistance." *International Labour Review* 137, no. 4, 501–16.

Karapin, Roger. 1999. "The Politics of Immigration Control in Britain and Germany." *Comparative Politics* 31, no. 4, 423–44.

Karasimeneov, Georgi. 1995. "Parliamentary Elections of 1994 and the Development of the Bulgarian Party System." *Party Politics* 1, no. 4 (October), 579–87.

———. 2004. *Party Systems in Post-communist Europe*. Bonn: Zentrum für Europäische Integrationsforschung, Rheinische Friedrich-Wilhelms Universität.

Karatani, Rieko, and Guy S. Goodwin-Gill. 2003. *Defining British Citizenship: Empire, Commonwealth and Modern Britain*. London: Routledge.

Katwala, Sunder. 2008. "Why Europe's Left Can Rise Again: The Policies the Center Left Promoted Remain Relevant, but They Are Now Failing as Politics." *Newsweek*, 22 September.

Katzenstein, Peter. 1985. *Small States in World Markets: Industrial Policy in Europe*. Ithaca: Cornell University Press.

Kautsky, Karl. 1910. *The Class Struggle*. Chicago: Charles Kerr.

Keech, William R., and Kyoungsan Pak. 1995. "Partisanship, Institutions, and Change in American Trade Politics." *Journal of Politics* 57, no. 4 (November), 1130–42.

Keman, Hans, Kees van Kersbergen, and Barbara Vis. 2006. "Political Parties and New Social Risks: The Double Backlash against Social Democracy and Christian Democracy." *The Politics of Post-Industrial Welfare Society*, ed. Klaus Armingeon and Giuliano Bonoli, 27–51. New York: Routledge.

Kenworthy, Lane. 2008. *Jobs with Equality*. Oxford: Oxford University Press.

Kesselman, Mark, and Joel Krieger, eds. 2008. *European Politics in Transition*. 6th edn. Boston: Houghton Mifflin.

King, Desmond, and David Rueda. 2008. "Cheap Labor." *Perspectives on Politics* 6, no. 2 (June), 279–97.

King, Desmond, and Mark Wickham-Jones. 1990. "Review Article: Social Democracy and Rational Workers." *British Journal of Political Science* 20, no. 3 (July), 387–413.

Kingdon, John W. 1999. *America the Unusual*. New York: St. Martin's / Worth.

Kitschelt, Herbert. 1992. "The Socialist Discourse and Party Strategy in West European Democracies." *The Crisis of Socialism in Europe*, ed. Christiane Lemke and Gary Marks. Durham: Duke University Press.

————. 1994. *The Transformation of European Social Democracy*. New York: Cambridge University Press.

————. 1999. "European Social Democracy between Political Economy and Electoral Competition." *Continuity and Change in Contemporary Capitalism*, ed. Herbert Kitschelt et al., 317–45. Cambridge: Cambridge University Press.

Kitschelt, Herbert, in collaboration with Anthony J. McGann. 1995. *The Radical Right in Western Europe: A Comparative Analysis*. Ann Arbor: University of Michigan Press.

Kitschelt, Herbert, and Philipp Rehm. 2005. "Work, Family, and Politics: Foundations of Electoral Partisan Alignments in Postindustrial Democracies." Paper presented at the annual meeting of the American Political Science Association, Washington.

Kjellberg, Anders. 1983. *Facklig organisering i tolv länder*. Lund: Arkiv.

————. 2009. "The Swedish Model of Industrial Relations." *Trade Unionism since 1945*, ed. Craig Phelan. Oxford: Peter Lang, forthcoming.

Kopstein, Jeffrey, and Sven Steinmo, eds. 2008. *Growing Apart? America and Europe in the Twenty-first Century*. Cambridge: Cambridge University Press.

Korpi, Walter, and Joakim Palme. 2003. "New Politics and Class Politics in the Context of Austerity and Globalization: Welfare State Regress in 18 Countries, 1975–95." *American Political Science Review* 97, no. 3 (August), 425–46.

Kotlikoff, Laurence J., and Scott Burns. 2004. *The Coming Generational Storm: What You Need to Know about America's Economic Future*. Cambridge: MIT Press.

Kriesi, Hanspeter, et al. 2008. *West European Politics in the Age of Globalization*. Cambridge: Cambridge University Press.

Krugman, Paul. 2005. *The Great Unraveling*. New York: W. W. Norton.

Kuttner, Robert. 2008a. "The Copenhagen Consensus." *Foreign Affairs* 87, no. 2 (March–April), 78–84.

————. 2008b. *Obama's Challenge: America's Economic Crisis and the Power of a Transformative Presidency*. White River Junction: Chelsea Green.

Kuzio, Taras. 2001. "Transition in Post-Communist States: Triple or Quadruple?" *Politics* 21, no. 3 (September), 168–77.

Labour Party Manifesto. 2005. http://image.guardian.co.uk/sys-files/Politics/documents/2005/04/13/labourmanifesto.pdf.

Laclau, Ernesto. 2005. *On Populist Reason*. London: Verso.

Ladrech, Robert. 2003. "The Party of European Socialists: Networking Europe's Social Democrats." *Journal of Policy History* 15, no. 1, 113–29.

Lamy, Pascal. 2004. *La démocratie-monde*. Paris: Autrement.

Laqueur, Walter. 1970. *Europe since Hitler*. New York: Penguin.

Lavelle, Ashley. 2008. *The Death of Social Democracy: Political Consequences in the 21st Century*. Aldershot: Ashgate.

LeBihan, Blanche, and Claude Martin. 2006. "A Comparative Case Study of Care Systems for Frail Elderly People: Germany, Spain, France, Italy, United Kingdom and Sweden." *Social Policy and Administration* 40, no. 1 (February), 26–46.

Lee, Frances E. 2009. *Beyond Ideology: Politics, Principles, and Partisanship in the U.S. Senate*. Chicago: University of Chicago Press.

Leibfried, Stephan. 2000. "Towards a European Welfare State?" *The Welfare State: A Reader*, ed. Christopher Pierson and Francis G. Castles. Cambridge: Polity.

Leonhardt, David. 2010. "Health Care Overhaul Becomes the Law of the Land: In the Process, Pushing Back at Inequality." *New York Times*, 24 March, § A, 1.

Letki, Natalia. 2002. "Lustration and Democratization in East-Central Europe." *Europe-Asia Studies* 54, no. 4 (June), 529–52.

Lewis, Paul G. 2004. "What Is the Right Way in East-Central Europe? Concluding Remarks." *Journal of Communist Studies and Transition Politics* 20, no. 3 (September), 133–48.

Lijphart, Arend. 1977. *Democracy in Plural Societies: A Comparative Exploration*. New Haven: Yale University Press.

———, ed. 1990. *Conflict and Coexistence in Belgium: Dynamics of a Culturally Divided Society*. Berkeley: University of California, Institute for International Studies.

Linz, Juan, and Alfred Stepan. 1996. *Problems of Democratic Transition and Consolidation: Southern Europe, South America, and Post-Communist Europe*. Baltimore: Johns Hopkins University Press.

Lipset, Seymour Martin, and Gary Marks. 2000. *It Didn't Happen Here: Why Socialism Failed in the United States*. New York: W. W. Norton.

Lipset, Seymour M., and Stein Rokkan. 1967. "Cleavage Structures, Party Systems, and Voter Alignments: An Introduction." *Party Systems and Voter Alignments: Cross-National Perspectives*. London: Free Press.

Little, Richard, and Mark Wickham-Jones, eds. 2000. *New Labour's Foreign Policy: A New Moral Crusade?* Manchester: Manchester University Press.

Lockhart, Charles. 2003. *The Roots of American Exceptionalism: Institutions, Culture and Policies*. New York: Palgrave Macmillan.

Ludlow, Peter. 1982. *The Making of the European Monetary System*. Oxford: Oxford University Press.

Lupu, Noam, and Jonas Pontusson. 2010. "The Structure of Inequality and the Politics of Redistribution." Paper presented at the annual meeting of the American Political Science Association, Washington, 2–5 September.

Luxembourg Income Study. n.d. "LIS Key Figures," http://www.lisproject.org/keyfigures.htm.

Lyon, Dawn, and Miriam Glucksman. 2008. "Comparative Configurations of Care Work across Europe." *Sociology* 42, no. 1 (February), 101–18.

Maas, Willem. 2006. "The Politics of Immigration, Employment and Amnesty in Spain." Paper presented at the annual meeting of the International Studies Association, San Diego, 22 March.

MacArthur, John R. 2000. *The Selling of "Free Trade": NAFTA, Washington, and the Subversion of American Democracy*. New York: Hill and Wang.

Madsen, Per Kongshøj. 2002. "The Danish Model of Flexicurity." *Labour Market and Social Reforms in International Perspective*, ed. Giuliano Bonoli and Hedva Sarfati. Burlington, Vt.: Ashgate.

Magone, José. 2007. "Conquering Electoral Hegemony: A New Beginning for Portuguese Socialism?" *Pôle Sud* 27, 121–43.

Mahon, Rianne. 2006. "The OECD and the Work/Family Reconciliation Agenda:

Competing Frames." *Children, Changing Families and Welfare States*, ed. Jane Lewis. Cheltenham: Edward Elgar.

Maier, Charles. 1981. "The Two Postwar Eras." *American Historical Review* 86, no. 2 (April), 327–52.

Maier-Braun, Karl-Heinz. 2006. "Der lange Weg ins einwanderungsland Deutschland." *Zuwanderung und Integration* [Landeszentrale der politischen Bildung Baden-Württemberg], vol. 4.

Mair, Peter. 2006. "Ruling the Void?" *New Left Review* 42 (November–December), 25–51.

Mair, Peter, and Cas Mudde. 1998. "The Party Family and Its Study." *Annual Review of Political Science* 1, 211–29.

Mair, Peter, and Ingrid Van Biezen. 2001. "Party Membership in Twenty European Democracies, 1980–2000," *Party Politics* 7, no. 1, 5–21.

Mansfield, Edward, and Diana C. Mutz. 2009. "Support for Free Trade: Self-Interest, Sociotropic Politics, and Out-Group Anxiety." *International Organization* 63, no. 3 (July), 425–57.

Marglin, Stephen, and Juliet Schor. 1991. *The Golden Age of Capitalism*. New York: Clarendon.

Martin, Andrew, and George Ross, eds. 1999. *The Brave New World of European Labor: European Trade Unions at the Millennium*. New York: Berghahn.

———, eds. 2004. *Euros and Europeans: Monetary Integration and the European Model Of Society*. Cambridge: Cambridge University Press.

Martin, Cathie Jo. 2004. "Reinventing Welfare Regimes." *World Politics* 57, no. 1 (October), 39–69.

Martin, Cathie Jo, and Kathleen Thelen. 2007. "The State and Coordinated Capitalism." *World Politics* 60, no. 1 (October), 1–36.

Mayer, Frederick W. 1998. *Interpreting NAFTA: The Science and Art of Political Analysis*. New York: Columbia University Press.

McGowan, Francis. 2001. "Social Democracy and the European Union: Who's Changing Whom?" *Social Democracy: Global and National Perspectives*, ed. L. Martell. New York: Palgrave.

McKibbin, Ross. 2009. "Will We Notice When the Tories Have Won?" *London Review of Books*, 24 September, 9–10.

Mehrtens, F. John, III. 2004. "Three Worlds of Public Opinion? Values, Variation, and the Effect on Social Policy." *International Journal of Public Opinion Research* 16, no. 2 (summer), 115–43.

Meidner, Rudolf. 1993. "Why Did the Swedish Model Fail?" *Socialist Register*, ed. Ralph Miliband and Leo Panitch. London: Merlin.

Mellman, Mark, Aaron Strauss, Anna Greenberg, Patrick McCreesh, and Kenneth D. Wald. 2006. "The Jewish Vote in 2004: An Analysis." Washington: Solomon Project.

Merkel, Wolfgang. 1992a. "After the Golden Age: Is Social Democracy Doomed to Decline?" *The Crisis of Socialism in Europe*, ed. Christiane Lemke and Gary Marks. Durham: Duke University Press.

———. 1992b. "Between Class and Catch-All: Is There an Electoral Dilemma for

Social Democratic Parties in Western Europe?" *Socialist Parties in Europe II: Of Class, Populars, Catch-all?*, ed. Wolfgang Merkel et al. Barcelona: ICPS.

—. 1992c. "After the Golden Age: Is Social Democracy Doomed to Decline?" *Socialist Parties in Europe*, ed. José Maravall et al. Barcelona: ICPS.

—. 2001. "The Third Ways of Social Democracy." *Multiple Third Ways*, ed. René Cuperus, Karl Duffek, and Johannes Kandel. Amsterdam: Wiardi Beckman.

Merkel, Wolfgang, Alexander Petring, Christian Henkes, and Christoph Egle. 2008. *Social Democracy in Power: The Capacity to Reform*. London: Routledge.

Meyer, Thomas, with Lewis P. Hinchman. 2007. *The Theory of Social Democracy*. Oxford: Polity.

Migration Policy Institute. 2004. "To Regularize or Not to Regularize." Briefing with Ferrucio Pastore, deputy director of the Center for International Policy Studies (CesPI), Rome, 30 June.

Miliband, David. 2008. "Against the Odds We Can Still Win, on a Platform of Change." *Guardian*, 30 July.

Miliband, Ralph. 1977. *Marxism and Politics*. New York: Oxford University Press.

Millard, Frances. 2003. "Poland." *Developments in Central and East European Politics*, ed. Stephen White, Judy Batt, and Paul G. Lewis, 23–40. New York: Palgrave Macmillan.

Miller, Susan, and Heinrich Potthoff. 1986. *A History of German Social Democracy*. New York: St. Martin's.

Mink, Georges, and Jean-Charles Szurek. 1998. "L'ancienne élite communiste en Europe centrale: Stratégies, resources et reconstructions identitaires." *Revue française de science politique* 48, no. 1, 3–41.

Mishra, Ramesh. 1984. *The Welfare State in Crisis: Social Thought and Social Change*. New York: St. Martin's.

—. 1999. *Globalization and the Welfare State*. Cheltenham: Edward Elgar.

Money, Jeannette. 1999. *Fences and Neighbors: The Political Geography of Immigration Control*. Ithaca: Cornell University Press.

Moravscik, Andrew. 1998. *The Choice for Europe*. Ithaca: Cornell University Press.

—. 2002. "In Defence of the 'Democratic Deficit': Reassessing Legitimacy in the European Union." *Journal of Common Market Studies* 40, no. 4 (November), 603–24.

Morel, Nathalie. 2006. "Providing Coverage against New Social Risks in Bismarckian Welfare States: The Case of Long-Term Care." *The Politics of Post-Industrial Welfare Society*, ed. Klaus Armingeon and Giuliano Bonoli, 227–47. New York: Routledge.

Morone, James A. 2005. "Storybook Truths about America." *Studies in American Political Development* 19, no. 2 (October), 216–25.

Moschonas, Gerassimos. 2002. *In the Name of Social Democracy: The Great Transformation, 1945 to the present*. London: Verso.

—. 2007. "The Party of European Socialists." *Encyclopedia of European Elections*, ed. Yves Déloye and M. Bruter. London: Palgrave Macmillan.

—. 2008a. "Reformism in a Conservative System: European Union and Social-Democratic Identity." *In Search of Social Democracy: Responses to Crisis and Modernisation*, ed. John Callaghan et al. Manchester: Manchester University Press.

———. 2008b. "Socialism and Its Changing Constituencies in France, Great Britain, Sweden and Denmark." Columbia University, Council for European Studies, Sixteenth International Conference, Chicago.

———. 2009. "Reformism in a 'Conservative' System: European Union, Political Parties and Social Democratic Identity." *Socialism and European Unity*, ed. Michael Newman. London: Junction.

Moschonas, Gerassimos, and George Papanagnou. 2007. "Posséder une longueur d'avance sur la droite: Expliquer la durée gouvernementale du PSOE (1982–96) et du PASOK (1981–2004)." *Pôle Sud* 27, 43–105.

Mucciaroni, Gary. 1990. *The Political Failure of Employment Policy, 1945–1982*. Pittsburgh: University of Pittsburgh Press.

Mudde, Cas. 2004. "The Populist Zeitgeist." *Government and Opposition* 39, no. 4 (January), 541–63.

Münz, Rainer. 2004. "New German Law Skirts Comprehensive Immigration Reform." Migration Information Source, August.

Nannestadt, Peter. 2007. "Immigration and the Welfare State: A Survey of 15 Years of Research." *European Journal of Political Economy* 23, no. 2 (June), 512–32.

Noel, Alain, and Jean-Philippe Therien. 2008. *Left and Right in Global Politics*. New York: Cambridge University Press.

Notermans, Ton. 2001. "The German Social Democrats and Monetary Union." *Social Democracy and Monetary Union*, ed. Ton Notermans. New York: Berghahn.

———, ed. 2001. *Social Democracy and Monetary Union*. New York: Berghahn.

Oberlander, Jonathan. 2003. *The Political Life of Medicare*. Chicago: University of Chicago Press.

Obinger, Herbert, Peter Starke, Julia Moser, Claudia Bogedan, Edith Obinger-Gindulis, and Stephan Leibfried. 2010. *Transformations of the Welfare State: Small States, Big Lessons*. New York: Oxford University Press.

OECD (Organization of Economic Co-operation and Development). n.d. "Social Expenditure Database," http://stats.oecd.org/Index.aspx?datasetcode=SOCX_AGG.

———. 1985. *Social Expenditure, 1960–1990: Problems of Growth and Control*. Paris: OECD.

———. 2000. *Literacy in the Information Age*. Paris: OECD.

———. 2004. *Employment Outlook 2004*. Paris: OECD.

———. 2007a. *Sweden: Achieving Results for Sustained Growth*. Paris: OECD.

———. 2007b. *OECD Factbook 2007*. Paris: OECD.

———. 2007c. *OECD Health Data 2007*. Paris: OECD.

———. 2007d. *Economic Survey of Sweden, 2007*. Paris: OECD.

———. 2007e. *International Migration Outlook: Sopemi*. 2007 edn. Paris: OECD.

———. 2008a. *StatExtracts: 2008 Annual Labour Force Statistics*. Paris: OECD.

———. 2008b. *Economic Outlook 2008* 84. Paris: OECD.

———. 2008c. *Employment Outlook 2008*. Paris: OECD.

———. 2008d. *Labour Force Statistics, 1987–2007*. Paris: OECD.

———. 2008e. *Growing Unequal? Income Distribution and Poverty in OECD Countries*. Paris: OECD.

Offe, Claus. 1983. "Competitive Party Democracy and the Welfare State." *Policy Sciences* 15, no. 3 (April), 225–46.

———. 1984. *Contradictions of the Welfare State*, ed. John Keane. Cambridge: MIT Press.

———. 1996. *Varieties of Transition: The East European and East German Experience*. Cambridge: Polity.

Oh, Jennifer. 2009. "Challenged to Open: A Comparative Study of Agricultural Market Reform in Japan and Sweden." PhD diss., Princeton University.

Orenstein, Mitchell. 1995. "Transitional Social Policy in the Czech Republic and Poland." *Czech Sociological Review* 3, no. 2, 179–96.

Palier, Bruno. 2002. *Gouverner la sécurité sociale*. Paris: Presses Universitaires de France.

———, ed. 2010. *A Long Goodbye to Bismarck? The Politics of Welfare Reform in Continental Europe*. Amsterdam: Amsterdam University Press.

Palier, Bruno, and Kathleen Thelen. 2010. "Institutionalizing Dualism." *Politics and Society* 38, no. 3 (September), 119–48.

Parness, Diane. 1991. *The SPD and the Challenge of Mass Politics*. Boulder: Westview.

Paterson, William E., and James Sloam. 2005. "Learning from the West: Policy Transfer and Political Parties." *Learning from the West? Policy Transfer and Programmatic Change in the Communist Successor Parties*, ed. Dan Hough, William E. Paterson, and James Sloam. New York: Routledge.

Paterson, William, and Alastair H. Thomas, eds. 1977. *Social Democratic Parties in Western Europe*. London: Croom Helm.

Pekkarinen, Jukka. 2001. "Finnish Social Democrats and EMU." *Social Democracy and Monetary Union*, ed. Ton Notermans. New York: Berghahn.

Pérez, Sofía A. 1999. "Constraint or Motor? Monetary Integration and the Construction of a Social Model in Spain." *Euros and Europeans: Monetary Integration and the European Model of Society*, ed. Andrew Martin and George Ross. Cambridge: Cambridge University Press.

Pérez, Sofía, and J. Fernandez-Albertos. 2009. "Immigration and Left Party Government in Europe." Paper presented at the annual meeting of the American Political Science Association, Toronto, 3–6 September.

Phillips, Kevin. 1969. *The Emerging Republican Majority*. New York: Arlington House.

Pierson, Christopher. 2001. *Hard Choices: Social Democracy in the 21st Century*. Oxford: Oxford University Press.

———. 2007. *Beyond the Welfare State: The New Political Economy of Welfare*, 3rd edn. University Park: Pennsylvania State University Press.

Pierson, Paul. 1994. *Dismantling the Welfare State: Reagan, Thatcher and the Politics of Retrenchment*. Cambridge: Cambridge University Press.

———. 1996. "The New Politics of the Welfare State." *World Politics* 48, no. 2 (January), 143–79.

———. 1998. "The Deficit and the Politics of Domestic Reform." *The Social Divide: Political Parties and the Future of Activist Government*, ed. Margaret Weir, 126–80. Washington: Brookings Institution.

———. 2002. "Coping with Permanent Austerity: Welfare State Restructuring in

Affluent Democracies." *Revue française de sociologie* 43, no. 2 (April–June), 369–406.

———, ed. 2001. *The New Politics of the Welfare State*. New York: Oxford University Press.

Piketty, Thomas, and Emmanuel Saez. 2003. "Income Inequality in the United States, 1913–1998." *Quarterly Journal of Economics* 118, no. 1 (February), 1–39.

Pittaway, Mark. 2003. "Hungary." *Developments in Central and East European Politics*, ed. Stephen White, Judy Batt, and Paul G. Lewis, 57–73. New York: Palgrave Macmillan.

Piven, Frances Fox, ed. 1992. *Labor Parties in Postindustrial Societies*. New York: Oxford University Press.

Pochet, Philippe, and Jonathan Zeitlin, eds. 2005. *The Open Method of Coordination in Action: The European Employment and Social Inclusion Strategies*. Brussels: Peter Lang.

PollingReport.com. 2009. "Federal Budget, Taxes, Economy." http://www.polling report.com/budget.htm.

Pontusson, Jonas. n.d. "Social Democracy, Varieties of Capitalism and Globalization." Unpublished paper.

———. 1992. *The Limits of Social Democracy*. Ithaca: Cornell University Press.

———. 1997. "Between Neo-liberalism and the German Model: Swedish Capitalism in Transition." *Political Economy of Modern Capitalism*, ed. Colin Crouch and Wolfgang Streeck, 55–70. London: Sage.

———. 2005a. *Inequality and Prosperity: Social Europe vs. Liberal America*. Ithaca: Cornell University Press.

———. 2005b. "Varieties and Commonalities of Capitalism." *Varieties of Capitalism, Varieties of Approaches*, ed. David Coates, 163–88. New York: Palgrave Macmillan.

———. 2006. "Whither Social Europe?" *Challenge* 49, no. 6 (November–December), 35–54.

Pontusson, Jonas, and Peter Swenson. 1996. "Labor Markets, Production Strategies, and Wage-Bargaining Institutions." *Comparative Political Studies* 29, no. 2 (April), 223–50.

Potrafke, Niklas. 2009. "Did Globalization Restrict Partisan Politics? An Empirical Evaluation of Social Expenditures in a Panel of OECD Countries." *Public Choice* 140, nos. 1–2 (July), 105–24.

Preda, Cristian, and Sorina Soare. 2008. *Regimul, partidele si sistemul politic din România*. Bucharest: Nemira.

Przeworski, Adam. 1985. *Capitalism and Social Democracy*. Cambridge: Cambridge University Press.

Przeworski, Adam, and John Sprague. 1986. *Paper Stones: A History of Electoral Socialism*. Chicago: University of Chicago Press.

Quatremer, Jean, and Thomas Klau. 1997. *Ces hommes qui ont fait l'Euro*. Paris: Plon.

Rajan, Raghuram G. 2010. *Fault Lines: How Hidden Fractures Still Threaten the World Economy*. Princeton: Princeton University Press.

Rattner, Sidney. 1972. *The Tariff in American History*. New York: Van Nostrand.

Rawnsley, Andrew. 2001. *Servants of the People: The Inside Story of New Labour.* London: Penguin.

Rentoul, John. 2008. "Daylight Robbery at the Library of Rhetoric." *Independent,* 29 March.

Reynié, Dominique. 2008. "L'avènement d'un stato-scepticisme en Europe." *L'opinion européenne en 2008,* ed. Fondation Robert Schuman. Paris: Lignes et Repères.

Richards, John. 2004. "Clusters, Competition and 'Global Players' in ICT Markets: The Case of Scandinavia." *Building High-Tech Clusters,* ed. Timothy Bresnahan and Alfonso Gambardella, 160–89. New York: Cambridge University Press.

Richardson, Jeremy, ed. 2006. *European Union: Power and Policy-making.* 3rd edn. London: Routledge.

Rieger, Elmer, and Stephan Leibfried. 2003. *Limits to Globalization: Welfare States and the World Economy.* Oxford: Polity.

Romano, Flavio. 2006. *Clinton and Blair: The Political Economy of the Third Way.* New York: Routledge.

Room, Graham. 2002. "Education and Welfare: Recalibrating the European Debate." *Policy Studies* 23, no. 1 (March), 37–50.

Ross, George. 1987. "Destroyed by the Dialectic: Politics, the Decline of Marxism, and the New Middle Strata in France." *Theory and Society* 16, no. 1 (January), 7–38.

———. 1995. *Jacques Delors and European Integration.* Cambridge: Polity.

Ross, George, Stanley Hoffmann, and Sylvia Malzacher, eds. 1987. *The Mitterrand Experiment.* New York: Oxford University Press.

Rothstein, Bo. 1992. "Labor-Market Institutions and Working Class Strength." *Structuring Politics,* ed. Sven Steinmo, Kathleen Thelen, and Frank Longsteth, 33–56. New York: Cambridge University Press.

Rueda, David. 2008. *Social Democracy Inside Out: Partisanship and Labor Market Policy in Advanced Industrial Democracies.* Oxford: Oxford University Press.

Ruggie, John G. 1982. "International Regimes, Transactions, and Change: Embedded Liberalism in the Postwar Economic Order." *International Organization* 36, no. 2 (spring), 379–415.

———, ed. 2008. *Embedded Global Markets: An Enduring Challenge.* Aldershot: Ashgate.

Russell, Meg. 2005. *Building New Labour: The Politics of Party Organisation.* London: Palgrave Macmillan.

Ryner, Magnus. 1999. "Neoliberal Globalization and the Crisis of Swedish Social Democracy." *Economic and Industrial Democracy* 20, no. 1 (February), 39–79.

Sainsbury, Diane. 1990. "Party Strategies and the Electoral Trade-off of Class-Based Parties: A Critique and Application of the 'Dilemma of Electoral Socialism.'" *European Journal of Political Research* 18, no. 1 (January), 29–50.

———, ed. 1999. *Gender and Welfare State Regimes.* Oxford: Oxford University Press.

SAP. 1932. *Social-Demokraten* 15 (September).

Sartori, Giovanni, and Giacamo Sani. 1983. "Polarization, Fragmentation and Competition in Western Democracies." *Western European Party Systems,* ed. Hans Daadler and Peter Mair. London: Sage.

Sassoon, Donald. 1996, 2010. *One Hundred Years of Socialism: The West European Left in the Twentieth Century.* London: I. B. Tauris.

Schain, Martin A. 2006. "The Politics of Immigration in France, Britain and the United States: A Transatlantic Comparison." *Immigration and the Transformation of Europe,* ed. Craig A. Parsons and Timothy M. Smeeding, 362–92. Cambridge: Cambridge University Press.

Scharpf, Fritz. 1987. *Crisis and Choice in European Social Democracy.* Ithaca: Cornell University Press.

Schatz, Joseph J. 2008. "Drawing a Fine Line on Trade." *CQ Weekly,* 8 December, 3230–38.

Scheiber, Noam. 2007. "The Centrists Didn't Hold." *New York Times,* 28 July, 15.

Scheve, Kenneth F., and Matthew J. Slaughter. 2001. "Labor Market Competition and Individual Preferences over Immigration Policy." *Review of Economics and Statistics* 83, no. 1 (February), 133–45.

———. 2006. "Public Opinion, Integration, and the Welfare State." *Globalization and Egalitarian Redistribution,* ed. Pranab Bardhan, Samuel Bowles, and Michael Wallerstein, 217–60. Princeton: Princeton University Press.

———. 2007. "A New Deal for Globalization." *Foreign Affairs* 86, no. 4 (July–August).

Schickler, Eric, and Devin Caughey. 2010. "Public Opinion, Organized Labor, and the Limits of New Deal Liberalism, 1936–1945." Paper presented at the annual meeting of the American Political Science Association, Washington, 2–5 September.

Schlesinger, Arthur. 1986. *The Cycles of American History.* Boston: Houghton Mifflin.

Schmidt, Vivien. 2006. *Democracy in Europe: The EU and National Polities.* Oxford: Oxford University Press.

Schnietz, Karen E., and Timothy Nieman. 1999. "Politics Matters: The 1997 Derailment of Fast-Track Trade Authority." *Business and Politics* 1, no. 2, 233–51.

Schröder, Martin. 2008. "Integrating Welfare and Production Typologies: How Refinements of the Variety of Capitalism Approach Call for a Combination of Welfare Typologies." *Journal of Social Policy* 38, no. 1 (January), 19–43.

Schumacher, Kurt. 1986 [1945]. "'What Do the Social Democrats Want?' Speech Delivered in Kiel on October 27, 1945." *A History of German Social Democracy from 1848 to the Present,* ed. Susanne Miller and Heinrich Potthoff. New York: St. Martin's.

Schwab, Susan C. 1994. *Trade-offs: Negotiating the Omnibus Trade and Competitiveness Act of 1988.* Boston: Harvard Business School Press.

Schwartz, Joseph. 1995. *The Permanence of the Political.* Princeton: Princeton University Press.

Seeleib-Kaiser, Martin, Silke van Dyk, and Martin Roggenkamp. 2005. "What Do Parties Want? An Analysis of Programmatic Social Policy Aims in Austria, Germany, and the Netherlands." Bremen: Universität Bremen. ZeS-Arbeitspapier 01/2005.

Seeleib-Kaiser, Martin, and Timo Fleckenstein. 2007. "Discourse, Learning and Welfare State Change: The Case of German Labour Market Reforms." *Social Policy and Administration* 41, no. 5 (October), 427–48.

Seldon, Anthony. 2007. "Conclusion: The Net Blair Effect, 1994–2007." *Blair's Britain, 1997–2007*, 645–50. Cambridge: Cambridge University Press.

———, ed. 2007. *Blair's Britain, 1997–2007*. Cambridge: Cambridge University Press.

Sen, Amartya. 1992. *Inequality Reconsidered*. Cambridge: Harvard University Press.

Shalev, Michael. 1983. "The Social Democratic Model and Beyond: Two Generations of Comparative Research on the Welfare State." *Comparative Social Research*, vol. 6, ed. Richard F. Tomasson, 315–51. Greenwich, Conn.: JAI.

Shaw, Eric. 2007. *Losing Labour's Soul? New Labour and the Blair Government, 1997–2007*. London: Routledge.

Sheils, John, and Randall Haught. 2004. "The Cost of Tax-Exempt Health Benefits in 2004." *Health Affairs* web exclusive (25 February), W4-106 to W4-112.

Shoch, James. 2000. "Contesting Globalization: Organized Labor, NAFTA, and the 1997 and 1998 Fast-Track Fights." *Politics and Society* 28, no. 1 (March), 119–50.

———. 2001. *Trading Blows: Party Competition and U.S. Trade Policy in a Globalizing Era*. Chapel Hill: University of North Carolina Press.

———. 2006. "From NAFTA to CAFTA: Trade Liberalization and Party Politics in the U.S. House of Representatives, 1993–2005." Paper presented at the annual meeting of the American Political Science Association, Philadelphia.

———. 2008. "Bringing Public Opinion and Electoral Politics Back In: Explaining the Fate of 'Clintonomics' and Its Contemporary Relevance." *Politics and Society* 36, no. 1 (March), 89–130.

Shonfield, Andrew. 1965. *Modern Capitalism: The Changing Balance of Private and Public Power*. Oxford: Oxford University Press.

Simms, Brendan. 2002. *Unfinest Hour*. London: Penguin.

Skidelsky, Robert. 2009. *Keynes: The Return of the Master*. New York: Public Affairs.

Skocpol, Theda. 1996. *Boomerang: Health Care Reform and the Turn against Government*. New York: W. W. Norton.

Smith, Steven S. 2007. *Party Influence in Congress*. New York: Cambridge University Press.

Soare, Sorina. 2004. "La construction du label social-démocrate roumain et la consolidation de deux pôles sociaux-démocrates à tendance antithétique." *Politique et société dans la Roumanie contemporaine*, ed. Alexandra Ionescu and Odette Hatto, 183–210. Paris: L'Harmattan.

———. 2006. "La reconversion sociale-démocrate des anciens partis communistes et leur adhésion à l'économie de marché: Le cas des sociaux-démocrates roumains." *La transition vers le marché et la démocratie: Europe de l'est, Europe centrale et Afrique du sud*, ed. Wladimir Andreff, 173–90. Paris: La Découverte.

Soare, Sorina, and Cristian Preda. 2008. *Regimul, partidele si sistemul politic din Romania*. Bucharest: Nemira.

Sombart, Werner. 1976 [1906]. *Why Is There No Socialism in the United States?* London: Macmillan.

Soskice, David. 1999. "Divergent Production Regimes." *Continuity and Change in Contemporary Capitalism*, ed. Herbert Kitschelt et al., 101–34. New York: Cambridge University Press.

Sotiropoulos, Dimitri A., Ileana Neamțu, and Maya Stoyanova. 2003. "The Trajectory of Post-Communist Welfare State Development: The Cases of Bulgaria and Romania." *Social Policy and Administration* 37, no. 6 (December), 656–73.

Spiliotes, Constantine J. 2002. *Vicious Cycle: Presidential Decision Making in the American Political Economy.* College Station: Texas A&M Press.

Spirova, Maria Stefanova. 2005. "Political Parties in Bulgaria: Organizational Trends in Comparative Perspectives." *Party Politics* 11, no. 5 (September), 601–22.

Spyropoulou, Vivian. 2008. *On a Tightrope? Electoral Dynamics and Governmental Stability of the European Social Democracy, 1950–2007.* Athens: Panteion University of Athens.

Stan, Lavinia. 2002. "Moral Cleansing Romanian Style." *Problems of Postcommunism* 49, no. 4 (July–August), 52–62.

Stanley, Harold W., and Richard G. Niemi. 2008. *Vital Statistics on American Politics, 2007–2008.* Washington: CQ Press.

Stephens, Evelyn Huber, and John D. Stephens. 2001. *Development and Crisis in the Welfare State.* Chicago: University of Chicago Press.

Stephens, John. 1986. *The Transition from Capitalism to Socialism.* Chicago: University of Illinois Press.

Stephens, John, Evelyne Huber, and Leonard Ray. 1999. "The Welfare State in Hard Times." *Continuity and Change in Contemporary Capitalism,* ed. H. Kitschelt et al. Cambridge: Cambridge University Press.

Stewart, Kitty. 2007. "Equality and Social Justice." *Blair's Britain, 1997–2007,* ed. Anthony Seldon, 408–35. Cambridge: Cambridge University Press.

Stimson, James A. 2004. *Tides of Consent: How Public Opinion Shapes American Politics.* New York: Cambridge University Press.

Stoesz, David, and Howard Jacob Karger. 1992. *Reconstructing the American Welfare State: Pragmatic Responses to the Welfare Crisis.* Lanham, Md.: Rowman and Littlefield.

Stoica, Catalin Augustin. 2004. "From Good Communists to Even Better Capitalists? Entrepreneurial Pathways in Post-Socialist Romania." *East European Politics and Societies* 18, no. 2 (May), 236–77.

———. 2005. "Once upon a Time There Was a Big Party: The Social Bases of the Romanian Communist Party." *East European Politics and Societies* 19, no. 4 (November), 686–71.

Stratman, Thomas. 2005. "Some Talk: Money in Politics: A (Partial) Review of the Literature." *Public Choice* 124, nos. 1–2 (July), 135–56.

Straw, Jack. 1993. *Policy and Ideology.* Blackburn: Blackburn Labour Party.

Summers, Lawrence. 2008. "America Needs to Make a New Case for Trade." *Financial Times,* 27 April.

Sundberg, Ian. 1999. "The Finnish Social Democratic Party." *Social Democratic Parties in the European Union,* ed. R. Ladrech and P. Marlière. Hampshire: Macmillan.

Sundstrom, Gerdt, Lennarth Johansson, and Linda B. Hassing. 2002. "The Shifting Balance of Long-Term Care in Sweden." *Gerontologist* 42, no. 3, 350–55.

Suro, Roberto, Richard Fry, and Jeffrey Passel. 2005. "Hispanics and the 2004 Election: Population, Electorate and Voters." Pew Hispanic Center.

Svallfors, Stefan, and Peter Taylor-Gooby, eds. 2007. *End of the Welfare State? Responses to State Retrenchment.* New York: Routledge.

Svensson, Torsten. 1994. "Socialdemokratins Dominans." PhD diss., Uppsala University.

Swank, Duane. 2002. *Global Capital, Political Institutions, and Policy Change in Developed Welfare States.* New York: Cambridge University Press.

Swank, Duane, and Hans-Georg Betz. 2003. "Globalization, the Welfare State, and Right Wing Populism in Western Europe." *Socio-Economic Review* 1, no. 2 (May), 215–45.

Swensson, Peter. 2002. *Capitalists against Markets: The Making of Labor Markets and Welfare States in the United States and Sweden.* New York: Oxford University Press.

Szczerbiak, Aleks. 1999. "Testing Party Models in East-Central Europe: Local Party Organisation in Postcommunist Poland." *Party Politics* 5, no. 4 (October), 525–37.

———. 2001. "Party Structure and Organisational Development in Post-communist Poland." *Journal of Communist Studies and Transition Politics* 17, no. 2 (June), 94–130.

Taylor-Gooby, Peter, ed. 2004. *New Risks, New Welfare: The Transformation of the European Welfare State.* Oxford: Oxford University Press.

Taylor-Gooby, Peter, and Trine Larsen. 2004. "The UK: A Test Case for the Liberal Welfare State?" *New Risks, New Welfare: The Transformation of the European Welfare State,* ed. Peter Taylor-Gooby, 55–82. Oxford: Oxford University Press.

Teitel, Ruti G. 2000. *Transitional Justice.* Oxford: Oxford University Press.

Teixeira, Ruy, and John Halpin. 2010. "Election Results Fueled by Jobs Crisis and Voter Apathy among Progressives." Washington: Center for American Progress Action Fund, http://www.americanprogressaction.org/issues/2010/11/pdf/election_results.pdf.

Teixeira, Ruy, and Joel Rogers. 2000. *America's Forgotten Majority: Why the White Working Class Still Matters.* New York: Basic Books.

Therborn, Göran. 2007. "After Dialectics: Radical Social Theory in a Post-communist World." *New Left Review* 43, 63–114.

Thurber, James, ed. 2009. *Rivals for Power: Presidential-Congressional Relations.* 4th edn. Lanham, Md.: Rowman and Littlefield.

Timonen, Virpi. 2004. "New Risks: Are They Still New for the Nordic Welfare States?" *New Risks, New Welfare: The Transformation of the European Welfare State,* ed. Peter Taylor-Gooby, 83–110. Oxford: Oxford University Press.

Tismăneanu, Vladimir. 2000. "Hypotheses on Populism: The Politics of Charismatic Protest." *East European Politics and Societies* 14, no. 2 (March), 10–17.

Toro-Morn, Maura I. 2004. *Migration and Immigration.* Westport, Conn.: Greenwood.

Touykova, Marta. 1997. "La stratégie de survie du Parti Socialiste Bulgare." *Études du CERI* 31, http://www.ceri-sciencespo.com/publica/etude/etude31.pdf.

Toynbee, Polly, and David Walker. 2010. *The Verdict: Did Labour Change Britain?* London: Granta.

Trentmann, Frank. 2008. *Free Trade Nation.* Oxford: Oxford University Press.

Tucker, Robert. 1970. *The Marxian Revolutionary Idea.* Princeton. Princeton University Press.

Ungerson, Clare. 2003. *"Commodified Care Work in European Labour Markets."* European Societies 5, no. 4 (October), 377–96.

Ungerson, Clare, and Sue Yeandle, eds. 2007. *Cash for Care in Developed Welfare States*. Houndsmill, Basingstoke: Palgrave Macmillan.

UNICEF. 2000. *A League Table of Child Poverty in Rich Nations*. Innocenti Report Card 1. Florence: Innocenti Research Centre, http://www.unicef-icdc.org.

———. 2007. *Child Poverty in Perspective: An Overview of Child Well-being in Rich Countries*. Innocenti Report Card 7. Florence: Innocenti Research Centre, http://www.unicef-icdc.org.

U.S. Bureau of the Census. n.d. "Historical Poverty Tables: People," http://www.census.gov/hhes/www/poverty/histpov/perindex.html.

———. 1992. *Measuring the Effect of Benefits and Taxes on Income and Poverty: 1979 to 1991*. Washington: U.S. Government Printing Office.

———. 2001. *Poverty in the United States: 2000*. Washington: U.S. Government Printing Office.

———. 2007. *The Effect of Taxes and Transfers on Income and Poverty in the United States: 2005*. Washington: U.S. Government Printing Office.

U.S. Congress, Joint Committee on Taxation. 2010. *Estimates of Federal Tax Expenditures for Fiscal Years 2009–2113*. Washington: U.S. Government Printing Office.

Van Biezen, Ingrid. 2003. *Political Parties in New Democracies*. London: Palgrave Macmillan.

Van Biezen, Ingrid, and Petr Kopecky. 2007. "The State and the Parties: Public Funding, Public Regulation and Rent-Seeking in Contemporary Democracy." *Party Politics* 13, no. 2 (March), 235–54.

Vedrine, Hubert. 2009. Interview in *Le Monde*, 30 May.

Veikou, Mariangela, and Anna Triandafyllidou. 2004. "Italian Immigration Policy and Its Implementation: A Report on the State of the Art." Report prepared for the research project "Does Implementation Matter? Informal Administration Practices and Shifting Immigrant Strategies in Four Member States" funded by the European Commission, Research DG, contract no. HPSE-CT-1999-00001.

Verba, Sidney, Kay Lehman Schlozman, and Henry E. Brady. 1995. *Voice and Equality: Civic Voluntarism in American Society*. Cambridge: Harvard University Press.

Victor, Barbard. 1999. *Le Matignon de Jospin*. Paris: Flammarion.

Vis, Barbara. 2010. *Politics of Risk-taking: Welfare State Reform in Advanced Democracies*. Amsterdam: Amsterdam University Press.

Visser, Jelle. 2006. "Union Membership Statistics in 24 Countries." *Monthly Labor Review* 129, no. 1 (January), 38–49.

Visser, Jelle, and Anton Hemerijk. 1997. *A Dutch Miracle: Job Growth, Welfare Reform, and Corporatism in the Netherlands*. Amsterdam: Amsterdam University Press.

Von Beyme, Klaus. 1985. *Political Parties in Western Democracies*. New York: St. Martin's.

Voulgaris, Yannis. 2008. "Les élections grecques de 2007: secousse passagère ou début d'un séisme?" *Pôle Sud*.

Wade, Robert. 2008. "Financial Regime Change?" *New Left Review* 53 (September–October), 5–21.

Wall, Stephen. 2008. *A Stranger in Europe: Britain and the EU from Thatcher to Blair*. Oxford: Oxford University Press.

Waller, Michael. 1995. "Adaptation of the Former Communist Parties of East-Central Europe." *Party Politics* 1, no. 4 (October), 473–90.

Wallerstein, Michael, and Miriam Golden. 2000. "Postwar Wage Setting in the Nordic Countries." *Unions, Employers, and Central Banks: Macroeconomic Coordination and Institutional Change in Social Market Economies*, ed. Torben Iversen, Jonas Pontusson, and David Soskice, 107–37. New York: Cambridge University Press.

Walter, Stefanie. 2010. "Globalization and the Welfare State: Testing the Microfoundations of the Compensation Hypothesis." *International Studies Quarterly* 54, no. 2 (June), 403–26.

Walters, William. 2004. "Secure Borders, Safe Haven, Domopolitics." *Citizenship Studies* 8, no. 3 (September), 237–60.

Watts, Julie. 2002. "The Unconventional Immigration Policy Preferences of Labor Unions in Spain, Italy, and France." San Diego: University of California, San Diego, Center for Comparative Immigration Studies. Working Paper 5.

Weatherford, M. Stephen, and Lorraine M. McDonnell. 1996. "Clinton and the Economy: The Paradox of Policy Success and Political Mishap. *Political Science Quarterly* 111, no. 3 (fall), 403–36.

Weaver, R. Kent. 2000. *Ending Welfare as We Know It*. Washington: Brookings Institution.

Wickham-Jones, Mark. 1995. "Anticipating Social Democracy, Pre-empting Anticipations: Economic Policy-Making in the British Labour Party, 1987–1992." *Politics and Society* 23, no. 4 (December), 465–94.

Wilensky, Harold L. 2002. *Rich Democracies: Political Economy, Public Policy, and Performance*. Berkeley: University of California Press.

Wilentz, Sean. 2008. *The Age of Reagan: A History, 1974–2008*. New York: Harper Collins.

Williams, K. 2003. "The Czech Republic and Slovakia." *Developments in Central and East European Politics*, ed. Stephen White, Judy Batt, and Paul G. Lewis, 41–56. New York: Palgrave Macmillan.

Wirls, Daniel. 1998. "The Consequences of Equal Representation: The Bicameral Politics of NAFTA in the 103rd Congress." *Congress and the Presidency* 25, no. 2, 129–45.

Wolf, Martin. 2008. "Keynes Offers Us the Best Way to Think about the Crisis." *Financial Times*, 24 December.

Wolff, Edward N. 2007. "Recent Trends in Household Wealth in the United States: Rising Debt and the Middle Class Squeeze." Annandale-on-Hudson, N.Y.: Levy Economics Institute. Working Paper 502, http://www.levy.org/pubs/wp_502.pdf.

Wolfreys, Jim. 2006. "France in Revolt, 1995–2005." *International Socialism* 109.

Women's Voices, Women Vote. 2007. "Unmarried America."

Yergin, Daniel, and Joseph Stanislaw. 1998. *The Commanding Heights: The Battle for the World Economy*. New York: Free Press.

Young, Alasdair R., and John Peterson. 2006. "The EU and the New Trade Politics." *Journal of European Public Policy* 13, no. 6 (September), 795–814.

Zaslove, Andrej. 2007. "Immigration Politics and Policy in Germany and Italy: The

End of the Hidden Consensus." Paper presented at the annual conference of the Political Studies Association, University of Bath, 11–13 April.

Zelizer, Julian E. 2003. "The Uneasy Relationship: Democracy, Taxation, and State Building Since the New Deal." *The Democratic Experiment: New Directions in American Political History*, ed. Meg Jacobs, William J. Novack, and Julian E. Zelizer, 276–300. Princeton: Princeton University Press.

Zielonka, Jan. 2006. *Europe as Empire: The Nature of the Enlarged European Union*. Oxford: Oxford University Press.

Zysman, John, and Abraham Newman, ed. 2006. *How Revolutionary Was the Digital Revolution? National Responses, Market Transitions, and Global Technology*. Stanford: Stanford Business Books.

About the Contributors

SHERI BERMAN is an associate professor of political science at Barnard College, Columbia University, in New York City. She is the author of *The Social Democratic Moment: Ideas and Politics in the Making of Inter-War Europe* (Cambridge: Harvard University Press, 1998) and *The Primacy of Politics: Social Democracy and the Making of Europe's Twentieth Century* (Cambridge: Cambridge University Press, 2006).

JAMES CRONIN is a professor of history at Boston College and an affiliate of the Center for European Studies at Harvard University. His most recent book is *New Labour's Pasts: The Labour Party and Its Discontents* (London: Longman, 2004). Among his earlier books are *The World the Cold War Made* (London: Routledge, 1996) and *The Politics of State Expansion: War, State and Society in Twentieth-Century Britain* (London: Routledge, 1991).

JEAN-MICHEL DE WAELE is dean of the Faculty of Social and Political Sciences, professor of political science, and associate of the Institute for European Studies at the Free University of Brussels. He is the author of *L'Europe des communistes* (with Pascal Delwit), *Les partis politiques en Belgique* (with Pascal Delwit), *L'extrême droite en France et Belgique* (with Pascal Delwit), and other books.

ARTHUR GOLDHAMMER is an affiliate of the Center for European Studies at Harvard. He has worked primarily as a translator specializing in French history, literature, philosophy, and social science. He has translated more than a hundred works by many of France's most noted authors, is on the editorial board of the journal *French Politics, Culture and Society*, and in 1996 was named Chevalier de l'Ordre des Arts et des Lettres by the French Minister of Culture. In 1997 he was awarded the Médaille de Vermeil by the Académie Française. He is currently working on a book about democracy after Tocqueville, whose *Democracy in America* he translated in 2004 and for which he received the Florence Gould Translation Prize. In addition, Goldhammer hosts a blog on French politics at artgoldhammer.blog spot.com.

CHRISTOPHER HOWARD is a professor of government at the College of William and Mary. He is the author of *The Welfare State Nobody Knows: Debunking Myths about U.S. Social Policy* (Princeton: Princeton University Press, 2007) and *The Hidden Welfare State: Tax Expenditures and Social Policy in the United States* (Princeton: Princeton University Press, 1997).

JANE JENSON is a professor of political science at the University of Montreal, where she holds the Canada Research Chair in Citizenship and Governance. Her most recent books are *L'état des citoyennetés en Europe et dans les Amériques* (Montreal: Presses de l'Université de Montréal, 2007), edited with B. Marquès-Perreira and E. Remacle; *La politique comparée: l'histoire, les enjeux, les approaches* (Montreal: Presses de l'Université de Montréal, 2003), written with Mamoudou Gazibo; and *Who Cares? Women's Work, Child Care and Welfare State Redesign* (Toronto: University of Toronto Press, 2001), with Mariette Sineau et al.

GERASSIMOS MOSCHONAS is a professor of political science at Pantheon University in Athens and a visiting professor at the Institute for European Studies, Free University of Brussels. He is the author of *In the Name of Social Democracy: The Great Transformation from 1945 to the Present* (London: Verso, 2002).

SOFÍA A. PÉREZ is an associate professor of political science at Boston University. She is the author of *Banking on Privilege: The Politics of Spanish Financial Reform* (Ithaca: Cornell University Press, 1997) and a co-author with Michael Loriaux et al. of *Capital Ungoverned: Liberalizing Finance in Interventionist States* (Ithaca: Cornell University Press, 1996). She is also the author of scholarly articles, reviews, papers, books, and book chapters on such topics as the politics of exchange rate regimes, monetary policy, wage bargaining, social pacts, and democratic transition. Her current research centers on the impact of European monetary integration on labor markets in countries of the European Union, in particular Italy and Spain, and the impact of immigration on politics.

JONAS PONTUSSON is a professor of political science at the University of Geneva. He has written, most recently, *Inequality and Prosperity: Social Europe vs. Liberal America* (Ithaca: Cornell University Press, 2005).

GEORGE ROSS is *ad personam* Chaire Jean Monnet at the University of Montreal, Morris Hillquit Emeritus Professor in Labor and Social Thought at Brandeis University, and faculty associate of the Minda de Gunzburg Center for European Studies at Harvard University. He is the author of *Jacques Delors and European Integration* (New York: Oxford University Press, 1995) and the editor, with Andrew Martin, of *The Brave New World of European Unions* (Oxford: Berghahn, 1999) and *Euros and Europeans: EMU and the European Social Model* (Cambridge: Cambridge University Press, 2005).

JAMES SHOCH is an associate professor of government at California State University, Sacramento. He is the author of *Trading Blows: Party Competition and U.S.*

Trade Policy in a Globalizing Era (Chapel Hill: University of North Carolina Press) and of articles on the politics of American trade and industrial policy.

SORINA SOARE is a researcher at CEVIPOL, le Centre d'Étude de la Vie Politique, at the Free University of Brussels.

RUY TEIXEIRA is a senior fellow at the Center for American Progress and the Century Foundation, as well as a fellow of the New Politics Institute. He has also held positions at the Economic Policy Institute, the Brookings Institution, and the Progressive Policy Institute. He is the author or co-author of five books including, with John Judis, *The Emerging Democratic Majority* (New York: Scribner, 2004); with Joel Rogers, *America's Forgotten Majority: Why the White Working Class Still Matters* (New York: Basic Books, 2001); and *The Disappearing American Voter* (Washington: Brookings Institution Press, 1992).

Index

Page numbers in *italics* refer to figures; those followed by a *t* refer to tables.

JAMES CRONIN is a professor of history at Boston College.

GEORGE ROSS is *ad personam* Chaire Jean Monnet at the University of Montreal.

JAMES SHOCH is an associate professor in the Department of Government at California State University, Sacramento.

Library of Congress Cataloging-in-Publication Data
What's left of the left : Democrats and Social Democrats in challenging times / edited by James Cronin, George Ross, and James Shoch.
p. cm.
Includes bibliographical references and index.
ISBN 978-0-8223-5061-3 (cloth : alk. paper) —
ISBN 978-0-8223-5079-8 (pbk. : alk. paper)
1. Political parties—United States—History. 2. Political parties—Europe—History.
3. Right and left (Political science) 4. Globalization—Political aspects. I. Cronin, James E. II. Ross, George, 1940– III. Shoch, James.
JF2011.W438 2011
324.2′17094—dc22
2011006368